The Quest for Justice

Aboriginal Peoples and Aboriginal Rights

This collection of many voices develops more deeply and exhaustively the issues raised in the editors' earlier volume, *Pathways to Self-Determination*. It contains some twenty-three papers from representatives of the aboriginal people's organizations, of governments, and of a variety of academic disciplines, along with introductions and an epilogue by the editors and appendices of the key constitutional documents from 1763.

The contributors represent a broad cross-section of tribal, geographic, and organizational perspectives. They discuss constitutional questions such as land rights; the concerns of Metis, non-status Indians, and Inuit; and native rights in broad contexts – historical, legal/constitutional, political, regional, and international.

The issue of aboriginal rights and of what these rights mean in terms of land and sovereignty has become increasingly important on the Canadian political agenda. The constitutional conferences between government and aboriginal peoples have revealed the gulf between what each side means by aboriginal rights: for the Indians these rights are meaningless without sovereign self-government, an idea the federal and provincial governments are not willing to entertain. Somewhere in the middle lies the concept of nationhood status.

Ultimately, the aboriginal peoples are asking for justice from the dominant society around them; if it is denied or felt to be denied, the editors conclude, the consequences for the Canadian self-concept would be costly and debilitating. The twenty-four contributors provide a fine guide to this profound and complex problem, whose solution depends on our understanding and our political wisdom.

The editors are both at the University of Lethbridge. MENNO BOLDT is a member of the Department of Sociology; J. ANTHONY LONG is a member of the Department of Political Science. With LEROY LITTLE BEAR, they are also the editors of *Pathways to Self-Determination: Canadian Indians and the Canadian State*.

The Quest for Justice

Aboriginal Peoples and Aboriginal Rights

Edited by
Menno Boldt and
J. Anthony Long
in association with
Leroy Little Bear

UNIVERSITY OF TORONTO PRESS
Toronto Buffalo London

© University of Toronto Press 1985
Toronto Buffalo London
Printed in Canada

ISBN 0-8020-2572-2 (cloth)
ISBN 0-8020-6589-9 (paper)

Canadian Cataloguing in Publication Data
Main entry under title:
The Quest for justice
  Bibliography: p.
  Includes index.
  ISBN 0-8020-2572-2 (bound). – ISBN 0-8020-6589-9 (pbk.)
  1. Indians of North America – Canada – Government
  relations – Addresses, essays, lectures. 2. Métis –
  Government relations – Addresses, essays, lectures.
  3. Inuit – Canada – Government relations – Addresses,
  essays, lectures. 4. Indians of North America –
  Canada – Constitutional law – Addresses, essays,
  lectures. 5. Métis – Constitutional law – Addresses,
  essays, lectures. 6. Inuit – Canada – Constitu-
  tional law – Addresses, essays, lectures.
  7. Indians of North America – Canada – Civil rights
  – Addresses, essays, lectures. 8. Métis – Civil
  rights – Addresses, essays, lectures. 9. Inuit –
  Canada – Civil rights – Addresses, essays, lectures.
  I. Boldt, Menno, 1930–
  II. Long, J. Anthony.
  III. Little Bear, Leroy.
  E92.Q48 1985   323.1′197′071   C85-098613-3

This book has been published with the help of grants from the Alberta
Law Foundation and the Publications Fund of the University of
Toronto Press.

Contents

Preface ix

Introduction 3

1 **Political and Philosophical Perspectives on Aboriginal Rights by Indian, Inuit, and Metis Leaders**

Introduction 17

OREN LYONS
Traditional Native Philosophies Relating to Aboriginal Rights 19

DAVID AHENAKEW
Aboriginal Title and Aboriginal Rights: The Impossible and Unnecessary Task of Identification and Definition 24

FRED PLAIN
A Treatise on the Rights of the Aboriginal Peoples of the Continent of North America 31

CHIEF JOHN SNOW
Identification and Definition of Our Treaty and Aboriginal Rights 41

PETER ITTINUAR
The Inuit Perspective on Aboriginal Rights 47

CLEM CHARTIER
Aboriginal Rights and Land Issues: The Metis Perspective 54

BILL WILSON
Aboriginal Rights: The Non-status Indian Perspective 62

2   **Aboriginal Rights in the Constitutional and Policy-Making Processes**

Introduction 71

ROY ROMANOW
Aboriginal Rights in the Constitutional Process 73

RICHARD DALON
An Alberta Perspective on Aboriginal Peoples and the Constitution 83

BRIAN SLATTERY
The Hidden Constitution: Aboriginal Rights in Canada 114

SALLY WEAVER
Federal Difficulties with Aboriginal Rights Demands 139

THE RIGHT HONOURABLE PIERRE ELLIOTT TRUDEAU
Statement by the Prime Minister of Canada to the Conference of First Ministers on Aboriginal Constitutional Matters 148

THE RIGHT HONOURABLE BRIAN MULRONEY
Notes for an Opening Statement to the Conference of First Ministers on the Rights of Aboriginal Peoples 157

MENNO BOLDT AND J. ANTHONY LONG
Tribal Philosophies and the Canadian Charter of Rights and Freedoms 165

3   **Historical and Contemporary Legal and Judicial Philosophies on Aboriginal Rights**

Introduction 183

JAMES YOUNGBLOOD HENDERSON
The Doctrine of Aboriginal Rights in Western Legal Tradition 185

WILLIAM B. HENDERSON
Canadian Legal and Judicial Philosophies on the Doctrine of Aboriginal Rights 221

THOMAS FLANAGAN
Metis Aboriginal Rights: Some Historical and Contemporary Problems 230

4   Negotiated and Supranational Approaches to Securing Aboriginal Rights

Introduction 249

GURSTON DACKS
The Politics of Native Claims in Northern Canada 251

BILLY DIAMOND
Aboriginal Rights: The James Bay Experience 265

LEON MITCHELL
Using Mediation to Resolve Disputes over Aboriginal Rights:
A Case Study 286

DOUGLAS SANDERS
Aboriginal Rights: The Search for Recognition in International
Law 292

RUDOLPH RYSER
Fourth World Wars: Indigenous Nationalism and the Emerging
New International Political Order 304

5   Aboriginal Rights and Indian Government

Introduction 319

PAUL TENNANT
Aboriginal Rights and the Penner Report on Indian Self-
Government 321

MENNO BOLDT AND J. ANTHONY LONG
Tribal Traditions and European-Western Political Ideologies:
The Dilemma of Canada's Native Indians 333

Epilogue 347

Appendices

A   Royal Proclamation of 1763 (excerpt) 357
B   A Declaration of the First Nations (1981) 359
C   Metis Declaration of Rights 361
D   First Ministers' Accord Pertaining to Aboriginal Peoples in the
     Constitution, November 1981 (excerpt) 362
E   Sections of the Constitution Act, 1982, Pertaining to Aboriginal
     Peoples 363

F   Resolution to Amend the Constitution Act, 1982 (1983) 364
G   Proposed Constitutional Accord on the Rights of the Aboriginal Peoples of Canada (1984) 366
H   Indian Treaty Areas 370
I   First Ministers' Conference on Aboriginal Constitutional Matters: Proposed Accord Relating to the Aboriginal Peoples of Canada (1985) 371

Table of Cases 379

Notes 381

Contributors 404

Preface

In our earlier volume on Indian self-government, *Pathways to Self-Determination: Canadian Indians and the Canadian State* (Toronto: University of Toronto Press 1984), we made the point that the aboriginal perspective is largely missing from published works on issues affecting aboriginal peoples. In this volume, as in the last, we have tried to correct that deficiency by drawing heavily on the views of aboriginal leaders. In particular, we wanted to provide a forum that would allow aboriginal perspectives to be widely disseminated at a time when a series of crucial constitutional deliberations are being conducted on aboriginal rights.

The assembling of papers for this anthology began at a conference on aboriginal rights held at the University of Lethbridge in the spring of 1982. We wish to acknowledge the contribution of others who have assisted us in the preparation of this volume. Our thanks are due first to the contributors to this collection: all except six of the articles were prepared especially for this book. We are grateful for the valuable secretarial and clerical assistance of Marg McKeen, Carol Tomomitsu, Lana Cooke, Liz Zorzetti, and Diane Bennett. The helpful comments provided by R.I.K. Davidson and Kathy Johnson of the University of Toronto Press, and by an anonymous reviewer, were greatly appreciated. Finally, we thank the Alberta Law Foundation for underwriting a significant portion of the cost of assembling and disseminating the papers in this volume.

The Quest for Justice

Aboriginal Peoples and Aboriginal Rights

Introduction

The issue of aboriginal rights is now firmly entrenched on the public-policy agenda in Canada. The constitutional status of aboriginal peoples and the constitutional affirmation and recognition of aboriginal rights commit both present and future generations of Canadians to seek a resolution of the issue. The issue subsumes difficult questions about the political, legal, and constitutional steps that should be taken to redress historic injustices to Canada's aboriginal peoples and, on a broader scale, how aboriginal people as culturally distinct ethnic groups should relate to the larger society.

Canada's Aboriginal Peoples

The aboriginal peoples of Canada are defined by the Constitution Act (1982) as Indian, Inuit, and Metis. Indians have traditionally been subdivided into two groups, status and non-status. A status Indian is a person registered or entitled to be registered as an Indian for purposes of the Indian Act. Status Indians are members of the 577 bands across Canada, which are located mainly south of the sixtieth parallel on reserve lands within the provinces. According to the Department of Indian Affairs and Northern Development, there are 323,782 status Indians in Canada.

Non-status Indians are those Indians or their descendants who have lost their right to be registered under the Indian Act. Loss of status has occurred in several ways. The most common reason for loss of status is marriage of a registered Indian woman to a non-Indian. Loss of status has also occurred in other ways, such as voluntary renunciation, compulsory enfranchisement, and failure of government officials to include some Indian families in the 'registry.' Non-status Indians do not have a distinct constitutional status, but are grouped with Metis. For most non-status Indians this situation will change when the federal government amends the Indian Act to restore registered Indian status to those women (and their progeny) who lost it when they married non-Indians. Census figures indicate that there are approximately 75,000 non-status Indians in Canada. The amendment to the Indian Act could cause a population shift from non-status Indian to status Indian of up to 60,000 people.

The Inuit are those aboriginal people who inhabit Canada's northernmost regions, including the Mackenzie Delta, the Northwest Territories, the area along Hudson Bay, Labrador, and the Arctic Islands. The Inuit are the smallest group of Canadian aboriginal peoples, numbering somewhat over 25,000.

The Metis are of mixed Indian and non-Indian ancestry. The term 'Metis' originally referred to people of mixed ancestry living on the prairies; Statistics Canada now includes under the category of Metis all people living in any part of Canada who claim mixed Indian and non-Indian ancestry. The 1981 census sets Canada's Metis population at slightly over 98,000. According to the census approximately two-thirds of the Metis live in Manitoba, Saskatchewan, Alberta, and the Yukon and Northwest Territories. The rest are scattered throughout the remaining provinces. The Native Council of Canada, which represents many Metis and non-status Indians, disputes the census figure. The council places the combined population of Metis and non-status Indians at close to one million. Much is at stake in these conflicting counts; if census figures are used as the basis for negotiating settlements with respect to Metis land claims, housing, economic development, and social services, then the Metis will receive much less in the way of benefits than they feel they are entitled to.

The History of Aboriginal Policy

Government policy toward aboriginal peoples can be classified according to three historical periods. The first, extending from the beginning of confederation to the late 1960s, can be described as a period of stable neo-colonialism for status Indians, government acceptance of limited responsibility for Inuit, and divestment or denial of responsibility for Metis and non-status Indians. Beginning in the late 1960s, government policy toward aboriginal peoples entered a period of instability as both government and aboriginal peoples sought to alter their relationship with each other. Policy developments during this second stage were influenced by Canadian court decisions on Indian and Inuit land claims, by increased activity of aboriginal political associations, by intensified demands for aboriginal self-government and aboriginal rights, and by pressures from various Indian band councils for social and economic improvements. The third and current period in aboriginal policy continues to be influenced by the same concerns, but the forum for resolving these issues has been expanded from the courts and the bureaucracy to include the constitutional conferences.

In the first two periods the Canadian government pursued the general strategy of treating each major aboriginal group (Indians, Inuit, and Metis) differently. In the case of Indians the Canadian government introduced, early in Confederation, a policy of internal colonialism to deal with Indian peoples. The main objective of this policy was to free Indian land for white settlement. The key mechanisms for carrying out this policy were the signing of treaties and the expropriation of Indian lands. These practices later were translated into a policy of insulation and amalgamation embodied in the Indian Act. The act established the legal category of 'status Indian,' a system of band governments with limited delegated power, an Indian administration system structured along colonial lines, and a system of land reserves that consigned Indians to small, geographically dispersed land areas. This approach to Indian policy, which prevailed until the late 1960s, was designed to prepare Indians for assimilation into the larger Canadian society. It was assumed that the social and economic advancement of Indians, a necessary requisite for assimilation, could be best achieved in an insulated environment under the tutelage of the federal government.

The first significant attempt to break away from the long-standing policy paradigm of internal colonialism occurred in 1969 when the Liberal government, under Prime Minister Pierre Trudeau, presented a White Paper on Indian policy which proposed that federal tutelage be quickly eliminated and that Indians be treated like all other Canadian citizens. This policy initiative encountered vigorous opposition from Indian leaders and was withdrawn by the federal government in 1971. Recognizing that Indian peoples did not want to give up their unique status and their historic claim to land and other rights, the federal government began to explore alternative approaches to improving the intolerable economic and social conditions prevailing in Indian communities.

Beginning in the mid-1970s, the government introduced a series of legislative and administrative initiatives designed to enlarge the Indian peoples' autonomy and capacity to manage their own affairs. The underlying assumption of these initiatives was that increased Indian self-government would produce improved economic and social conditions among Indians, thus reducing their cost to the federal government.

By and large, this policy thrust, with some alterations, was continued into the 1980s and culminated in the introduction of legislation in 1984 by the Liberal government that ostensibly was designed to allow a greater degree of political autonomy for Indian peoples. The proposed legislation, however, did not recognize self-government as an inherent right of Indian peoples. Special legislation allowing for a greater degree of Indian self-government as well as reform of the Indian Act was proposed as a parallel action to the ongoing constitutional negotiations on aboriginal rights and self-government. The Conservative government, elected in 1984, appears to have abandoned a legislatively based approach to Indian self-government. Instead, it has chosen to entrench the principle of Indian government in the constitution. Specific forms and jurisdictions of Indian governments would be developed through negotiated settlements between Indian communities, the provinces, and the federal government.

The policy of the federal government toward the Inuit is one of long-standing indifference and neglect. Unlike Indians and Metis, who came into contact and conflict with the Canadian government early in the history of Confederation, the Inuit have until recently remained socially and geographically isolated. The expansion of the natural resource extraction industry into the Arctic, particularly during the last decade, has resulted in an influx of non-natives into the Yukon and Northwest Territories which threatens the traditional Inuit hunting and fishing areas as well as their traditional way of life. This situation has spurred initiatives on both sides to negotiate agreements that will minimize negative impacts and hostile confrontations.

Historically, the Inuit, like the status Indians, have come under the authority of the federal government. By virtue of the Quebec Boundaries Extension Act of 1912, however, a number of Inuit residing in the James Bay area were brought under the provincial authority of Quebec. In 1939, the Supreme Court ruled that the Inuit came under the federal Parliament's authority to 'make laws for Indians and lands reserved for Indians' (section 91(24) of the Constitution Act, 1867). Although the Inuit now come under the mandate of the Department of Indian and Northern Affairs, they are not subject to the provisions of the Indian Act.

The federal government's policy toward the Metis was to buy out their aboriginal claims on an individual basis. The buy-out was accomplished either through individual land grants or through payment in government scrip. The government's policy, until the passage of the Constitution Act, 1982, was not to recognize the existence of group rights for Metis and non-status Indians; this resulted in their being denied aboriginal group status. Metis and non-status Indians have come under the social, economic, and legislative jurisdiction of the provincial governments and in some cases of the territorial governments. With one notable exception, they have been treated like other Canadian citizens; the exception is in Alberta, where a group of Metis has been singled out for special treatment by the Alberta government. The Alberta Metis Betterment Act, passed in 1939, established, among other things, a distinct land base for Metis in northern Alberta. The provincial government maintains, however, that this act was spurred by the perceived social and economic needs of individual Metis, and does not imply any recognition of Metis aboriginal rights.

Beginning in the early 1970s, the federal government began to develop a 'native' policy which involved entering into a limited relationship with both Metis and non-status Indians. This new relationship has been ad hoc in approach – that is, it lacks a comprehensive policy framework. Different federal departments give financial support to Metis and non-status Indian political associations, subsidize their housing, and provide limited funding for land claims research. The two groups still lie in an undefined borderland between provincial and federal government responsibility.

Recent Developments

Beginning in the late 1960s, a number of events and factors converged to propel aboriginal policy-making into political and social prominence in Canada. Space does not permit us to identify and assess the relative significance of all the events and factors that have influenced recent aboriginal policy-making; however, we will single out several for consideration.

The White Paper

Many consider the 1969 White Paper to be the single most important catalyst in raising the political consciousness of Indian peoples. Introduced by the Trudeau government as part of its 'Just Society' program, the White Paper blamed the economic and social stagnation of Indians and their condition of dependency on the existing policy of internal colonialism. The White Paper proposed that the only acceptable solution to the 'Indian problem' was to integrate Indians fully and equally into Canadian society. To achieve this objective, the White Paper recommended the repeal of the Indian Act, the removal of special status for Indians, the elimination of the Indian Affairs Department, and the extension of all provincial economic, social, educational, health, and other services to Indians. The

8   Introduction

White Paper generated immediate and vociferous opposition from all segments of the Indian community. Indian leaders viewed the proposals as a subterfuge for dispossessing Indian peoples of their lands and aboriginal rights, with the ultimate goal being the cultural genocide of Indians.

The White Paper policy initiative had at least two important consequences for Indians. First, in preparing the White Paper the government accelerated a trend that had begun a few years earlier to bring Indians into a consultative role in the development of Indian policy. For most of its history the Department of Indian Affairs had initiated and implemented policy on a unilateral basis. In preparation for the 1969 White Paper, however, the Department of Indian Affairs undertook a number of steps designed to bring about a consultative process involving Indian peoples. This approach set a precedent from which the government has been unable to retreat in subsequent Indian policy-making. Second, the White Paper heightened Indian awareness and appreciation of their cultural and political heritage. This cultural revival provided an issue around which Indian peoples across Canada could unite and rally in opposition to detrimental federal Indian policies.

The Development of Aboriginal Political Associations

The White Paper and the associated consultative process produced some significant side-effects for all aboriginal peoples. One of these was the establishment of a program under the jurisdiction of the secretary of state to provide core funding to political associations representing aboriginal groups. The funding was originally intended to help aboriginal political organizations participate in the consultative process. During the 1970s and 1980s the number of government departments involved in funding aboriginal associations increased, and at the same time the mandated purposes for which funding could be used were expanded to allow aboriginal groups to research land and treaty claims, to prepare constitutional proposals, and to provide limited delivery of services.

By giving financial support to the aboriginal groups, the federal government helped create the organizations and structures that aboriginal peoples now use to influence the public policy-making process. They now have the means to bargain for aboriginal government, aboriginal rights, land claims, and other benefits on a sustained basis. If they had to rely solely on financial support from their respective constituencies, there is little question that the Assembly of First Nations, the Inuit Committee on National Issues, and the Native

Council of Canada, among others, could not have mounted a sustained campaign for the recognition of aboriginal peoples and rights in the Constitution Act, 1982. These publicly funded political organizations also have created an ongoing structure through which new aboriginal leaders can be recruited to replace the older leadership.

The New Aboriginal Elite

One of the most significant factors in the political evolution of aboriginal peoples has been the development over the past two decades of a university-educated aboriginal élite. Beginning in the 1970s, a number of universities in Canada began to develop native American studies programs. At the same time, some professional faculties, such as education and law, began to be more receptive to aboriginal students, encouraging their enrolment and developing programs to take into account their special needs. With improved access, the university enrolment of Indian students catapulted from under 100 to over 2,600 in the period from 1957 to 1979.

The effects of expanded educational opportunities for aboriginal peoples are twofold. First, they are producing an aboriginal leadership that is skilled in handling political, legal, and administrative matters, and that is able to function effectively in the dominant society. This new élite will assume a position of dominance during the next decade. Second, the emerging educated élite has the expertise to establish and staff the political and administrative infrastructures needed for aboriginal self-government. Without question, one of the most urgent needs confronting aboriginal peoples today is for personnel trained to facilitate economic and social development within their communities.

Judicial Interpretation of Aboriginal Title

Along with their increased activity in the political arena during the 1970s, Indian and Inuit leaders began to press their claims to aboriginal land title through the courts. Indians and Inuit have had mixed results in gaining judicial acceptance of their claims. The Supreme Court's judgment in the *Calder* case (1973), which involved a claim based on aboriginal title by the Nishga Indians of British Columbia, is especially noteworthy. Although the Nishga suit was dismissed on a technicality, the Supreme Court divided on the question of whether aboriginal title still existed. The court, in splitting its decision, in effect did not reject the doctrine of aboriginal title to land.

The true significance of the Supreme Court's split decision on aboriginal title, however, lies beyond the judicial arena. The court's indecision spurred the federal government to develop a policy of negotiating land claims based on historical claims to aboriginal title. Federal officials feared that if, in some future test case, aboriginal title should be affirmed by the judiciary, the claims settlements that might be awarded to aboriginal peoples could exceed the government's capacity to pay. To avert this eventuality, in July 1974 the federal government created a Native Claims Office in the Department of Indian and Northern Affairs, as well as a process to deal with specific and comprehensive claims. Thus, the federal government in effect confirmed that unresolved land claims based on aboriginal title -- that is, 'comprehensive land claims' – should be settled on the basis of negotiated agreements between the government and the Indians and Inuit. This policy has contributed to the redefinition of aboriginal rights as a broadly based political concept. Having achieved constitutional and political recognition for aboriginal title, Indian and Inuit leaders could now turn their attention to other types of claims within the framework of aboriginal rights. This has led to the redefinition of aboriginal rights to include a general demand for self-governing status and cultural preservation.

Patriation of the Constitution

The current debate over aboriginal rights has focused on the meaning of aboriginal rights provisions contained in the Charter of Rights and Freedoms. However, we must not allow this debate to overshadow other effects resulting from patriation of the constitution. The patriation process involved a reconstruction of the basic nature of the Canadian state. It introduced new parameters for defining the relationship between the two founding peoples, the relationship between federal and provincial governments, and the relationship of Canada's peoples with each other and with the state.

The patriation process thus provided a unique opportunity for aboriginal peoples to redefine their relationships with the Canadian state. The federal government assisted them in this redefinitional process by granting aboriginal associations several million dollars to develop their own constitutional positions and to participate in the constitutional debates. This government assistance did not make the negotiations between aboriginal peoples and the governments any less problematic. Aboriginal leaders demanded that their unique status as Canada's first peoples, and their aboriginal rights, be entrenched in the constitution. Moreover, aboriginal leaders demanded that they be allowed to participate fully and equally in the discussion of issues affecting them. During the patriation process many felt that they were being relegated to the level of other minority groups. When their demands for full, ongoing, and equal participation in the constitutional process were denied, some leaders protested by boycotting the constitutional deliberations.

Subsequently, a combination of factors, including extensive public lobbying on the part of the aboriginal groups inside Canada and in the British Parliament, forced the federal government and the provinces to concede to aboriginal demands for a recognition of their unique status. When the Constitution Act, 1982, was proclaimed, aboriginal peoples were elevated to a special constitutional status; their existing aboriginal rights were recognized and affirmed. Moreover, the constitution guaranteed an ongoing forum in which these new relationships could be defined and specified. Significantly, entrenchment of existing aboriginal rights in the constitution stands as a commitment from which the Canadian state cannot retreat.

Constitutional recognition of existing aboriginal rights has introduced a major new variable into the aboriginal policy arena: the involvement of provincial governments. Historically, Indians and Inuit have eschewed formal relationships with the provinces, considering themselves to be a federal responsibility. With the notable exception of the James Bay and Northern Quebec Agreements (1975) and the Northeastern Quebec Agreement (1978), status Indians and Inuit have not entered into any extensive political arrangements with the provinces. It is ironic, therefore, that the entrenchment of existing aboriginal rights in the constitution, a concession the Indians and Inuit fought hard to achieve, has had the effect of bringing the provinces into the negotiations on aboriginal issues. The provinces' part in the constitutional amending process gives them a key role in future efforts to define aboriginal rights.

Negotiated Settlements

The prominence given to the constitutional conferences on aboriginal rights has overshadowed other negotiations between governments and the Indians and Inuit. These negotiations, which have centred on settling disputes over land and other issues, have produced substantial gains for Indian peoples. Collectively, these individually negotiated settlements involve benefits of hundreds of millions of dollars, millions of acres of land, and significant increases in political autonomy. Moreover, some of these agreements, such as those affecting land north of the sixtieth parallel, will determine the direction of political and economic development in those territories for decades to come.

The context in which these settlements have been negotiated is the government's native claims policy, initially developed in 1973 and modified during the early 1980s. Basically, this policy acknowledges that aboriginal peoples have inherent interests in certain land areas and that claims can be negotiated where aboriginal interests can be shown not to have been previously settled. This type of claim has come to be known as a 'comprehensive' claim. Under its native claims policy the government has also acknowledged that Indians may have legitimate grievances in regard to unfulfilled treaty obligations and the maladministration of lands and other assets under government control. The Department of Indian Affairs considers these grievances 'specific' claims.

Between 1970 and 1983, the federal government provided over $95 million in the form of grants, contributions, and loans to aboriginal political groups to conduct research into treaties and aboriginal rights and to develop and negotiate their comprehensive and specific claims. Two of the most important settlements effected under the comprehensive claims policy are the James Bay and Northern Quebec Agreements and the Western Arctic Claim by the Inuvialuit of the Mackenzie Delta and the western Beaufort Sea. The James Bay and Northern Quebec Agreements provide for cash grants of many millions of dollars, the allocation of lands for exclusive use by the Indians and Inuit, hunting and fishing rights, strengthened self-government, aboriginal control over education, and ownership of renewable and non-renewable resources.

Concurrent with the negotiations leading up to these comprehensive claims settlements have been a number of ongoing negotiations related to specific treaty and other entitlements of Indians. During 1982 and 1983 specific claims were settled with the Penticton, Osoyoos, Clinton, West Bank, Squamish, and Okanagan bands in British Columbia alone. Moreover, tripartite negotiations between federal, provincial, and Indian representatives have been under way for some time in Alberta, Saskatchewan, and Manitoba with respect to specific claims submitted by numerous Indian bands.

The positive results of claims negotiations, in process and completed, over the past several years may indicate that the best hope for progress on aboriginal issues lies outside of the constitutional, judicial, and parliamentary processes.

Supranational Activities

Although the federal government is determined to treat aboriginal rights as a domestic issue, aboriginal peoples have long sought support for their claims in international forums. In their quest for justice, status Indians as a group have been the most frequent users of supranational initiatives to bring international pressure to bear on the Canadian government.

Indians have pursued the supranational strategy on two fronts. On the home front, Indian leaders have interjected their historic treaty relationship with the British crown into their negotiations with the federal government. On many occasions since Confederation, Indians have petitioned Britain to pressure the Canadian government into recognizing the principle of Indian nationhood that is implied in the treaty agreements between the Indians and the crown. The latest and most extensive manifestation of this strategy occurred during the final stages of the constitutional patriation process, when Indian leaders lobbied the British crown and House of Commons to delay patriation and force concessions from the Canadian government. On the international front Indians and Inuit have joined forces with indigenous peoples in other nations to draw the attention of the United Nations and other international bodies to their aboriginal claims to land, cultural integrity, and a greater measure of independence.

International pressure can be credited with bringing about some changes in Canada's policies toward non-status Indians. The United Nations Human Rights Commission's decision in the *Sandra Lovelace* case offers one example of such an induced policy change. The Canadian government, acting under the authority of the Indian Act, had denied Indian status to Lovelace because she married a non-Indian. For this action the Human Rights Commission found Canada in violation of the International Covenant on Civil and Political Rights. The Lovelace decision impelled the government to act quickly to amend the discriminatory section of the Indian Act.

It is difficult to measure the cumulative effect of international lobbying by aboriginal peoples. But Canada takes pride in its international image as a civilized country, dedicated to humane treatment of all its peoples, and therefore any action that has a potential for creating international disapprobation of Canada for its treatment of aboriginal peoples is likely to stir the government into taking corrective measures.

Aboriginal Rights in the 1980s

If there is a watershed in government policy toward aboriginal peoples it is represented by the proclamation of the Constitution Act, 1982. The significance of that event lies not so much in any major shift in government policy, but rather in the fact that the constitution placed aboriginal peoples on a new footing in their relationship to the Canadian government. For the first time in Canadian history Indians, Inuit, and Metis have been identified in the constitution as distinct groups with a special status in the Canadian state, and their existing aboriginal rights have been recognized and affirmed. For the Metis this represents a change not merely in degree but in their basic status: a departure from their previous position as Canada's forgotten people. Moreover, the constitution has given aboriginal peoples access to the highest political forum in the land for the purpose of negotiating a new relationship with the Canadian state. Aboriginal policy-making by virtue of the constitutional conferences can now occur outside the parliamentary political process. These constitutional provisions will also strengthen the aboriginal peoples' claims in future when they deal with aboriginal issues in the courts.

Aboriginal leaders, especially Indian leaders, are beginning to question the benefits of constitutional recognition of their rights, however. The federal government's promises that native peoples would have a strong voice in the constitutional process of defining aboriginal rights, like other promises made in the past, are quickly turning to ashes. Although three constitutional conferences on aboriginal rights have taken place, aboriginal peoples have gained little from their participation. Their rights have yet to be defined. It is becoming increasingly clear to aboriginal leaders that the definition of aboriginal rights will be determined in negotiations between the provincial and federal governments. Aboriginal peoples will have little say in the matter.

Aboriginal peoples are not faring much better in the Canadian political forum. Indians now find themselves confronted with federal government legislative initiatives on sexual equality and self-government that they have had small part in framing, that many Indian leaders oppose, and that are proving divisive to them and to their relationships with non-status Indians. The Metis, meanwhile, are caught in political wrangling over which government, federal or provincial, should carry legal and financial responsibility for them. They face the prospect of a lengthy jurisdictional struggle that will delay solutions to their urgent social and economic problems. Ultimately, they may have to seek clarification of their status in the courts. Only the Inuit, who have made significant progress in negotiating land claims settlements, and who have succeeded in obtaining government approval in principle for division of the territories, seem to be in control of their future.

1 Political and Philosophical Perspectives on Aboriginal Rights by Indians, Metis, and Inuit Leaders

THE PURPOSE OF SECTION INTRODUCTIONS in this book is not to represent or criticize the authors' perspectives. The authors speak for themselves and all papers deserve to be read in their entirety. In the introductions we will briefly identify selected salient themes, perspectives, and issues that interest us in the contributions, and we will attempt to 'tease out' some of the connections among the diverse perspectives presented in the collection.

In this section native leaders discuss aboriginal rights. The first four authors (Lyons, Ahenakew, Plain, and Snow) speak from the status Indian perspective; Ittinuar from the Inuit point of view; and Chartier and Wilson, respectively, from the Metis and the non-status Indian positions.

Several significant themes run through most of these presentations. One is the idea expressed by the status Indian leaders that their claim to aboriginal title, and hence to aboriginal rights, rests on spiritual premises. Their aboriginal title and their right to self-government, they assert, are based on a covenant with the Creator from time immemorial. Because their rights are derived from the Creator they are therefore inalienable by any human action, whether through law, politics, or coercion. Although Indian leaders stand ready to negotiate on aboriginal rights, we will discover in sections 2 and 3 how problematical it is to accommodate their spiritual premises in the Canadian constitutional, legal, and political frameworks.

Chartier and Wilson take a different approach. They emphasize the political and social injustices suffered by the Metis and non-status Indians, and they build a legal-political case rather than a spiritual case for aboriginal rights. However, like the status Indian leaders and Ittinuar, they stress that aboriginal rights are derived by virtue of their descent from the first peoples, and that aboriginal rights reside in the aboriginal collectivities, not in the individual.

All of the writers explicitly or implicitly express an apprehension that the Canadian government, motivated by its desire to assimilate aboriginal peoples and gain control over aboriginal lands and resources, will use the Canadian constitutional, legal, and political systems to deprive aboriginal peoples of their aboriginal land title and rights. Consequently, they emphasize the need for a unified political front among the various aboriginal groups and factions in asserting the reality of aboriginal rights and their just claim to the land.

OREN LYONS

Traditional Native Philosophies
Relating to
Aboriginal Rights

The issue of aboriginal rights presents a difficult problem for the governments of Canada. Statements are issued by government ministers about what aboriginal rights are; batteries of lawyers are running about trying to define aboriginal rights; constitutional amendments are passed. Do we have aboriginal rights or don't we? Lawyers talk about the issue as though they understand it, and judges make decisions about it, but afterwards everyone asks, 'What did he say?' No one knows. Aboriginal rights must exist, or else the Canadian and provincial governments wouldn't be so worried about them.

Aboriginal rights were given to us by the Creator when we were put here. The prime minister of Canada knows that we have aboriginal rights. He is thinking, 'We have to move fast before they find out they have them, because those Indians are getting smarter every day.' We understand everything about aboriginal rights except the legal talk, so governments try to make a legal issue out of it. When our white brother can go to his highest tribunal and gain from it (by an act of Parliament) the right to never have to drink water again, then I will respect their legal version of our aboriginal rights. There is no tribunal on earth that can change the natural law, because it is outside our jurisdiction. The matter of aboriginal rights is outside our jurisdiction; it is the natural law.

What are aboriginal rights? They are the law of the Creator. That is why we are here; he put us in this land. He did not put the white people here; he put us here with our families, and by that I mean the bears, the deer, and the other animals. We are the aboriginal people and we have the right to look after all life on this earth. We share land in common, not only among ourselves but with the animals and everything that lives in our land. It is our responsibility. Each generation must fulfil its responsibility under the law of the Creator. Our forefathers did their part, and now we have to do ours. Aboriginal rights means aboriginal responsibility, and we were put here to fulfil that responsibility.

Just the other day, I was talking to one of our old chiefs. He was going around our nation from house to house to gather up certain things for the ceremony planned for the next day. He and his partner stopped for tea, and when I said to him, 'You must be tired,' he answered, 'Well, you know how it is with Indians, they always have to work. That is the way it will always be. If you are going to be an Indian, you will find that you can never rest because there is something that needs doing every day and you have to get up and do it. The way white people have got it figured out, they don't have to do that. They can sit and watch television or do nothing; but not Indians, they always have to be doing something.'

The elder then told me how a young clan mother became very discouraged when he told her that her work would continue for the rest of her life. She said, 'I don't want to do this work for the rest of my life.' He explained it to her as he explained it to me. He said, 'How would you feel if the rest of creation felt the way you did? You know how it is in the winter-time when everything is asleep and how good you feel in the spring when you see the trees start to throw out their leaves. Doesn't it make you feel good to see everything renewed again? Even the old men feel young again in the spring; it renews their drive. What if the trees said the same thing that you just said – "I'm tired; I don't think I want to have leaves this spring." What would you think if spring came and no leaves came out on the trees; how would you feel? How would you feel if the grass didn't grow or the birds didn't come back?' She said, 'I would feel pretty bad.' He said, 'Well, they would feel the same way if you were to quit working. We have to keep working together.' It is hard work being an Indian. There are a lot of responsibilities. You always have to do this or that, but that is what we were given to do. That is our aboriginal responsibility, our aboriginal right.

The concern of our elders is for our children, and what is going to happen to them. The elders know they will not always be here to teach them their responsibilities. If the children don't learn their responsibilities, how will they survive? The elders don't like to move away from home. You can hardly get them to go to town, never mind going to another nation. So some of us offered to act as 'runners' for the elders. We offered to travel to various places and talk to the young people and their folks to remind them of their aboriginal responsibilities. The elders instructed us to go around the country and meet at least once a year in Navajo country, in Six Nation country, and so on.

When we were in Navajo country we were visited by a runner from the

United Nations. The runner said the United Nations wanted advice from us. He asked, 'If you were ruling the earth, what would you do?' Indians don't think in terms of ruling the earth, but we understood what he was trying to ask. We began to think about it.

The person seeking our advice was the undersecretary-general of the United Nations. We sat down in a circle and talked about the world's problems. When we had a statement ready, the elders sent it to the United Nations General Assembly on 29 August 1982:

Brothers and Sisters the natural law is the final and absolute authority governing 'Etinohah' – the earth we call our mother. This law is absolute, with retribution in direct ratio to violations. This law has no mercy; it will exact what is necessary to maintain the balance of life. This law is timeless and cannot be measured by the standards of mankind. All life is subject, absolutely, to this authority. Water is our bodies; water is life. Fresh water is maintained by the thundering grandfathers, who bring rain to renew the springs, streams, rivers, lakes and oceans. We are nourished by our mother – the earth – from whom all life springs. We must understand our dependence on her and protect her with our love, respect and ceremonies. The faces of our future generations are looking up to us from the earth; and we step with great care not to disturb our grandchildren.

We are part of the great cycle of life, with four seasons and endless renewal, as long as we abide by this absolute law. When we disturb this cycle by interfering with the elements, changing or destroying species of life, the effects may be immediate or they may fall upon our children who will suffer and pay for our ignorance and our greed. The natural law says that the earth belongs to our children – seven generations into the future – and we are the caretakers who must understand, respect and protect 'Etinohah' for all life.

The natural law is that all life is equal in the great creation; and we the human beings, are charged with the responsibility (each in our generation) to work for the continuation of life. We the human beings, have been given the original instructions on how to live in harmony with the natural law. It now seems that the natural world people are the ones who have kept to this law. The Elder circle of indigenous people of the Great Turtle Island, charged with keeping the first law of life (spirituality), are concerned that the validity of this law no longer is recognized in today's life. We are concerned that the basic principles of the law are no longer being passed on to the next generation. This could be fatal to life as we know it.

The natural law will prevail regardless of man-made laws, tribunals and governments. People in nations who understand the natural law are self-governing, following the principles of love and respect that ensure freedom and peace. We come together because we are alarmed by the destruction of vital life structures. Our faith is intertwined with one another; what affects one will affect all.

Water is primary to life; corn is next. Poisoned water will poison all life; lack of water causes droughts, deserts and death. The nations that sit in the great council of the United Nations must relearn the natural law and govern themselves accordingly, or face the consequences of their actions. There are people in nations among you who understand this message; and we ask you to stand with us and support our songs and ceremonies in defense of 'Etinohah' (our mother the earth). We are, respectfully, a traditional circle of Elders.

When I was a child we never had much, but we all played together and had fun. We didn't have much to eat and sometimes we didn't have any shoes. No one ever noticed that because everyone was in the same boat. We didn't know we were poor. We didn't feel poor. We had a grandmother and a grandfather, and when we were in trouble they were there. We had uncles and aunts (we had them by the tens) all over the place. They were always glad to see us. If we were at a friend's house, we were invited to eat. My mother sometimes didn't know half the children in the house, but they sat down and ate with us. That was the way it was; that is the right way. Today people say, 'You better not put out the food just now because company is coming.' That is no good because the kids learn to be stingy that way. Then when you are older and in need, your children will not help you. It all comes back to you. The aboriginal responsibility is to share, and that is the basis of our aboriginal rights. Our good fortune in being born one of 'the real people' carries responsibility, and that is something we have to work at. We will lose our aboriginal rights if we don't meet our aboriginal responsibilities.

We are all subject to the same natural law. That is what we are talking about when we talk about aboriginal rights. We are talking about the survival of ourselves and of the earth. If we don't work together on this, our children will suffer. The time to do something is now, not later. Work in your communities, look after your families, look after your ceremonies, fulfil your aboriginal responsibilities – that is the way to keep your aboriginal rights.

Our aboriginal responsibility is to preserve the land for our children. Everything on and in the land belongs to our children. It doesn't belong to us. We have no right to sell it, or give it up, or make a settlement. If we do that we will 'settle' our great-grandchildren right out of their aboriginal rights. We will spend the money that they give us and our children won't get a thing. They will suffer because we were greedy. Aboriginal rights are higher than politics or legal jargon. They are part of the natural law, which is higher than all politics; we must adhere to it or else we are all going to disappear.

DAVID AHENAKEW

Aboriginal Title and Aboriginal Rights: The Impossible and Unnecessary Task of Identification and Definition

The most precious aboriginal right of the First Nations is the right to self-government. Just as the wording of section 91(24) of the Constitution Act, 1982 refers to 'Indians and lands reserved for the Indians,' the concept of First Nation self-government is usually understood to mean two broad groups of jurisdictions: each First Nation governing its own people and their affairs, and governing their land and its use. Traditionally among First Nations, these two concepts are combined. The Creator gave each people the right to govern its own affairs, as well as land on which to live and with which to sustain their lives. These Creator-given rights cannot be taken away by other human beings.

Before the European settlement of North America, it was unknown among the First Nations for one nation to deprive another nation by force of its right to self-determination and to sufficient lands and resources to maintain the lives of its people. In Europe, however, conquest and domination were frequent occurrences. Entire peoples were displaced and forced to submit to government by others. The right of land was a royal prerogative. Although title carried with it the right of use and occupation, it was only at the continuing pleasure of the crown. It did not carry with it rights of self-determination.

International law has been struggling for several centuries to deal with this situation. Since the Second World War and the ostensible demise of colonialism, the collective human right of self-determination has been advanced and entrenched in international conventions. Because First Nation concepts are generally not recognized in Canadian law, the federal government has taken the position that self-government and aboriginal title are not 'existing,' but must be 'identified and defined.' This places the First Nations in the situation of having to discuss these concepts not only from their own viewpoint but from the Western European perspective which separates rights from title and title from self-determination.

The First Nations assert that the right of their people to govern their lands and resources is a right that flows from their aboriginal title. Their people's right to live on their own land, and to have use and occupancy of it, equally flows from their aboriginal title. Their right to permit settlement by others while at the same time retaining certain rights for themselves, as well as all residual rights, also flows from aboriginal title. But the right to govern their own lives and affairs is a collective human right that would accrue to them if they were living collectively, no matter where they might live.

As well, there are extraterritorial rights that do not stem from title but from maintenance of sovereignty. The pre-existing right, that is, the aboriginal right, to cross the U.S.-Canada border freely and to engage in trade and commerce with other First Nations has never been surrendered. The limits of this class of rights are not easily discerned. While it might be possible to claim that a right is exempt from the application of municipal traffic laws on the ground that such application violates a pre-existing right, that seems to be going beyond reasonable limits, and First Nation governments are likely to press the rights of their people only where it is necessary for political, cultural, and economic survival.

Thus, it is possible that there may be three classes of aboriginal rights: (1) the rights that flow to a people from aboriginal title to govern and control land and resources; (2) the rights to a people's cultural survival and elements of self-determination, which flow from common identity, language, culture, and values; (3) the right of a people to be exempt from or protected from the application of the laws of another jurisdiction to which it has not agreed to be subjected, and which would have the effect of unreasonably abrogating pre-existing rights or privileges.

With whom do aboriginal rights lie? Can an individual aboriginal person demand that the federal government recognize his aboriginal rights, or must those rights be demanded by the First Nation to which the individual belongs? Does an aboriginal person have special rights by reason of being 'aboriginal,' or by virtue of his being part of an aboriginal collective, such as a First Nation? If the former is the case, just what is an 'aboriginal person,' and who is to define that term? An aboriginal collective – particularly one that has a governmental structure through which it can determine who is and who is not a member of that collective – can simply be recognized as existing; it need not be defined. International relationships between countries are exactly like this; an ambassador and his country need not submit to definition.

It seems, then, that although an aboriginal right may be exercised by an individual member of a First Nation, the protection of the right is through a government-to-government relationship. By including self-government as an aboriginal right First Nations are, in effect, distinguishing between those rights an individual aboriginal person might have and those he has by virtue of membership in a First Nation. Could an individual aboriginal person, for instance, demand that the federal government protect his right to fish a certain lake when his First Nation, for conservation purposes, prohibited fishing? Could a First Nation government manage its relationship with the federal government if some of its members individually pressed rights which the collective had determined were not in its best interests? And do aboriginal rights apply to all aboriginal persons in all parts of Canada? Can a Micmac demand, as an aboriginal right, that the federal government permit him to fish Pacific salmon which the Nishga have determined are part of their own aboriginal title and rights? Or must the Micmac obtain permission of the Nishga? It seems obvious that the latter is the case, and was the case long before Europeans arrived in Canada.

Although no examples of individually held aboriginal rights come to mind, there may be some. If there are, then there is another categorization of aboriginal rights: (1) aboriginal rights that belong to the individual aboriginal person, and (2) aboriginal rights that accrue to an individual by virtue of his membership in a First Nation. This distinction is particularly crucial in such self-government questions as membership and access to lands, resources, and services. Unless the distinction is clear, First Nation self-government may be undermined by federal governments intervention on behalf of individuals who claim land, resources, and services as individual aboriginal rights. The distinction is essential to the argument that some aboriginal rights flow from aboriginal title, since it is presumed that the undivided title is held collectively by a particular First Nation. If these rights are said to be held individually and severally, they cannot simultaneously be held collectively and jointly.

This distinction in aboriginal title and aboriginal rights must be fully understood in order that the concepts can be correctly applied. As well, it is essential that discussion take place in the context of the First Nation concept of title, which contains rights that are not included in the Western European concept of title. At the same time, it is important that the full extent of the Western European concept of title be utilized to destroy the notion that aboriginal title means only 'use and occupation,' since the Western European concept of title holds that an 'owner' may retain title and all residual rights while at the same time permitting others to have use and occupation of the property.

For many years ambitious settlers circumvented the prohibitions against buying land contained in the Royal Proclamation of 1763 by signing 999-year leases that gave them use and occupation without disturbing title. These leases were subsequently made invalid by the Indian Act, although in most cases the federal government proceeded to protect the right of the settlers by obtaining surrenders of the land or by passing new legislation which operated notwithstanding the Indian Act. The federal government also permitted settlers to obtain title as well as to enjoy use and occupation of Indian land by failing to protect Indian interests. Currently, a restrictive land claims policy which limits the ability of First Nations to press their claims allows non-Indians to retain de facto title to Indian lands.

The federal position, often sustained by the primitive nature of Canadian law on aboriginal rights, is that an aboriginal right must be proved to have existed and to have been exercised before any claims can be made with regard to the right. For instance, the federal government is willing to consider the claim of the Coppermine Indians to copper in their area in a quantity sufficient for them to make their own utensils, since expert witnesses can testify that in ancient times the Coppermine Indians did make their own copper utensils. The federal government, however, will not consider the claim of the Coppermine Indians to petroleum under their lands on the premise that they did not make use of it historically, and thus are not considered to have an aboriginal right to it. By this faulty logic, the Arabs of Saudi Arabia should be denied the right to exploit oil resources, and the United Kingdom and Norway should be precluded from drilling for North Sea oil. Does one need more examples of the silliness of the federal argument?

Incongruously, the federal government claims all rights in aboriginal areas, although obviously it did not make use of those rights historically. Incongruously, the federal government claims that it can make agreements regarding the extinguishment of aboriginal title and rights (such as it is now proposing in the Yukon) but that it cannot pass laws recognizing aboriginal title and rights.

Another incongruous situation arises from a restrictive interpretation of aboriginal rights by the federal government, which concludes that a First Nation can exercise its right only in the precise way it did in pre-settlement times. If a First Nation used bone rather than steel fish-hooks, then it can only exercise its aboriginal right to fish with bone hooks. The fact that settlers have been able to move from bone hooks to fishing trawlers in no way mitigates this ludicrous position. Canadians seem to be able to maintain continuity of identity and rights despite their technological evolution from horses and buggies to jets. Knickers and three-cornered hats are no longer fashionable. Why must Indian people be limited to a particular anthropological time in order to qualify for the exercise of an aboriginal right? Do Canadian taxpayers really want to maintain a bevy of federal lawyers in comfort to produce such puerile and intellectually insulting arguments in order to protect vested interests and an outdated, racist historical perspective?

What has happened, in effect, is that the federal and provincial governments have nearly succeeded in turning the historical relationship with the First Nations on its head. As relative newcomers to the scene, the governments have arrogated to themselves the right to determine what is and what is not an aboriginal right, what criteria will be applied regarding the exercise of an aboriginal right, and the legal system under which any actions will be heard. Their own title, and their own rights in Canada, are considered to be absolute, and thus are not open to discussion.

The federal government has protected itself with a number of catch-22 policy positions. As an example, federal officials say aboriginal rights could be considered at a political rather than a legal level if the right to self-government could first be established. To establish that right, however, one must rely upon the current law, which does not recognize First Nation government. This is a classic example of arguing in a circle.

Federal officials pretend that they are unable to make a political determination of the question of aboriginal rights because it is essentially a legal question. This policy is itself a political decision, no matter how much federal officials might deny it. Worse, it seems that federal officials themselves made this political decision. Perhaps this is why they deny its political nature; no minister of government is prepared to take responsibility for it.

There are two options open to the federal government: it can approach the question of aboriginal title and rights as a political matter, or it can have the matter resolved through the use of international arbitration. Currently, a United Nations working group is engaged in a five-year plan to draft an international convention regarding the rights of the 'entrapped nations' – indigenous peoples encircled by a dominant government not of their own making. When this work is completed, the First Nations will be strengthened in their efforts to obtain the justice to which their cause is entitled.

When other societies attempted to identify and define their rights in a constitutional manner, they did not find it an easy task. One historical parallel is the framing of the United States constitution. Interestingly enough, it was a process in which the First Nations were very much involved. The authors of the Declaration of Independence and the Bill of

Rights were compelled by the example of freedom-loving First Nations to revise their concepts about the fundamental nature of human beings. Benjamin Franklin and others wrote lengthy treatises on the political structure of First Nations, particularly the one closest to them, namely, the Iroquois Confederacy. They did not attempt to devise an exhaustive list of the individual and collective human rights 'the People' of the new nation were to have once they had been cut loose from the authority of the king. Instead, they defined those powers that the people were willing to permit their government to exercise. The people retained for themselves all powers not specifically delegated to government. Special care was taken with regard to those rights the people considered to have been violated by the king's agents. The constitution made it clear that freedom of press, religion, and speech, the right to bear arms, and the protection against search and seizure were to be retained by the people, and Congress was prohibited from passing any laws affecting the free exercise of those rights.

What would the constitution of the United States look like today if, instead of leading a revolutionary army, George Washington had gone to London to hold a special conference with ministers of the crown 'to identify and define' the rights of the American people in the same way the First Nations and other aboriginal peoples are forced to submit to in Canada? If such a meeting had been held, the king would have called together colonial governors to identify and define the rights of the people, and he would have allowed the people to send a few representatives. Would it have been possible for the people to make an exhaustive list of the rights they believed they had? And even if such a list had been made, would it have been valid for decades and centuries ahead, or would changing circumstances have rendered the list invalid before the narrow interpretations of the king's lawyers? If the king had said he could not grant rights without the participation of the colonial governors, is there any real likelihood that they would have given their approval according to a formula they had insisted upon in order to protect their own vested interests?

Basically, the First Nations find themselves now in such a situation – they must 'identify and define' all the natural human rights, rights the Creator gave to them when he placed them on this land. They are asked to define these rights in a manner that will suffice for all time and that will meet with the approval of the provincial governments. It is as impossible a task now for the First Nations as it would have been in 1775 for George Washington.

The way to achieve protection of aboriginal rights is not to identify and define them. Such a process will result in limiting rights, not protecting them. International standards will soon make it clear, if they do not already do so, that Canada has no jurisdiction to interfere with any right that the peoples of the First Nations enjoyed before Europeans arrived in Canada and that the peoples of the First Nations have not expressly and voluntarily delegated or surrendered to the crown. That, in essence, is what aboriginal rights are all about. Is any further 'identification and definition' necessary?

Once Canada has accepted these rational standards and perspectives, then the First Nation governments and the federal government can sit down in a spirit of mutual accommodation and begin to readjust the balance between the two titles – aboriginal and settlement. Their common goal will be to find a balance so that the peoples of the First Nations and the settler peoples can be free and prosper in a multi-national democratic state.

FRED PLAIN

A Treatise on the Rights of the Aboriginal Peoples of the Continent of North America

I want to deal in this paper with our understanding of the meaning of 'aboriginal rights.' First of all, I want to quote from a paper produced by the Union of Ontario Indians in 1970. I was president of the union at that time, and I authorized the following statement, which was presented to a special committee dealing with the constitution of Canada.

As Indian people we will always see our special status and our legal right as flowing from the original sovereignty of our nations. The colonial legal system to a large degree denied that sovereignty, but they never denied the existence of rights based on the aboriginal possession of tribal territories. It was the unauthorized violation of these rights that led to the unrest which prompted the Royal Proclamation of 1763.

That document, the first written constitutional document for British North America, recognized the existence of Indians' territorial rights, and established legal procedures for the surrender of these rights. The lands which today comprise Ontario were Indian lands. In the words of the Proclamation, they had not been ceded to or purchased by the colonial power. The procedures established by the Royal Proclamation for ceding Indian lands remain in force today. The last treaty signed under these procedures was in 1956, the Soto adhesion to Treaty #6.

Areas remain today in Ontario for which no valid treaty or surrender exists. Therefore, the procedures of the Royal Proclamation are still of practical consequence even in Ontario. Section 91.24 of the British North America Act of 1867 gave jurisdiction over Indians and lands reserved for the Indians to the Federal Government. This was not enacted as seems popularly believed out of a paternalistic concern for Native peoples.

It was enacted to make clear the power of the Federal Government to engage in colonial expansion in the West. The phrase 'lands reserved for Indians' included lands not ceded by treaty as of 1867, which for Ontario comprised by far the greater part of the present territory of this Province. If the Indians and their lands had not been crucial to the opening of the West, it would have been more logical to place Indians under Provincial jurisdictions as somewhat different terms of Indian policy developed in each colony of 1867.

Following the surrender of the Hudson's Bay Company Charter in 1869/70, the Governor General, exercising prerogative power in compliance with the procedures established by the Royal Proclamation, began negotiating a series of treaties with the Indian nations in Ontario and the Northwest. The treaties were constitutional documents. They were seen by both sides as establishing basic patterns of interrelationship for the future. They were based on the idea of mutual consent and the understanding that the Indians had legal rights in their patrimony. To violate these documents is to compromise the integrity of the Canadian legal system. The Migratory Birds Convention Act, and the decisions in Regina vs Sekina in 1964, and in Regina vs George in 1966, and Daniels vs White and the Queen in 1968, to Indian people represent violations of basic legal commitments.

The basic rights of the Indian peoples are of constitutional significance. Yet, these rights have not been uniformly safeguarded under the present constitutional structure. This should change.

What Are Aboriginal Rights?

In white society there has always been confusion as to what actually is meant by the term 'aboriginal rights.' In 1970, for example, Prime Minister Pierre Trudeau was reported to have said that the concept of aboriginal rights is so complicated as to be unworkable. But to us, the Nishnawbe-Aski, the concept is basic, simple, and unambiguous. Our definition of aboriginal rights can be summed up in one phrase: 'the right of independence through self-government.' When we say that our right to self-government, our right to self-determination, our right to nationhood must be recognized in any new Canadian constitution, we are defining aboriginal rights. This is the goal of the Nishnawbe-Aski as outlined in the Declaration of Nishnawbe-Aski of 1977.

Aboriginal rights defined in this way include the right to develop our own life-style and our own economy, and to protect and encourage the practice of our sacred traditions as we know them. We, the Nishnawbe-Aski, have the inherent right to determine what our future will be. We shall determine the destiny of our land. We want to see the continued development of our people under their own governing systems. Aboriginal rights were a mere concept in Prime Minister Trudeau's mind, but to my people they are a reality. We have the inherent right to develop and grow under our own system, and our own system will flow from our own people, who will develop our own constitution. Our Indian constitutions have every right to be recognized in any new Canadian constitution. This is the true meaning of aboriginal rights.

What Is an Aborigine?

The aborigines are the indigenous inhabitants of a country. For instance, the people that we know as the Indian nations of North and South America are the aborigines of these two continents. They were the first people to live in this part of the world.

Because we were the first people to live here we have a claim to certain rights. These rights include human rights – that is, the basic right to life claimed by all people. However, when we talk about aboriginal rights, we are also talking about the inherent right to self-determination that applies to all aborigines.

What Is Civilization?

To understand aboriginal rights we must understand the meaning of civilization. Civilization is the accumulation of the traditions and culture of a people: their ability to express themselves in a variety of ways – in dance, music, art, law, religion, the telling of stories, the writing of books, and so on. The aboriginal people of North and South America constituted a number of different civilizations.

Aboriginal rights guarantee each indigenous nation the right to develop its own traditions and culture – its own civilization. Each aboriginal nation has the inherent right to seek happiness and a comfortable way of living, and to develop itself at its own pace. This was a right of each aboriginal nation from its beginning, and it exists today. Each nation exercised aboriginal rights within its own lands and boundaries and under its own sovereignty.

To recognize that the aboriginal people were a civilization long before the white man came to North America is to acknowledge that as an aboriginal people we exercised our aboriginal right to govern ourselves. Conversely, to acknowledge that we have aboriginal rights is to recognize that these rights flow from our long-standing civilization.

Aboriginal and European Attitudes toward the Land

Nishnawbe-Aski means 'the people and the land.' Our links with the earth are sacred links that no man can ever sever. We are one with the earth, and the earth is one with us. The Nishnawbe-Aski Declaration states that we have the right to govern and control our own people in our own land, and the right to remedy our own situations. The efforts that are made to meet our needs must come from our own people.

As nations of people we made laws to govern ourselves. Among the laws that we made were laws governing our use of the land and its resources. But our attitude toward the land and its use was and still is very different from the European attitude. We aboriginal people believe that no individual or group owns the land, that the land was given to us collectively by the Creator to use, not to own, and that we have a sacred obligation to protect the land and use its resources wisely. For the Europeans, the idea that land can be owned by a person or persons and exploited for profit is basic to the system. The European political and legal systems have been developed to reflect this concept of the land.

Many European and Canadian laws have to do with regulating private property in one form or another and with governing relations among people with respect to private property. The sovereign government has created laws to govern the distribution of the scarce resource of property. The most basic form of property, other than one's own body, is land.

The idea that land can be bought and sold, or that you can exercise some rights but not others in the land, is absolutely foreign to the Nishnawbe-Aski way of thinking. Yet this is the basis for all legislation that has been enacted since the coming of the Europeans to North America.

Legislation Affecting Aboriginal Rights

The Royal Proclamation of 1763 was passed in the British Parliament because of the struggles between Indians and Europeans over the land. This document recognized the existence of Indians' territorial rights and established the legal procedures for the giving up of those rights.

The Constitution Act, 1867, established Canada as a nation. The act sets out the division of powers between the provinces and the federal government. Section 91(24) of the act gives jurisdiction over Indians and lands reserved for Indians to the federal government.

The act was intended to make clear the power of the federal government to engage in colonial expansion in the west. This was done because we Indians and our lands were crucial to the opening of the west, and the federal government wanted to be able to control us and our land in order to consolidate its power over the country.

After the royal proclamation, and until as recently as 1956, treaties were signed between the government and the Indian nations. These treaties were seen by both sides as establishing basic patterns of future interrelationships. They were based on the idea of mutual consent and on the understanding that the Indians had legal rights in and control of the land.

The treaties were a recognition by colonial law that we Indian people had sovereignty in our land. In fact, there was a widespread acknowledgment that the aboriginal occupants of the land had certain legal claims because of their historical sovereignty over the land. The English legal system developed a theory that those claims were limited in certain ways, but that aboriginal tribes had the legal right to possess their tribal territories. Under the English legal system, if the lands passed into non-Indian hands, then the Indian claims had to be extinguished by a formal treaty and by some form of compensation.

The treaties were negotiated sometimes before white settlement, sometimes after. The effect of the treaties was to extinguish many aboriginal rights; to preserve some residual rights, such as hunting, fishing, and trapping; and to create some new rights, such as schooling, medical care, and annuity payments.

While the treaties have not been totally in our favour, the law has never denied that the aboriginal tribes have legal rights to possess their tribal territories.

What Does It Mean to Be a Nation?

Our aboriginal right allows us to determine our future as the Nishnawbe-Aski Nation. What does it mean to be a nation? In 1977, an international conference on discrimination against indigenous populations of the Americas put forward a declaration of principles aimed at gaining recognition for indigenous or aboriginal peoples as nations under international law. The criteria for recognition as a nation are: that the people have a permanent population; that they have a defined territory; that they have a government; that they have the ability to enter into relations with other states. We can assure Canada and the international community that using these criteria we can define ourselves as a nation. We have a population that is permanent; we have always existed and we are not going to die out or fade into oblivion. We have a defined territory stretching from James Bay and Hudson Bay west to the Manitoba boundary; from Hudson Bay and James Bay southward to the height of land known as the Arctic watershed and east to the borders of Quebec. We have a democratic government given to us by the Creator. The Royal Proclamation of 1763 refers to our sovereignty, and the government of Canada approached us as a nation to enter into a treaty with them. We continue to have the right to enter into relations with other states.

Under these criteria, the Nishnawbe-Aski have a solid basis for claiming our aboriginal right to determine what our future will be and to determine how we are going to attain our goals.

Do the Indian People Have a System of Government?

When the white man first came to America, there were systems of government in operation in this new land. The democratic system employed by the great Six Nations Confederacy was studied by the Europeans, and was picked up and incorporated into their governing systems. Democracy was already flourishing in North America before the white man came. The right to govern one's people, the right to govern one's destiny, the right to determine the paths that a nation will follow to reach its objectives must be recognized as sovereign and aboriginal rights.

We had a government. That government has been dormant because of the influx of federal law, particularly the Indian Act and its administrators, the Department of Indian Affairs. Our government has remained hidden in the hearts of our people, but it has never died. Our government will come forth under the careful guidance and leadership of the Nishnawbe-Aski Commission. We will be prepared to put the constitution of the Nishnawbe-Aski on paper, if that is what is required. Our government is a reality.

We must draw out from our people what they want to see developed in their community with regard to their own governing structure. Only then can we begin to educate our people in the traditional ways of living, traditional Indian government, and the traditional right to determine our future.

What Does It Mean to Be Independent?

When the Nishnawbe-Aski made their declaration in 1977, they stressed that their objective was to see the full development of cultural, economic, spiritual, and political independence. We think that we have to come to grips with the fact that cultural independence and economic independence cannot be divorced. One cannot exist without the other.

At the time the white man came here, our educational system was complete. The educational system and the political development of the various Indian nations in Canada determined the life-style of the particular tribe in whatever area of America they lived in. For instance, the economy of the Ojibway and the Cree living in this part of North America was based on the presence of animal, fish, bird, and plant life destined to give sustenance to the people. Hunting, fishing and trapping, and gathering were not separate issues to be dealt with at a political level by certain components of government; they were part of the socio-economic system of our people, and they are included in the overall definition of aboriginal rights. Before the white man came, all Indian nations were independent and exercised their aboriginal rights within their own lands.

The Nishnawbe-Aski and the Constitution

We did not question the statement of Prime Minister Pierre Trudeau that the people of this country have a right to their own constitution. We support the principle of patriation; Canadians have a right to determine the instrument by which government is going to make laws that apply to them.

When the constitutional negotiations became an issue, we told the British parliamentarians that we were not fighting the patriation of the constitution to Canada. We felt that the Canadian people had a right to their own constitution, but we also believed that the Nishnawbe-Aski Nation, which existed before the Europeans came to North America, have a right to their own constitution, and that they must not be deprived of the right to make their own laws and determine their own destiny through their own governing system. Because the Canadian government was unwilling to recognize our right to our own constitution, we challenged the patriation of the British North America Act.

We, the aboriginal people, must clearly spell out the true aboriginal rights that must be recognized in any Canadian constitution. These rights are non-negotiable. But we must take a united stand, or we will find it difficult to persuade Canada's first ministers to heed our claims.

What the Canadian Government Wants from the Aboriginal People

We are in the heat of a tremendous battle; a battle that is focused on jurisdiction. The premiers of the provinces and the prime minister are trying to reduce the aboriginal rights question to a series of legal issues that they can contest or disregard. At the same time, they attempt to placate the Indian people by saying, 'We will look after you; we will improve your conditions; we will accommodate your needs.' But ultimately they will try to consolidate their jurisdiction over our land and our resources. The first ministers have only one goal in mind in the constitutional negotiations: they hope to gain complete control over all Indian lands and resources. This is what the constitutional process is all about.

The Canadian Government's Attitude to Aboriginal Rights

The Honourable Jean Chrétien had these words to say about aboriginal and treaty rights: 'We will honour our lawful obligations to the aboriginal people.' Precisely what did he mean? He meant that Canada has obligations to native people only if such obligations will stand the test of the law. If the law decrees that certain obligations must be met, and if those obligations are defined in such a manner that the government can accept the definition, then they will be honoured. But what does the term 'law' mean? Law, in the modern liberal state, is the creation of an autonomous and general legal system composed of: private parties; a legitimate legal sovereignty and its administrative agencies (the governor-in-council, or Parliament, or the government of Canada, and its cabinet and various departments); and the independent judiciary.

When the explorers from the European nations came to America, they found a land with people and law. The Europeans had no right to come and trample that system of laws underfoot and impose a new legal system in North America. But this fact is not readily going to be recognized and acknowledged by the people who in the first instance denied the existence of the aboriginal system of law. They will fight any attempt to bring truth to bear.

Let us go back to the quotation from the Nishnawbe-Aski declaration. In the minds of our people who hunt, trap, and fish the forests, lakes, and rivers of Nishnawbe-Aski land, there is a clear concept of what our land tenure is. However, according to the government of Canada, which makes the laws, aboriginal rights are to be determined by a court interpretation. As far as the courts are concerned aboriginal rights are conceptual rights only; that is to say, they are a concept that exists only in the mind until drafted into some kind of law that makes sense in a legal system. The government makes the law defining aboriginal rights, and the government appoints judges who interpret the law dealing with aboriginal rights. If the government of Canada has its way, the white man's law and the white man's courts will determine how the concept of land tenure is defined in practice.

Who Will Decide What Our Aboriginal Rights Are?

Court cases have never solved the riddle of aboriginal rights. The *Baker Lake* case is a prime instance of what happens when the dominant governing society, through its enacted laws and its judicial system, decides what constitutes aboriginal rights. In the *Baker Lake* case, the court said that the Inuit do have aboriginal rights because they have been here from time immemorial. Because of that one basic fact, the court recognized that aboriginal rights do exist. However, the Supreme Court of Canada took it upon itself to define what the aboriginal right is not. The judgment states that the aboriginal right is not a proprietary right. In other words, the right of the aboriginal people does not relate to the land, and therefore the land is open to those exploiters who want to extract the gas and the oil, destroy the environment, and then move out. The indigenous population is then left with evil consequences that greatly outweigh any potential benefits that might come to them from the resource exploitation.

In the communities of the Nishnawbe-Aski Nation, our fishermen, our trappers, our hunters, our schoolchildren, and our women who maintain our homes understand what our aboriginal rights are. Aboriginal rights are a riddle only to those who do not want to hear or face the truth, who do not want their taking of the land interfered with by the aboriginal owners of this continent.

The aboriginal people have a clear concept of land tenure in their minds; therefore our chiefs, our elders, our people, our children, should define our aboriginal rights – not the federal government, the provinces, or the Canadian courts. It is we who must protect our aboriginal right to self-determination as a nation and our right to develop and use the resources of the land free of interference and intimidation. We have an obligation to preserve the rights granted to us by the Creator. We have that right now. We have always had that right. We are determined to have that right in the future. We don't have to beg the prime minister of Canada and the provincial premiers to recognize that we have certain basic human and aboriginal rights.

Conclusion

I close this paper with a prayer. Great Grandfather, our hearts and our minds are joined together. We rejoice to know that our right to live and enjoy the beauty of this great land was given to us, not by any foreign government, but by yourself. Great Grandfather, you gave us the land and its resources; you made us one with the birds, the animal life, the fish life; you made us one with nature itself. This is our aboriginal right. It is a right that no government can interpret for us.

Because you gave it to us, no man has a right to take it away from us. Many times, our hearts have been made heavy when we have seen the devastation of our land by those who seek only to mine it for its wealth and then leave it. Our hearts have been made heavy because other powers have come in and made laws that have restricted our free movement of spirit. Yet you have put it in our hearts this day to stand upon our feet once again, and boldly claim that our aboriginal right is forever.

Breathe upon us with your spirit of life, and give us greater determination to press for this right to be fully restored to us and recognized by all people. Great Grandfather, be with us in all of our deliberations, for without your leadership and guidance we are weak and helpless. Cause the sound of the drum to be loud and clear to our hearts and minds in this crucial hour.

CHIEF JOHN SNOW

Identification and Definition of Our Treaty and Aboriginal Rights

These are difficult and trying times in our history. We have been in difficult situations before, but today we have come to perhaps the most critical crossroads in our lives. Today we are being asked to spell out our Indian rights in a foreign language – the English language – in constitutional form. We are accustomed to talking about our rights in our own languages with our elders. Because of problems in interpretation we have always been in a weak position in our dealings with government. We have experienced an additional disadvantage because we have had to pursue our rights through the English legal and legislative systems.

Explaining our rights in a foreign language is almost impossible, because sometimes we cannot find English words equivalent to our Indian words. I also question whether it is possible to draft a single definition that will accommodate the different interests of Indian people across Canada. Furthermore, there is a time problem. The federal government seems to want a 'quick fix,' but I believe the process of definition will take years of bilateral discussions and negotiations between the Indian people and the government of Canada. The definition of these rights cannot be concluded without the consent of our people.

One major point I want to make is this: our treaties with the crown are of great importance to us. It is because of the treaties our forefathers signed that we still retain our aboriginal Indian rights. We have never surrendered those rights to the federal government or to the provincial governments. If it was not for these treaty agreements – the written

This is an edited version of a speech given at a treaty conference held in Saskatoon, 12–13 January 1983, two months prior to the first ministers' conference held in Ottawa, 15–16 March 1983.

documents and the associated oral promises and agreements – we might have lost all of our rights as aboriginal people. But because of the existence of these treaty agreements the federal government finds itself in a difficult position when it attempts to do away with our rights.

The Indian treaties with the crown are real, and we must see to it that the terms of those treaties and related documents are fully included in the new constitution. Without our treaties we would be in the same unfortunate situation as the non-status and non-treaty Indians. I remind all treaty and registered Indians that the treaties are sacred covenants; they are binding documents; and they must not be altered unilaterally by the government of Canada. The treaties, the Royal Proclamation of 1763, the Declaration of the First Nations, and all other materials related to the treaties should be the basis of our constitutional discussion with the government of Canada.

The federal government has repeatedly reaffirmed, through the office of the prime minister and through the minister of Indian affairs, that our treaty rights will be respected. But the government has subordinated the treaty agreements to other legislation. In effect, the federal government has arbitrarily changed the rules when it didn't like them. It has used this tactic to abridge our hunting, fishing, and trapping rights. That is why the constitutional discussions must truly be a bilateral process between two equal and consenting parties, and not a case of one party dictating the terms to the other. I am convinced that the government will manipulate the constitutional discussions to try once again to deprive us of our special status as the original people of this continent. Our treaties present a dilemma to the federal government because they confirm that we are not just another minority group in Canada, but that we are the original peoples with special rights and special status.

I know that many recent studies on the treaties by historians, anthropologists, lawyers, and others have stated that our forefathers were forced to sign a prepared treaty text with no other option available to them. I don't fully agree with such a simple interpretation. No doubt we were misled by the legal jargon and the gestures of friendship by the treaty commissioners, missionaries, and the mounted police. Perhaps we were naïve in accepting government promises without understanding the bureaucratic strings that would be attached. But our forefathers signed the treaties in good faith. We have not broken our treaty promises to live in peace with the white man, to share use of the land with settlers, and to work with the queen's people in establishing a better life for all people on this Mother Earth.

We are now all aware that the federal government's long-standing policy has been to assimilate the Indian people. They tried to do this by

'Christianizing and civilizing' our children through the residential school system. This policy was a clear betrayal of the spirit and intent of the treaties. As a result, we are now struggling for cultural survival in our own land. We have endured attacks on our language, our religious beliefs, our homelands, and our traditional ways of life. We have experienced many forms of subjugation, abuse, and discrimination, yet these trials have deepened our faith and made us stronger. They have brought us together and made us aware of our common purpose. We are survivors, and we will always survive, given any circumstances, because we have faith in the Creator. We are confident that the Creator will guide us into the future.

Women have always been partners with men in the historical battle for survival of the Indian peoples, and women are once again making important contributions in our present struggle to survive. They have met with cabinet ministers in Ottawa. Some members of Parliament are aware of our position on aboriginal and treaty rights because of the work of our women. Their contribution must not be ignored. So too, the contributions of all other parts of Indian society must be acknowledged. The elders must be recognized as well as the young people; the elected leaders as well as those who elected them. In 1970, we responded to the federal government's White Paper on Indians by developing our own Red Paper. At that time, we demonstrated that we can be a united people. We, the treaty Indians, must continue to work together toward achieving our aboriginal and treaty rights. We will never give up these rights or our freedoms!

Section 37 of the Constitution Act, 1982, states that the constitutional conferences on aboriginal issues will be 'composed of the Prime Minister of Canada and the First Ministers of the Provinces,' while members of the Indian nations will attend only as invited 'representatives.' Our status at the conferences is that of a powerless minority group, which may deserve some kind of special recognition but which is not entitled to share in any real power. As things stand there is no consent clause to commit or legally oblige the first ministers to entrench aboriginal title and treaty rights. Moreover, any Indian rights that may be written into the constitution now are subject to the amending formula. This means that at any time in the future such rights could be altered or even eliminated without our consent by agreement between the federal and provincial governments. Before we will accept the Canadian constitution, we must be certain that our aboriginal and treaty rights cannot be changed without our consent; that condition must be recognized in the amending formula.

Ever since the treaties were signed there have been at least two major and different interpretations of their meaning. There is the Indian version of the treaties and there is the government version, and the difference is like day and night. This difference must be resolved before the constitution can be finalized. The government of Canada must sit down with the Indian people at the conference table and try to bring these two versions of treaty rights together. The government must face the facts of life; it must acknowledge that the treaties give us special rights and status, and that it cannot do away with these by a mere stroke of the pen. The government cannot say to us, 'Here is the new constitution. You have no special rights in the new constitution.' The basis of our aboriginal rights is the treaties, and the legal recognition of the treaties must be entrenched in the constitution.

We must be constantly on guard against further legislated limitations on our aboriginal and treaty rights. The first step must be to spell out and to clarify our aboriginal and treaty rights so that each party coming to the negotiating table will fully understand the issues involved. The second step must be to resolve our land claims. There are many land claim settlements to be negotiated right across this continent. The government has attempted to resolve some of these claims and, in doing so, has begun to settle some of its long-standing debts to the First Nations of this land.

There remain many other outstanding debts incurred by the government of Canada to Indian people, and payment on these debts is long overdue. Our elders tell us that we never surrendered the mineral rights or natural resources of our Mother Earth, yet Indian people have not shared in Canada's resource wealth. The question of resource ownership and resource revenue, like our land claims, must be resolved. Also, some specific promises in the treaties were never ratified by the Canadian Parliament. These commitments must be recognized, ratified, and entrenched in the new constitution.

The new constitution must also guarantee in a more meaningful way some of our special treaty rights. I am referring here to our rights to education, medical services, and economic development; to our rights to our own language, religion, and cultural traditions; and to our rights to hunt, fish, and trap. For instance, in regard to medical services the 'medicine chest' provision in the treaties is not being honoured. I have listened to many elders, and they say our forefathers used to have their own medicine people and special places where they would go for healing purposes. My own people used to go to Radium, the mountain hot springs, a sacred area. This area is no longer available to us. It is now a tourist resort. My people also used to go to the Lake Louise area, to Pipestone River, to get pipestone for ceremonial purposes. This is no longer available to us either; it is now a national park owned by the federal government. My people used to go to the Cypress Hills area to gather herbal medicine; this is no longer possible because of settlement in that area.

By taking the use of these lands away from us the government has assumed a great responsibility. The government must now be responsible for all medical services for native people. Because the government has taken almost all traditional medicine and sacred areas from us, the 'medicine chest' provisions in the treaties must be interpreted to mean that the government will provide us with hospitalization, modern medicine, and drugs. This can also be said about our means of livelihood. The places where we made a good living have been taken from us with a stroke of a pen. Essentially, all our natural resources have been taken from us, and now the government is trying to say, 'You have no rights.' This is a gross injustice.

With the new constitution the prime minister and the provincial premiers are saying to us that we have no special rights, and that in future we will be classed as immigrants to this country. Why did the British crown and the federal government bother to make treaties with us in the first place? When the Europeans first came over they knew that we were the owners of this land. That is why they made treaties with us. Why are they trying to get out of honouring these treaties today? This must not be allowed to happen. We must stand together, and these treaty rights must be entrenched in the constitution. We must carefully prepare our position papers, spelling out our aboriginal and treaty rights in the modern context, to meet our present and future needs. The Indian people must come to a consensus with respect to our position on aboriginal rights and treaty rights. Let us give direction, let us appoint spokesmen, and let us stand with them and support them.

In the old days when there was a crisis in the encampment our forefathers took action to correct the situation. If there was no meat in the camp, the hunters provided food for everyone. If enemy warriors were approaching, our brave warriors defended their people. We were always ready for any challenges. Today we, the descendants of a great people, must be ready to meet any challenge, even the challenge of the new Canadian constitution. We must be ready to take a stand, to state our position. We must be ready to discuss, to negotiate, and to make the constitution work for the benefit of the First Nations of this great island. In this task it seems that the odds are against us, but our history tells us that we have been in similar situations before and we have survived.

I am confident as we approach the constitutional conference table that we will not be going there alone. The Creator who put us here will be with us. I am sure that the Great Spirit, the Creator, will be at our side during these difficult times. He will give us understanding, patience, strength, courage, and wisdom as we make plans for the future of our people. The Great Spirit has created us for a purpose, and has placed us on this great island. We are the Great Spirit's people, and there will always be Indian people on this great island. The Great Spirit has been good and kind to us. In the past, he guided our forefathers. Today he guides us. We, the descendants of a great people, must stand united. Let us walk together in unity, and go forward as the Great Spirit's people.

Dagu-wichawaa, zena iwaach. My relatives, my kinsmen, I have spoken!

PETER ITTINUAR

The Inuit Perspective on Aboriginal Rights

Any discussion of the Inuit perspective on aboriginal rights must begin with the recognition that we have existed as a distinct people in the North for thousands of years. We have maintained our own culture, our own religion, our own economy, our own language, and our own decision-making structures. Our long survival in one of the harshest environments in the world should attest to the viability of our culture. To put our historical experience in more contemporary terms, one could say that we have exercised our aboriginal rights freely for countless generations. In the context of the present discussions over aboriginal rights, therefore, our position is that we must have the right to continue exercising these historical 'rights' both now and in the future. The challenge we face is to ensure the preservation of those rights in the context of an evolving Canadian federalism. I suspect the Indian and Metis peoples see their struggle in much the same way.

Like the other aboriginal groups in Canada, our particular culture has always been based on a close relationship to the land. Our identity as a distinct people is derived from and dependent on the continuation of that relationship. In contrast to the Europeans we, like the other aboriginal groups, have never viewed land as a commodity that can be bought and sold any more than the air we all breathe can be bought and sold. Our traditional attitude toward the land is expressed best by the man from Gjoa Haven who recently said in a letter, 'This land does not belong to anyone, it's just borrowed for a time. Neither the government nor the Inuit have more authority over it.' I doubt if anyone can say it any better than that.

If the Inuit approach to the aboriginal rights question differs from that of other aboriginal groups, however, the difference probably is a result of our historical and geographical relationship to the rest of Canada.

Unlike the other aboriginal groups, we have not felt the impact of European culture and institutions until relatively recently – until my own generation, in fact. This means that our essential ties to the land have not yet been effectively broken, as they have been for many aboriginal peoples in the South. We have not had to live under the burden of a century of control under the Indian Act, for example. Neither have we had to deal with the legacy of unscrupulous land dealers who robbed us of our land entitlements. In comparison, we have been left relatively free, at least until recently, to carry on our lives as we traditionally have, with our ties to the land still relatively intact.

The government's long-standing indifference to our part of the country was reflected in a remark by former Prime Minister Louis St Laurent, who admitted in the early 1950s that the government 'had administered those vast territories of the North in an almost continuing absence of mind.' In the light of the historical experience of other native peoples in the South, we in the North should be thankful for this lack of interest on the government's part.

Our historical experience leads us to take a slightly different approach to the current discussions on aboriginal rights. Inasmuch as our culture and economy still remain closely tied to the land, we see our chief task in the aboriginal rights debate as securing a guarantee from the federal government for the continuation of our historical rights. For the purposes of making a distinction, it is probably accurate to say that the principal struggle other native groups face is to regain the rights that have been eroded or taken away from them in the past; our chief task is to maintain our rights against the erosion that may occur in the future.

Over the last ten years we have attempted to protect our aboriginal rights in the courts, through the land claims process, and in constitutional negotiations. I will review some of our efforts in each of these areas.

Legal

The courts are the primary forum within which aboriginal groups have been pursuing their aboriginal rights. If there is one word that describes the legal status of the concept of aboriginal rights, that word is 'ambiguous.' During the last ten years almost every legal initiative taken to clarify the concept has resulted in further ambiguities being created.

Aboriginal rights can be expressed in different forms, such as treaty rights or constitutional guarantees, but perhaps the most critical element at stake is that of aboriginal title. Our collective identity as indigenous peoples has been and will continue to be dependent on our relationship to the land and all that it provides. The key legal issue that has to be resolved is the meaning of aboriginal title.

In the absence of any clear decisions on the matter, the federal government in the late 1960s was content to act as if aboriginal title had no legal basis. In its 1969 White Paper the federal government signalled its intention to forget about such rights once and for all. In doing so it did all aboriginal peoples a favour, because this action motivated us to organize ourselves more effectively to defend our rights. All aboriginal groups owe a debt to those who, like the Nishga, were courageous enough to use the courts to secure the recognition of aboriginal rights. The 1973 Supreme Court ruling in the *Calder* case did not remove the ambiguity surrounding the issue, but it did serve to put the two sides on a more nearly equal legal footing. This had a significant impact on the federal government's approach to land claims inasmuch as it now felt compelled to set up a formal process for negotiating land claims settlements.

Since 1973 it has been the Inuit who have pressed the legal question further. In 1979, the people of Baker Lake went to the Federal Court of Canada for an injunction to stop mineral exploration in their area, claiming it interfered with their aboriginal right to the land. This effort served to clarify some aspects of the legal meaning of aboriginal title, but once again it also created ambiguities. On the positive side, the court did establish that the Inuit have an aboriginal title to the land in common law, and that it has never been extinguished by any legislation, either directly or indirectly. The court was not asked to define what aboriginal title actually meant, but Mr Justice Mahoney did say that aboriginal title conferred the right to hunt and fish but it did not confer property rights. On the negative side, he held that it was within the powers of the government to legislate aboriginal title out of existence if it so desired.

The *Baker Lake* decision was a mixed blessing. It left unclear the implications of existing legislation such as the Canadian Mining Regulations and the Territorial Lands Act. It also confirmed that the precise meaning of aboriginal title is still far from resolved. Pursuing the resolution of this question through the courts is an extremely risky proposition, because each side has a great deal to lose by a definitive ruling. That is why we now prefer to seek a solution through other forums, such as the land claims process or the constitutional negotiations.

Land Claims

Prior to the *Calder* decision, the federal government felt it could deal with outstanding native claims in the North at its own discretion because our claims had no sound legal basis. The decision in the *Calder* case gave our own claims a much greater legal validity and prompted the government to enter into a process of meaningful formal negotiations. In preparation for these negotiations we conducted a comprehensive land-use and occupancy study to document Inuit ties to the land. Based on the evidence produced by the study, our formal claim to the government called for the recognition of those rights we had never ceased to enjoy – the right to control the use of lands and waters in our traditional territories and the right to use and preserve our language and our culture. Additionally, we claimed the right to benefit from the new forms of wealth resulting from economic exploitation of our territories and the right to establish a political jurisdiction and government within Confederation based on traditional Inuit political institutions.

Since we submitted our first claim in the mid-1970s negotiations have proceeded at varying rates, with increasing progress being made in the last two years. The process is one of translating a claim based on an undefined title into concrete rights and obligations. In many respects, the critical issues all revolve around the question of power – who will have it and how it will be used. Are the decisions affecting our region going to be made by Inuit or non-Inuit, and will they be made in the regional or the national interest?

Since we began preparing our claim, it has become obvious to us that if our ties to the land are to continue we must retain a certain amount of control over what happens in the North. In today's terms, this means a degree of both economic and political control. Given the rush to develop the resources of the North, it becomes imperative that we develop institutional arrangements that will ensure we are not pushed aside in the federal government's pursuit of the 'national interest.' We are convinced that it is possible to do this.

The Inuit have developed a policy position on land claims which I think can be described as moderate. We do not take the position that we own everything in the North. Rather, we accept the fact that we are a part of Canada, and that we can make a contribution to the country as a whole by sharing the wealth that can be drawn from our lands. Such sharing is consistent with our traditional philosophy of life. But at the same time we insist that the sharing arrangement must protect and guarantee our cultural integrity, which is dependent upon our continuing links to the land.

This willingness to share on an equitable basis is evident in our approach to claims negotiations. Instead of trying to retain all the power for ourselves, we have opted for an approach that emphasizes our right to have a meaningful say in the decision-making process as it relates to our most fundamental needs. Put another way, we are prepared to recognize the legitimate needs of the country as a whole if it in turn is prepared to recognize our legitimate needs as a distinct northern people.

A concrete example of our willingness to share power and control can be found in the wildlife agreement signed by ourselves and the federal negotiator in the fall of 1981. It represents the first component of an eventual agreement in principle which we hope can be finalized within the next two years. Our main purpose was not to assume complete control over decision-making, but rather to secure for ourselves a significant role in the decision-making process for the future. We have proposed an arrangement, for example, which does not take away the minister's ultimate responsibility for decisions. We are willing to accept the principle of a ministerial veto if the Inuit are given the power to make decisions in the first instance, and if the minister's right to overrule those decisions is subject to certain agreed-upon criteria. In practical terms, we are advocating the establishment of a wildlife management board with an equal number of representatives from both the Inuit and the federal government. The board would have the primary power to regulate wildlife harvesting and conservation. Its decisions would be law, unless the minister saw fit to overrule them, which he could only do under certain negotiated conditions.

We believe that this type of shared decision-making is the best way to administer an area that is critical to our future. We hope to negotiate similar types of decision-sharing arrangements on issues relating to environmental protection and economic development. The main issue will continue to be how decision-making power will actually be shared. The government is more than willing to let us act as adviser's to the decision-makers; the challenge for us is to find procedures that will ensure our advice carries real weight. Our goal in the land claims process is to translate our undefined aboriginal rights into more precisely defined arrangements for sharing administrative control over the lands we live on.

The Inuit have always realized that political authority is essential if we are to exercise some control over our lives. Here too our distinct geographical and historical relationship to the rest of Canada influences the way we approach our goal of self-government. Unlike other native groups, we are in a majority in our region, and will likely remain so for a long time to come. This gives us options that other native groups do not have. If we cannot secure our political rights through the land claims process, for example, we can pursue them through other forms of public government.

In our claims submission we proposed the creation of a new political jurisdiction in the eastern Arctic called Nunavut. It would initially have powers equivalent to those of the existing Northwest Territories government, with additional powers over land-use planning and land-use controls. Under our proposal Nunavut would achieve full provincial-type powers during a transition period of about fifteen years. Although it would be based on our aboriginal claim to the area, the Nunavut government would also protect the rights of non-Inuit.

While the Nunavut proposal is an integral part of our overall claim, the federal government has not yet accepted it as a subject for negotiation. In fact, the federal government has resisted negotiating any types of political rights through the claims process with aboriginal groups. In the presence of this standoff we have pursued the political issue on another front, by pushing for the division of the Northwest Territories into two territories, one of which would be Nunavut. Through lobbying in Ottawa and with the support of the territorial government, we have persuaded the federal government to agree in principle to the concept of division. What we may not be able to achieve through land claims we hope to achieve through the political evolution of the North.

The Constitution

As land claims negotiations have been proceeding, another even more important forum has emerged for the resolution of the aboriginal rights question – the constitutional conferences. With the government's decision to patriate the constitution in the fall of 1980, a historic opportunity was created for resolving the long-standing issue of aboriginal rights.

At first the federal government showed no interest in including any positive recognition of our rights in its draft resolution. Only after intense lobbying by many people were we able to get the federal and provincial governments to include a formal recognition of aboriginal and treaty rights of the Inuit, Metis, and Indian peoples. However, some provinces insisted that this recognition be limited to those rights that were in existence at the time of patriation. Since the extent and meaning of those rights has never been defined in law, the constitution merely entrenches the ambiguities that have always existed.

While section 35 of the Constitution Act, 1982, does not by itself resolve any of the ambiguities about what our rights actually mean, it does give us a foot in the door to work out a solution at the highest political level. As I have said, there is much to lose by relying on the courts to define our rights. But in section 35 we now have available to us another forum for settling the matter; we can engage in actual negotiations rather than relying on a judge.

I think the issue of aboriginal rights should be resolved through the political process rather than in the courts because it is a political issue. Our relationship to the rest of Canadian society should be determined by public policy, not by legal technicalities. While the political route is not without its own hazards and obstacles – most notably the provinces – it also carries certain advantages for us. For one, it is a much more public process. We will be able to put our case not just to a judge in a courtroom but to the country as a whole. If there is doubt as to how much potential support exists among the Canadian public for the aboriginal position, and how important that support can be in persuading the government to move, we need only reflect on the support that emerged for our cause after the original version of section 34 of the draft constitution act was rejected. To overcome the government's resistance to a meaningful definition of our rights, we must take advantage of that public support and we must do the work necessary to mobilize it on our behalf.

There are two main threats to our success in future constitutional negotiations. The first is the inability of the several aboriginal groups to come to the table with a united position. The second major impediment to a successful outcome will, of course, be the provinces. This is where the biggest potential conflict of interests lies. If we are to overcome it, we must be prepared to mobilize our allies in the general public to give us the support we will need.

CLEM CHARTIER

Aboriginal Rights and Land Issues:
The Metis Perspective

Legal terms relating to the rights of the aboriginal peoples of Canada have often been used interchangeably. 'Aboriginal title,' 'Indian title,' 'native title,' 'usufructuary rights,' and 'aboriginal rights' have at one time or another been used to attempt to describe the rights the colonizers felt aboriginal peoples possessed.

In the early 1500s, after America became known to the Europeans, several writers and theologians spoke on behalf of the Indian peoples. They stated that Indians, although heathens and non-Christians, nevertheless were capable of ownership of land and had sovereignty over their territories. Spain, Portugal, France, and England did not accept these views, but nevertheless found it useful to recognize some of the rights possessed by the aboriginal inhabitants. They also quickly realized that the Americas were vast and that they need not fight over them. They essentially came to a gentleman's agreement: whoever got to a piece of land first could claim it for his sovereign. The principal right remaining for the aboriginal people was the right to continue the peaceful enjoyment of their way of life and the use of their territories.

In the early 1800s the United States Supreme Court began to define this theory as the 'doctrine of discovery.' Basically, this meant that the country that arrived first could claim it for its king or queen. In order to perfect their title, the discoverers had to settle the land. They further stated that the aboriginal peoples had a right to continue using the land until they either gave up that right or were conquered. That is how the concept of aboriginal title or rights was created. There is still no clear, definitive statement to be made about what exactly is covered by the term 'aboriginal title.' It is clear that hunting, trapping, and fishing are some of the aboriginal rights that exist. In Canada, the privy council in the *St Catherine's Milling* case (1888) stated that aboriginal title was merely a usufructurary right and that Indian peoples did not own the land. They went on to state that they did not have to describe what those usufructuary rights were. (A usufruct is the right to use the property of another to one's own advantage so long as the property is not altered or damaged.)

In the *Calder* case (1973) the Supreme Court of Canada also stated that it did not have to define what aboriginal title was composed of. The judgments of Chief Justice Hall and Justice Judson addressed aboriginal title in a cursory fashion. The chief justice held that the Nishga still had valid aboriginal title:

... this is not a claim to title in fee but is in the nature of an equitable title or interest ... a usufructuary right to occupy the lands and to enjoy the fruits of the soil, the forest and the rivers and streams which does not in any way deny the Crown's paramount title as it is recognized by the law of nations. Nor does the Nishga claim challenge the Federal Crown's right to extinguish that title. Their position is that they possess a right of occupation against the world except the Crown and that the Crown has not to date lawfully extinguished that right.

Justice Judson, ruling that the aboriginal title of the Nishga had been extinguished, expressed the following opinion with respect to Indian title: '... the fact is that when the settlers came, the Indians were there, organized in societies and occupying the land as their forefathers had done for Centuries. This is what Indian Title means and it does not help one in the solution of this problem to call it a "personal or usufructuary right."'

However, the Federal Court–Trial Division, in the *Baker Lake* case (1979), said that although the Inuit of Baker Lake retained valid aboriginal title, they did not own minerals below the surface. Basically, the court stated that aboriginal title relates only to hunting, trapping, and fishing – elements of a traditional life-style – and that uranium mining and Inuit hunting at Baker Lake could continue jointly. The decision was not appealed.

Briefly stated, the legal position in Canada at present is that the crown has the underlying title to the land and the aboriginal peoples have merely a 'possessory' right, that is, a right to the use of the land. In addition, this possessory right can only be surrendered to the crown, and once it has been surrendered the crown title becomes absolute. Although this severe limitation on the sovereign rights of the aboriginal peoples has always been denied by them, there appears to be a willingness to negotiate a political and legal relationship that would provide for entrenchment of aboriginal rights in the constitution of Canada.

The first major instrument to recognize the rights of the aboriginal people was the Royal Proclamation of 1763, which required 'consent' before the lands of the Indian peoples could be legitimately ceded. The proclamation provided that the lands of the Indian people could only be purchased by the crown at a public meeting with the Indians convened for that purpose. This proclamation, which was essentially the first constitution of British North America, still has the force of law as an imperial statute. In addition, section 25 of the new Charter of Rights and Freedoms lends protection to whatever rights the royal proclamation affords the aboriginal peoples.

The next major recognition of the aboriginal peoples' distinctive position within Canadian society is reflected in section 91(24) of the British North America Act, 1867 (now known as the Constitution Act, 1867). That section gives the federal government jurisdiction over 'Indians, and the lands reserved for the Indians.' The government interprets this clause to mean that it has exclusive legislative authority over Indian peoples and land; the aboriginal peoples maintain that section 91(24) indicates only that the federal government has jurisdiction to enter into relationships and discussions with aboriginal nations.

It should be noted at this time that the term 'Indian' was used both in the royal proclamation and in the Constitution Act, 1867. However, neither document defined the term. In the *Re Eskimos* case (1939) the Supreme Court of Canada ruled that the term 'Indian' as used in the Constitution Act, 1867, included the Eskimos (Inuit). It is the opinion of the Metis National Council and the Association of Metis and Non-status Indians of Saskatchewan as well as some legal scholars that the Metis are also included in the category of 'Indian.' The opinion that it is not necessary to be defined as an Indian under the Indian Act to be a constitutional 'Indian' is based on the fact that the current Indian Act still excludes the Inuit despite the ruling in *Re Eskimos*.

Support for this proposition can also be found in the Constitution Act, 1982. Section 35(2) defines aboriginal peoples as the 'Indian, Inuit and Metis peoples of Canada.' In *Re Eskimos*, Justice Kerwin stated that 'the majority of authoritative publications and particularly those that one would expect to be in common use in 1867, adopt the interpretation that the term "Indians" includes all the Aborigines of the territory subsequently included in the Dominion.' That the Metis are Indians (constitutionally) also finds support in section 31 of the Manitoba Act, 1870, which expressly recognized that the Metis shared in the Indian title to land. This legislation was subsequently given constitutional force by the British North America Act, 1871. There can be no further doubt with respect to this issue; the Manitoba Act, 1870, is now included in schedule 1 of the Constitution Act, 1982.

The participation by half-breeds in Indian title to the land was also specifically recognized in the rest of the Northwest Territories and Rupert's Land by the Dominion Lands Act, 1879. Support for this proposition can be found in the adhesion of Rainy River half-breeds to Treaty 3 in 1875. The order-in-council for Treaty 10 in northern Saskatchewan also provided for the relieving of the claims of the 'Aborigines,' a category made up of the Indians and Metis resident in that part of the province.

The first piece of legislation to refer specifically to the Metis people was the Manitoba Act, 1870, which provided for the distribution of lands 'towards the extinguishment of the Indian Title to the lands in the Province.' By section 31 the government set aside 1,400,000 acres to be divided among the children of the half-breed heads of families residing in Manitoba at the time of the transfer, 'in such mode and on such conditions as to settlement or otherwise, as the Governor General in Council may from time to time determine.' The government allowed gross injustices to be perpetrated against the half-breed people through the implementation of a grant and scrip system, leaving the half-breeds landless and in abject poverty which persists to this day. In 1879, the Dominion Lands Act extended this attempted unilateral extinguishment of rights to the rest of the Northwest Territories, although the provisions were not implemented until the 1885 War of Resistance at Batoche.

The Manitoba Metis Federation has challenged as unconstitutional subsequent federal and provincial legislation allowing this injustice to take place. The federation is seeking a declaration that the federal and provincial legislation purporting to extinguish their rights is outside the legislative competence of both levels of government.

A brief overview of the implementation of this form of so-called extinguishment will help in understanding the injustices suffered by the Metis. While treaties with the Indians set apart communal tracts of land and recognized other rights, the scrip issued to the half-breeds was for a specific amount of land which was fully alienable. In addition, by this method of unilateral dealing, the government of Canada also purported to extinguish all aboriginal title rights possessed by the Metis, including the right to hunt. As a consequence of this imposed scrip system, most of the land fell into the hands of speculators.

The Canadian government, in dealing with the Metis, issued land and money scrip. Land scrip was a certificate describing a specified number of acres and naming the person to whom the land was granted. Only that person could register the scrip in exchange for the land selected. Because they lacked information and knowledge about the land scrip system most Metis never registered the scrip; most registrations were done by opportunistic speculators and swindlers, who would appear at the registry office with any aboriginal person who was readily available. To facilitate the transaction, the speculator would have a transfer or quit-claim signed by the unwitting Metis or else would forge his signature, usually an X.

Money scrip was in essence a bearer bond. It was easily negotiable for money, goods, services, or land. Anyone who presented it would be able to redeem it in exchange for dominion land, which at the time was selling at one dollar per acre. Money scrip was introduced after a considerable amount of lobbying by speculators who stood to gain in their dealings with Metis who had no experience or familiarity with such transactions. Both money and land scrip were redeemable at one dollar per acre. After a number of years, however, the price of land and the value of land scrip increased. Thus, money scrip became less desirable.

Both land and money scrip could only be used for dominion lands in surveyed areas. Scrip was only issued to the Metis in what are now the provinces of Manitoba, Saskatchewan, and Alberta, although a limited amount was given to Metis who had moved to the northern United States. This was so even though a portion of Treaty 8 covered the northeast portion of British Columbia. Because scrip could only be applied against surveyed land, a significant number of Metis were immediately at a disadvantage. For example, in the 1906 Treaty 10 area of northern Saskatchewan, 60 per cent of the scrip issued was land scrip. To this day there is virtually no surveyed land in that area. As a consequence, the Metis of northern Saskatchewan were deprived of their land base and their opportunity to acquire ownership of land. With respect to the Northwest Territories, when Treaty 11 was entered into in 1921, the Metis were allotted a cash grant of $240 rather than land or money scrip.

Researchers for the Association of Metis and Non-status Indians of Saskatchewan have documented evidence that of the scrip issued, one-third was land scrip and two-thirds money scrip, for a total of 31,000 certificates or 4,030,000 acres (these figures are based on 80 per cent of the known remaining files). Over 90 per cent of the scrip was delivered into the hands of banks and speculators. The banks received over 52 per cent of the issued scrip. The Department of the Interior, which was responsible for the scrip program, facilitated the transfer of scrip to corporations and individual speculators by keeping scrip accounts for them.

Although scrip was meant to be used for land only, the notes were used for other purposes. Because of the desperate and destitute situation of the Metis, scrip was often sold for cash, bringing the equivalent of twenty-five cents on the dollar or acre in 1878, and rising to five dollars per acre for land scrip in 1908. The majority of scrip, however, was sold for approximately one-third of its face value. Scrip was also exchanged for farm animals, implements, seed, food, and other supplies.

Most of this speculative activity took place outside the area covered by the Manitoba Act, 1870. Therefore, the constitutional implications of section 31 of that act did not apply. Nevertheless, there is a line of thought that holds that all aboriginal peoples in Rupert's Land and the Northwest Territories had their aboriginal title constitutionally entrenched by virtue of section 146 of the Constitution Act, 1867. That section provided for the entry into confederation of those two areas, and decreed that 'the provisions of any Order-in-Council in that behalf shall have the effect as if they had been enacted by the Parliament of the United Kingdom of Great Britain and Ireland.'

On 19 November 1869, the Hudson's Bay Company surrendered its charter to the crown. Following the negotiations between the provisional government and the Canadian government, the British Parliament passed an order-in-council on 23 June 1870 making Rupert's Land a part of Canada effective 15 July 1870. Section 14 of that order-in-council stated that 'any claims of Indians to compensation for lands required for purposes of settlement shall be disposed of by the Canadian Government in communication with the Imperial Government; and the company shall be relieved of all responsibility in respect of them.' Also incorporated into the order-in-council were addresses to the queen by the Senate and the House of Commons. The first one, dated December 1867, asked for the transfer of Rupert's Land to Canada: 'Upon the transference of the territories in question to the Canadian Government, the claims of the Indian tribes to compensation for lands required to purposes of settlement will be considered and settled in conformity with the equitable principles which have uniformly governed the British Crown in its dealings with the aborigines.' The order-in-council does not specifically refer to half-breeds, although it does refer to 'aborigines'; it was issued after the Manitoba Act expressly recognized the half-breeds right to land under Indian title.

In the *Paulette* case (1973) Mr Justice Morrow, then of the Northwest Territories Supreme Court, was of the opinion that the provisions or conditions of the order-in-council had 'become part of the Canadian Constitution and could not be removed or altered except by Imperial Statute.' But for the provisions found in section 31 of the Manitoba Act, 1870, it is clear that the Canadian Parliament is precluded from dealing unilaterally with the aboriginal title of the aboriginal people covered by the order-in-council, that is, those aboriginal people living within the area covered by the Hudson's Bay Company charter. Any doubt about the referential incorporation of the order-in-council under the provisions of section 146 can arguably be laid to rest by the specific inclusion of the order-in-council as the Rupert's Land and the North Western Territory Order under schedule 1 of the Constitution Act, 1982.

It is argued by the Metis National Council and the Association of Metis and Non-status Indians of Saskatchewan that the action of the federal government, coupled with its knowledge of the fraud that was being perpetrated, was illegal, immoral, and inequitable, and that the aboriginal title of the Metis remains unextinguished.

Also of concern to the Metis is the Constitution Act, 1930, which ratified the Natural Resources Transfer Agreements between the provinces of Manitoba, Saskatchewan, and Alberta and the federal government. By these agreements the provinces were given ownership and control of the natural resources within their boundaries. Contained in the agreements is a provision that the provinces would allow 'Indians' to continue hunting, trapping, and fishing for food on all unoccupied crown lands and lands to which they have a right of access. This constitutional provision cuts down the aboriginal and treaty right to hunt, trap, and fish for commercial purposes. The places of hunting are also restricted. It is of great concern to the Metis and non-status Indians that the term 'Indians' is not defined. In a judgment rendered on 20 July 1978, the Saskatchewan Court of Appeal ruled that the term 'Indian' as used in the agreement did not include the accused, a non-treaty, non-status Indian. This decision prevented all aboriginal people not entitled to be registered under the Indian Act from exercising their right to hunt, trap, and fish, even for food. This decision was not appealed and the issue has still not been resolved.

It is the belief of the Metis that the long-standing denial of our rights, economic deprivation, poverty, and the displacement of our people have to be rectified in a manner that is meaningful to us. We require a cultural, social, economic, and political regeneration as well as an adequate land base and resource rights. The concept of Metis nationalism and accepted principles of international law indicate that these goals can be reached through political expression and in a spirit of goodwill. Our right to self-determination is on a higher plane than the legal fiction of aboriginal title. As a nation of aboriginal people, we have a right to a homeland and self-government no less than the Palestinians or the blacks of South Africa. This right is a right of choice, a right to choose statehood, assimilation, or anything in between. The Metis have chosen to exercise this right within the Canadian federation, and will seek to have it acknowledged in all forthcoming constitutional conferences. It must always be kept in mind that the conferences are for the purpose of identifying and defining all the rights of aboriginal peoples, not merely their aboriginal and treaty rights.

The Metis will insist on a charter of rights, which will be in addition to the current recognition and affirmation of our existing aboriginal rights. This charter will provide the legal basis for a third level of government for and by aboriginal people, and by implication will necessarily alter the current jurisdictional division of powers under sections 91 and 92 of the Constitution Act, 1867, including section 91(24) respecting Indians and the lands reserved for the Indians. The Metis, while not rejecting aboriginal title, are striving for the entrenchment of our right to self-determination. The primary attributes of that right are a land base and Metis self-government.

BILL WILSON

Aboriginal Rights:
The Non-status Indian
Perspective

To ask 'What is the non-status Indian perspective on aboriginal rights?'
is to admit to a basic misunderstanding of aboriginal title. Aboriginal
rights flow from aboriginal title. All the descendants of the original
occupants of the land retain aboriginal title to the land as well as the
rights that flow from that title. This will always be the case because no
generation or special group has the right to sign away the rights of any
future generation. Even if land claims are resolved today, the future
descendants of the original occupiers of the land will be entitled to
negotiate their own bargain in regard to aboriginal title and rights. Had
all this been clear to Indian leaders over the last hundred years, the
question of non-status Indian peoples' claim to aboriginal title would
never have arisen.

Federal government Indian policy over the past one hundred years has
served to muddy the waters in regard to aboriginal title. Even a cursory
look at this policy reveals a systematic attempt to separate Indians from
their land, their rights, and each other. Non-status Indians today exist as
a function of the Indian Act and the federal government's Indian policy.
Let us look briefly at the creation of the group of native Indian people
now referred to as 'non-status.'

The Indian Act, by establishing criteria governing who was eligible to
belong to the status Indian group, created a charter group of eligible
persons; moreover, it stipulated a formula for the perpetuation of that
group. The formula, while perhaps liberal in the beginning, became
exclusionary over time. Perhaps the best evidence of the exclusionary
nature of the formula is found in its affirmation of patrilineal preference,
which became increasingly rigid and which persists to the present
day. That this patrilineal preference flew in the face of the matrilineal

tradition of most Indian tribes only serves to reinforce the assumption of a deliberate policy to divide and confound Indian people.

It must be remembered that the ultimate goal of the Canadian government's Indian legislation has always been the integration or assimilation of Indians into the dominant society. In 1950, H.E. Harris, then minister of Indian affairs, announced a 'new' Indian policy: 'The ultimate goal of our Indian policy is the integration of the Indians into the general life and economy of the country. It is recognized, however, that during a temporary transition period of varying length ... special treatment and legislation are necessary.'[1]

This policy of integration or assimilation had the effect of reinforcing the exclusionary formula for perpetuation of the charter group. It served as a rationale for getting Indians off the lists and into non-Indian society as quickly as possible. Despite the exclusionary formula, the charter group grew in numbers and came to be a large financial burden on the treasury. This provided an additional important motive for rigorous enforcement of the exclusionary formula.

The practice of enfranchisement, which was adopted even before Confederation, was an expedient to accelerate integration or assimilation. Enfranchisement was designed to remove all distinctions between Indians and other Canadians. In 1857, legislation was passed describing a procedure of enfranchisement which, unchanged, formed the basis of federal legislation until 1918. This legislation was titled An Act to Encourage the Gradual Civilization of the Indian Tribes in This Province.[2] In the event that the title of this legislation did not make clear the government's intent, federal policy was made explicit by Duncan Campbell Scott, deputy superintendent-general of Indian affairs. Speaking to a House of Commons committee in 1920, Scott stated that the enfranchisement policy would be continued 'until there is not a single Indian in Canada that has not been absorbed into the body politic, and there is no Indian question, and no Indian Department.'[3]

Enfranchisement ostensibly would provide a mechanism whereby Indians would move from a dependent protected status into full citizenship, on a par with their white neighbours. Initially the federal government characterized enfranchisement as a privilege. Because few Indians were willingly enfranchised, the federal government passed compulsory enfranchisement legislation in 1920 and 1923. This legislation gave the Department of Indian Affairs the power to initiate the removal of Indians from their band lists, their families, their tribes, and their land. The racist assumption that white people knew what was best for Indians was alive and well.

The manner in which the original band lists were compiled must also be considered in order to understand the non-status Indian question. In 1951, the 'Indian register' was formed from various band lists that had existed within the department before that time. These lists included band fund lists, treaty pay lists, and other lists used by the department to identify members of the charter group. Although all native people supposedly were given the opportunity to be included on the lists, many were left off. This can be attributed partly to the incompetence and carelessness of the officials responsible for compiling the lists. Personal or family favouritism also played a part. In many cases whole families or clans were left off the band lists, with the result that the Indian register of 1951 was incomplete. The incomplete register resulted in the ludicrous situation of many full-blooded Indian parents and their children losing their Indian status because the father had not been included in the original lists. Aboriginal heritage, blood quantum, and culture seemed irrelevant.

The Indian Act had the effect of breaking up the tribal system and removing the land from Indian control. In this regard the government's potlatch laws, directed at the heart of Indian culture, were the most explicit threat to the tribal system. The potlatch laws and enfranchisement, especially compulsory enfranchisement, seemed designed to break up band lands into small pieces. Both initiatives were bitterly resisted by Indians, and the potlatch laws were defied even to the point of incarceration.

Exclusion from the band lists meant that non-status Indians were not eligible for any services provided by the Department of Indian Affairs. Inadequate though those services may have been, they were more than the non-status Indian could look forward to in white society.

Non-status Indians were discriminated against in all aspects of their lives by non-Indians, and at the same time were excluded from participating in their ancestral communities. Forced to live in a society that did not welcome them, non-status Indians could be forgiven for looking longingly to their status Indian brothers and sisters. The federal government not only created two classes of Indian people, but also played off the two groups against each other. Status Indians often viewed non-status Indians as a threat to their own well-being. Internal racism was masked with the excuse that the money or land allocated by the government was insufficient to include non-status Indians for distribution purposes. Although the attitudes of Indians have changed, this excuse is still put forward when the status–non-status question is discussed in regard to band lists.

The non-status Indians truly became the forgotten people. Even supposedly informed status Indian leaders assumed that their non-status Indian brothers and sisters must have done something wrong to find themselves in their excluded position. Instead of experiencing the 'privilege' of enfranchisement, non-status Indian people found themselves totally disfranchised from almost all tribal or band functions.

The introduction of the elected band council system further alienated non-status Indians from their own people. Formerly, they had been able to participate in Indian life through their shared culture and through their hereditary tribal institutions, regardless of the Indian Act. After the introduction of the so-called democratic electoral system, however, they found no place in band society.

Non-status Indian people were also excluded from the national and provincial Indian organizations on the assumption that the only bona fide Indians were those recorded on the band lists. This, of course, was a racist assumption based on the white man's legislation. Many Indians accepted this assumption despite what our history and our culture told them. Although remnants of this racist assumption exist to this day, in the past twenty years Indian people have progressed to the point where they are throwing off these non-Indian assumptions. The best example of this is the present movement among Indians to re-identify with tribal institutions and Indian culture.

We Indians passed through a stage where we assumed that big Indian organizations at the provincial and national levels could best represent people at the community level. We were told this by such people as the late Arthur Laing when he was minister of Indian affairs in 1965. These directives came from non-Indian people and non-Indian institutions, and we followed them. The renewed political and cultural activity in Indian communities from 1960 to the present has led us back to our family and tribal structures. In every province and territory in Canada, Indians are now identifying with their traditional land base and tribal system. Pockets of racism still exist within the Indian community in various parts of the the country, but in general the new attitude seems to be that non-status Indian claims to aboriginal title represent an aboriginal right, not a favour extended to them by their status Indian brothers and sisters. This is the most significant development that has taken place in Indian communities across the country in the last fifteen years.

Indian organizations have existed in British Columbia since the late 1800s, but before 1969 the provincial organizations were almost exclusively composed of status Indians. In April 1969, an organization known as the British Columbia Association of Non-status Indians (BCANSI) was formed by Butch Smitheram. Its purpose was to organize,

educate, and unite non-status Indian people in the province of British
Columbia. In November of the same year, the Union of British
Columbia Indian Chiefs (UBCIC) was formed. Membership in BCANSI was
open to non-status Indians and Metis. UBCIC was composed of chiefs or
their designated representatives, all of whom had to be status Indians.
UBCIC was formed to pursue land claims at the provincial level.
Throughout the union's early years, it acted exclusively on behalf of
status Indian people. In British Columbia in 1969, the assumption was
that only status Indians could be included in any claim based on
aboriginal title and that non-status Indians had no place in the land
claims process. BCANSI at first made no representations in the area of
land claims. Its members felt excluded from the entire land claims
process. Not until 1971 was the whole question of aboriginal title,
aboriginal rights, and land claims even discussed at a BCANSI convention. The association had to be convinced that its members had a right to
be involved in land claims negotiations.

BCANSI's initial attempts to be included in the land claims process
were vigorously rebuffed by UBCIC and by status Indians in British
Columbia. But the struggle continued, led by younger people in both
associations. Ultimately, a new awareness developed in the province of
peoples' rights as opposed to chiefs' rights or provincial association's
rights. This awareness, coupled with a new emphasis on tribal councils,
made it easier to deal with the question of who was qualified to assert
land claims. Over time it became accepted that the historical rights that
flow from aboriginal title cannot be defined or restricted by the Indian
Act or any other legislation passed by federal or provincial governments.

The years 1975 and 1976 saw attempts to amalgamate UBCIC and
BCANSI. This was more than an amalgamation of two provincial
organizations; it marked the rejection of discrimination and internal
racism. These years also signalled an end to the 'big Indian association'
mentality. Tribal councils re-emerged, and they flourish today; the
majority make no distinction between status and non-status Indians.

This change in attitude is reflected across the country. We see claims
being put forward on the basis of traditional lands and culture, not on
the basis of some artificial status definition imposed by non-Indians.
Much work still has to be done to remove the pockets of racism that
exist among status Indian people on the reserves. The discrimination
that exists among non-status Indian people, who are suspicious of their
status Indian brothers and sisters, must also be eradicated. We have
broken down the attitudinal barriers that separated us; we have returned
to our Indian family structures and tribal institutions, and are now
attempting to work our way out from under the colonial oppression of

the Department of Indian Affairs and all that it represents. Regardless of what Parliament or the Department of Indian Affairs says or does, Indian people are taking the instruments of self-government into their own hands. The most important instrument is that of control of our membership, a membership defined according to our history, culture, and traditions, not in accordance with Victorian patrilineal assumptions.

What does all this have to do with aboriginal rights viewed from a non-status Indian perspective? The thesis of this paper is that the question of aboriginal title and the rights that flow from that title, as well as the exercise of those rights, is the same for non-status Indians as it is for status Indians. It could perhaps be said that non-status Indians have a larger historical grievance, given that they have been ignored for over one hundred years, but this is not what is being said by non-status Indian leaders. Non-status Indian leaders want to be involved in their tribal councils and in their bands not as a favour but as a right. The only difference is that they are seeking some 'extra' provision for urban non-status Indians, who may not know with which band or tribal structure they should affiliate.

The consensus of position and purpose among Indians is not yet perfect, but it is clear where we are heading. Ultimately the term 'non-status Indian' will be purged from our vocabulary, and we will refer to ourselves by our traditional band or tribal names. Land claims are now being formulated and advanced on behalf of tribes – that is, the descendants of the original inhabitants of a particular area of land – without regard to the racial distinctions contained in the Indian Act. This is the way it should be.

Land claims will be resolved so that this generation of Indians will have an increased land base, control of its institutions, control of its resources, and, most important, decision-making authority in regard to all the things that affect Indians within their traditional land base. The aboriginal rights of all of the original inhabitants of the land will be negotiated on the basis of the existence of aboriginal title to that land.

It has taken a long time for Indian people to get back to their roots and rid themselves of non-Indian assumptions. We can only hope progress will continue at the rate it has in the last twenty-five years. The constitutional conferences have demonstrated that Indian people are capable of standing toe-to-toe with any non-Indian leader in the country. This is no surprise to the Indian people, of course.

We recognize that many barriers still stand in our way, not the least of which are our internal political differences and personality conflicts. We also have federal policies that are of little or no help and provincial policies of outright opposition and racism to contend with. We have seen in the preparations for the constitutional conferences an attempt by the provinces and the federal government to force Indian, Inuit, and Metis people into amalgamations not of their own design. We must remember that while we share many common interests, we are all different peoples and our differences must be respected. We do not see only one political party or only one church among the white people. Why should all Indians be expected to conform to one mould?

There remains another obstacle, not often talked about or admitted to, and that is the role played by white lawyers and consultants. It has been said that they are the only people who benefit from claims to aboriginal title and aboriginal rights or from the constitutional discussions. Although this is true, it will remain true only in the short term. Even more important than the money the white lawyers and consultants make at our expense is the power they exercise on behalf of Indians in the constitutional process. We have it within ourselves to make all the decisions and do all the work now being done by white lawyers and consultants. They are not needed, but they remain as a vestige of the colonial mentality native Indian people have accepted for far too long.

Politics and personalities: these are things with which we must deal. Many of our leaders have had as their primary goal co-operation with non-Indians; seeking benefits for their people has been of secondary importance. Such leaders must be replaced, just as we must rid ourselves of the 'convenience Indians,' the 'self-proclaimed Indians,' and the other pretenders who have attached themselves to our fight. The elimination of the status question from all discussions in regard to aboriginal title and rights makes our fight much simpler. We can now work toward the full exercise of our aboriginal rights without regard to the Indian Act or other non-Indian dictates.

2 Aboriginal Rights in the Constitutional and Policy-Making Processes

THE 1982 CONSTITUTIONAL ACCORD formally signalled the end of the exclusive relationship that historically existed between status Indians and the federal government. The policy and process of integrating Indians into provincial political, administrative, economic, and social institutions has been in evidence since the Second World War, and was fuelled by the 1969 federal government White Paper. However, the Constitution Act, 1982, which entrenches existing aboriginal and treaty rights, represents a watershed in Indian–Canadian relations because it set these relations on a course that now requires formal participation by the provinces in the development of future Indian policy. This change carries profound political, economic, social, and legal implications for the future direction of Canadian Indian policy. Henceforth, the provinces will be fully and formally involved in the definition of aboriginal rights, Indian government, land title, and services to Indians. There is a bitter irony here for status Indians. Although they fought hard to have their aboriginal rights entrenched in the constitution, now part of the control over status Indians has been transferred to the provinces, thus introducing ambiguity into their historic claims to nationhood and aboriginal and treaty rights.

In this section the contributors consider the constitutional process as an approach to resolving aboriginal rights claims. It is readily apparent that the governments of Canada start out with a fundamentally different set of premises from those expressed by aboriginal leaders in section 1. One fundamental difference is that aboriginal title and rights are thought by the governments to be subject to the will of legislatures, not to the will of the Creator. Another difference is that aboriginal leaders believe that rights are vested in the collectivity, while the governments see rights as vested in the individual. Whereas aboriginal leaders say there is no problem with the definition of aboriginal rights – they know what the term means – federal and provincial governments see insoluble problems in defining the concept. While aboriginal leaders emphasize principles, such as justice, the governments emphasize pragmatism and political expedience.

There are differences not only in premises but in priorities. Aboriginal leaders view their claim to aboriginal rights as a matter of survival for their people. The federal and provincial governments deal with aboriginal rights in the context of of federal–provincial–aboriginal jurisdictional arrangements. Although the federal and provincial governments express concern and empathy for the aboriginal peoples' condition, and although they project a desire for an equitable solution that will ensure the survival of aboriginal cultures and language, it is clear that to them solutions outside the framework of delegated authority are unacceptable.

Taken together, sections 1 and 2 demonstrate the virtual impossibility of achieving any meaningful consensus on aboriginal rights. Aboriginal leaders cannot agree among themselves on policy positions; federal and provincial governments and even departments cannot agree on their policy positions. Moreover, the entire negotiating process appears stalled in a catch-22 situation: each side is reluctant to develop its policy position in the absence of a policy position on the other side. In addition to all this, serious questions are surfacing on both sides as to whether the constitutional forum is the appropriate one for resolving the issue of aboriginal rights.

ROY ROMANOW

Aboriginal Rights in the Constitutional Process

In this paper I will briefly review the key events relating to aboriginal rights as I saw them in the constitutional process during the period of patriation from about 1978 to 1982. Unfortunately, most of the activities took place without any written transcripts or minutes of proceedings, so I will present my version of the key events that transpired during that period. Second, I will consider some questions regarding the section 37 conferences, and offer some advice based on my experience with the constitutional discussions. As I reflect on the constitutional proceedings, I realize how frequently the arguments were circular, and how old positions were abandoned only to be re-adopted. Often the bargaining dealt exclusively with pragmatic concerns, with little consideration given to principles.

It cannot be said that the constitutional negotiations started at any particular moment. I see the process as having started in the mid-1970s, when concurrence of the centrifugal political forces of Quebec separatism and western Canadian economic alienation strained Canadian unity, bringing Canadians (and in particular the federal government) to the realization that some form of constitutional renewal was imperative. As an expression of its concern the federal government in 1978 tabled a White Paper on constitutional reform entitled 'A Time for Action.' This was followed shortly after by Bill C-60. The White Paper is important to any discussion of aboriginal rights. In it recognition of aboriginal rights was set out as one of the principles to guide the renewal of federation. Although the document failed to make a specific commitment to legislative or constitutional entrenchment of aboriginal rights, the principle was joined in the mind of the federal government with other principles pertaining to language rights and regional alienation – principles thought to be fundamental to renewing the federation.

The White Paper and Bill C-60 provide an insight into how the federal government approached the process and timing of constitutional change. Both documents argued in effect that there should be two phases of reform. The first phase would focus on those things the federal government believed lay within its own constitutional authority, thus allowing it to act without provincial consent. These included a statement of aims, a charter of rights, and a reformed Senate. In this first phase the provinces would be consulted. If agreement could be obtained, so much the better; if not, the federal government was determined to move unilaterally. In the second phase, at some later date there would be a fundamental discussion with the provinces on restructuring the division of powers between the federal and provincial governments. Apart from the recognition of the principle of aboriginal rights, nothing more was said on this issue.

The task of formulating a response by way of policy and tactics to the federal government's initiatives was relatively easy for the provincial governments. After all, since the 1976 federal–provincial conference the provinces had been formulating their own notions of constitutional reform aimed at restructuring the division of legislative powers to the advantage of the provinces. So, in 1978, when the premiers met at their annual premiers' conference, they issued the Regina Communique. This document restated their philosophical approach to the constitution; in it they rejected the idea of breaking up the constitutional reform process into two phases. The premiers also asserted that there could be no deadlines on the constitutional process and that the federal government could not put its own priorities, such as a charter of rights, to the top of the agenda while neglecting provincial priorities. As a consequence of the stand taken by the provincial governments, the two agenda items – the revision of federal institutions and the division of powers – were merged at the 1978 first ministers' conference. Thereafter, the federal–provincial negotiating process was continued in the form of the Continuing Committee of Ministers on the Constitution (CCMC).

Canada's aboriginal leaders bore the unenviable burden of trying to overcome three impediments to a full consideration of their rights. First, the debates surrounding the constitution were dominated by the federal and provincial governments, and their concerns were paramount. Aboriginal rights were not one of those concerns. Second, the mounting political pressure to get on with constitutional negotiations dictated an extremely tight timetable. The pressure to proceed came less from the public than from Prime Minister Pierre Trudeau, who was determined that reform must begin sometime during 1978–9. As a consequence of the tight schedule, native concerns were neglected. Finally, aboriginal peoples faced the task of articulating – legally, conceptually, and historically – exactly what 'aboriginal rights' meant. This difficult task was made more complicated for Indian leaders by the federal government's concurrent announcement of its intention to amend the Indian Act. The proposed amendments to the act would transfer authority from the Department of Indian Affairs to band governments. This new policy thrust was confusing, because it was a complete reversal of the federal government's 1969 proposed Indian policy to detribalize Indians and take away their special status. Quite apart from any other considerations, the notion that Indian self-government could be created unilaterally by federal legislation implied an unacceptable inferior constitutional position for Indians and contradicted the Indians' claim that they had an inherent right to self-determination, self-government, or sovereignty, as some described it.

The rigidity of the constitutional timetable was a source of great irritation to the provinces as well as the aboriginal leaders. The premiers not only rejected the arbitrary deadlines set by the federal government, but initiated tactics designed to stall the constitutional negotiations. Concurrently, Indian leaders, acting through the general assembly of the National Indian Brotherhood (NIB), endorsed a resolution to advise the queen that patriation should be halted until aboriginal rights were fully recognized. But none of these various initiatives succeeded in delaying patriation. Although the timetable was seriously disrupted by the federal elections, by the referendum in Quebec, and by the Supreme Court's deliberations on the federal government's authority to patriate the constitution, the final outcome was not affected. Sensing its impending defeat in the 1978 federal election and apprehensive over the sovereignty-association issue in Quebec, the Liberal government was determined that nothing should deter it from its quest to attain reform and patriation of the constitution.

Once the federal and provincial agendas were merged, the structure of the CCMC was established. Marc Lalonde was appointed federal co-chairman, and I was appointed provincial co-chairman. The issue of aboriginal rights was not on our agenda. It fell victim to the obsessive concerns over the future of Quebec, the mounting economic alienation in western Canada, and public pressure to get the job of patriation done. So, as Canadians embarked once more on that elusive quest to finalize their constitutional independence, aboriginal rights became a casualty of other priorities.

In 1979, after the defeat of the Trudeau government, the Clark government took over for a period of approximately nine months. In my judgment this period was characterized by a failed but none the less genuine attempt to establish a role for aboriginal leaders in the constitutional process. During the summer of 1979 a series of meetings took place between Prime Minister Joe Clark and the leaders of aboriginal organizations in Canada. Although these negotiations did not produce any agreement, aboriginal people made one modest gain: agenda item 11, 'Native Peoples in the Constitution of Canada,' was added to the constitutional agenda.

After a meeting with Prime Minister Clark, Chief Noel Starblanket of the NIB, in a letter dated 2 October 1979, summarized their negotiations as having produced an agreement that 'our request for ongoing and full participation has been accepted and that equal participation will be limited to Agenda Item 11 that flows from the February Meeting of First Ministers'.' This statement manifests a major misunderstanding between the federal government and Indian leaders. The minutes of the CCMC meeting with the aboriginal organization on 3 December 1979 record that, in addition to restating its view of self-determination, the brotherhood insisted on full, equal, and ongoing participation in the constitutional discussion on *all* issues, including participation in economic and energy meetings. But Prime Minister Clark's minister, Bill Jarvis, specifically insisted on limiting the scope of native involvement to agenda item 11 only and did not accept the principle of equal participation. The idea of 'ongoing and full participation' by Indian leaders in economic and energy meetings was clearly not acceptable to the provinces or to the federal government. Thus, the initially hopeful signs that the prime minister, the provinces, and the aboriginal organizations would be able to agree on the details of process floundered on a significant procedural misunderstanding.

The Clark government felt that it could not hold meaningful negotiations on the substantive issues of the constitution until Quebec decided whether it was going to remain in Confederation. Accordingly, questions of constitutional process and procedure were placed on the back burner. The return to power of the Trudeau government in 1980, marked the return of the constitutional issue to the top of the public agenda.

On the question of the Indians role in the constitutional discussions, Trudeau endorsed direct participation by the Indian leadership on those constitutional issues which directly affected Indian rights. On the remaining agenda items, the prime minister was to meet with the aboriginal representatives 'to obtain [their] views on constitutional matters prior to the next First Ministers' Conference.' Although a promise had been made in February 1979 to include the item 'Native Peoples in the Constitution of Canada' on the new agenda, the item never appeared. The reason for its exclusion is unclear. On 9 June 1980 a private first ministers' meeting, at which only the premiers and the prime minister were present, struck the agenda. Whether or not a full consideration of the 'native peoples' item took place I have been unable to determine. The prime minister sent a letter to Chief Starblanket on 11 August 1980 defining the general item of 'native peoples' as it stood in the constitution to mean 'aboriginal rights, treaty rights, internal Native self-government, Native representation and political institutions, and responsibilities of the federal and provincial governments for the provision of services to Native people.' In effect, this represented a restatement of his speech to the First Nations Constitution Conference (FNCC) in April 1980. Again, the detailed consideration of aboriginal rights was postponed.

During this period of constitutional activity, the notion of self-determination and sovereignty was becoming firmly entrenched in the policy positions of the aboriginal peoples. In 1978 and thereafter the Federation of Saskatchewan Indians mounted a number of persuasive legal and historical arguments for the right to self-determination and full sovereignty. There emerged from the 1980 FNCC a declaration of principles laying claim to full control of land, water, air, minerals, timber, and wildlife on all Indian lands on the basis that Indian sovereignty had never been surrendered. In effect, this declaration was an assertion of full Indian sovereignty without any constraint or limitation by the federal government. This constituted a major policy cleavage between the Indians and the other governments. No further meetings took place between Indian leaders and the ministers or their bureaucrats until the last week of August 1980, a clear indication of the gap between the two sides.

The only reference to aboriginal rights in the 1980 CCMC constitutional discussions appeared in an 'undeclared rights' section of the constitutional draft, which said that rights not specifically mentioned in the Charter of Rights and Freedoms would not be derogated from, 'including those that may pertain to Native people.' This was a change from the 1978 Bill C-60 provisions, which had the same general protection for undeclared rights, but in which the reference to the rights of native people read 'including those of Native people under the Royal Proclamation of 1763.'

In 1978 the provinces were already resolved to oppose the inclusion of the undeclared rights section on the ground that it suggested there were additional overriding rights in the constitution which had not yet been articulated by the Charter of Rights and Freedoms. The provinces argued that a court might limit some specifically enumerated rights set out in the Charter on the ground that they violated some undeclared right. For example, there might be an undeclared right not to be harassed, or a right to live in an orderly society, or some other such undeclared right which, depending on how it was defined by a court, could limit the specifically enumerated right of free speech. In this manner undeclared rights would override specifically enumerated rights and would achieve constitutional status. This would open the door for the judiciary to recognize an open-ended series of new constitutionally entrenched rights.

Applying this logic to the question of aboriginal rights, the provinces were concerned that if the judiciary were to find the right to self-determination and full sovereignty to be an undeclared right of aboriginal people, the impact of such a finding would have serious consequences for the provinces with respect to land and jurisdictional authority. Of course, that was only one aspect of a much larger issue concerning the Charter of Rights and Freedoms. The provinces believed that an entrenched Charter would involve the appointed judiciary in the political process, thereby diminishing the supremacy of the legislatures. In a more general sense, an entrenched Charter would pose the fundamental question whether the definition and protection of human rights are better served by the democratic political process or through legal interpretations by the judiciary. The provincial governments were no doubt mindful of Thomas Jefferson's statement: 'The constitution is a mere thing of wax in the hands of the judiciary which they may twist and shape into any form that they please.'

The provinces' apprehension over the prospect of the judiciary's shaping the constitution was not shared by aboriginal leaders. By supporting constitutional entrenchment of aboriginal rights, aboriginal leaders in effect expressed a willingness to accept considerable judicial involvement in shaping their peoples' future.

The NIB's determination to oppose patriation until agreement was reached on entrenchment of aboriginal rights disrupted the federal and provincial governments' priorities. In the summer of 1980 the federal and provincial negotiators hoped for a breakthrough on the amending formula and other issues. But a significant group in our society – aboriginal people – was adamantly saying 'no' to patriation. Even those provinces that were opposed to the patriation process were not willing to defy the growing political momentum for patriation. Accordingly, the aboriginal peoples stood alone and were excluded from the constitutional talks.

When the first ministers' conference in September 1980 failed to reach agreement, the Trudeau government, true to its word, moved unilaterally. As a result, the provinces joined the aboriginal people on the sidelines. We then witnessed a period of confrontation and bitterness. The scene of constitutional activity shifted to the joint parliamentary committee, but most provinces ignored this process. They felt that the procedure violated their notion of federalism. Why, they asked, should the provinces submit to the authority of the federal government when they are equals in Confederation?

In response to public pressure, the federal government suddenly and dramatically reversed itself on the question of entrenching aboriginal rights in the constitution. The government proposed an amendment that would give positive recognition to treaty and aboriginal rights. This was followed by a remarkable about-face by aboriginal leaders. Some now said that as a consequence of the amendment on aboriginal rights they would join the federal government in urging the British government to approve the constitution resolution despite the objections of the provinces. The spectacle of the aboriginal peoples joining hands with the federal government raised apprehension in the provinces. The accord between the Indians and the federal government was short-lived, however. Within days Indian organizations reverted to their original positions before the joint parliamentary committee, taking a very antagonistic stance against the proposed government amendment.

By the time the first ministers met in November 1981, the constitutional flip-flop by Indian leaders had become extremely important. Simply stated, the antagonistic actions by Indian leaders before the joint parliamentary committee were interpreted by the federal government and many provincial governments to mean that anything short of self-determination or full sovereignty was unacceptable to the Indian leadership, and that the provisions of the proposed section 34 of the draft Constitution Act recognizing and affirming aboriginal and treaty rights of the aboriginal peoples were either of no value or of no interest to most of the Indian organizations. By the time this question was being considered in November 1980 in a closed session of first ministers, the Indians' antagonistic conduct before the joint parliamentary committee was being re-enacted in a public political battle in London. The aboriginal peoples' London lobby confirmed in the minds of the federal and provincial governments that the original section 34 should not be retained because it was contrary to the wishes of the Indian community. Of course, there were other factors. The demand for entrenchment of aboriginal rights was not fully understood by many of the governments, and those who thought they did understand it expressed reservations about its implications for provincial jurisdiction.

All of these matters came to a head in the immediate post-constitutional accord period. During this period womens' organizations across Canada, followed by some aboriginal groups, demanded that certain changes be implemented to the Charter of Rights and Freedoms. The government of Saskatchewan responded with a telex to the minister of justice on 18 November 1980, stating that if the accord was to be opened to accommodate the wishes of the womens' lobby, then section 34 in its original form would have to be reinstated. Two days later, the premier of Alberta expressed the uncertainty of a number of premiers as to the meaning of the original section 34. Premier Lougheed suggested that if a new section 34 was introduced it should read thus: 'Aboriginal and treaty rights of the aboriginal peoples of Canada, as those rights existed prior to the coming into force of this part, are affirmed.' The final wording of section 35 of the Constitution Act, 1982 (formerly section 34) read as follows: 'The existing aboriginal and treaty rights of the aboriginal peoples of Canada are hereby recognized and affirmed.' This restatement, with its potentially unknown consequences, failed to quell the opposition of the aboriginal people, which continued until patriation.

In summary, it is no fault of the aboriginal peoples that in its preoccupation with Quebec nationalism and western Canadian alienation the federal government neglected the question of aboriginal rights. Aboriginal peoples lacked effective economic and political bargaining weapons with which to reinforce their arguments for entrenchment of aboriginal rights. Aboriginal arguments were based on legal and moral principles and on historical and cultural obligations. Important as these considerations are in the practical world they were not as effective as the threat to hold up a major economic enterprise such as the James Bay project.

There was and still is no effective instrument for dealing with the key issues on the aboriginal peoples' agenda. There is no appropriate or adequate mediation or arbitration forum. Perhaps the political process could have performed some of those functions, but when one considers that the entire constitutional process was characterized by confrontation and bitterness, it is unlikely that a civilized and reasoned discussion of the complex legal issues would ever have taken place. In addition, the governments of Canada simply did not understand the aboriginal position. Because they did not go through a period of orientation and become knowledgeable about the question of aboriginal rights, their natural tendency was to put it aside.

Where do we go from here? First, the most important accomplishment of future constitutional conferences on aboriginal rights will be the establishment of an ongoing mechanism for the negotiation of those rights. That is, both sides must be committed to a political process. Given the neglect and discrimination suffered by the aboriginal peoples of Canada in the past, their reluctance to participate in such a process can be readily understood. Some would argue that there are better mechanisms – for example, the judicial process – for achieving aboriginal goals. The patriation experience, despite the problems, is nevertheless a testament to the efficacy of the political process. My own province, Saskatchewan, did not get everything it wanted in the field of resource ownership, but we did make some gains. When the process of constitutional reform resumes, we will want to further expand and extend those gains. We must bear in mind Judge Learned Hand's comment about the lack of moderation in society: 'This much I do know: that a society which is so riven that the spirit of moderation is gone, no court can save; but a society where that spirit flourishes, no court need save.'

Second, we need to clarify section 35 of the Constitution Act, 1982. What does the phrase 'existing aboriginal and treaty rights' mean? Does it mean only those rights that were recognized by the courts on 17 April 1982, the date on which the act was proclaimed? If so, the section falls far short of the goals of aboriginal peoples. One can argue that the purpose of inserting 'existing' might be to freeze aboriginal rights as defined on 17 April 1982. That view, which is offered by many credible constitutional lawyers, is one that I do not share. When the province of Saskatchewan ultimately agreed to the insertion of 'existing' in section 35, it said that rights do not exist merely because courts say they exist; courts can confirm rights, but a court does not make rights. The province held that aboriginal rights to self-government may or may not exist. If they exist, they exist independently of the courts. If there is a genuine difference of opinion as to the meaning of the word 'existing,' then the definition of the word should be placed near the top of any future conference agenda. I advocate restoring the wording of the original section 34.

There is the larger question of the relationship of section 35 to other sections of the constitution. Section 35, which forms part 2 of the constitution, is not subject to the enforcement procedures in part 1 (the

Canadian Charter of Rights and Freedoms). Viewed one way, it is possible that section 35 means that aboriginal rights are inviolate and no other federal legislation or policy can supersede them. Another interpretation holds that section 35 is too generally worded; it is not enforceable and therefore it means nothing. In my own view, section 35 falls somewhere between these two extremes. The section places a high constitutional value on aboriginal rights. Under section 91(24) of the Constitution Act, 1867, those rights can be limited by the political process only on the grounds of strong moral and legal necessity. But who decides whether there are strong moral or legal grounds for limiting aboriginal rights? At present we have no constitutional yardstick for resolving such a question.

The aboriginal peoples will have to decide whether section 35 should be linked to part 1 of the Constitution Act, 1982. Part 1 establishes high standards that must be met before legislative incursions can be made on entrenched rights and freedoms, and thus would provide protection for aboriginal rights. On the one hand, there is a down-side to such a linkage, because it may diminish the inviolability of section 35. On the other hand, leaving its status totally unspoken also raises the prospect that someday, somewhere, a judge will decide if and when incursion of the legislature is permitted. I think the judges will allow incursions on strong grounds, and if they do allow it they will define the standard permitting those incursions. That is a forfeiture of the political process and of our right to define those standards.

I conclude by saying that we must come to grips with the concept of Indian self-government. In my view the Federation of Saskatchewan Indians' position that Indian self-determination cannot be violated by anyone is too extreme. The other view, held by the federal and provincial governments, that Indian self-government is at the sufferance of legislative actions pursuant to section 91(24) of the Constitution Act, 1867, is too restrictive. I urge both sides to start looking for the middle ground of constitutionally recognized limited self-government. Once entrenchment of limited self-government is achieved, we can move on. The words of Malcolm Ross, a distinguished scholar, should be our guide in making the commitment to process and seeking the middle ground: 'As Canadians we take our life from the fruitful collision and interpretation of many inheritances and thus, we grow.'

RICHARD DALON

An Alberta Perspective on Aboriginal Peoples and the Constitution

This essay has three distinct but related purposes. It provides a historical account of events of the aboriginal constitutional process during the period between November 1981 and March 1984. It provides an analysis of particular events and an interpretation of certain sections and amendments to the Constitution Act, 1982. Needless to say, this analysis is not exhaustive or entirely unbiased. As Nietzsche put it in *The Will to Power*, 'There are no facts, everything is in flux, incomprehensible, elusive; what is relatively most enduring is – our opinions.' As in most such analyses, a particular perspective is presented. In this case it is a provincial, though not necessarily a provincial government, view-point. Finally, the essay contains speculations about future events and outcomes.

Federal–provincial discussions on native issues and the constitution did not begin formally until the November 1981 first ministers' conference on the constitution. The earlier constitutional discussions cannot be easily separated from later events, however, and the entire constitutional process was a prerequisite for the later discussions on aboriginal issues and the constitution. Nevertheless, it is fair to say that the most significant events occurred between 1978 and 1983. These events culminated in the historic first ministers' conference in March 1983. I will try to render these events understandable by placing them in a historical context.

The Constitutional Struggle

Federal–provincial discussions on aboriginal rights and the constitution did not occur until events were rapidly and inevitably pushing

The views expressed in this paper are those of the author and do not represent those of the government of Alberta.

the constitution toward patriation in a climate of federal–provincial hostility. This fact had several serious and unanticipated consequences. First, there was little time for discussions to take place between 30 January 1981, when the relevant amendments to the constitution were introduced to Parliament, and 17 April 1982, when patriation occurred. Moreover, there was no established forum in which discussions could take place. Second, the provinces were preoccupied with their efforts to stop the federal government's unilateral patriation of the constitution, and all other issues received scant attention. This is not to say that the provinces were uninterested in aboriginal issues and the constitution; ineluctable events forced them to focus their attention elsewhere. Finally, and perhaps most important, not enough time remained to discuss and examine the specific wording of the aboriginal amendments, and as a result the long-term implications were neither well thought out nor well understood. This mistake was, for various reasons, repeated at the March 1983 first ministers' conference, with the contentious proposed amendment to the Constitution Act, 1982, section 35(4).

At the November 1981 first ministers' conference on the constitution, agreement was reached among nine provinces and the federal government on the issues of patriation, the amending formula, and a charter of rights. The resolutions then before Parliament included three sections referring to native people:

25 *The guarantee in this Charter of certain rights and freedoms shall not be construed so as to abrogate or derogate from any aboriginal, treaty or other rights or freedoms that pertain to the aboriginal peoples of Canada including (a) any rights or freedoms that have been recognized by the Royal Proclamation of October 7, 1763; and (b) any rights or freedoms that may be acquired by the aboriginal peoples of Canada by way of land claims settlement.*

34 *(1) The aboriginal and treaty rights of the aboriginal peoples of Canada are hereby recognized and affirmed.*
(2) In this Act, 'aboriginal peoples of Canada' includes the Indian, Inuit and Metis peoples of Canada.

36 *(1) Until Part VI [the amending formula] comes into force, a constitutional conference composed of the Prime Minister of Canada and the first ministers of the provinces shall be convened by the Prime Minister of Canada at least once in every year.*
(2) A conference convened under subsection (1) shall have included in its agenda an item respecting constitutional matters that directly

affect the aboriginal peoples of Canada, including the identification and definition of the rights of those peoples to be included in the Constitution of Canada, and the Prime Minister of Canada shall invite representatives of those peoples to participate in the discussions on that item.

The provinces were trying to draw up an accord that they could present to the prime minister during the conference. There are conflicting accounts of what took place during the process of drafting the provincial accord in which section 34 of the draft Constitution Act, the section recognizing and affirming aboriginal rights, was dropped. Robert Sheppard and Michael Valpy in their book *The National Deal* describe it this way:

No explanation that is completely satisfying has ever been given for dropping the rights clause in the accord. Accounts from provincial delegations vary; some say it was given up almost by accident, or by a kind of osmotic, unspoken agreement; others stick to the line that it was discarded because the native peoples themselves did not accept it. On the federal side, there are reports that the Prime Minister was surprised to see it missing when the proposals drawn up by the provinces were placed before him – but that he shrugged and accepted it. No one from any delegation, federal or provincial, says the issue was debated at any length in the private sessions.[1]

In any event, the final federal–provincial accord included sections 25 and 36, but not section 34.

The various native organizations objected strongly to the omission of section 34, which to their minds guaranteed aboriginal rights. In an attempt to accommodate their objections, Premier Peter Lougheed met with Alberta Metis leaders and others to work out specific wording that would be acceptable to all parties. The wording was ultimately agreed to by the other provinces and the federal government. Just three weeks after the conference of 5 November, the Commons voted to restore section 35 (formerly section 34) in the constitution. Section 35 reads: as follows.

35 (1) The existing aboriginal and treaty rights of the aboriginal peoples of Canada are hereby recognized and affirmed.

(2) In this Act, 'aboriginal peoples of Canada' includes the Indian, Inuit and Metis peoples of Canada.

The only difference between the old section 34 and the new section 35 is the word 'existing.' Much has been made of this addition by the aboriginal representatives. A host of lawyers have spent and are still spending a great deal of time and effort attempting to uncover the underlying meaning of the word. The legal meaning, of course, will only become clear when the courts interpret the section, although it is possible to speculate on what the outcome might be. I will leave this speculation for the later discussion of the relevant sections. As to Alberta's intentions in introducing the word 'existing,' Premier Lougheed made clear in his opening remarks at the March conference what those intentions were:

Our difficulty, Mr. Chairman, was that the force of the aboriginal rights provision was unclear. The Government of Alberta supported and still does fully support existing aboriginal and treaty rights. The proposed aboriginal rights provision was open to the interpretation, however, that it would create new aboriginal rights that were not previously recognized in law. Not having been part of the earlier discussion between the federal government and Indian leaders, the Premiers on November 5th, 1981 were not prepared to include any additional provisions without understanding fully what was being requested and the consequences of such requests ...

I want to emphasize that the intent of the Alberta Government in agreeing to the present wording of section 35 was neither to freeze the legal status quo of aboriginal and treaty rights for all time, nor to deny any modern treaty or agreements between governments and aboriginal peoples the protection of section 35. In effect, it was a commitment by governments to protect the aboriginal rights which exist now and to recognize those which may come into existence as a result of this conference.

The 1982–3 National Constitutional Process

The constitution was patriated on 17 April 1982. Within one year of that date a first ministers' conference on the constitution had to be convened, with natives and their constitutional rights being one item on the agenda. The process initially involved a lengthy series of meetings between officials of the federal, provincial, and territorial governments and representatives of the aboriginal peoples. The aboriginal organizations that participated in these initial meetings were the Inuit Committee on National Issues, representing the Inuit, and the Native Council of Canada, representing the Metis and non-status Indians. The Assembly of First Nations, representing status Indians, did not participate in any of the meetings of officials until after the ministerial meeting on 31 January 1983. Quebec did not participate, but observers were sent to all the meetings.

The purpose of the pre-conference meetings, from the federal, provincial, and territorial governments' perspective, was twofold: first, to set an agenda for first ministers that realistically could be dealt with in two days; second, to obtain an appreciation and understanding of precisely what was meant by the various proposals put forth by the aboriginal people. The aboriginal representatives, however, had another purpose in mind. They wanted the governments to respond to their proposals, ostensibly to enable the aboriginal organizations to adjust their positions in the light of the various government responses. This expectation on the part of the aboriginal people was to be a continuing source of frustration for them because the governments were simply not prepared to put their positions on the table. It was only at the last ministerial meeting before the first ministers' conference that most of the provinces reluctantly outlined tentative positions on the various agenda items.

The reluctance of governments to state their positions in the preparatory process was understandable given that the governments were developing their policies in response to aboriginal proposals, which could only be done after the issues and the aboriginal positions were clearly understood. Moreover, until the ministers had approval from their cabinets, it was difficult for ministers and impossible for officials to react on behalf of their respective governments. In retrospect, it would not have been helpful had the governments reacted, since none of the aboriginal organizations was willing to alter its position or remove items from the agenda prior to the first ministers' conference. Even when the governments were unanimously opposed to a particular aboriginal position (such as the proposal that all constitutional amendments affecting aboriginal rights would require their consent), the aboriginal representatives would not remove the item from the agenda. This attitude is reflected in a comment made by Chief Billy Diamond at the ministerial meeting of 28 February 1983: 'Our view is that nothing short of consent on matters respecting aboriginal rights is fair and reasonable.' Their strategy was to keep all items on the agenda until they had government agreement. While this lack of compromise was an unorthodox approach to what is normally considered 'negotiation,' it was understandable in view of the aboriginal peoples' long and disappointing experience negotiating with governments.

The national preparatory process for the first ministers' conference culminated with a ministerial meeting on 28 February and 1 March

1983. The governments, at least, had partly accomplished their objectives. They certainly had a clearer, albeit not a definitive, understanding of the aboriginal issues and they had agreement on an agenda, which contained the following six items:

1 *Charter of Rights of the Aboriginal Peoples*
   Preamble
   Removal of 'existing,' and expansion of section 35 to include recognition of modern treaties, treaties signed outside Canada and before Confederation, and specific mention of 'aboriginal title' including the rights of aboriginal peoples of Canada to a land base
   Statement of the particular rights of aboriginal peoples
   Statement of principles
   Equality
   Enforcement
   Interpretation
2 *Amending formula revisions, including:*
   Amendments on aboriginal matters not to be subject to provincial opting out (section 42)
   Consent clause
3 *Self-government*
4 *Repeal of section 42(1)(e) and (f)*
5 *Amendments to part III, including:*
   Equalization   ⎫
   Cost-sharing   ⎬ *Resourcing of aboriginal governments*
   Service delivery ⎭
6 *Ongoing process, including further first ministers' conferences and the entrenchment of necessary mechanisms to implement rights.*

Metis Representation

During the preparatory process a frustrating and contentious issue arose concerning who would represent the prairie Metis – that is, the Alberta, Saskatchewan, and Manitoba Metis. The Native Council of Canada (NCC), a national organization, claimed to represent both the Metis and the non-status Indians. The NCC is structured along federal lines with one vote per provincial or territorial organization. There was a great deal of tension between the Metis and the non-status Indians represented by the NCC. This tension was due in part to the different approaches taken by the two groups. The non-status Indians based their arguments on legal grounds and wanted to come under federal jurisdiction. In short, they wanted the same rights that status Indians have under section 91(24) of

the Constitution Act, 1867, and the Indian Act. The Metis, however, did
not take a legalistic approach and did not want to come under sole federal
jurisdiction. This was of particular importance to some of the Alberta
Metis, since if they were to come under federal jurisdiction the Alberta
Metis Betterment Act could be found ultra vires, and the Metis living on
settlements might lose their land. The tension was eased somewhat by
the creation of a Metis constitutional committee within the NCC that
would represent Metis interests at the conference table.

The Metis constitutional committee consisted of the presidents of
the Manitoba Metis Federation, the Saskatchewan Non-status and
Metis Association, the Metis Association of Alberta, and the Federation
of Metis Settlement Associations of Alberta. At the ministerial meeting
of 28 February the Metis constitutional committee was denied a seat at
the table by the NCC. After that meeting the Metis broke their ties with
the NCC. Three of the provincial Metis organizations (excluding the
Federation of Metis Settlement Associations of Alberta) formed a new
group called the Metis National Council (MNC). The MNC was registered
in Saskatchewan under the title of the Metis Brotherhood. The MNC
then claimed that it represented all the prairie Metis and demanded a
seat at the conference table. This request was denied.

Less than a week before the first ministers' conference was to take
place the MNC sought a court injunction in Ontario to prevent the conference from proceeding without proper Metis representation. In the end
an agreement was reached that the MNC would be given one seat. There
were now four native organizations represented at the conference.

The Provincial Process

While the national preparatory process was under way, a similar and
parallel process was going on in Alberta and other provinces. In Alberta,
the process was limited to discussions with the province's two Metis
associations. There were no discussions between the Alberta government and the Indian Association of Alberta because their national
organization, the Assembly of First Nations, felt that its relationship
was solely with the federal government – a view presumably shared by
the Indian Association of Alberta.

At the suggestion of Sam Sinclair, president of the Metis Association
of Alberta, and Elmer Ghostkeeper, president of the Alberta Federation
of Metis Settlement Associations, a two-tiered consultative process was
established in Alberta to prepare for the 1983 constitutional conference.
The Honourable Dick Johnston, minister of federal and intergovernmental affairs, chaired the ministerial committee, which consisted of

the Honourable Don McCrimmon (minister responsible for native affairs), Elmer Ghostkeeper, and Sam Sinclair. I co-chaired the officials' committee with a representative either from the Metis Association of Alberta or from the Alberta Federation of Metis Settlement Associations. The committee had representation from the departments of Municipal Affairs (the department responsible for administering the Metis Betterment Act), the Attorney-General, the Native Secretariat, Culture, and Federal and Intergovernmental Affairs. The committees' terms of reference were contained in Premier Lougheed's letter to Mr Sinclair and Mr Ghostkeeper.[2]

As I understand it, the purpose of the discussion in the committee [the ministerial committee] and in the working group [the officials' committee] will be to share views and information on our respective positions with a view to identifying areas where there may be a consensus. I should note, however, that we anticipate that Alberta's position will be formulated in part in response to the views presented by your Associations and by other governments and interested parties. Consequently, it is probable that we will not be able to provide much more than a tentative reaction to the views of your Associations in the early stages of the process.

One of the difficulties with the Alberta process was that the terms of reference of the officials' committee and ultimately of the ministerial committee were never resolved to the satisfaction of the Metis. The Metis tended to view the officials' committee as a negotiating body. They would put forward a position expecting the officials to tell them whether or not it was acceptable. This procedure, of course, was impossible from the officials' perspective, because any acceptance or indeed any rejection of a Metis position presupposed an existing Alberta position. At that early stage, however, there was no Alberta position, a situation that created frustration on both sides.

In an attempt to ease this frustration, the government agreed to provide some preliminary and tentative reactions to the positions put forward by the Metis representatives. Unfortunately, a provincial election was announced on 5 October 1982, and no responses were given to the Metis positions until after the appointment of a new cabinet.[3] In retrospect, however, it is unlikely that provincial responses would have significantly affected the outcome of discussions.

The meetings between the province and the Metis culminated with a joint report from the Federation of Metis Settlement Associations, the Metis Association of Alberta, and the Department of Federal and

Intergovernmental Affairs. In the final analysis, the report was not much more than a listing of Metis demands for constitutional change with some sketchy implementation proposals. It contained, among other things, a proposed charter of rights that would recognize land and resource rights, political rights, social rights, cultural rights, and economic rights.

The newly appointed Alberta ministers met with Metis leaders on 21 February 1983. By that time it was clear that most of the issues identified in the joint report were also covered by the national aboriginal constitutional agenda items. Therefore, any response given to the Alberta Metis would also be a response to the national organizations. The ministers reiterated their commitment to a co-operative approach with the Metis. They recalled that this co-operation had begun in the fall of 1981 with the discussion of section 35 and had continued throughout 1982 through the efforts of the joint working group. At the national level, as members of the Alberta delegation, the Alberta Metis participated in all national meetings leading up to the first ministers' conference as required by section 37 of the Constitution Act, 1982. During this period Alberta had provided almost a quarter of a million dollars in support of the Alberta Metis' constitutional work.

The ministers made it clear that Alberta supported the often-stressed Metis' goal of collective survival, and would do everything it could to help them achieve this objective. Moreover, the government of Alberta recognized and accepted a responsibility for the Alberta Metis, and consequently took a policy position that would ensure its programs and policies were consistent with that objective. This policy position, with its subsequent practical application, led the province to take a cautious approach to any constitutional change. Alberta's view, partly influenced by its earlier position on the charter of rights, was that much could and should be done to solve the Metis problems through provincial rather than national initiatives, and that provincial legislative, program, and policy changes were the best vehicles for achieving the goals and objectives of the Alberta Metis. This was later to become known as the 'made-in-Alberta solution.' As for actual constitutional amendments, they were to be kept to a minimum. In fact, of the six proposed constitutional amendments that were to make up the agenda items for the 1983 first ministers' conference, the Metis were told that Alberta would probably support only two inclusions in the constitution. These were the provision for future constitutional conferences on aboriginal rights and guaranteed sexual equality for native women. Alberta rejected out of hand the entrenchment in the constitution of any form of guaranteed representation in Parliament and the legislatures and the removal of the word 'existing' from the current section 35 of the Constitution Act, 1982. I will return to the latter issue.

The Metis expressed a different perspective at their meeting on 21 February 1983 with Alberta government ministers. While they appreciated the provincial willingness to offer a made-in-Alberta solution to some of their problems, they would not accept non-constitutional solutions to what they felt were constitutional problems. They did not want to be placed at the mercy of a provincial government which could at any time revoke provincial legislation and change its programs and policies. In short, they wanted a constitutional guarantee of their aboriginal rights.

Sam Sinclair and Elmer Ghostkeeper reacted to the February 1983 meeting by writing to Premier Lougheed on 2 March 1983. Their letter carried a tone of disappointment and frustration. Premier Lougheed responded with a four-page letter and an invitation to meet at Government House on 12 March, just three days before the first ministers' conference was to take place in Ottawa. Both in his letter to Mr Sinclair and Mr Ghostkeeper and at the meeting with them, the premier reiterated many of the points made by Mr Horsman and Mr Pahl. The Alberta government was willing to consider the possibility of some form of ongoing national process; it was willing to support a constitutional requirement for consultation with aboriginal people prior to any amendment of those sections of the constitution that directly affected them; and it was willing to consider a statement of principles that could outline the commitments of governments to the aboriginal people. Finally, and most important, while the significance of the issues raised by the Metis in a constitutional context was recognized, it was not believed that constitutional change was the only means, or for that matter the most efficacious means, of addressing those issues.

Representatives of the Alberta government were attempting to be pragmatic, to help the Metis solve their problems, but the solution was to be 'home-made.' This position was based partly on an evaluation of the historical relationship between the Metis and the province. Alberta is the only province to have provided land to its Metis; it has a land tenure program that gives individuals in northern communities (where most of the Metis in Alberta live) the opportunity to obtain title to a parcel of land; it is the only province with a Metis Betterment Act; and it is attempting to give more decision-making powers to northern native communities. It is not surprising, therefore, that Alberta favours a pragmatic home-made approach rather than a more cumbersome constitutional approach which in the end may not provide the solutions to many of the problems unique to the Alberta Metis.

The Metis meeting with Premier Lougheed brought to an end the Metis–Alberta consultative process for the 1983 first ministers' conference. It was, for all practical purposes, to be the end of all formal constitutional discussions with the Metis. Discussions on the made-in-Alberta process continued for some time, but they did not address the problem of constitutional amendments.

The Major Issues of the 1983 First Ministers' Conference

Equality Rights

Section 25 of the Constitution Act, 1982, which guarantees that aboriginal rights and freedoms will be unaffected by the Charter, is relatively straightforward. It only becomes problematic when read with section 15, the equality rights section. The concern expressed by the Inuit and the Metis is that equality under the law guaranteed in section 15 may not apply to section 25. Therefore, native women, for example, who are discriminated against by statutory enactment of aboriginal and treaty rights may not be protected by the constitution. Both the federal government and the provinces argued that women's rights were protected under section 15 and section 28, which reads, 'Notwithstanding anything in this Charter, the rights and freedoms referred to in it are guaranteed equally to male and female persons.' Nevertheless the governments were willing to amend the constitution and to make doubly sure of aboriginal sexual equality. This goal was achieved at the first ministers' conference by an agreement to amend section 35 which, ironically, turned out to be the most contentious point of all.

At the 1983 first ministers' conference the federal government tabled a document containing a draft of proposed constitutional amendments. Included was the following amendment to section 25 of the Constitution Act, 1982, ensuring equal application of rights (this wording parallels the wording of section 28): '(2) Notwithstanding any other provision of this Act, the aboriginal, treaty and other rights and freedoms that pertain to the aboriginal peoples of Canada apply equally to male and female persons.' The document was discussed by federal, provincial, territorial, and aboriginal representatives. This particular section was agreed to in principle, but it was thought that it could be placed more appropriately in section 35 than in section 25. This was not a contentious issue, and in fact the federal government was willing to place it in either section or in both. The Metis representatives also wanted the words 'apply equally' changed to 'are guaranteed equally.' The next morning a draft accord prepared by the federal government was presented to the conference. The accord was intended to reflect the discussions of the previous day. The relevant clause appeared in section 35(4): 'Notwithstanding any other provision of this Act, the aboriginal and treaty rights referred to in subsection (1) apply equally to male and female persons.' Ministers and officials were asked to review the federal government draft while the first ministers continued the conference. The Native Council of Canada made the point once again that it wanted the word 'apply' changed to 'guaranteed equally.' This change was agreed to, and when the final text was signed by all parties and released it read as follows: '35(4) Notwithstanding any other provision of this Act, the aboriginal and treaty rights referred to in subsection (1) are guaranteed equally to male and female persons.' The day after the meeting the Inuit and the Native Council of Canada objected to the wording and argued that they had been deceived by the drafters of the document. They argued that everyone had agreed to the following wording: 'Notwithstanding anything in this part, the rights of the aboriginal peoples of Canada are guaranteed equally to male and female persons.' This wording was never discussed or agreed to by the provinces. One thing is certain, however: all governments and aboriginal groups, with the possible exception of the Assembly of First Nations, wanted to ensure that whatever the rights of aboriginal people turned out to be, they should be enjoyed equally by men and women.

What is the difference between the two wordings? Is the issue really one of sexual equality? To answer these questions we have to look at section 35(1): 'The existing aboriginal and treaty rights of the aboriginal peoples of Canada are hereby recognized and affirmed.' It is probable that this section does not have the force of a guarantee, as is the case in the first thirty-four sections, which make up the Charter of Rights and Freedoms. Sections 1 through 34 are further protected by the enforcement provision of section 24(1): 'Anyone whose rights or freedoms, as guaranteed by this Charter, have been infringed or denied may apply to a court of competent jurisdiction to obtain such remedy as the court considers appropriate and just in the circumstances.' Since this section is restricted to those rights and freedoms guaranteed by the Charter, it cannot be invoked to protect any rights obtained in section 35.

As Kenneth M. Lysyk points out, however,

by recognizing and affirming existing aboriginal and treaty rights, however, section 35 may be taken to 'constitutionalize' these rights to the extent at least of attracting the protection of subsection 52(1) of the Constitution Act: '52(1) The Constitution of Canada is the supreme law of Canada, and any law that is inconsistent with the provisions of the Constitution is, to the extent of the inconsistency, of no force or effect.'[4]

The courts would therefore be in a position to declare any federal or provincial law that was inconsistent with such rights to be of no force and effect. It appears that governments did not want to guarantee these rights in the strong sense – that is, in the sense that rights in sections 1–34 are guaranteed. It also appears, however, that the governments did want to afford at least the constitutional protection of section 52(1) to existing aboriginal and treaty rights.

Now we can examine the difference between section 35(4) in the final agreement and what the aboriginal peoples apparently wanted. The main difference is the extent of the rights to be applied equally to men and women. In the agreement the rights are restricted to the aboriginal and treaty rights referred to in section 35(1), namely, 'existing aboriginal and treaty rights.' The aboriginal peoples' text was much broader in scope; they wanted all their aboriginal rights, whatever they might turn out to be, to apply equally to men and women. In part, the wording of section 35(4) was chosen by the governments because it conforms to the prevailing wording of section 35. The proposed amendment originally had been written to conform to the wording in section 25. In fact, in my opinion, it would have been more effective and certainly more encompassing if the proposed amendment had been put in section 25, which refers to aboriginal and treaty rights as well as to other rights and freedoms.

Why did the aboriginal people insist on their amendment? Perhaps it was an attempt to guarantee rights in section 35(4) that are neither guaranteed nor contained in 35(1). If this is a reasonable claim, then it will have to be shown that the proposed wording would guarantee additional rights not contemplated by section 35. It appears obvious that the aboriginal proposal is broader in scope in so far as it does not restrict the notion of rights to existing aboriginal and treaty rights or even to aboriginal and treaty rights without the 'existing' qualification. This broadening of rights becomes much more important if we give a different reading to the words 'are guaranteed equally to male and female persons.' I think it is fair to say that the governments' intention was to have the rights mentioned in section 35(1) apply equally to male and female persons. However, another interpretation of the wording is that it performs two functions: first, it guarantees those rights contained in section 35(1); second, it guarantees that they will be applied equally to male and female persons. If this interpretation is correct, then it appears that governments have said something in section 35(4) they did not intend to say, and the aboriginal representatives are attempting to capitalize on this error.

What did the aboriginal people want? If it was aboriginal sexual equality, then there appears to have been another way of achieving this, namely, by an amendment to section 25. If they were concerned with guaranteeing rights they thought were not guaranteed in section 35, then they should have put forth a different section 35(1). Apparently they were concerned with both matters. This has been a topic of discussion since the first ministers' conference, and I shall return to it.

The problems with section 35(4) clearly illustrate the importance of having enough time to consider properly the wording of any new amendments to the constitution and their possible implications. In this case, while ministers and officials were frantically attempting to arrive at an acceptable wording for what appeared on the surface to be a straightforward problem – sexual equality – the first ministers were in front of television cameras anxiously awaiting the final wording. The first ministers were understandably eager to achieve some positive results at that meeting, particularly when the entire nation was watching. At the 1984 first ministers' conference the eagerness to achieve results was felt even more strongly by a federal government about to face an election. Such pressure often leads to ill-conceived solutions which, if placed in the constitution, will be around to cause problems for a long time.

The Term 'Existing'

I would like to return for a moment to section 35(1) and the problem of the word 'existing.' As I mentioned earlier, Alberta added this word to the old section 34 in order, as Premier Lougheed stated at the 1983 first ministers' conference, 'to protect those aboriginal rights which exist now and to recognize those which may come into existence as a result of this conference.' This implies that section 35(1) should be read in conjunction with section 37. In other words, as new aboriginal rights come into existence, they will be accorded the protection of section 35(1). The aboriginal people were concerned that rights that may be acquired through future land claims agreements would be excluded by 'existing.' This problem was eventually solved through an agreement to amend section 25(b) and section 35(3):

25(b) any rights or freedoms that now exist by way of land claims agreements or may be so acquired.

35(3) For greater certainty in subsection (1) 'treaty rights' includes rights that now exist by way of land claims agreements or may be so acquired.

But no one is yet sure what 'aboriginal rights' are. Some think the term refers only to hunting, fishing, trapping, and land rights. Some think the term is synonymous with 'aboriginal title,' the meaning of which is equally unclear. Still others use it as a catch-all term to include all rights people acquire by virtue of their aboriginality.

Once these rights are defined, would they or should they apply equally to all aboriginal groups? For the first time, for example, Metis are defined in section 35(2) as an aboriginal people, although it is not clear that they are aboriginal people in the same sense as the Indian or Inuit. Indian and Inuit people obtain their aboriginality by virtue of the 'time immemorial' or 'original peoples' characterization, meaning that their ancestors occupied the land prior to the white man's arrival; they have an interest in the land that was subsequently taken from them. People who worked the land prior to its appropriation acquire a property right in the land. According to Locke, the original inhabitants retain the right to property and the right to rid themselves of any form of government they have not agreed to.[5]

Although this argument may support the aboriginality of Indians and Inuit, the Metis acquired their aboriginality by virtue of section 35(2) of the Constitution Act, 1982. Presumably, they are therefore not aboriginal in the same sense that the Indian and the Inuit are. One might grant them a portion of the latter type of aboriginality (if it makes sense to speak at all of 'partial' aboriginality) since at least part of the aboriginality stems from the original peoples argument, but it could never be complete. This partial aboriginality may entail a political or moral as opposed to a legal claim.

The question I pose here is whether aboriginal rights could flow from different notions of aboriginality. It is relatively clear, for example, that Indians and Inuit have certain aboriginal rights, such as hunting, fishing, trapping, gathering, and land rights. It is true that the precise nature of these rights is unclear, but it is nevertheless assumed that they exist. The existence of these rights is not quite as clear in the case of the Metis. This presumably was one of the reasons that the prairie Metis, at least, argued their aboriginal rights on political rather than legal grounds; that is, they based their rights on section 37 rather than section 35 of the Constitution Act, 1982. They have not altogether abandoned the legal argument, but it is being held in abeyance.

I point this out only to illustrate how complicated the issue is and the magnitude of the problem of attempting to define aboriginal rights. It is for this reason that the 1983 first ministers' conference could not have been expected to be more than a preliminary step in that direction. Until these rights are defined more precisely, the governments could only be expected to protect existing rights within the constitution. This point was made quite clearly by Prime Minister Trudeau speaking in Parliament on 7 November 1980: 'I think the simple claim of aboriginal rights, without anyone knowing exactly what it means, is not a matter which one can convincingly argue should be put in the constitution at this time. First of all, the courts would be called upon to interpret such a constitutional amendment, and I think everyone would want to know what aboriginal rights are, what [is] their extent, to whom they apply, and so on.'

Three Additional Issues

Three remaining topics were discussed at the conference. The first appeared on the agenda as 'statement of principles,' the second as 'self-government,' and the third as 'consent clause.' The aboriginal groups were seeking the entrenchment of guaranteed aboriginal rights in an aboriginal charter of rights with a provision for enforcement that would have afforded them the same guarantee and protection that now exists for the first thirty-four provisions in the present Charter of Rights and Freedoms. During the preparatory process they proposed general wordings for aboriginal rights, arguing that this would accommodate necessary differences across Canada in the specific implementation of the various rights. The governments argued that any wording of guaranteed rights would have to be precise in order to limit the degree to which the courts could determine the nature of the rights conferred and in order to allow governments to assess the implications of any rights before agreeing to include them in the constitution.

As an alternative to guaranteed rights, some governments have advocated the development of a statement of principles constituting political commitments by governments to aboriginal peoples. These principles, if included in the constitution, would have to be worded in such a way that they would not derogate from federal or provincial legislative jurisdiction; like the equalization provisions in section 36, they would not be legally enforceable.

The first ministers' resolution proposed by the federal government at the 1984 conference contained a number of such non-justiciable principles, but, surprisingly, some of the aboriginal representatives were opposed to them. They were raised again during the meeting of first ministers on the second day of the conference, but they did not attract a great deal of support from anyone. In the end, it was easier to obtain a consensus on the accord without them, and in the interest of obtaining an agreement they were dropped. Just what function they would have performed had they been accepted was unclear, and perhaps that was the main reason for omitting them.

The discussions on self-government encompassed models ranging from a government that would determine its own citizenry but still somehow exist within confederation to a quasi-municipal form of government. For example, Jim Sinclair, the representative for the Metis National Council, spoke of a partnership within the country that would allow natives to control their own lives and decide their own future. What form these self-governing institutions would take was unclear. What was clear, however, was that all aboriginal groups required some form of land base in order to govern themselves. This point was particularly important to the Metis who, with the exception of some 3,500 Alberta Metis living on settlements, have no land base. Everyone agreed that this subject should be placed on the agenda of the ongoing process.

The aboriginal groups wanted to include a consent clause in the constitution that effectively amounted to veto power over any amendments directly affecting the aboriginal peoples. The aboriginal representatives argued that this was necessary in order to ensure that future governments would not arbitrarily amend the constitution and remove the native rights they had fought so hard to entrench in the constitution. This was unacceptable to virtually all governments on the ground that it undermined the democratic principle of supremacy of Parliament and provincial legislatures. The compromise, and I think it is a good one, was a consultation clause which went into section 35:

35(1) The Government of Canada and the provincial governments are committed to the principle that, before any amendment is made to Class 24 of section 91 of the Constitution Act, 1867, to section 25 of this Act or to this Part,

(a) a constitutional conference that includes in its agenda an item relating to the proposed amendment, composed of the Prime Minister of Canada and the first ministers of the provinces, will be convened by the Prime Minister of Canada; and

(b) the Prime Minister of Canada will invite representatives of the aboriginal peoples of Canada to participate in the discussions on that item.

This was a significant achievement and one that will make it difficult for governments to amend any section of the constitution that directly affects aboriginal people.

The 1983–4 National Constitutional Process

Beginning in October 1983, a number of meetings took place between the aboriginal leaders and the various governments. The first meeting succeeded primarily in recommending to ministers and aboriginal leaders an agenda and a process that would allow the participants to discuss all the issues and prepare for the second first ministers' conference, scheduled for March 1984. The agenda was to include equality rights, aboriginal title and aboriginal rights, treaties and treaty rights, land and resources, and aboriginal or self-government. Under the category of aboriginal title and aboriginal rights, the following subcategories were proposed by the Assembly of First Nations: aboriginal title, aboriginal rights, treaties, treaty rights, removal of the term 'existing,' First Nations government (including fiscal relations, jurisdiction, land, culture, education, and religions), and implementation. Under the category of land and resources, the following subcategories were proposed by the Metis National Council: Metis self-identification, Metis land base, Metis self-government on land base (including economic development, education, training, language and culture, services, and resourcing of Metis government), resources on and off existing and future Metis lands, existing Metis land base, and implementation. Under the category of aboriginal or self-government, the following subcategories were proposed by the Metis National Council under the general heading of Metis government outside Metis lands: economic development, education and training, language and culture, services, resourcing of aboriginal governments, and implementation.

The ministers agreed that four working groups would be established to address each of these items in detail. Working groups 1, 2, and 4 (responsible for equality rights, aboriginal title and aboriginal rights, treaties and treaty rights, and aboriginal or self-government, respectively) were chaired by the federal government. Working group 3, land and resources, was chaired by a deputy minister from the Northwest Territories. The reports of these groups were presented to ministerial meetings in January and February 1984.

Two obvious but important facts emerge from a close examination of the agenda and the process. First, the agenda, with all its categories, is essentially the entire agenda included in the 1983 constitutional accord on aboriginal rights. The enormously lengthy and complicated agenda could not be discussed in detail or even superficially at a single meeting.

This was recognized by most governments early on in the process, and while many attempted to reduce the agenda to a manageable number of items, they were unsuccessful. No aboriginal leaders were willing to remove any items for future discussions. Moreover, as mentioned earlier, no aboriginal representative was prepared to forgo discussion on an item even if it was rejected out of hand by all governments. It is difficult to see how this intransigent strategy could achieve any long-term objectives. At worst, it tends to substantiate the views of some that the aboriginal representatives are not prepared to negotiate, and at best it simply delays progress.

Second, the process was inadvertently structured along aboriginal organizational lines. For example, working group 2 (aboriginal title and aboriginal rights, treaties, and treaty rights) was almost exclusively dominated by the Assembly of First Nations; working group 3 was dominated by the Metis National Council; working group 4 was dominated by the Inuit Committee on National Issues. The Native Council of Canada was present in all the groups, but to a much lesser extent than the Indian and Inuit groups. All the delegations could participate equally in each working group, but they chose not to. In many ways this had a salutary effect on the process in so far as there was an uninterrupted set of positions or arguments presented by one aboriginal organization. Because of the diversity in their positions, there had always existed the problem of limiting the discussions to one topic and by one aboriginal organization.

The Major Issues of the 1983–4 Constitutional Process

The process leading up to the March 1984 first ministers' conference was completed with the February ministerial meeting. What were the issues and what was accomplished? In response to these questions I will review some of the main issues discussed during this period, issues that are an extension of the 1983 first ministers' conference.

Equality Rights

Let us start with the equality rights issue, which in some senses is the most manageable. The basic legal question relative to this issue is whether the equality sections of the Constitution Act, 1982, including section 35(4), prevent discrimination in all aspects relevant to the rights of aboriginal peoples. The difficulties with the various sections of the constitution dealing with equality were discussed earlier, but some additional concerns were brought up during the 1983–4 discussions.

One obvious problem is with section 35(4), because it does not address all rights pertaining to aboriginal peoples. It refers only to 'existing aboriginal and treaty rights' and therefore probably does not make illegal the discriminatory sections contained in the Indian Act. It is true that this problem becomes irrelevant if the federal government amends the appropriate sections of the Indian Act as they have stated they will. Nevertheless, even if the appropriate amendments were made it might not satisfy all the aboriginal people, since they could argue that there is nothing, other than political acumen, to prevent any future government from changing its policy.

Other questions remain unresolved; for example, will the other equality sections of the Constitution Act, 1982 – sections 15 and 28 and their relationship to section 25 – prohibit discrimination in all aspects relevant to the rights of aboriginal peoples? The various governments and their legal advisers disagree on the answer. The federal government still maintains that the existing sections are sufficient, but in the final analysis only the courts can determine if that is correct. One thing is certain, however: everyone intends the provisions to ensure that discrimination against aboriginal women is prevented.

Aboriginal Title versus Aboriginal Rights

The second issue of significance is the problem of defining the terms 'aboriginal title' and 'aboriginal rights.' The basic position of the Assembly of First Nations is that all their aboriginal rights flow from aboriginal title; consequently, they would like to see the words 'aboriginal title' added to section 35(1). Furthermore, they believe that aboriginal title cannot be and must not be extinguishable. It does not appear to me that a great deal of progress has been made in this area since the March 1982 first ministers' conference. The Indians continue to make the same points that they made during that first conference. Indeed, the ministers have never forgotten the words of Chief James Gosnell, who spoke to the issue of aboriginal title at the 1983 first ministers' conference.[6]

Our land started eroding by this and that and so on. So when we talk about title, we are talking about our land ownership and I want to make it very clear so there is not misunderstanding when we say 'aboriginal title.' Don't get mixed up with aboriginal title and aboriginal rights, they are two different things and you cannot have aboriginal rights unless you have the title. This is our interpretation. When you have the title, your rights flow from the title, your aboriginal rights flow from the title and I said, 'Where did you get your title?' It has always been our belief that God gave us the land, the lands that we are talking about and we say that no one can take our title away except he who gave it to us to begin with.

Now, the title as we talk about it, the aboriginal title is our ownership of this land and if you want me to put it like, lock, stock, and barrel or total ownership, whether it is the mountains, inside the mountains, up in the air, the snow, the sea, you name it, subsurface rights and everything that there is in the land was given to us by God for our use to survive. This is the way we believe it to be, the question of aboriginal title ... This is our title, Canada, the whole of Canada is our title and then it is divided here, there and so on and some of the lands have been negotiated and others haven't.

The idea that God or the Creator gave aboriginal people aboriginal title is difficult to deal with. One might accept the wording of the American constitution that man has certain inalienable or natural rights; that is, rights which one acquires either from God or by virtue of being human, as opposed to civil or legal rights which one acquires simply by belonging to a particular society. This is quite different, however, from the declaration that the Creator gave aboriginal title to aboriginal people, a title that cannot be extinguished.

One might further accept the idea that natural rights, unlike civil or legal rights, *ought* not be extinguishable. It may be advisable here to bear in mind Hume's warning concerning the passage from 'is' to 'ought' statements. Governments can and do take away both civil and natural rights; whether they ought to, is of course another question. Presumably, what they cannot do is grant natural rights, which are either innate or given by God; governments simply legalize them. This legalization, however, is important, since a natural right outside any political or legal system has no meaning, or at least is legally impotent. For this reason the Indians' views of a God-given title are not practically useful. In the end all natural rights that are entrenched in the constitution or legalized in some manner will be subject to interpretation by the courts. There is no escape from this inevitability. The point is made succinctly by Leslie C. Green:

Having failed in their efforts to abort the Constitution and Charter by way of the judicial process, Canada's Indians sought to have what they regarded as their aboriginal rights spelled out in the Charter. They were unwilling to put their trust in abstract statements that would have to be interpreted by the courts in order to flesh them out. What the

Indians overlooked is that every right embodied in the Charter, however specifically it might be spelled out, requires judicial interpretation to give it meaning. It is only through the medium of the courts that the concept of legally recognized or protected aboriginal rights has been developed.[7]

Even though it may be reasonable to argue that one may have natural rights, in my view doing so does not advance the Indians' case much further. If we all have the same natural rights, as it is reasonable to assume, then presumably these rights are protected by the Canadian Charter of Rights and Freedoms. The aboriginal people must therefore be talking about additional rights that are not shared by non-aboriginal people. These 'rights' (I prefer to call them 'aboriginal claims') are claims, in the case of the Indians and Inuit, that exist by virtue of the 'time immemorial' argument. In the case of the Metis, they are claims that exist by virtue of section 35(2) and section 37 of the Constitution Act, 1982. These claims, I would argue, are legitimate or not depending on the circumstances of the inhabitants at the time, how the indigenous people were treated, whether they were deprived of a certain land or life-style by illegal or immoral means, and so on. If these were the grounds on which the aboriginal people based their claims to aboriginal rights, then it would be easier to accept or reject them and to know if it was reasonable to place them in the constitution. As it now stands, the term 'aboriginal rights' is either so general that it includes almost everything imaginable, or it is so ambiguous that it lacks any meaning.

This problem is exacerbated by the confusing relationship between aboriginal title and aboriginal rights. I have tried to argue that if we accept the definition given by the Indians the former is virtually devoid of any practical meaning, and the latter is more reasonably understood when it is interpreted to mean 'aboriginal claim.' It should also be pointed out that the aboriginal people themselves do not agree on a definition of aboriginal title. It is not surprising, then, that governments are reluctant to put such an ambiguous term in the constitution and that they insist on a clearer description of aboriginal rights. Moreover, even when governments do have a clear idea of what a particular aboriginal right is, it does not follow that they must agree to it. It seems to me that the aboriginal people often interpret a statement of disagreement as evidence that governments do not understand what the aboriginals are seeking. In the hope of making them understand, the aboriginal people explain their position once again rather than advancing a new or modified position.

The Term 'Existing'

Associated with section 35 is the continuing request that the word 'existing' be removed. It is, of course, not certain how the courts will interpret the word. The aboriginal representatives fear that at best it means nothing, and at worse it might be limiting. Does it refer to only those rights that existed as of 17 April 1982, or does it extend to any new rights that may be acquired in the future? The Alberta perspective is that the word 'existing' should remain in section 35(1) until such time as all the rights referred to in section 35 are defined. If and when the governments agree to new rights, then, in my opinion, they will be afforded the protection of section 35 since they will then exist.[8] The federal government's argument was rather different. It held that putting the word 'existing' in section 35(1) had no significance because if one were to ask what rights section 35 recognized and affirmed, the answer would have to be existing rights. What other rights are there except those that exist? The federal government contended that removing the word 'existing' would have significance for the courts because they would then be forced to give some meaning to its removal. The force of this argument is difficult to evaluate until the courts have had an opportunity to consider the matter. For example, the courts may be just as interested in the word's inclusion as in its exclusion.

Land and Resources

The issue of land has long been an overriding concern for the Metis. Alberta is the only province that has set aside land for the use of Metis, and the only province that has specific legislation dealing with the Metis. In 1938 the legislative assembly of Alberta passed the Metis Betterment Act which, among other things, allowed the minister, with the approval of the lieutenant-governor-in-council, to set aside lands for occupation by members of a settlement association.

Several sites were set aside in 1938 and 1939 by orders-in-council for use by the Metis settlement associations. The title to the land remained in the provincial crown, although association members were entitled to use and occupy specific plots. This was not done in recognition of any aboriginal right to the land, but because the scheme was viewed as one means of alleviating the Metis' deplorable living conditions. This point of view, however, is not shared by the Alberta Federation of Metis Settlement Associations; it argues that the establishment of settlements constitutes a recognition of Metis political and aboriginal rights.

Paradoxically, Alberta is in both a strong and a weak position when it comes to the question of land and self-government for Metis. On the one hand, at least 3,500 Metis live on settlements in Alberta and have an excellent opportunity to increase the level of decision-making on those settlements. On the other hand, if the Metis are correct, the province may have already conceded an existing aboriginal right for the Metis – namely, the right to land. This does not, of course, solve the problem for the thousands of Metis who do not live on the settlements, but at least it points the way to possible solutions for them as well.

It is not at all clear how the Metis land issue will be resolved in the other provinces, particularly in Saskatchewan and British Columbia. It is unlikely that either of those provinces will agree to entrench a right to land in the constitution. It is possible, however, that the Alberta government may agree to protect existing Metis settlements through an amendment to the Alberta Act, which is part of the constitution. The land issue is further complicated by the fact that most of the provinces and both national Metis organizations want the Metis to come under federal jurisdiction within the meaning of section 91(24) of the Constitution Act, 1867. Some provinces apparently hope that that will solve their problems, and that the federal government will have to provide the Metis with land. But this shift of jurisdiction will not solve anything. Since the federal government's jurisdiction under section 91(24) is discretionary, it need not, and probably would not, be exercised. Moreover, since the federal government does not own significant portions of land in the prairie provinces, any land claims settlement for the Metis would have to come from provincial crown land. In any event, the jurisdiction problem simply side-steps the land question for the Metis and does nothing to solve many of the immediate and desperate problems they face at the local level.

The Metis land issue is made more difficult by the lack of information available on the number of Metis in Canada. There are two parts to this problem: the first is to decide on a definition of 'Metis' and the second is to have a reasonably accurate enumeration taken. The two organizations that represent the Metis differ in their approaches to the problem of definition. The Native Council of Canada defines 'Metis' according to blood lines; that is, one is a Metis by virtue of his 'Indianness.' Using this definition, many aboriginal people who are now classified as non-status Indians would qualify as Metis. The Metis National Council uses other criteria for defining who is a Metis: aboriginal ancestry, self-identification as a Metis, and community acceptance. The MNC tends to use the term 'Metis' to refer to a mixed-blood population that formed a cohesive social band and occupied a Metis homeland in Rupert's Land, parts of Northwestern Ontario, and parts of the Northwest Territories. The major problem with the MNC criteria is that if an aboriginal person satisfied the first two – that is, aboriginal ancestry and self-identification as a Metis – a Metis community could not reject that individual as a Metis unless the community itself used hidden criteria. In other words, it seems to me that the first two criteria together are both necessary and sufficient. The community-acceptance criterion is either irrelevant or, through sleight of hand, becomes the only significant one, thereby making the first two criteria necessary but not sufficient.

Although both national Metis organizations maintain that they know who the Metis are, they spend a great deal of time and effort dealing with definitions. This causes a serious conflict between the two Metis organizations, a conflict which they look to the governments to solve. On the one hand they maintain that they know who the Metis are and that they want to define their own membership; on the other hand they are asking the governments to tell them who the Metis are under section 35(2) of the Constitution Act, 1982. It seems to me that both the MNC and NCC approaches to the definition question are legitimate. It is nevertheless important to resolve the issue, because the amount of land required for the Metis is in part dependent on the number of Metis. Until governments have a better idea of the amount of land and the number of services they are to provide, it will not be easy to get any agreement from them.

Self-Government

The issue of self-government for aboriginal people is so large and complex that it is impossible to do justice to it in this paper. Various options have been presented to the governments from all the aboriginal organizations. The Report of the Special Committee on Indian Self-Government in Canada (the Penner Report) was released and the federal government tabled its response on 5 March 1984. In the government's response, Indian Affairs Minister John Munro indicated a willingness to proceed along the lines of the special committee's recommendations and to deal legislatively with Indian government. The Inuit have made significant progress with their proposal for a Nunavut territorial government in the Northwest Territories, the Western Arctic Regional Municipality (WARM) in the Beaufort Sea Region, and the Kativik Regional Government in Quebec. The Metis have developed three options for self-government, but their proposals are much more difficult to come to terms with than those of other aboriginal groups. This difficulty is due to many different factors: the Metis are not a large homogeneous people with a common language; except in Alberta, they have no land base; they live, in many cases, in large urban centres; their number is uncertain; and their aboriginal claims do not have the same basis as those of other aboriginal peoples. It is true that Indian proposals for self-government also present difficulties, but to a much lesser extent. The Inuit are ahead of most of the other aboriginal peoples in terms of self-government precisely because they are a homogeneous people with a common language and an identifiable homeland. They base their self-government models on non-ethnic grounds, which the government and Canadians generally find easier to accept.

The Penner Report made some significant recommendations which, if implemented, will constitute an important step toward self-government for the Indian people. This is not to say that the Metis aspirations for self-government can be ignored simply because they present more difficult problems. Indeed, in Alberta, the Metis settlements are making good progress toward more control over their own affairs.

The one element that appears common to all proposals for self-government is the creation of a 'third order' of government with powers similar to those of a province, a proposition that most existing governments have rejected. There were many arguments throughout the 1983 and 1984 constitutional discussions about what constitutes a third order of government, and very little agreement. In my opinion, when the powers or jurisdiction of any institution are incorporated within the constitution, another order of government is constituted. That is why the provinces resist any suggestion that the powers of municipalities be placed in the constitution. Municipalities are not, strictly speaking, a third order of government; they obtain their authority from the provinces, not from the constitution.

In some cases the proposals for self-government amount to creation of a sovereign state capable of signing international treaties and issuing valid passports. These proposals are easy for governments to deal with by rejection. However, even the more moderate proposals do not appear at present to have much of a chance for entrenchment in the constitution. Before the governments will agree to entrench an aboriginal right to self-government in the constitution, they will have to be fully cognizant of the practical implications. That is why the activity on self-government outside the constitution – such as the Kativik and Nunavut models, the Penner Report, and the Alberta Metis settlements – is so important. These practical approaches to self-government will give governments the information they need to make a decision on constitutionalizing self-government for aboriginal people. All of the implications of self-government will become obvious once the systems are actually in existence and functioning. Until that point is reached, it

is doubtful that any government will risk the constitutional entrenchment of self-government for aboriginal people.

The Major Issues of the 1984 First Ministers' Conference

Only two items of the cumbersome agenda of the 1984 first ministers'
conference were discussed at length: equality rights and aboriginal or
self-government. The entire first day was taken up with opening
speeches and the equality rights issue. The equality rights issue carried
over to the second day, and the remainder of the time was spent
discussing self-government. The federal government surprised everyone by tabling a proposed 1984 constitutional accord on the rights of the
aboriginal peoples of Canada. The accord contained a provision for
amendments to section 25 and part II of the Constitution Act, 1982. The
proposed amendment to section 25, intended to solve the equality rights
problem, read as follows: 'Nothing in this section abrogates or derogates
from the guarantees of equality with respect to male and female persons
under section 28 of this Charter.' Presumably this was intended to make
clear that section 28, which guarantees equality of men and women,
applies to aboriginal people in general and to section 35 in particular.
This would have allayed the fears of those who argued that section 28
did not apply to section 35. Near the end of the conference a group of
officials, ministers, and aboriginal representatives worked on a new
wording for the amendment to section 35(4): 'Notwithstanding any
other provision of this Act, the aboriginal and treaty rights referred to in
subsection (1) are guaranteed equally to male and female persons, and
this guarantee of equality applies in respect of all other rights, and all
freedoms, of the aboriginal peoples of Canada.' This was rejected by the
leaders of the Assembly of First Nations on the ground that the existing
section 35(4) could arguably be said to imply that section 35(1) rights are
guaranteed rather than simply reconized and affirmed. The Assembly
of First Nations, however, did agree to study it further. It was
anticipated that they would table a new wording to this proposal.
   The second proposed amendment was to Part II, and read as follows:

COMMITMENTS RELATING TO ABORIGINAL PEOPLES OF CANADA

*35(2) Without altering the legislative authority of Parliament or of the
provincial legislatures, or the rights of any of them with respect to the
exercise of their legislative authority,*
   *(a) Parliament and the legislatures, together with the government of
Canada and the provincial governments, are committed to (i) preserv-*

ing and enhancing the cultural heritage of the aboriginal peoples of Canada, and (ii) respecting the freedom of the aboriginal peoples of Canada to live within their heritage and to educate their children in their own languages, as well as in either or both of the official languages of Canada;

(b) the aboriginal peoples of Canada have the right to self-governing institutions that will meet the needs of their communities, subject to the nature, jurisdiction and powers of those institutions, and to the financing arrangements relating thereto, being identified and defined through negotiation with the government of Canada and the provincial governments; and

(c) are committed to participating in the negotiations referred to in paragraph (b) and to presenting to Parliament and the provincial legislatures legislation to give effect to the agreements resulting from the negotiations.

This proposed amendment was modelled along the lines of section 36 (the equalization and regional disparities section) of the Constitution Act, 1982. This section has always been interpreted as a weak, non-justiciable statement of moral obligation to the principle of economic equality among all Canadians. The federal government argued that the force of the proposed amendment to part II was equivalent to the moral obligation imposed by section 36. It would certainly not take away any powers from either jurisdiction, nor would it impose any fiscal commitments on the governments. Still, there is a degree of uncertainty as to its precise meaning and effect. Unlike section 36, which has never been challenged in the courts – partly because there appears to be general agreement among the governments as to its force and meaning – the proposed amendment to part II would probably be challenged sooner or later in the courts. It is unlikely that the aboriginal people and the governments would agree on its meaning or purpose, and a legal battle seems inevitable. How the courts would interpret it and what obligation they might place on the governments is difficult to say. In any event, the proposed amendment may not turn out to be as innocuous as the federal government presented it to be.

The accord was supported in principle by the aboriginal people, Manitoba, New Brunswick, and to a lesser extent, Ontario. However, on the eve of 9 March no one supported the accord in its entirety; virtually all those who supported it in principle wanted some amendments made. The extent of the amendments was never learned: because it did not receive enough support for adoption, no one pursued additional changes to it.

It seems to me that the accord was rejected for several reasons. First, no one had enough time to study it in detail. The federal tactic of tabling it on the first day ensured its demise. As was pointed out by Premier Lougheed, Prime Minister Trudeau, and others, they had not even left Ottawa in 1983 before the aboriginal people were maintaining that the equality amendment that was adopted did not do what everyone intended it to do. Therefore, few politicians were willing to repeat this mistake; most were determined not to be forced into a quick decision or into drafting hasty amendments to the constitution.

Second, the approach of the federal government, Ontario, Manitoba, New Brunswick, and the aboriginal people is fundamentally different from that of the other provinces. They want to begin with general principles that commit the governments to negotiations on self-government in the hope that the details can be worked out later. This approach has the advantage of giving some kind of constitutional recognition to the process and perhaps even to the right of self-government itself. The other provinces want to approach self-government from the opposite end; that is, they want to start outside the constitution, to negotiate and discuss self-government with the aboriginal people before they commit themselves to entrenching anything in the constitution. Both are equally legitimate approaches to the issue of self-government. The latter, however, is premised on the precise understanding of the implications of constitutional changes. It is clearly a more cautious approach, and given the repercussions of hasty action and the seriousness of any amendment to the constitution, it seems preferable.

One additional item that surfaced at the conference was the issue of responsibility for the Metis. The Metis and most provinces argue that the Metis are a federal responsibility under section 91(24) of the Constitution Act, 1867. Alberta, which had accepted responsibility for the Metis of Alberta, said that in the light of the presentations made by the Native Council of Canada and the Metis National Council, it was going to study the issue with a view to reconsidering its position if necessary. It was agreed by everyone that this should be a subject for the next first ministers' conference.

The conference ended on an unhappy note. The aboriginal people were disappointed that there was no agreement on any amendments to the constitution, and their closing remarks reflected their frustration. Whether the outcome of the conference was as bleak as portrayed by the aboriginal peoples depends in part on the expectations of the participants. The aboriginal people certainly had high expectations, which were to some extent thwarted. It could be argued that their expectations were too high – indeed, completely unrealistic – and that the absence of an agreement may have the salutary effect of forcing the aboriginal representatives to become more realistic. Governments, for the most part, were not looking for any new amendments at the conference. They were satisfied to try to reach some practical agreements on a negotiating process for self-government outside the constitution.

By the end of the conference the federal government had discussed its initial reaction to the Penner Report, tabled a proposal for the review of social, cultural, and economic programs and services for aboriginal people, announced its intention to introduce legislation to remove discrimination on the basis of sex from the Indian Act, and promised to proceed with the framework legislation for self-government. In an attempt to bring some focus to future work, Manitoba Premier Grant Devine suggested the following five tasks be carried out in preparation for the 1985 first ministers' conference:

1 Examine the definitions and implications of various forms of self-government outlined in the federal response to the Penner Report.
2 Proceed with a process of community consultation and negotiations for self-government.
3 Proceed with the process of identification and enumeration of Metis.
4 Proceed with Senator Austin's project to review services and programs for aboriginal people.
5 Proceed with the process for attempting to resolve the question of jurisdictions and responsibilities for aboriginal people, including section 91(24) and who is responsible for the Metis.

Most governments appeared to agree with this approach, although the aboriginal representatives seemed to be preoccupied with both their perception of the failure of the conference and their poignant closing remarks. In my opinion, the agreement of the governments in itself represents another step forward. To be sure, it will not satisfy the immediate desires of the aboriginal people, but it will continue to move the process toward some resolution of outstanding problems.

Toward a Conclusion

Most of the issues raised by the aboriginal peoples can be resolved outside the constitution. This is encouraging, because non-constitutional solutions are usually less complicated, do not require decisions from the courts, involve local governments which are sensitive to local needs, and result in practical solutions to real problems. Non-constitutional solutions, it is true, do not address the more basic problem of providing a constitutional guarantee for aboriginal rights, which is the overriding concern of all aboriginal representatives. They want a guarantee of their aboriginal rights, which from their perspective can only be achieved by placing those rights within the constitution.

What is more likely to occur in the subsequent conferences scheduled for 1985 and 1987 is the advancement of some general non-justiciable principles along the lines proposed by the federal government in the 1984 first ministers' conference. The first ministers are painfully aware of the problems encountered in amending the constitution. It is difficult to draft an amendment that everyone accepts, and even then the amendment does not always say or mean what everyone thought it said or meant. The proposed section 35(4) is a good example.

At least two more first ministers' conferences must be held before 17 April 1987. There is ample time to think through all the implications of any proposed constitutional amendments. In the meantime, the aboriginal people will be able to raise their concerns in the highest forum in the country, which will provide an opportunity for all Canadians to better understand the problems and frustrations facing the aboriginal people of Canada. The solutions will not be easy, and constitutional amendments by themselves will not solve these problems. Let us hope that through the long constitutional process both aboriginal people and government representatives will be able to make the compromises needed to ensure the survival of the aboriginal people of Canada.

BRIAN SLATTERY

The Hidden Constitution: Aboriginal Rights in Canada

Most countries have a national myth – an account that purports to relate the central events of a country's history in compressed form, that explains how the country has come to be and what it stands for. National myths are useful and perhaps indispensable ways of making the complex past relevant to the perplexing present. They provide the framework for much historical writing, and subtly influence lawyers and judges on constitutional issues. All national myths involve a certain amount of distortion, but some at least have the virtue of broad historical accuracy, roughly depicting the major forces at work. The myth that underlies much legal thinking about the history of Canada lacks that redeeming feature.

It is commonly assumed that North America was juridically a vacant land when it was first encountered by Europeans. Bit by bit, lands were wrested from the wilderness and settled or exploited under grants from a European monarch who had obtained complete sovereignty and title to the soil upon discovery. All land rights in Canada, other than prescriptive rights, stem directly or indirectly from crown grants. Our laws, legal institutions, and constitutional arrangements were all derived from Europe or created by European settlers. Our law-making bodies ultimately owe their authority to the British Parliament or the crown. There are, in a word, no truly indigenous laws, rights, legislatures, or courts in Canada.

This account has marked shortcomings. North America was not, of

This paper appeared previously in a slightly different form in 32 *American Journal of Comparative Law* (1984) 701–44. I would like to express my appreciation to Messrs Daniel Gormley and Keith Boswell and Professors Louise Arbour, Paul Emond, and Peter Hogg for their kind assistance in preparing this work, and to the Social Science and Humanities Research Council of Canada for its generous financial support.

course, uninhabited when first explored and settled by Europeans. It was the domain of a variety of independent peoples, who possessed their own territories, laws, and governmental institutions.[1] These groups often had military capabilities sufficient to make them respected and feared by the settler communities and their parent states. Native Americans were jealous of their independence and quick to avenge intrusions on their lands and offences against their persons. Unless the aboriginal peoples could be conquered – a hazardous enterprise at best – their co-operation and consent were necessary for sufficient lands to be obtained for white settlement and held in safety. But Indian nations were not viewed simply as obstacles to European penetration.[2] During the seventeenth and eighteenth centuries in particular, they were valued as trading partners and as military allies in struggles with rival Christian powers.

European imperial efforts in America usually proceeded on at least two levels simultaneously. At one level, European states grappled among themselves for exclusive access to the advantages offered by the New World, be these precious minerals, skins and furs, fish, timber, or land for settlement. In the effort to improve their position relative to one another, the colonial powers at times advanced extraordinary claims and sought to justify them by resort to extraordinary principles. At various points, papal bulls, early discoveries or explorations, symbolic acts, or token coastal settlements were invoked by European nations to support pretensions to vast territories, territories they neither occupied nor controlled. These claims had little foundation in either fact or reason and usually met with the scorn of competing European powers, even if the same powers on occasion indulged in similar diplomatic fantasies. As Elizabeth I of England tartly observed to the Spanish ambassador, to sail to and fro, to build huts, to name a river or a promontory could not confer ownership, since prescription without possession was of no effect.[3] All that mattered in the final analysis was what a state could gain and hold by force or coerce its rivals to recognize in a treaty settlement.[4]

At another level, European states had to deal with the various native peoples who were the real masters of North America. France and England might sign a treaty whereby the lands around Hudson Bay would be left to the British crown, but this document was of little assistance when it came to controlling or even influencing the aboriginal inhabitants.[5] The imperial powers were thus obliged to maintain extensive sets of diplomatic relations with native American peoples, to enter into alliances, sign treaties, and exchange gifts. Incoming Europeans often attempted to secure some authority over the indigenous groups they dealt with; frequently, however, they were in no position to do this, and it was some time before the situation changed.

Interesting complications resulted from the coexistence and interaction of these two diplomatic spheres. The tendency of many commentators has been to wish the complexities away by focusing on one sphere (usually the inter-European) to the exclusion of the other. This blessedly uncomplicated view can no longer be sustained. Yet if the historical role of native peoples is now widely recognized, it has not been accommodated by the standard intellectual framework that influences legal thinking. What we lack is a proper understanding of when and how the native peoples of Canada were won to the allegiance of the crown and what effect this process had on their original land rights, customary laws, and systems of government. Did the crown gain sovereignty over Canada with or without the consent of the aboriginal peoples? On what terms was it achieved? Did native groups come to occupy the same status as other Canadian subjects, or did they have some special relationship with the crown? It is a remarkable fact that coherent answers to these questions cannot be found in standard treatises on Canadian constitutional law and history, or even in more specialized works.

The Constitution Act, 1982, invites us to remedy this deficiency.[6] Section 35 provides that '(1) the existing aboriginal and treaty rights of the aboriginal peoples of Canada are hereby recognized and affirmed; (2) in this Act, "aboriginal peoples of Canada" includes the Indian, Inuit and Metis peoples of Canada.'

This section has a curious past. It was not found in the original draft of the act, but was inserted in a slightly different form on the unanimous recommendation of the parliamentary special joint committee on the constitution after strong representations from native organizations. The government's decision to include the section was treated by all parties as a historic occasion and given wide publicity. When the section was later dropped from the draft as the result of the federal–provincial agreement of November 1981, there was a sharp reaction among both native and non-native Canadians. Intensive lobbying and public demonstrations led to the section's reinstatement with one change: the word 'existing' was added to the phrase 'aboriginal and treaty rights.'[7] In announcing the new version, the minister of justice assured the House of Commons that the amendment did not alter the substance of the provision.[8]

Section 35 has undergone further discussion since the enactment of the Constitution Act, 1982. Section 37 of the act required that a constitutional conference be called within one year to deal with matters concerning the aboriginal peoples of Canada, including the identification and definition of their rights, and stipulated that representatives of aboriginal Canadians be invited to participate. In March 1983, the first ministers' conference on aboriginal constitutional matters met at Ottawa, attended by the prime minister of Canada, the provincial premiers or their delegates, territorial representatives, and representatives from four national native organizations. The conference agreed, in an accord dated 16 March, to make certain changes in the existing provisions, and to meet again within one year.[9] I will discuss here the constitutional provisions in their amended form.

Under the agreement of 16 March, two further subsections are added to section 35. The first serves to remove doubts as to whether the phrase 'treaty rights' in section 35(1) covers rights gained under existing and future land claims agreements, a number of which have recently been concluded with native peoples or are in the process of being negotiated.[10] The second specifies that the aboriginal and treaty rights referred to in section 35(1) are guaranteed equally to male and female persons.[11] The recent agreement also adds a new section 35(1), which stipulates that any future amendments to the major constitutional provisions regarding aboriginal peoples will first be discussed at a conference of first ministers to which aboriginal representatives will be invited.

These sections make up part II of the Constitution Act, 1982, entitled 'Rights of the Aboriginal Peoples of Canada.' They fall outside the Canadian Charter of Rights and Freedoms found in part I of the act. They are supplemented by a provision located within the Charter proper that serves to shield native rights from the possible adverse effects of other Charter provisions. Section 25 states:

The guarantee in this Charter of certain rights and freedoms shall not be construed so as to abrogate or derogate from any aboriginal, treaty or other rights or freedoms that pertain to the aboriginal peoples of Canada including:
(a) any rights or freedoms that have been recognized by the Royal Proclamation of October 7, 1763; and
(b) any rights or freedoms that may be acquired by the original peoples of Canada by way of land claims settlement.

The agreement of 16 March changes the wording in paragraph (b) of section 25 so as to indicate that both past and future land claims agreements are covered.[12] The agreement also adds a new section 37(1) requiring that two further first ministers' conferences be convened before April 1987 to discuss aboriginal constitutional matters.

The most important of these various provisions is that found in section 35(1), which states that the existing aboriginal and treaty rights of the aboriginal peoples of Canada are hereby recognized and affirmed. I will focus exclusively on this provision here, leaving aside a range of issues relating to its companion sections.[13] It will be helpful first to identify the two groups of rights referred to, namely, 'aboriginal' and 'treaty' rights, before considering the precise scope and effect of the provision.

Section 35(1) adopts and confirms the common-law doctrine of aboriginal rights.[14] This doctrine holds that the crown's acquisition of North American territories was governed by a principle of continuity whereby the property rights, customary laws, and governmental institutions of the native peoples were presumed to survive, so far as this result was compatible with the crown's ultimate title, and subject to lawful dispositions to the contrary. Aboriginal groups presumptively assumed the status of domestic dependent nations united by special ties to the crown as ultimate sovereign. The United States Supreme Court articulated this doctrine in the early cases of *Johnson* v *M'Intosh* (1823)[15] and *Worcester* v *Georgia* (1832).[16] The doctrine figured prominently in a number of Canadian decisions over the years, and was recently reiterated by the Supreme Court of Canada in *Calder* v *Attorney-General of British Columbia* (1973).[17]

The Quebec case of *Connolly* v *Woolrich* (1867)[18] provides an interesting example of the doctrine's operation. There the courts upheld a marriage contracted under Cree customary law between a white man and an Indian woman in the Canadian North-West, even though the same man later married another woman in a Christian ceremony recognized by Quebec law. In attempting to discredit the first marriage, the second wife argued, among other things, that English common law had been introduced into the North-West before the marriage took place, thus invalidating Indian custom. In any case, she said, the marriage customs of pagan and uncivilized nations such as the Crees could not be recognized even between the natives themselves, much less between a Christian and a native. These arguments did not persuade the courts. The trial judge noted that the first English and French settlers in the North-West found the country in the possession of numerous and powerful Indian tribes. Even if the settlers brought with them the laws of their mother countries,

Yet, will it be contended that the territorial rights, political organization such as it was, or the laws and usages of the Indian tribes, were

abrogated – that they ceased to exist when these two European nations began to trade with the aboriginal occupants? In my opinion, it is beyond controversy that they did not – that so far from being abolished, they were left in full force, and were not even modified in the slightest degree in regard to the civil rights of the natives.[19]

The doctrine of aboriginal rights draws on two main sources, namely, French[20] and English[21] state practice regarding Indian nations from early colonial times and the Royal Proclamation of 1763.[22] The first subject cannot be pursued here. The second, however, deserves more than a passing mention, because it provides essential background for an understanding of section 35(1).

The Royal Proclamation of 1763

By 1763, Great Britain's long struggle with France for American empire was over. At the Peace of Paris, France ceded all its remaining territories in Canada to the British Crown, as well as its territories east of the Mississippi River. Britain also obtained Florida from the Spanish Crown, thus completing its claims to the eastern and northern sectors of America.[23] Only one area was left to another European power, namely, the lands west of the Mississippi that France had relinquished to Spain the previous year.[24]

These treaties temporarily sorted out the claims of the three main European rivals among themselves. But the French crown could not give Great Britain what it did not possess, namely, authority over the native groups inhabiting the ceded territories. These nations were in many cases trading partners of the French and sometime military allies. If they were not prepared to accept direct French authority, neither were they willing to accept that France might deposit them in the pocket of the English king. As the Chippewa leader, Minivavana, told an English trader: 'Englishman, although you have conquered the French, you have not yet conquered us. We are not your slaves. These lakes, these woods and mountains, were left to us by our ancestors. They are our inheritance; and we will part with them to none.'[25]

A similar viewpoint was expressed by certain Wabash River Indians: 'You tell us, that when you Conquered the French, they gave you this Country. That no difference may happen hereafter, we tell you now the French never conquered, neither did they purchase a foot of our Country, nor have [they a right] to give it to you, we gave them liberty to settle for which they always rewarded us and treated us with great Civility.'[26]

Britain was well aware in 1763 of the precarious nature of its relations with the old Indian allies of France and the growing dissatisfaction of its own native allies and trading partners. Since mid-century the British government had been increasingly occupied with Indian affairs, and the war with France had emphasized the importance of native friendship and support. For some time a plan had been afoot to assure the Indians of the crown's good intentions by removing a principal cause of Indian discontent – white intrusion on Indian lands. This plan culminated in the publication of a royal proclamation on 7 October 1763.[27] The interest of the document is not purely historical, for its main terms have never been generally repealed in Canada.[28] Although it must be read in the light of later developments, it still forms a principal basis for aboriginal rights in many areas.

The proclamation is one of those legal instruments that do simple things in complicated ways. The central idea of its Indian provisions is simple: to ensure that no Indian lands in America are taken by British subjects without native consent. This objective is secured by three main measures: colonial governments are forbidden to grant any unceded Indian lands, British subjects are forbidden to settle on them, and private individuals are forbidden to purchase them. A system of public purchases is adopted as the official mode of extinguishing Indian title. The British government was particularly concerned at the prospect of white settlement spreading indiscriminately into the American interior, and so the proclamation temporarily sealed off much of that area to settlers, designating it an exclusive Indian territory. But the document's main measures are not confined to the Indian territory; they apply throughout British North America.

The Indian provisions of the proclamation begin with a preamble wherein the king explains his basic aims:

And whereas it is just and reasonable, and essential to our Interest and the Security of Our Colonies, that the several Nations or Tribes of Indians, and with whom We are connected, and who live under Our Protection, should not be molested or disturbed in the Possession of such Parts of Our Dominions and Territories as, not having been ceded to, or purchased by Us, are reserved to them, or any of them, as their Hunting Grounds.

Although the king asserts ultimate sovereignty over the Indians, he also acknowledges their semi-autonomous status, describing them as nations or tribes 'with whom We are connected, and who live under Our Protection.' He recognizes that the Indians are entitled to undisturbed possession of the lands reserved to them, and, in an important formula repeated later in the text, defines these reserves as any Indian lands that have not been ceded to or purchased by the crown. The king claims these lands as part of his dominions, but at the same time recognizes the existence of an Indian interest requiring extinguishment by cession or purchase. In technical terms, the Indian interest constitutes a legal burden on the crown's ultimate title until surrendered.

In 1763, most of the American territories claimed by Britain were unceded lands held by native peoples. Under the proclamation such lands were automatically deemed Indian reserves. Their boundaries were determined negatively by past Indian cessions and positively by current Indian possessions. Much of the unorganized American interior was still unceded, but other unceded lands lay within the undisputed boundaries of existing colonies, including the northern colonies of Rupert's Land, Quebec, Newfoundland, and Nova Scotia.

It is sometimes argued that the proclamation recognized aboriginal land rights only in the exclusive Indian territory created in the American hinterland.[29] On this supposition, Indian title was not recognized in areas specifically excluded from the territory, such as the coastal belt east of the Appalachian mountains and the colonies of Quebec and Rupert's Land.[30] But the text does not support this view. After describing the boundaries of the territory, the proclamation orders the removal of all persons who have settled either within the territory 'or upon *any other Lands*, which, not having been ceded to, or purchased by Us, are still reserved to the said Indians as aforesaid' (emphasis added). This provision clearly assumes that unceded Indian lands located outside the Indian territory are reserved for Indian use. The king also forbids colonial governors to make grants of 'any Lands whatever, which, not having been ceded to, or purchased by Us as aforesaid, are reserved to the said Indians, or any of them.' The ban applies to unceded Indian lands generally, wherever they happen to be located. Finally, the proclamation provides that no private person shall make any purchases from the Indians 'of any Lands reserved to the said Indians, within those Parts of Our Colonies where We have thought proper to allow Settlement,' and specifies that if the Indians are ever inclined to dispose of such lands, they shall be purchased for the crown in a public assembly. Since the provision only applies in areas where settlement was permitted, and the Indian territory was, for the time being, expressly closed to 'any Purchases or Settlements whatever,' it could only refer to unceded Indian lands found outside the territory, in eastern and northern colonies where settlement was still allowed.

In brief, the proclamation recognized that lands possessed by Indians throughout British territories in America were reserved for their exclusive use unless previously ceded to the crown. Prior to a public cession of such lands, they could not be granted away or settled. These provisions applied not only to the Indian territory but to the full range of British colonies in North America, no matter how humble or peripheral. In this respect, Rupert's Land, Quebec, Nova Scotia, Newfoundland, the Thirteen Colonies, and the Floridas were brought under a uniform legal regime.[31] The Indian territory was placed in a special position. Whereas in other areas Indian lands might still be purchased by public authorities, in the territory such purchases were forbidden altogether for the time being. The idea was to divert the flow of white settlement from the American interior to the northern and southern colonies, which were still relatively sparsely settled. However, the crown envisaged that in due course parts of the territory might be opened up, in which case the standard regime governing purchase of Indian lands would take effect.

There has been some controversy as to whether the proclamation applied to the far western reaches of the American continent, notably modern British Columbia and the Yukon Territory.[32] The question has usually been treated as depending on how much territory Great Britain claimed in 1763. The historical evidence indicates that British claims extended indefinitely westward to the Pacific Ocean in latitudes now occupied by Canada.[33] But a better basis exists for resolving the issue. Many of the proclamation's provisions are framed in general terms, referring broadly to 'Our Dominions and Territories' and 'Our Colonies or Plantations in America.' Imperial enactments using such terms were normally given a prospective application so as to apply not only to colonies and territories held when the legislation was enacted but also to those acquired subsequently, unless this result was clearly excluded. The purpose of the proclamation was to establish a uniform set of rules governing Indian lands throughout British territories in North America. There is no reason to think that Indian lands located in territories acquired after 1763 needed less protection than those acquired earlier. It is natural to infer that the proclamation applied to both.[34]

The Royal Proclamation of 1763 has a profound significance for modern Canada. Under its terms aboriginal peoples hold continuing rights to their lands except where these rights have been extinguished by voluntary cession. Treaties of cession have been signed for large parts of Canada, notably in Ontario and the prairie provinces, but no such treaties exist for the Atlantic provinces and parts of Quebec, British Columbia, the Yukon, and the Northwest Territories, as well for pockets of land elsewhere. Moreover, there is doubt as to whether

Canadian legislatures were competent to override the proclamation's terms prior to 1931, when the Statute of Westminster was enacted.[35] So native peoples may today hold subsisting aboriginal rights to large tracts of Canadian land.

The Adaptability of Aboriginal Rights

As noted earlier, the doctrine of aboriginal rights extends not only to property rights but also to customary laws and governmental institutions. It is important to understand that the internal development of such rights was not arrested at the time the crown acquired sovereignty. Rather, these rights retained a certain amount of inherent flexibility, allowing for adaptation to new circumstances. For example, the customs of a native group were not permanently frozen at the time the crown first asserted sovereignty, in 1670, in 1763, or at some other date. They remained responsive to changes in group behaviour and attitudes. Likewise, the right of self-government was not tied down to institutions and arrangements prevailing at some distant historical period. In principle, a native group remained free to adopt new governmental structures.

The position of aboriginal land rights is more complex. As we have seen, the Royal Proclamation of 1763 laid down a uniform legal regime governing native title whereby native groups were recognized as holding communal rights to their unceded lands, subject only to a restriction of alienation. The same position has been held to obtain in common law. At the communal level, the title was a uniform one, not varying in character from group to group or affected by local native custom. It was the same for a nation of farmers as for a band of hunters. In all cases, it allowed for full possession and use of the land. But within a group, the extent to which a particular subgroup, family, or individual might take advantage of the group's collective title was determined by rules particular to the group itself as dictated by customary law and group organs of self-government. In a nutshell, the rights of the group as against the crown and other outsiders were governed by uniform rules flowing from the proclamation and the common law, while the rights of group members inter se were governed by rules peculiar to the individual group. The latter could be altered in the same manner as other group customs, by a general change in attitude and practice, or deliberate amendment by competent bodies.

Aboriginal title imported full rights of possession and use. Native groups were not confined in law to any particular mode of land use, much less to 'traditional' uses. An Indian band that originally lived by hunting or fishing might turn to farming when wild game became depleted, or to ranching, lumbering, or mining. To hold that native peoples were permanently wedded to certain historical practices would in some cases have been to sentence them to slow starvation; in any case it would have denied them the right to adapt to new conditions or exploit their lands more productively.

The proclamation did not establish any boundaries between native groups. In practice, such boundaries tended to fluctuate in response to demographic, economic, or military pressures. It could hardly be held that an Indian band that migrated in search of better hunting conditions or security from its enemies forfeited any claim to aboriginal title. So it was recognized that native peoples were entitled to the unceded lands they actually possessed at any given period. When the crown wanted to negotiate the surrender of certain lands, it dealt with the people actually controlling them. There was usually no inquiry as to whether the people had been there from 'time immemorial' or the date the crown first claimed sovereignty. Such an approach would have quickly proved unworkable. Of course, once native lands had been validly ceded by a group holding title to them, they were permanently withdrawn from the pool of lands available for aboriginal possession.

Indian Treaties

As we have seen, many of the native peoples inhabiting the territories claimed by Great Britain in 1763 were independent; at best they were allies and trading partners of the crown, at worst declared enemies. In areas remote from the eastern colonies, there were numerous groups that had little if anything to do with the British.

The crown thus faced the task of consolidating its territorial claims by slowly earning the allegiance of the native inhabitants. From time to time it also needed to obtain Indian lands for settlement, and here the Royal Proclamation of 1763 required a voluntary public cession. The practice of making treaties with the Indians was well adapted to both purposes. It was followed in many British colonies until 1867, and continued by the federal government for many years after that date.[36] Indeed, treaties with native peoples have recently been revived in the shape of land claims agreements.[37]

Indian treaties have taken many forms over the years. Some treaties, usually those concluded during the early stages of European contact, were drafted as international pacts whereby a European state negotiated on equal terms with an Indian group regarding such matters as peace, friendship, trade, and alliance.[38] Other agreements, which became more common as European states gained the upper hand, defined the relationship between the crown and what was described as a dependent, protected, or tributary aboriginal nation, one that in some respects owed allegiance to the crown but in other respects remained autonomous.[39] Another variety of agreement was more on the style of a voluntary submission, in which the members of an Indian group acknowledged their subordination to the crown and undertook to behave as good and faithful subjects in return for the crown's protection and other advantages.[40] These types of agreements all had international or broadly constitutional aspects. Others were more mundane. The most common was a simple cession of Indian land to the crown in return for stated consideration, with no attempt to define the overall position of the Indian signatories vis-à-vis the crown.[41]

Many historical agreements were a mixture of types. An example is provided by Treaty 3, known as the North-West Angle Treaty, signed in 1873 between the crown and the Saulteaux tribe of Ojibway Indians, inhabiting an area that straddles the border of Ontario and Manitoba.[42] The treaty served a number of goals, broadly described in the opening paragraphs as obtaining the Indians' consent to the settlement of their country and establishing peace and goodwill between them and the crown. The initial clauses refer to the Indians as subjects of the queen, but subsequent provisions make it clear that one function of the treaty is to secure the Indians' formal adherence to the queen as sovereign. Thus, the Indians promise to conduct themselves as good and loyal subjects of Her Majesty, to obey the law, to maintain peace with both whites and Indians, to refrain from molesting the persons or property of other inhabitants, and to help apprehend any Indians infringing the law or the treaty provisions.

These were not mere pro forma undertakings. The independent attitude of the Indians is illustrated by the statement of their spokesman, Mawedopenais, during negotiations with crown officials:

We think it is a great thing to meet you here. What we have heard yesterday, and as you represented yourself, you said the Queen sent you here, the way we understood you as a representative of the Queen. All this is our property where you have come ... This is what we think, that the Great Spirit has planted us on this ground where we are, as you were where you came from. We think where we are is our property. I will tell you what he said to us when he planted us here; the rules that we should follow – us Indians – He has given us rules that we should follow to govern us rightly.[43]

This statement suggests that from the Indians' perspective they negotiated the treaty as autonomous peoples with their own countries and laws. The undertakings made in the treaty to adhere to the queen and her laws represent an important voluntary alteration in their status, if those terms were fully explained to the Indian parties and accepted by them.

The Indians also cede to the crown 'all their rights, titles and privileges' to a defined tract of land. In return the crown undertakes to set aside certain lands as Indian reserves, to make annual payments to the Indians, to maintain schools on the reserves, to furnish annual supplies of ammunition and twine, and to bestow other specified benefits. In a clause of great practical significance to the Indians, the crown also agrees that they shall continue to have the right to hunt and fish throughout the lands surrendered, subject to any regulations made by the government of Canada, and excepting any lands to be taken up for settlement, mining, lumbering, or other purposes.

The Constitutional Guarantee

We are now better equipped to interpret section 35(1) of the Constitution Act, 1982. That section states that 'the existing aboriginal and treaty rights of the aboriginal peoples of Canada are hereby recognized and affirmed.' A number of difficult questions arise regarding the scope and effect of the provision. These depend in part on the meaning of the word 'existing.' It can be argued that the word has three distinct effects. First, it restricts the application of section 35(1) to those rights in existence when the Constitution Act, 1982, came into force, and excludes rights arising after that date. Second, it ensures that the section only covers rights that already existed under common law, statute, or other instrument. Third, it preserves the existing subordination of aboriginal and treaty rights to statute, and prevents the Constitution Act, 1982, from entrenching them. I will consider these arguments separately.

The Time of Recognition

Does section 35(1) apply to any aboriginal or treaty rights that happen to exist from time to time, or is it confined to those existing on the date the Constitution Act, 1982, came into force – on what I shall call the 'commencement date'? In other words, does the section establish 'floating' categories that attach to any rights meeting the section's description regardless of when they arise, or does it establish 'fixed' categories covering a finite body of rights identifiable on the commencement date? On the first view, rights under a treaty signed in 1990 would benefit; on the second view they would not.

A standard rule of statutory interpretation provides that the law is always speaking and applies to new facts as they arise.[44] But this presumption can be overturned by the statute's wording, and arguably the word 'existing' has that effect here. Turning to judicial decisions, we find that 'existing' has sometimes been held to have a prospective application, but in other cases to mean 'existing at the time of enactment,' depending on the context.[45] The question comes down to what section 35(1) intends to say.

Several factors can be cited in favour of the view that the section refers only to rights identifiable on the commencement date. There is a notable difference in phraseology between section 35(1) and the protective provision found in section 25 of the Charter. The latter refers to 'any aboriginal, treaty or other rights or freedoms that pertain to the aboriginal peoples of Canada,' and does not use the qualifier 'existing.' The presence of that word in section 35(1) arguably intimates that a narrower range of rights is singled out for positive recognition, namely, those identifiable on the commencement date. This conclusion is bolstered by the statement that the rights in question 'are hereby recognized and affirmed.' The wording suggests a discrete act of recognition, pinpointed in time, rather than a continuing process of recognition. The inference seems stronger, however, in the English version than in the French, where no equivalent of 'hereby' appears.[46]

Standing alone, then, section 35(1) might be interpreted as covering only rights existing on the commencement date. However, this interpretation cannot easily be sustained in the light of section 35(3). It states, 'For greater certainty, in subsection (1) "treaty rights" includes rights that now exist by way of land claims agreements or may be so acquired.' This provision specifies that the word 'treaty' includes land claims agreements of the modern type. It also indicates that section 35(1) covers rights arising from agreements signed after the commencement date. Rights that 'may be ... acquired' under land claims agreements are mentioned along with those that 'now exist' – a clear reference to rights acquired in future. Moreover, section 35(3) is presented not as an exception to the rule laid down in section 35(1), but as a clarification of that rule, enacted only 'for greater certainty.' If the partial definition of 'treaty rights' given in section 35(3) is inserted in section 35(1), it specifies in effect that the expression 'existing ... treaty rights' includes '*existing* rights that *now* exist by way of land claims agreements or *may be so acquired* (emphasis added).' This does not make sense unless the word 'existing' means 'existing from time to time.'

On balance, then, section 35(1) is best interpreted as embracing not only aboriginal and treaty rights that existed on the commencement date but also those arising later; so, rights acquired under treaties signed after that date will be covered. A different effect may occur in the case of aboriginal rights. The particular form that such rights assume has in principle always been open to change under the doctrine of aboriginal rights. We saw, for example, that native customary law and governmental institutions were not petrified at the moment the crown assumed sovereignty, but remained living entities open to development in accordance with group needs. Likewise, while aboriginal land title was uniform at the group level, it flowered into any number of distinct species within native groups in accordance with customary law and rules laid down by communal organs. Such rules could be altered from time to time. The enactment of section 35(1) did not bring to a sudden halt all evolutionary processes in these spheres; to the contrary, it reaffirmed the doctrine allowing for such evolution.

If rights can be added by treaty to those already covered by section 35(1), it may be inferred that rights covered there can also be modified or extinguished by the same method, without constitutional amendment. As we will see later, the wording of section 35(3) strongly implies that aboriginal land rights can be exchanged for treaty rights through land claims agreements.

The general picture that emerges is this. Any aboriginal and treaty rights that stem from acts or circumstances occurring or existing prior to the commencement date qualify for coverage in section 35(1). These rights may be supplemented by means of voluntary agreements ('treaties') signed with the crown after that date. Rights flowing from such agreements will automatically be captured by section 35(1) without need for constitutional amendment. By the same token, rights covered by the section may be diminished by agreement. The latter point will receive fuller treatment later, but for the moment it can be adopted as a working hypothesis.

The Effect of Recognition

A second effect can arguably be attributed to the word 'existing.' For a right to qualify under section 35(1), it must not only be an 'aboriginal' or a 'treaty' right within the section's meaning; it must also have a sound legal basis apart from the Constitution Act, 1982.

The reasoning in support of this conclusion runs as follows. The section is confined to 'existing' rights. But rights are intangibles; their existence cannot be demonstrated in the same way as that of teacups and toadstools. A right 'exists' only to the extent that it can be justified by reference to some sort of normative framework. The only framework which qualifies for this role is that provided by Canadian law. So, for a right to be an 'existing right' within the meaning of section 35(1), it must already be recognized in Canadian law apart from the Constitution Act, 1982.

This requirement, if correct, has several consequences. Section 35(1) does not bolster the position of rights whose legal status is otherwise uncertain or defective. Moreover, it cannot heal any blemishes in the legal rights it covers; it takes them as they are, warts and all. In short, the section has no remedial effect in respect to the status or character of the rights it addresses.

However, this interpretation is not wholly convincing. Consider the position of a right to an annuity held under an Indian treaty that was signed by the crown under the royal prerogative but never confirmed by Parliament. Arguably, the right is unenforcible in Canadian law in the absence of Parliamentary approval.[47] Assuming this is correct, does it necessarily follow that the right is not an 'existing treaty right' within the meaning of section 35(1)? It seems more natural to read the section as referring to rights existing under the terms of the treaty without reference to the larger question of their status in Canadian law. On this view, one effect of the section is to remedy any imperfections in that status.

So it can be argued that the word 'existing' does not require that the rights recognized by section 35(1) already have a firm basis in Canadian law. Rather, the phrase 'existing aboriginal and treaty rights' can be interpreted as referring to any rights of that description that have not previously been extinguished by acts valid under Canadian law. Which interpretation is right? The issue turns less on a bald exegesis of the word 'existing' than on a reasonable reading of the provision as a whole. We are drawn once again to the statement that the rights in question 'are hereby recognized and affirmed.' These words express the section's main purpose and effect and supply the key to a balanced understanding of its terms.

The phrase 'are hereby recognized' can be read in two main ways: it can mean 'are hereby acknowledged to be valid or genuine' or simply 'are hereby accorded notice or consideration.' If the second construction is correct, then the Constitution Act, 1982, does no more than 'note' the rights in question; in that case, why does it bother to deal with them at all? It seems more likely that the act means to acknowledge officially the validity of these rights. In fact, the first meaning is the ordinary legal one. *Black's Law Dictionary* says that 'recognition' is equivalent to 'ratification' and 'confirmation.' And a provision stating that courts 'shall recognize and take notice of all equitable estates, titles, and rights' has been interpreted judicially as directing courts to give effect to those rights.[49]

A similar choice confronts us in interpreting the phrase 'are hereby ... affirmed.' It can mean 'are hereby confirmed or ratified' or, alternatively, 'are hereby strongly asserted.'[50] Again, the first sense is the ordinary legal one, as dictionaries testify. *Black's Law Dictionary*, for example, says that 'affirm' means to 'ratify, make firm, confirm, establish, reassert,' and *Jowitt's Dictionary of English Law* notes, among other things, that where a party to a voidable contract waives his right to avoid it he is said to 'affirm' the contract. Given the doubts surrounding aboriginal and treaty rights, it seems likely that the Constitution Act, 1982, uses 'affirm' in its normal legal sense of 'confirm' or 'ratify.'

This conclusion is supported by the French version of section 35(1), which has equal authority with the English. It provides that the rights in question are 'reconnus et confirmés.' 'Confirmés' is presented as the equivalent of 'affirmed.' The choice of words is significant. Le Petit Robert tells us that 'confirmer,' as used in the present context, means 'to render certain; to affirm ... the existence of something.'[51] Moreover, a standard French-English dictionary supplies only one English meaning for 'confirmer,' namely, 'to confirm,' and gives as an example the phrase 'confirmer un traite,' that is, 'to ratify a treaty.'[52] It follows that the phrase 'are hereby ... affirmed' in section 35(1) means 'are hereby confirmed'; only then does it have a common core of meaning with the French text. There are numerous authorities on the juridical meaning of 'confirm.' They hold, in effect, that to confirm something is to complete or establish what was previously imperfect or uncertain, or to ratify what was done earlier insufficiently or without authority.[53] In particular, it seems that to confirm a document may mean to give it a life that it otherwise lacked, as when an invalid document is confirmed by another document.[54] In land law, a 'confirmation' is the conveyance of an estate or right in lands or tenements to someone who already has possession thereof or of some estate therein, whereby a voidable estate is made sure and unvoidable or a particular estate is increased or enlarged.[55]

These authorities suggest that section 35(1) has a broad remedial effect. It addresses itself in part to rights that arguably lacked legal status or were uncertain or defective in various respects and recognizes them as legal rights, not mere moral or political rights or precarious rights dependent on the will of the sovereign. It follows that the word 'existing' does not confine the section to rights already recognized at law or prevent it from remedying defects in those rights. There would be little point in recognizing and affirming rights if the effect were restricted in advance to rights that needed no recognition or affirmation. Rather, the word 'existing' should be read in the second sense considered above, as meaning 'unextinguished' or 'subsisting' – as excluding rights terminated by lawful acts prior to the commencement date, but not as requiring any unextinguished rights to have been fully recognized in Canadian law before that date.

One point needs explanation. To say that certain rights are now confirmed as legal rights or that defects in their legal character are cured does not necessarily mean that such rights are immune to statutory override. It means that they are full-fledged legal rights, enforcible in the courts, and secure against possible invasion by executive act under the prerogative. Whether the Constitution Act, 1982, also shields aboriginal and treaty rights from statutes is a distinct question, which I shall now consider.

Entrenchment

Before the Constitution Act, 1982, took effect, aboriginal and treaty rights could in principle be modified by the acts of a competent legislature.[56] Has this position now changed? The answer depends in part on section 52(1) of the act: 'The Constitution of Canada is the supreme law of Canada, and any law that is inconsistent with the provisions of the Constitution is, to the extent of the inconsistency, of no force or effect.' The term 'Constitution of Canada' is defined in section 52(2) as including the Constitution Act, 1982. Is a law that infringes a right in section 35(1) void for inconsistency with the constitution of Canada? In answering this question it will be simplest to deal first with statutes passed after the commencement date, then with those passed before that date. Suppose that in 1990 Parliament enacts a statute expropriating a tract of aboriginal land covered by section 35(1). The Constitution Act, 1982, directs the courts to recognize the aboriginal title in question, but the statute tells them to disregard it. The courts cannot do both. In the absence of any special factors justifying the expropriation (to be discussed later) the constitutional provision must take precedence and nullify the conflicting statute.

Nevertheless, it could be argued that the word 'existing' in section 35(1) preserves aboriginal and treaty rights in the state they were in at the commencement date, a state which in principle included a subordination to statute. If a legislature was competent to curtail aboriginal and treaty rights before the Constitution Act, 1982, took effect, it is still competent to do so. But we have already seen that the phrase 'are hereby recognized and affirmed' gives the section a broad remedial effect, disposing of the notion that it preserves the status quo. Moreover, the argument confuses the section's scope with its legal effect. The fact that the section only covers 'existing' rights does not necessarily mean that the act's effect on these rights is controlled by the law formerly in force.[57]

Another factor must be considered. Section 35(1) can only be amended in accordance with part V of the act. Under the ordinary procedure laid down in section 38, an amendment requires the approval of Parliament and of two-thirds of provincial legislatures accounting for 50 per cent of the total population of the provinces. Yet the argument set out above holds, in effect, that section 35(1) could be eviscerated by an ordinary federal statute stating that 'the existing aboriginal and treaty rights of the aboriginal peoples of Canada are hereby extinguished.' It seems unlikely that the amending formula can be circumvented so easily.

This conclusion is supported by the wording of section 35(4): 'Notwithstanding any other provision of this Act, the aboriginal and treaty rights referred to in subsection (1) are guaranteed equally to male and female persons.' The word 'guaranteed' is significant because it plainly indicates an intent to entrench. Yet if section 35(1) did not guarantee aboriginal and treaty rights at all, what would be the point of stating that it guarantees them equally to both sexes?

I conclude that section 35(1) entrenches aboriginal and treaty rights against statutory override.[58] But entrenchment does not completely preclude legal limitation of those rights. In determining whether a statute infringes a section 35(1) right, the courts will have to define the proper bounds of the right. In doing so they will be guided in part by standards of reasonableness. Once those reasonable bounds have been determined, it will not ordinarily be possible for statutes to overstep them.

The question arises whether there might be unusual circumstances in which a protected right, as properly defined, may be overridden by ordinary statute. Imagine that in wartime a particular tract of land is needed for defence installations, and for various good reasons no other tract will do. It happens the land is subject to aboriginal title. Can the federal government expropriate the land by simple statute, or must it follow the cumbersome procedure laid down for constitutional amendments? It can be strongly argued that section 35(1) is governed by an implicit standard of reasonableness, not only in its definition of the rights recognized but also in the protection it affords to such rights. If this view is correct, then considering the urgency of the situation the government can probably proceed by statute.

The implicit standard postulated here is clearly more demanding than that found in section 1 of the Constitution Act, 1982, which provides that the Charter of Rights and Freedoms guarantees the rights set out in it 'subject only to such reasonable limits prescribed by law as can be demonstrably justified in a free and democratic society.' It seems that section 35 was placed outside the Charter precisely to put it beyond the reach of section 1. Moreover, certain aboriginal and treaty rights need special protection because they are capable of being exhausted. If all aboriginal lands were taken, aboriginal land rights would cease to exist. By contrast, a Charter right such as freedom of speech is capable of infinite renewal.

These considerations suggest that section 35(1) erects a high barrier against statutory interference, one that can be surmounted only in emergencies to meet a pressing public need. Aboriginal and treaty rights are not, in ordinary circumstances, subject to statutory expropriation, even if generous monetary compensation is provided. The Constitution Act, 1982, guarantees the right itself, not its supposed monetary equivalent. Had the act contemplated such a substitution, clear language would have been used.

Prior Statutory Extinguishment

We have been considering laws passed *after* the commencement date that violate a section 35(1) right. What about laws passed before that date? We saw earlier that the phrase 'existing aboriginal and treaty rights' does not cover rights extinguished by legislation or other acts before the commencement date. In principle, then, no conflict can arise between rights 'existing' on that date and acts passed before then, because the former are defined and limited by the latter. The real problem is determining whether an act passed before the commencement date actually extinguished the right in question.

Treaty rights present particular difficulties. For example, when a statute in force on the commencement date was inconsistent with a right conferred by a treaty, and the enacting legislature was competent to modify the treaty, did the treaty cease to 'exist' for purposes of section 35(1)? Suppose a nineteenth-century Indian treaty guarantees an unrestricted right of fishing in a certain area, and a federal statute in force on the commencement date restricts fishing in that area for all persons, including Indians. Clearly, the Indians do not have an unrestricted statutory right to fish. But does their treaty right still exist?

The answer depends on the statute's wording. We must distinguish between a statute that nullifies a treaty right and one that merely fails to implement or observe it. The latter would not relieve the crown of its obligations under the treaty. Where the statute's wording does not indicate that the treaty was present to the mind of Parliament and consciously repudiated, the treaty promise remains intact if unfulfilled. Explicit words seem necessary to release the crown from promises made to private parties in return for substantial benefits gained at the expense of those parties. When a statute in force on the commencement date is inconsistent with a treaty promise but does not explicitly repudiate it, the Constitution Act, 1982, arguably affirms the promise and renders the legislation ineffective to that extent.

The distinction is clear in principle, but not always in practice. Some Indian treaties expressly say that certain promises are subject to future governmental regulation. In Treaty 3 of 1873, discussed earlier, the queen agrees that the Indian parties shall have the right to continue hunting and fishing throughout the lands surrendered in the treaty, 'subject to such regulations as may from time to time be made by her Government of her Dominion of Canada,' and saving any tracts taken up for settlement or other purposes. By contrast, certain earlier treaties containing similar promises make no reference to future governmental regulation.[59] If section 35(1) entrenches the actual rights guaranteed in Indian treaties, what effect does it have on the promise made in treaty 3?

On the one hand it could be argued that the treaty right is explicitly characterized as subject to governmental regulation; the constitutional entrenchment of the right does not remove its liability to legislative erosion or extinguishment. On the other hand it could be said that the treaty simply makes explicit what would in any case be understood: rights are subject to parliamentary regulation unless specially entrenched. On this view, since the Constitution Act, 1982, alters the principle of parliamentary supremacy referred to in the treaty, it also places the treaty right beyond legislative interference.

The question boils down to the correct interpretation of the treaty. On a reasonable view of the written text and related negotiations, what does the crown undertake to do? In 1873, hunting and fishing were the mainstay of many Indian groups. It seems unlikely that the Indians would have agreed that in return for ceding away most of their lands they would receive a right of hunting and fishing characterized as liable to complete suppression. The reference to governmental regulation is arguably something more than the expression of a standard constitutional rule, however. At least in the written text, it seems to qualify the scope of the crown's undertaking directly.

These reflections suggest a middle road between the two opposing views. What the crown promises is that the Indians shall have the right to hunt and fish, subject to future *regulation* as opposed to *suppression*. That is, the government reserves the power to regulate the manner in which the rights are exercised, short of substantial interference with the right itself. Of course, as a matter of constitutional law, the crown in Parliament remained free to impose whatever statutes it wished; but as a matter of treaty, the crown undertook to confine its interference to mere regulation. If this interpretation is correct, the Constitution Act, 1982, reaffirms the treaty promise and nullifies any legislation that crosses the line between regulation and suppression.

Voluntary Extinguishment

A further question now arises. Can rights governed by section 35(1) be modified or extinguished by the voluntary act of the native people concerned without a constitutional amendment? To take a concrete example, can aboriginal land rights be ceded to the crown by agreement coupled with ordinary legislation, or must an amendment to the Constitution Act, 1982, be secured?

Forceful arguments can be made for the validity of voluntary surrenders, at least in the case of aboriginal land rights. The purpose of section 35(1), it can be said, is to insulate the rights of aboriginal peoples from external threat, not to protect native peoples from themselves. There is no apparent reason why a total of seven provinces should have to sanction a land claims settlement, as would be required under the amending formula in section 38. Neither would such a requirement better protect the interests of the native peoples themselves. It has always been considered possible for a native people to cede aboriginal lands to the crown by treaty, and this historical practice is reflected in the wording of section 35(1), with its reference to both aboriginal and treaty rights.

What is more striking, both sections 25 and 35(3) refer to rights acquired under future land claims agreements.[60] These references indicate that aboriginal land rights may be voluntarily exchanged for treaty rights and are not inherently inalienable. They also imply that this exchange can take place without constitutional amendment. Thus, section 35(3) provides in effect that when an aboriginal land claim is settled the agreement will be automatically entrenched in the constitution. But if rights conferred in return for aboriginal lands are entrenched without constitutional amendment, it follows that the surrender itself may take effect without such amendment. It goes without saying that for a surrender to be valid it must be fully voluntary, and that section 35(1) harbours rules ensuring this.

Conclusion

If we survey the results of our analysis, we are struck by the potential of section 35(1) to provide solutions to a number of long-standing problems and grievances. I have argued that the section officially confirms the doctrine of aboriginal rights whereby the original rights of native American peoples are held to have survived the crown's acquisition of sovereignty, except in so far as these were incompatible with the crown's ultimate title or were subsequently modified by statute or other lawful acts. It also confirms that aboriginal rights are legal rights maintainable at law as against the crown and private parties. The section likewise recognizes that rights conferred on native peoples in treaties signed by the crown are enforcible in the courts, regardless of whether the treaties were previously confirmed by statute. But the section does not resurrect any aboriginal or treaty rights that were extinguished by lawful acts before the Constitution Act, 1982, came into force. Rights covered by the section are shielded against encroachment by ordinary statutes, except perhaps in cases of emergency. Nevertheless, they can be supplemented or diminished by voluntary agreement with the native peoples concerned, without resort to constitutional amendment.

A distinguishing feature of section 35(1) is its flexibility, both in its openness to change by voluntary act and in the latitude it allows to courts in resolving disputes regarding aboriginal and treaty rights. I cannot explore these matters in any depth here, but a few illustrations drawn from the areas of aboriginal land claims and rights of self-government may be helpful.

Section 35(1), I suggest, empowers courts to handle aboriginal land claims in a broadly equitable manner, one that takes account of current realities and needs while honouring the spirit of the doctrine of aboriginal rights. Three types of claims are likely to arise.

The first and simplest is the situation in which an aboriginal people possessed certain lands on the commencement date, and aboriginal title to the lands had not been extinguished. If the people hold substantial historical links with the lands, then section 35(1) confirms their right to exclusive use and possession under aboriginal title. The requisite historical links must be sufficient to identify the claimants, as opposed to other possible native claimants, as the true title-holders. But possession from 'time immemorial' need hardly be established, nor indeed possession from the time the crown first asserted sovereignty. In most instances, a period of some twenty to forty years would be adequate.

A more difficult case arises when, prior to the commencement date, a native people was factually dispossessed of its lands by acts attributable to the crown, but the acts did not lawfully terminate the aboriginal title. If title was not otherwise extinguished prior to the commencement date, the people hold subsisting aboriginal rights to the land, and in principle are entitled to regain possession. But in some instances it may not be possible for them to do so without hardship to innocent third parties who have assumed possession in the interim. Here I suggest that the courts may award compensation in lieu of possession, or a mix of the two, in the exercise of a broad equitable jurisdiction.

The third case is one in which, before the commencement date, a group's aboriginal land rights were compulsorily extinguished by statute or acts carrying statutory authority, without payment of appropriate compensation. Where the act did not explicitly rule out compensation, a right to compensation arguably arose under the doctrine of aboriginal title and also under general common-law principles governing compulsory acquisitions.[61] This right to compensation, where it exists, is itself an aboriginal right recognized by section 35(1) and may be enforced by the courts.

Claims to subsisting rights of self-government pose different problems. How far these rights have been eroded by statutes and other acts over the past centuries is a matter requiring detailed consideration. But over and above any particular governmental rights that may have survived, section 35(1) arguably recognizes the existence of an inchoate right of native self-government. The concrete form this right assumes must be specified in agreements between the native group concerned and the federal crown. Rights recognized in such agreements will automatically be entrenched in the constitution under section 35(1), either as concrete instances of the abstract aboriginal right of self-government or as treaty rights. As such, they can be modified only by constitutional amendment or voluntary agreement. The result will in effect be a third order of government within Canadian federalism, paralleling federal and provincial institutions. How far the federal crown may legally go in recognizing native governmental powers is unclear; but so long as such agreements do not overstep the existing limits of federal jurisdiction over native peoples under the Constitution Act, 1867, they probably are valid.[62]

Beyond its practical effect, section 35(1) has an important symbolic significance. The constitution now clearly acknowledges the historical role of native peoples in the making of Canada. That this should rank as an achievement is itself a sad comment on the modern position of native peoples. It is now over two centuries since the Royal Proclamation of

1763 was issued. The bicentenary of that event passed twenty years ago without a trace of public recognition in Canada. The Constitution Act, 1982, is the measure of how far we have come in the past two decades. Canada now seems poised to reclaim as its own the constitutional structures that developed during almost five centuries of European relations with native Canadian peoples.

SALLY WEAVER

Federal Difficulties with Aboriginal Rights Demands

In this paper I will identify the major reasons for the federal government's difficulties in dealing with aboriginal rights demands from native groups. I will provide some observations on this complex issue, and I will illustrate them with references to the evolution of 'native policy' in the 1970s. I see aboriginal rights as a political not a legal matter, and I understand 'aboriginal rights' to be a broader term than 'aboriginal land rights.' First, however, I will define what I mean by native policy and aboriginal rights.

Native Policy

In my view, the major federal policy innovation of the past decade with respect to aboriginal peoples in Canada has been the evolution of a *native* policy. I am referring here to the federal government's extension of its traditional interests in Indians and Inuit to include Metis and non-status Indians in some of its programs and policy processes. During the 1970s a broadly conceived native policy perspective emerged in Ottawa. This policy development is notable not because the federal government effectively grappled with Metis and non-status Indian issues, but because it attempted to do so.[1]

From the outset the federal government's native policy has been characterized by a series of unplanned, uncoordinated, ad hoc policy initiatives, motivated in part by a humanitarian concern for the Metis and non-status Indians and in part by political expediency. Native policy is an inclusive rubric under which policies are established for all aboriginal groups. It is and always has been a collage of policies rather than a consistent policy framework with guiding principles or goals.

The evolution of a native policy began in the late 1960s, in the prairies, under the federal government's Agriculture and Rural Development Act, which funded native communications workers. This initiative took fuller form starting in 1970 under the secretary of state's 'core funding' program, which funded the operating costs of national and regional native political organizations. The evolution of a native policy gained momentum with the introduction of the Canadian Mortgage and Housing Corporation's rural and native housing program in the early 1970s. Subsequently, in 1974–5, the federal cabinet's policy priorities exercise produced the 'Native Policy' document.[2] In 1976, acting on the recommendations contained in this document, the cabinet approved the establishment of a joint cabinet–Native Council of Canada (NCC) committee.[3] Concurrently, it approved funding of 'mutually acceptable' land claims research by Metis and non-status Indian organizations.[4]

The federal government's continuing interest in the Metis and non-status Indians was evident again when the Privy Council Office (the central bureaucratic agency advising the cabinet) established the 1978 task force to study the socio-economic development of Metis and non-status Indians. This initiative died in the fall of 1980 when the task force report was shelved and no ministerial action was forthcoming. A year later, in November 1981, the government announced its intention to establish a native economic development fund of $345 million. The most recent federal native policy initiative emerged in the context of the Canadian constitutional renewal process. One result of this process has been that the federal government acknowledged the Metis as one of the aboriginal peoples of Canada, and recognized and affirmed their 'existing aboriginal and treaty rights.'[5]

The implications of including Metis and non-status Indians as a federal responsibility are extensive, and raise vexing questions of cost, jurisdiction, administrative machinery, and government relationships with status Indians. The magnitude of these questions partly accounts for the federal government's reluctance to accept responsibility for the Metis and non-status Indians who are deemed to be 'the responsibility of the provinces' as ordinary citizens.

Aboriginal Rights

Aboriginal rights are a broad but fundamental political claim by aboriginal peoples against the state for recognition of their unique ethnicity and for resources flowing from this recognition. Advocates of aboriginal rights seek to alter the power relationships between aboriginal peoples and the governments of Canada. As a political symbol, the issue of aboriginal rights has what anthropologists call a 'multivalent' quality: that is, the symbol has many different layers of meanings depending on the speaker, the context of its use, and the time at which it is evoked. Multivalent symbols can be a unifying force, a focus of common identity in a political movement, because of their high level of inclusiveness (generality), and because of their 'condensation' of meanings. They are flexible in that they can be changed over time to include new demands, and they can be operationalized or translated differently by diverse native groups to serve their unique historical or regional purposes. Because of its multivalence, the symbol 'aboriginal rights' lacks any single clear referent among native groups. Its legitimacy derives primarily from the values and sentiments in the political cultures of aboriginal groups; it is only partially legitimized by the federal government on legal, moral, or conventional grounds.

To sum up, 'aboriginal rights' is a complex, emotionally charged, multivalent symbol that represents native demands for recognition as a unique cultural group; that is, as aboriginal people. On the basis of this uniqueness, they demand special resources from the state. These demands are rationalized by native groups in part on the ground of their cultural uniqueness and their historical special status in Canada. Moreover, they believe their cultural idioms can survive only in the context of a special relationship with the state.

Federal Perspectives

Any attempt to identify why the federal government experiences difficulties in dealing with native demands for aboriginal rights should emphasize that the federal government is not a monolithic corporate entity whose component parts think and act in concert. Rather, its organizational complexity and scale inevitably lead to internal conflict among its various departments and agencies and to contradictory philosophies and policies. This has evidenced itself in recent years in a lack of co-ordination between government actions and policies. In the following pages I will discuss some of the sources of policy confusion.

Ideology

Assertions by public servants and academics that ideology plays little part in policy-making are belied by the recent history of Indian and native policy development. Policy-making is not a pragmatic exercise devoid of principles and beliefs, but a process in which values that will guide government actions are selected and rationalized. Indian policy in Canada is made by individuals who hold strong feelings about whether or not native groups should be treated differently from other Canadians. One of the most pervasive forces underlying the federal government's resistance to aboriginal rights demands is its steadfast commitment to liberal-democratic ideology. Liberal-democratic ideology stresses equality, individualism, and freedom from discrimination on the basis of race, religion, nationality, and so on.[6] For most policy-makers in government, demands for aboriginal rights are problematical because they call for the administration of services, programs, and laws on the basis of special status, collective rights, and cultural uniqueness.[7] All of these concepts are viewed by the government as contradicting liberal-democratic ideology.

The federal government's policies under the Trudeau administration have persistently reflected the attitude that special treatment is discriminatory treatment. When provisions for special treatment of Indians have been incorporated into government policies, they have always been characterized as transitory or temporary measures and rationalized on the basis of economic need (socio-economic class), not on the basis of cultural recognition (ethnicity). Programs developed to include the Metis, for example, are rationalized on economic grounds such as economic disadvantage, social deprivation, or rural poverty. The federal government thus avoids explicit recognition of Metis ethnicity and defines the goals of its policies in terms of alleviating social and economic disadvantages.

Personalities

Personalities are a key factor in the development of policies. This is evident in former Prime Minister Pierre Trudeau's role and views on special status for Quebec or the Indians. The prime minister opposed policies or laws that implied recognition of racial or ethnic categories. Less visible than elected officials but nevertheless influential in the development of policy initiatives on aboriginal rights are public-servant activists who are sympathetic to the aboriginal cause. One can trace most of the policy initiatives in the 1960s and 1970s back to sympathetic officials in various federal departments and agencies. These officials usually have direct contact with native spokesmen and leaders and have acquired a good grasp of native issues. They function as action-oriented brokers between the government and native groups. They work to make government more responsive to native peoples by keeping native issues alive and before ministers. They also attempt to recast polemical native rhetoric into constructive language acceptable to ministers, and they rationalize native demands in terms that reflect government priorities. No doubt these activists have their own agendas; indeed, most hold strong views on how native leaders should act, what strategies they should adopt, and when they should implement them. Their career positions are tenuous because their loyalty is questioned by government and their sympathies are questioned by natives. They are aware of the risks they run, however, and most of them enjoy the political intrigue. They maintain a characteristically positive outlook as they move policy issues along in a way that is intended to accommodate both government and native needs.

In the 1970s the public-servant activists were sufficient in number and status in various departments and agencies to promote and broker aboriginal rights demands within government. The Native Policy document of 1976, for example, although intensely disliked by the Department of Indian Affairs and Northern Development (DIAND) and status Indians alike, is attributable to their work. Today, however, such activists are few and have little influence in the departments that house them. Although individual ministers can be and have been sympathetic to native demands, they have neither the time nor, often, the skill or influence to translate native demands into policy forms acceptable to cabinet. The absence of activists has left government with a diminished capacity to respond creatively and meaningfully to aboriginal rights demands.

Political Priorities of the Federal Government

Public servant activists tend to exploit government priorities to advocate and rationalize their preferred native policies. However, the recent shift of government priorities away from a social-justice emphasis to one of economic concern has made such rationalization extremely difficult. By the mid-1970s government interest began to focus on the economy, inflation, and unemployment. Concomitantly, there was an increasing emphasis in government on more rigorous financial control and management and on spending restraint. This emphasis has affected aboriginal rights demands in many ways, including an increased difficulty in getting native issues dealt with in any systematic and sustained fashion. Native issues are located at the periphery of government concern in terms of both policy interests and the assignment of ministers and public-service personnel to the issues. For example, the high priority that is placed on financial restraint has provided ready ammunition for those in government who stand opposed to aboriginal rights demands or who feel the federal government should not accept responsibility for Metis and non-status Indians. Thus, aboriginal rights demands are far less congruent with federal priorities today than they were in the early 1970s, and those officials who are sympathetic to these demands have little political leverage.

Ministerial Incentive

Ministerial incentive is always a vital aspect of any policy-making process, but in recent years it has become a particularly significant variable in the federal government's reaction to aboriginal rights demands. In the early years of the Trudeau administration there was considerable support and goodwill among the public, the cabinet, and the civil service for native aspirations. In recent years we have witnessed a general disenchantment with 'excessive' Indian demands. This disenchantment has resulted in ministers' finding little incentive to address native issues. Nor do they perceive themselves as being rewarded by Indian and Metis leaders for their efforts in behalf of native interests. The negotiations on the constitution are a case in point. Initially, government negotiators believed their concessions satisfied native demands. When native leaders subsequently changed their stance and resumed lobbying in London against patriation, cabinet ministers experienced a sense of betrayal and intense displeasure.

The confrontational posture of native organizations (Inuits excepted) also embittered some ministers and officials toward native organizations and convinced them that nothing will please native leaders. During the Trudeau administration, diminishing ministerial incentive stemmed from the Liberals' preoccupation with the declining political fortunes of their party and the knowledge that natives were not a significant electoral force. When native issues were addressed by ministers, it appeared to be for instrumental reasons. For example, the concessions on constitutional issues were made to gain native support for a smoother patriation process. Similarly, resumption of negotiations on a comprehensive claims settlement in the north was initiated to make way for much-needed energy developments.

In regard to the Metis and non-status Indians, ministerial interest in aboriginal rights remained problematic during the 1970s. Indeed, it is difficult to identify a single minister who took any policy initiative in this field. A humanitarian concern for the Metis and non-status Indians exists in cabinet, but there is little incentive for ministerial leadership or initiative to advance the issue of their aboriginal rights.

Government Structures and Co-ordination

Since the late 1960s policy-making relative to aboriginal peoples has become exceedingly complex. The policy-making arena has expanded from DIAND and its Indian and Inuit clientele to government and its native clientele. The emergence of additional government departments as participants in the native policy-making process has created a need for better co-ordination to ensure that the government's native policies are not only internally consistent but also compatible with other government policy initiatives. Although complete co-ordination of policies is not a realistic goal, it is still necessary to provide some modicum of assurance that the government knows what it is doing in the field of native policy. It must avoid serious contradictions in its policies and programs.

Expansion of the native policy-making arena has also made it necessary for the central agencies in government to referee disagreements between different departments. This role reflects the increased powers of the central agencies and has diminished the capacity of DIAND to move its preferred policies through the system. At the same time, the central agencies have not had much success in preparing an overall (governmental) native policy strategy acceptable to cabinet. For example, the promised $345 million native economic development fund, which involved the participation of several ministers, departments, agencies, and consultants, remains without a coherent policy vehicle after two years of work. This lack is attributable to the absence of a politically sanctioned native policy framework within which departments and agencies can formulate their submissions to cabinet.

As a result of these and other deficiencies, problems arise in setting native policy directions. For example, should DIAND's desire to proceed with Indian Act revisions pre-empt or precede the planned constitutional discussions on aboriginal rights? Does the affirmation in the constitution of 'existing aboriginal and treaty rights' conflict with the government's comprehensive land claims settlement policy, which is based on the extinguishment of Indian title? These and similar unanswered questions increase uncertainty and apprehension within government, which in turn fosters a general reluctance actively to engage native issues. The consequence of all this is that instead of addressing substance or content of policies, the government stresses the process of policies and resorts to evasions and tactical manoeuvres in dealing with native demands (for example, more and more meetings with native groups to discuss policy issues). In keeping with this style, the government has adopted a reactive and usually negative mode for dealing with aboriginal rights demands.

Federal–Provincial Relations

Federal–provincial relations as they pertain to native issues are uncharted territory. Because of the constitutional division of powers, federal–provincial relations have significant implications for the future of aboriginal-rights demands. To date there has been no concerted or systematic effort by the federal government to develop a clear policy direction for engaging the provinces in native affairs. The federal government will first have to sort out its own role, especially in regard to Metis and non-status Indians, before it can begin dealing with the provinces in any serious or systematic way.

Concepts of Ethnicity

Federal difficulties in dealing with aboriginal rights demands arise in part from a conception of ethnicity that is very different from that held by native groups. Much of government policy reflects what I call the 'hydraulic Indian' view of ethnicity. This view depicts an Indian or native person as a cylinder which, at some undefined point in history, was full to the top with 'Indianness,' that is, traditional Indian culture. As time passed, and as Indians adopted non-native ways, the level of 'Indianness' dropped to the point where the cylinder now is nearly empty. Elsewhere in this book Billy Diamond illustrates this approach to ethnicity in his description of how government lawyers at the James Bay hearings (conducted by Judge Malouf) tried to discredit the Crees' claim to Indianness by asking if they ate pizza or liked Chinese food. This view of Indian ethnicity holds that real Indians don't eat pizza. This is a truncated and static understanding of ethnicity, one that freezes cultural idioms in some historic moment. It fails to comprehend that ethnicity is a process that unfolds over time as groups continually select and reinterpret diverse cultural forms around them (native and non-native) in defining themselves as distinct from the larger society.

Under the static view of ethnicity, culturally non-traditional native peoples are cast as having a spurious, ethnicity. According to this view, for example the Metis are held to have died with Riel, and the Mohawk high-steel workers are not seen as legitimately expressing the Mohawk cultural idiom. The fallacy of this approach is evident in the fact that what once were non-traditional Indian cultural forms are today understood to be 'traditional' (for example, the Iroquois longhouse religion, a synthesis of Quaker and Iroquois religious systems). The static perspective of ethnicity is not static but the product of a time-lag, a sliding historical scale in which Indian and white cultural forms are synthesized by Indians and in time come to be regarded as 'traditional' or genuine by non-Indians. In this sense, ethnicity is always in the past tense. The concept of ethnicity contained in native demands for aboriginal rights embodies the notion of the ongoing process of ethnicity, not the frozen time-lag notion of ethnicity. For this reason aboriginal rights demands will continually change in the future as native groups reformulate their ethnicity in the context of the broader societal changes that impinge on them. This is already evident in Indian demands to 'renegotiate' historic treaties in contemporary terms: they seek to assign them a new meaning in today's context. Hence, attempts to freeze recognition of aboriginal rights at some moment in time will inevitably be unsuccessful, whether the attempts are promoted by native groups or by governments.

Conclusion

I have attempted to identify some of the reasons for the federal government's difficulties in responding to aboriginal-rights demands from native groups. I have interpreted aboriginal rights as a multivalent symbol representing a broad political claim by aboriginal peoples against the state for recognition of their unique ethnicity and for the resources (laws, jurisdiction, programs, land) flowing from this recognition. Given this interpretation, I have argued that federal resistance to these demands lies as much in the culture of policy-making (the liberal-democratic ideology and static concepts of ethnicity) as it does in the social roles (activist personalities and motivated ministers) and social structures (organizations, co-ordination, and jurisdiction) of policy-making. Relating these observations to future meetings on the constitution, I suggest that 'existing aboriginal and treaty rights' cannot be defined and specified in a way that will be meaningful to all parties. If 'aboriginal rights' is construed as a broad political claim, then no single act of accession to that claim is possible or even desirable.

The Right Honourable PIERRE ELLIOTT TRUDEAU

Statement by the Prime Minister of Canada to the Conference of First Ministers on Aboriginal Constitutional Matters, 8–9 March 1984

A study the government made a few years ago of the conditions of the Indian peoples presents a sorry state of affairs.

- Their life expectancy is ten years less than for the population as a whole.
- Violent deaths are three times the national rate. Suicides, particularly in the 15–24 age group, are more than six times the national rate.
- Between 50 and 70 per cent receive social assistance.
- One in three families lives in overcrowded conditions. Less than 50 per cent of Indian houses are properly serviced, compared to a national level of more than 90 per cent.

I do not think the latest figures, if they were available, would show any great change. No study of this kind has been made of the conditions of the Inuit or the Metis, but we cannot expect that such a study would lead to a very different result.

These statistics illustrate that aboriginal peoples have long been victims of severe injustices that are not tolerable in Canadian society. As a small but significant segment of our population they have suffered and for the most part continue to suffer acutely from economic disadvantage, social degradation, and political obscurity. But perhaps the greatest injustice is the hard fact that their condition has been almost totally ignored by the mainstream society, including its governments. Both levels of government have some degree of responsibility for the aboriginal peoples, either as citizens or as descendants of the original inhabitants of this country.

Yet in spite of these acknowledged adversities the aboriginal peoples have managed to survive as identifiable groups in our population. Will-power, patience, and determination to sustain themselves in a hostile social environment have enabled the aboriginal groups to persevere in their quest for the justice, respect, and consideration they have been denied since the dawn of our Canadian history; this by an ever-expanding and energetic society with particular pride in its capacity for tolerance and social compromise.

In the past decade or so, the aboriginal groups have succeeded, with encouragement from the government but largely through their own efforts, in making themselves heard. As their voices have become clearer and as the dialogue has enlarged, the disposition of governments to listen has grown. This positive approach to questions long ignored or treated negatively has led us to this conference table and to the agenda we face in this series of conferences.

We started in 1982 by inserting in our constitution section 35, in which aboriginal and treaty rights were recognized and affirmed. We were aware at the time that these rights needed to be identified and further defined through a constitutional process. My own view is that the problem of identification of rights is well advanced. On both sides we now have a clearer idea of the subject matters the aboriginal peoples have in mind when they speak about their rights. However, neither they nor we have the same clarity of ideas when it comes to the definition of those rights. That is not surprising, given the complexity of the subjects identified. We will find appropriate formulations for inclusion in the constitution when they have emerged with some precision from our ongoing discussions.

In the meantime, we should try to avoid the further complications that frequently flow from misinterpretation or misapprehension of words that have cropped up in the course of our ongoing consultations. One of these is the word 'extinguishment,' which has long been used in connection with aboriginal rights, whether referring to the treaties concluded with Indian groups in historic times or to the more recent comprehensive claims agreements already reached or in the process of negotiation. It is a word that has attractions for lawyers because of its tidiness, especially in situations where one set of rights is being exchanged or substituted for another. But the beneficiaries of those rights, in this case the aboriginal peoples, fear that extinguishment contains a threat of finality or extinction – a snuffing of the flame of aboriginal culture which the peoples concerned have strived so long and hard to sustain.

If we think back to the time when the contact between aboriginal and non-aboriginal peoples began, we know that the rights of the aboriginal peoples were not written down in formal documents. They were being exercised freely by the aboriginal groups found in various parts of the country. As the newcomers began to occupy the country, they gave expression to those aboriginal rights in legal documents of their own devising. The Royal Proclamation of 1763 was one such document; so were the treaties concluded with various Indian nations or tribes. There were further expressions of aboriginal rights in federal laws referring in particular to provincial boundaries and resource transfers. Changing situations at various times in our history have required new or enlarged formulations for giving expression to the rights of aboriginal peoples in Canadian law.

The treaty-making process and the land claims settlement process in which we are now engaged have the same goal: the transformation of uncertain, ill-defined aboriginal rights that have proved to be difficult to enforce into clearly stated, justiciable, written rights. These new rights rise, phoenix-like, from the ashes of the old. And so today we are looking for a further formulation or expression of aboriginal rights that will be suitable for inclusion in the constitution and that will serve as a sound base for the future relationships of the aboriginal groups with others in Canadian society, including governments. We do this at a time when our constitution is just beginning to serve all Canadians as a safeguard for rights. If a better word than extinguishment can be found to characterize the process I have just described, I will be disposed to agree to its use.

Another word that tends to irritate our discussions is 'entrenchment.' It is a word that often seems to get in the way of progress. In the business of building a solid constitutional base for aboriginal rights, one does not necessarily begin with the inclusion in the constitutional document of barely perceived propositions and prescriptions. We do not have to look very far afield in the world to see places where fine constitutional phrases and pronouncements are but a cover-up for a general denial of rights to some groups in the society concerned. We in this country do not seek a constitution that is nothing but a paper monument for rights that are buried under a pile of empty words. We seek constitutional provisions that have practical meaning and benefit for the people they concern. We will reach that goal by threshing and sifting ideas thoroughly until the right ones fall into place in workable formulas. We should know that they will work, if only on a trial basis, even as our discussions continue. When we have the right stuff, we will have little difficulty in finding place and expression for it in the constitution. That is a process solidly based in the Canadian way of achieving workable consensus and compromise.

In aboriginal matters, in all Canadian matters deserving constitutional treatment, we will succeed by striving energetically for formulas and prescriptions that work for the benefit of all concerned, because they will take into account the aspirations and interests of all concerned. And we will end up with a constitution that is alive and well and a source of pride and comfort for all of us.

Before suggesting some of the ways in which I think these matters should move in the immediate future, I want to refer briefly to another phrase which in recent years has troubled our discussions. I refer to 'equality of rights' for aboriginal men and women.

My own view is that equality of the sexes is protected for all Canadians including the aboriginal peoples by the Charter of Rights and Freedoms. But I do not preclude an additional provision for the sake of greater clarity. Such a provision was included in the resolution to amend the constitution we agreed upon last year. Should we conclude that further amendment is called for, the government of Canada will raise no objection.

On the subject of equality, legislation will be introduced shortly to repeal the discriminatory provisions of the Indian Act, and in particular section 12(1)(b). Repeal of this section will mean that status under the Indian Act will not be lost or acquired by marriage.

I would now like to propose our objectives at this conference. In the field of rights the major preoccupation of the aboriginal peoples is with self-government. This should be the principal subject of our discussions. But inclusion in the constitution of rights to self-government cannot alone meet the real day-to-day needs of Indians, Inuit, and Metis living in their own communities. Another item on our agenda should be the need to build the socio-economic infrastructure the aboriginal peoples need if they are to fulfil their reasonable expectations both as Canadians and as persons of aboriginal ancestry. Then there is a third question to which we should address ourselves. Peoples are distinguished one from another as much by language and culture as by history and geography. If our aboriginal peoples are to preserve their heritage and keep their identity in our society, their cultures and languages must be preserved and enhanced.

If you agree, I suggest that the underlying thrust of our discussions should be directed to these three ends:

- self-government, a broad subject-heading that can encompass most if not all of the particulars in the prepared agenda;
- building the socio-economic infrastructure;
- protection and enhancement of aboriginal cultures and languages.

I will deal briefly with each of these in turn.

There is nothing revolutionary or threatening about the prospect of aboriginal self-government. Aboriginal communities have rightful aspirations to have more say in the management of their affairs and to exercise more responsibility for decisions affecting them. These functions are normal and essential to the sense of self-worth that distinguishes individuals in a free society.

The government of Canada remains committed to the establishment of aboriginal self-government, and it is my impression that the provinces are of the same mind. We are not here to consider whether there should be institutions of self-government, but *how* these institutions should be brought into being; what should be their jurisdictions, their powers; how they should fit into the interlocking system of jurisdictions by which Canada is governed. Democratic institutions of government come into being as a result of an evolutionary system of trial and error, by learning while doing. The aboriginal peoples can look back on thousands of years of managing their own affairs, albeit at a time and in circumstances where government was a simpler matter than it is today.

Institutions of self-government may turn out to be different for different communities in different parts of Canada, not just among Indians, Inuit, and Metis, but among communities within each of these peoples as well.

Indians

The Report of the Special Committee on Indian Self-Government (the Penner Report) proposes institutions of self-government for the Indians deriving from both legislated delegation of federal powers and constitutional entrenchment. The government's response to the report envisages framework legislation to provide for self-governing institutions by delegation of federal powers. There will be consultations between the government and representatives of the Indian people to assist in the development of the proposed legislation. Parallel discussions will take place with provincial governments, since they have their own responsibilities toward the aboriginal peoples. Moreover, though the government can, within constitutional limits, delegate some of its responsibilities to aboriginal institutions of self-government, such delegation is bound to have its effect on the provinces. As we develop federal enabling legislation for early introduction in Parliament it is my hope that the provinces will develop complementary legislation to help ensure that the aboriginal governments mesh effectively with other governmental institutions.

Inuit

I now turn to the subject of self-government for the Inuit. The Inuit are to be found in the provinces of Quebec and Newfoundland and in the Northwest Territories, in both the western and the eastern Arctic. The provisions of the James Bay Agreement respecting local and regional government should meet the reasonable aspirations of the Inuit in northern Quebec. The Inuit of the western Arctic have the same expectations of the settlement there. The Inuit living in Labrador also look to the land claims settlement process to provide the needed governmental institutions.

The great majority of the Inuit, who live in the eastern Arctic, are also engaged in the land claims settlement process. In the matter of self-government, however, their aspirations are very different. They advocate division of the Northwest Territories and the setting-up in the eastern part of Nunavut – a public or non-ethnic government on the model of a territorial government. The government of Canada has agreed in principle to the division of the Northwest Territories, and is ready to give favourable consideration to the Inuit proposals.

The Metis

The provincial governments are mainly responsible for the Metis. While in the view of the federal government they do not fall within the definition of the word 'Indian' in section 91(24) of the Constitution Act, 1867, the federal government accepts a measure of responsibility for them as disadvantaged people. At this conference we must come to grips with the question of the complementary responsibilities of the federal and provincial authorities and strive to resolve it in the interest of the Metis.

If we approach the subject of self-government for the Metis in the context of legislated delegation of powers, the provinces and the Metis might wish to consider whether the necessary framework legislation should be put in place by the provincial governments. Any necessary complementary legislation could then be introduced in the Parliament of Canada.

I acknowledge and understand the importance the aboriginal peoples attach to self-government. But self-government is not an end in itself; it can be no more than a means to the attainment of the political and social objectives of a people.

I now come to the second issue that should engage our attention:

developing social and economic programs and services for the aboriginal peoples. As our aboriginal peoples take their affairs into their own hands increasingly in the years to come, federal and provincial governments, in close contact with the aboriginal peoples, must work together to put in place the socio-economic infrastructures that will enable them to fulfil their reasonable expectations as citizens of Canada. If this is to be achieved it will call for the maximum effort from all concerned. The provinces will have to fulfil their own obligations to the aboriginal peoples as Canadians resident in the provinces. The federal government must fulfil its special obligations to the aboriginal peoples that derive from their ancestry. The aboriginal leaders too must share in the design and management of these programs and services to help ensure that they are properly in place to meet the needs of their people.

Housing, schools, social services, roads, water supply, sewage systems, and electrification are essential to the health, comfort, and economic development of communities. These have come to be seen as entitlements that flow from Canadian citizenship and residence. I can find no reason to continue to deny them to so many of our aboriginal compatriots. As in all things, I believe we must help first those who need help most. We must first have a better understanding of the services and programs now being delivered by the federal government and the provinces, their effectiveness, and what gaps remain to be filled. I have asked Senator Austin, the minister of state for social development, to undertake this task, working in concert with the provincial governments and the representatives of the aboriginal peoples.

The third issue before us is the protection and enhancement of aboriginal cultures and languages. Aboriginal peoples are deeply concerned, and rightly so, about the maintenance of their cultures and languages, including arts, religion, and, above all, the education of their children. This is a concern that all Canadians can readily comprehend. In due course self-governing institutions will prove to be important bulwarks for culture and language. The design of the necessary social, cultural, and economic programs and services can be tailored so as to protect and enhance aboriginal cultures and languages. I suggest that it is the responsibility of us all to see that it is done.

Movement on these three issues – self-government, socio-economic development, and culture and language – would be real progress. To secure this progress, I am proposing that we strive to reach agreement on an accord. Such an accord would bind us to undertake amendment of the constitution. The draft amendment that will be distributed takes the form of a commitment to

- preserve and enhance the cultural heritage of the aboriginal peoples;
- respect the freedom of the aboriginal peoples to live within their own heritage and to educate their children in their own languages as well as within either or both of the official languages of Canada;
- include in the constitution the right of the aboriginal peoples to self-governing institutions;
- negotiate the nature, jurisdiction, and powers of those institutions and the financial arrangements relating to them.

The draft accord contains a further amendment regarding equality should this be found necessary. It also contains a political commitment to review all aspects of programs and services directed to the aboriginal peoples. The results of this review will be reported to the conference to be held next year.

Self-government for those communities that can meet agreed criteria is coming. As the years pass, more and more communities will take advantage of the enabling legislation. Individual communities unable to qualify alone could join together to achieve the critical mass needed for the development of self-governing institutions. But for many communities, isolated, remote, lacking any solid economic base, reliance on the Indian Act or, in the case of the Metis, provincial legislation will continue for many years to come. As we set up framework legislation for institutions of self-government, so must we also review existing legislation to minimize bureaucratic intervention and to delegate to communities not yet ready to adopt their own institutions of self-government whatever measure of decision-making and program management they can comfortably assume.

Building the socio-economic infrastructure can help break the cycles of poverty and dependency in which so many of our aboriginal peoples feel themselves to be trapped. Self-government and the enhancement of aboriginal cultures can return to the aboriginal peoples the pride of race and the sense of self-worth that is theirs by right.

My predecessor, Mike Pearson, once said that he had had as many lives as a cat. I've had a few myself, and I look forward to several more. But this is the last time I will address this assembly from this chair. For this reason I would like to say a few words to the aboriginal peoples of Canada not so much as prime minister or as chairman of the conference, but rather out of my own mind and heart.

Together we have embarked upon a journey that can lead you into full partnership in Canada, secure to you your own place in Canadian society with your own institutions of self-government, provide you with the infrastructure you need if you are to achieve economic success, and protect and enhance your cultures and languages. I am proud to have walked the first mile of this journey with you for there can be no turning back. The constitution guarantees you that.

But in the end your fate, and the fate of your children's children, is in your own hands. You are the custodians of an ancient spirituality. Your lives are rich in culture and tradition. The extended family that is the tribe or community can be your strong support.

Take advantage of all that a modern society can offer, but for your soul's health stand on your own feet on the sure foundation that spirituality, tradition, and family have laid.

The Right Honourable BRIAN MULRONEY

Notes for an Opening Statement to the Conference of First Ministers on the Rights of Aboriginal Peoples

It is an honour and an important duty for me to participate with you in this unique undertaking, this conference of first ministers on constitutional matters relating to the Inuit, the Indians, and the Metis of Canada. Although many of you have attended the two previous conferences, this is my first. As such, I want to set out my objectives for what I consider to be an essential undertaking for our federation.

It is not my intention, nor that of the new federal government, simply to follow the course which has been charted before. I believe there is new ground which can be explored, new understandings which can be reached.

In these two days of meetings, I wish to affirm and demonstrate the government's commitment to the further identification, definition, and constitutional protection of the rights of the aboriginal peoples. I look to the goodwill of all participants to produce tangible progress by the time we adjourn. I will make specific commitments on behalf of the federal government. I look for specific commitments from the provincial and territorial governments and from the representatives of the aboriginal peoples. Given Canada's long-standing traditions of fairness, tolerance, and understanding, I know that all Canadians expect this of me and of each of us.

My objective at the Regina conference on the economy, and again at the national economic conference, was to encourage the key actors in the Canadian economy to recast their dialogue in terms that made issues into shared concerns, not jurisdictional disputes. And so no one should be surprised that one of my objectives for this conference is to

Presented at the first ministers' conference on the rights of aboriginal peoples, Ottawa, 2–3 April 1985 encourage all participants to accept their share of responsibility in the search for new understandings. You know of my commitment to national reconciliation. You know of my determination to breathe new life into and restore harmony to federal-provincial relations. We have seen the advantages of moving to consensus and the new hope it offers us.

To all participants, I want to say that we in the federal government will demonstrate our new approach at this conference by not surprising you with initiatives for which you are not prepared, nor adopting pressure tactics to move you into positions with which you are not agreed. We will be up front and open.

To the aboriginal leaders, I want to say that, having been a labour negotiator, I know what it means to be sitting on one side of the table looking at powerful interests on the other. But this is not the situation today. We are here together to try to come to grips with problems common to us all.

The Current Situation and Its Background

It is important that we have a common understanding of why we are here. In 1982, after years of attempting to be heard, the Indian, Inuit, and Metis peoples convinced governments that there was unfinished business on the national agenda fundamental to their future and to the future of Canada.

I am here today not only as the prime minister, but as the member of Parliament for Manicouagan, one of the largest ridings in Canada, home to Cree, Montagnais, Naskapi, Huron, and Inuit. I take pride in the fact that it was Gaston McKenzie, a Montagnais leader, who seconded my nomination as the Progressive Conservative candidate there.

I am well aware of the issues and problems faced by the aboriginal peoples I represent, as well as those faced by aboriginal peoples across Canada. As prime minister, I have a responsibility to lead, a responsibility to initiate change. And so I say to you that I will spare no effort to establish the conditions to bring about the changes which must occur. It is to create change that we are engaged in this process, a process which can be frustrating, slow, and tortuous. Yet, we cannot afford to abandon it simply because the task is too daunting or because vested interests will be disturbed. On the contrary, we must renew our efforts.

It is an important task that Canada embarked on in 1982, when three articles were included in the Constitution Act dealing specifically with the aboriginal peoples. In doing so, a commitment was made that we were going to engage in fundamental, substantial, and positive change respecting aboriginal peoples. In 1983, governments signed an accord which, among other things, extended constitutional protection to land claims agreements and committed governments to the principle that before any amendment is made to the constitution respecting aboriginal peoples, a conference would be convened in which they would participate.

Although the 1984 conference did not produce tangible results, new foundations have since been established during the course of the preparatory meetings with Mr Crosbie and Mr Crombie. I have followed these meetings with interest and noted the positive will demonstrated by all participants to get the job done, to put forward new ideas, to challenge existing concepts, to draw upon specific experiences, to move toward a consensus.

Ontario, Manitoba, and Saskatchewan have made important contributions to moving discussions forward on all elements of our endeavour. I note as well the significant contribution by the governments of Nova Scotia and New Brunswick to the discussions on self-government for aboriginal peoples and to those on the clarification of existing provisions relating to equality between aboriginal men and women. Alberta has brought to these discussions its useful experience based on a relationship with the Metis which remains unique in Canada, under the provincial Metis Betterment Act.

I understand that British Columbia, Newfoundland, and Prince Edward Island, among other provinces, have stressed the importance of a full and open-exchange of views on aboriginal matters, and I welcome it. I was pleased to learn that the national assembly of Quebec recently adopted a resolution recognizing the special rights of aboriginal peoples. The two territories have offered us their special insights, and inspiration as they explore changes in their political institutions. For their part, the representatives of the aboriginal peoples have articulated their concerns in a frank and open manner and have contributed constructively to the preparatory discussions.

And so it is no surprise to me that many participants have come to this table expressing a willingness to consider constitutional provisions relating to self-government. The goodwill and momentum which has been generated over the last few months will sustain us in the difficult deliberations ahead and will lead us to concrete results.

Relations between Governments and Aboriginal Peoples in Canada

The aboriginal leaders present here today and their colleagues at the tribal council, band, community, or association level together represent the descendants of the original peoples of Canada. They have persevered and maintained their cultural identity through many years of adversity.

This is part of our national heritage, part of how we define ourselves as a society, something to be celebrated, not ignored.

There is another side, however, to this heritage of tenacity and perseverance. In describing the current situation, I could read you the litany of social indicators on the disparities suffered by aboriginal peoples in unemployment, in lives of despair ending in alcoholism or suicide, the waste in human potential caused by inadequate educational facilities and substandard housing. But I do not want to trade in sorrow. We are familiar enough with the statistics and I know some of you live with them on a day-to-day basis and see them reflected in the eyes of your children.

These social indicators are symptoms of an underlying problem which we must address. They are social indicators which we here in this room can change.

There are those who would say that the answer is more welfare. More social workers. More programs. But that is the way to dependency and misery. As was said by George Manuel, the Shuswap leader whose work in Indian politics has contributed greatly to our being here today, 'Indians are not seeking the best welfare system in the world.'

So, if more welfare is not the answer, then what is? I say the answer lies in aboriginal peoples assuming more responsibility for their own affairs, setting their own priorities, determining their own programs. As Zebedee Nungak of the Inuit Committee on National Issues said at the ministerial meeting held last month in Toronto, our task here is to do 'some constructive damage to the status quo in Canada.' We are here to chart a new course and to set out on it.

I have come across Hugh Brody's book, *Maps and Dreams*, about the Beaver Indian people in northern British Columbia. It is the title which sticks in my mind because that is very much what this is all about: maps and dreams. Maps to find our way to Canada's twenty-first century. Dreams to guide and sustain us.

The Canada we are building for the twenty-first century must have room for self-governing aboriginal peoples. Where our ongoing arrangements have failed to leave room for aboriginal peoples to control their own affairs, we must find room. Canada is big enough for us all. We need to rethink our understanding of Canada, so that the aboriginal peoples too will have their own space in our own time.

Self-Government for Aboriginal Peoples

Different forms of self-government already exist in Canada and most Canadians take them for granted. Apart from electing their federal and provincial governments, Canadians run their own school boards and village and town councils. Canadians also created regional governments when urban centres became too complex to be administered by a single city council.

In Canada, we assume that we can participate in the charting of our destinies, in determining how we are represented, in holding our representatives accountable. But the Indian, Inuit, and Metis peoples do not feel they have the same degree of participation.

In Canada, we assume that our cultural and linguistic backgrounds and traditions will be respected, even cherished and enhanced. But Indian, Inuit, and Metis peoples do not have this assurance, or the power to determine their own cultural development. In fact, there were times when aspects of their cultures were subject to legal sanctions and suppression.

The key to change is self-government for aboriginal peoples within the Canadian federation. We are a cautious people and self-government is a term which is worrisome to some of us. But self-government is not something that I fear. It is not an end in itself, but rather a means to reach common goals. It is the vehicle, not the destination. The challenge and satisfaction is in the journey itself.

The federal government's approach to self-government for aboriginal peoples takes account of these realities, of the inventiveness and creativity that Canadians have always shown in developing their democratic institutions. It is through self-government that a people can maintain the sense of pride and self-worth which is necessary for productive, happy lives.

As a Canadian and as prime minister, I fully recognize and agree with the emphasis that the aboriginal peoples place on having their special rights inserted into the highest law of the land, protected from arbitrary legislative action. Constitutional protection for the principle of self-government is an overriding objective because it is the constitutional manifestation of a relationship, an unbreakable social contract between aboriginal peoples and their governments.

In seeking constitutional change, I recognize that this alone cannot resolve social and economic problems. Constitutional change is not enough to reduce disparities and correct injustices. Rather, improvements to the economic and social circumstances of aboriginal peoples must be pursued at the same time as changes to our constitution are sought to define the rights of aboriginal peoples. Action is required on both fronts and these two sets of endeavours, while separate, are mutually supportive.

The new federal government has already initiated actions in regard to aboriginal peoples leading to increased self-government and to increased well-being. In doing so, it has sought the co-operation, participation, and contribution of the provinces, territories, and aboriginal groups in ensuring the success of these endeavours. These are smaller steps to larger dreams. They are important signals with real significance. Our early track record has already been posted.

Since September, my colleague John Crosbie has ably directed preparations for this conference by advancing constitutional proposals and exploring possible avenues of compromise with all participants.

For his part, my colleague David Crombie has undertaken a number of important initiatives. He has stated the government's intention to support the political evolution of the Northwest Territories in a way which will lead to the building of Nunavut in the eastern Arctic and give the aboriginal peoples of the western Arctic protection and a strong voice. He has also begun to explore models of self-government as well as changes to policy and legislation that may be needed to create or enhance those models. He is considering block funding through which Indian governments would have more freedom to determine their own priorities and establish their own programs.

He has introduced a process of renovation of Treaty 8, which involves Indian bands living mostly in northern Alberta, Saskatchewan, and British Columbia, to deal with past grievances and to establish a sound relationship to move into the future. This renovation process should provide us with a guide for building a positive, constructive relationship with other aboriginal communities. The minister has also undertaken an examination of the claims settlement process, giving consideration to alternatives to current policy. He has begun discussions with provinces to address the problems encountered by many urban aboriginal persons.

These are critical initiatives; they underpin our constitutional discussions and root them in reality.

My Expectations for This Conference

Canadians have rightfully objected to excessive intrusion of government into their lives. Governmental control is resented by us all. Yet the most regulated, controlled, and intruded-upon in Canada are the aboriginal peoples. One of the changes which must be made in the current state of affairs is the removal of these excessive interventions. The alternative – which is our main agenda item – is self-government.

Governments require a better grasp of aboriginal peoples' needs and aspirations. If they demonstrate sufficient creativity and flexibility, then all of Canada will benefit from aboriginal peoples who are secure in their own cultures and full partners in Canadian society.

Aboriginal peoples need a better understanding of the constraints faced by governments, one which takes into account the realities of the current economic environment.

Canada's aboriginal peoples face difficult choices in the years to come. They will have to decide what mix of traditional and modern life they find appropriate to meet their needs. These are trade-offs that they will have to make as they seek to define their rightful place in Canadian society. But they alone can strike that critical balance between old and new.

This is a challenging prospect for aboriginal peoples and for the rest of us. And if this prospect is to become a reality, it will call for an act of faith and imagination on all sides. The aboriginal peoples will have to be able to count on the continuing understanding and support of governments as they move toward an ever-greater control of their lives and circumstances. We all look forward to a new sharing of responsibility. We all look forward to a new life for the aboriginal peoples of Canada, one in which the opportunity to release creativity and entrepreneurship is fostered and enhanced.

But this cannot be achieved at the expense of cultural identity. I see the aboriginal peoples making their special contribution to Canadian society as Indians, Inuit, and Metis. There is no need to sever one's roots.

For those who wish to remain within their communities, that choice should not preclude their ability to lead a rewarding life. The Indian reserve, the Metis settlement, and the Inuit community must remain places of retreat and spiritual renewal for those who opt to live in an environment away from the one into which they were born. There are Inuit on Arctic drilling rigs, Metis farmers on the prairies, and Indian lawyers in southern cities.

As Mr Richard Nerysoo pointed out at Regina last February, in reference to the activity in the Northwest Territories on natural resources development, it is not a case of newer technologies destroying older ways, but rather of the new coexisting with the old.

And a renewed sense of self-assurance and self-worth, flowing from the acceptance both by aboriginal peoples and governments in Canada of mutual responsibilities and common objectives, is essential to reduce poverty and dependency. It will enable Indians, Inuit, and Metis to play their full roles as active and important contributors to the national economy and as holders of a unique and special place in the national mosaic.

The challenges we face at this conference will test our wisdom and generosity of spirit as political leaders. These challenges, moreover, will test our ability to translate political will into practical action.

As you know, the Constitution Act, 1982, and the subsequent accord of 1983 require that four aboriginal constitutional conferences be convened in the five-year period from 1982 to 1987. In effect, then, this conference represents the midpoint in the aboriginal constitutional process.

Ministers and aboriginal leaders have developed an agenda which, in my view, shows great promise. Over the next two days, we will be discussing self-government for aboriginal peoples, equality between aboriginal men and women, and a mandate for more intensive discussions in the next two years. The measure of agreement reached here will determine the shape and pace of events to come over the next two years.

I believe it is within our grasp to make this conference not just the midpoint but the turning point in our efforts to identify and define the rights of aboriginal peoples. Let us decide at this conference that our constitution shall acknowledge that aboriginal peoples have a right to self-government. Let us agree that we will work out together, over time and on a case-by-case basis, the different means, constitutional and otherwise, that will be required to respond to the special circumstances of different aboriginal communities. Such an achievement would be historic in nature, the first step toward a new relationship between self-governing aboriginal communities and governments in Canada, a relationship upon which we may hope to build the mutual trust and confidence that has eluded us for so long.

The Iroquois teach us that it is the obligation of chiefs and elders in councils such as this to keep in mind the unborn generations whose faces are coming toward us. Decisions are to be made with the well-being of the seventh generation in mind. That wisdom should impress upon us the seriousness of our task in these discussions as we work together toward creating a Canada for the twenty-first century, for the descendants of all those who sit around this table unto the seventh generation.

MENNO BOLDT AND J. ANTHONY LONG

Tribal Philosophies and the Canadian Charter of Rights and Freedoms

On 17 April 1982, the Canadian government proclaimed the Constitution Act, incorporating the Charter of Rights and Freedoms. In introducing the Charter the Canadian government was inspired by its liberal-democratic cultural and political tradition. From this perspective the provisions of the Charter are deemed to be progressive and beneficial for all Canadian citizens, but especially for members of disadvantaged minority groups. It is ironic, therefore, that the Charter's severest critics have been native Indians, the most disadvantaged of Canada's minorities.[1] In this paper we will probe into the philosophical, social, and political ideas that underlie the objections raised by Indian leaders to the Charter's provisions. Our thesis is that the western-liberal tradition embodied in the Canadian Charter of Rights and Freedoms, which conceives of human rights in terms of the individual, poses yet another serious threat to the cultural identity of native Indians in Canada.[2]

Two Theories of Man and Society

It is beyond the scope of our paper to deal fully with western-liberal and native American tribal philosophies of the individual and the state. A brief review, however, is necessary.

In the western-liberal tradition the dominant conception of society is that of an aggregate of individuals, each with his own self-interest. The state is a product of collective agreement, an emanation from the individual will, created to perform functions necessary for the common good. As such, the state is an artificial creation, not based in any natural

This paper appeared previously in a slightly more expanded form in 7 *Ethnic and Racial Studies* (1984) 482–95.

order. Individuals within the state place themselves under common political authority and agree to a common political obligation to the state. The individual is considered to be morally prior to any group and, in relation to the state, individuals are viewed as acting for themselves, not as members of any collectivity.

The generic individualism of liberal political theory is illustrated by the political philosophies of Rousseau, Hobbes, Locke, Mill, and others. For example, Rousseau believed in the individual who is born free even though he is everywhere in chains. The chains Rousseau referred to were created by the social group that superimposed itself on the individual. Hobbes conceived of society as reducible to individual wills in possession of certain natural and inalienable rights. An underlying premise for both Rousseau and Hobbes was that individual self-interest ought to take pre-eminence over group rights and claims. They saw no middle ground between the individual and the state. Their liberal political philosophy finds contemporary expression in the Universal Declaration of Human Rights, which states, in part, that rights go to every *individual* 'without distinction of any kind such as race, color, sex, language, religion or social origin, property, birth or status.'

North American Indians had a very different conception of man and society. Society was conceived of as cosmocentric rather than homocentric. Robert Vachon states that their reference point was not the individual but the 'whole,' which is the cosmic order.[3] Their conception of the individual was one of subordination to the whole. This conception was derived from their experience of the interrelatedness of all life (human, animal, plants, and objects) and the need for harmony among all parts. The whole and the parts can survive only if each part fulfils its role. In the cosmocentric perspective animals, plants, and objects were regarded as having souls or spirits and were dealt with as 'persons' who had human qualities of thinking, feeling, and understanding, and who had volitional capacities as well. Social interaction occurred between human beings and other-than-human 'persons' involving reciprocal relations and mutual obligations.

When the world of social relations transcends those that are maintained among human beings, this holds implications for the way one sees oneself in relation to all else. Within this encompassing web of social relations the individual is characterized as the repository of responsibilities rather than as a claimant of rights. Rights can exist only in the measure to which each person fulfils his responsibilities toward others. That is, rights are an outgrowth of every person's performing his obligation in the cosmic order. In such a society there is no concept of inherent individual claims to inalienable rights.

In the Hobbesian political philosophy the exercise of authority was deemed necessary to protect society against rampant individual self-interest. But in tribal society individual self-interest was viewed as inextricably intertwined with tribal survival. That is, the general good and the individual good were virtually identical. Hence, the social relations that give rise to individuality did not exist. Peter Laslett provides an apt analogy to illustrate the mythical quality of individuality in traditional Indian society.[4] To apprehend the individual in tribal society, he says, we have to peel off a succession of group-oriented and derived attributes as if they were layers of onion-skin. The individual turns out to be a succession of metaphorical layers of group attributes that ends up with nothing remaining. Laslett asserts that a face-to-face society is not a political society in the contemporary sense, but a cohabitation of a number of people whose whole experience has been derived from immediate contact with one another. They are always present at whatever is going on. They share not only a language and a history but all conceivable social purposes and a sense of spiritual brotherhood. The society is unified and internally consistent. Thus, the very structure of tribal Indian society inhibits the development of individual self-consciousness and the ability to conceive of rights in individualistic terms.

Michael Melody proposes that whereas western-liberal philosophies define man in terms of individualism, competition, and self-interest, traditional Indian philosophies define man in terms of spiritual unity, consensus, co-operation, and self-denial.[5] In short, the western-liberal tradition and native American tribal philosophies represent two very different theories of the nature of mankind. Each society built its model of human rights and dignity on its own conception of mankind.

Social Structure and Human Rights

Conceptions of appropriate human rights that grow out of a face-to-face communal experience will necessarily be different from those that grow out of a society of individuals acting for themselves. Pollis and Schwab propose that indigenous economic, political, social, and cultural arrangements bear a direct relationship to the way human rights are conceptualized.[6] In their cross-cultural analysis of human rights they make a convincing case that the liberal-democratic doctrine of human rights, as embodied in the Universal Declaration of Human Rights, is essentially a western capitalist ideology and is not relevant to societies with a non-western, non-capitalist cultural tradition. An urbanized industrial-capitalist society with an individualistic emphasis requires a different set of rules to protect its citizens against the arbitrary exercise of power than does a small face-to-face communal society. David Miller similarly subscribes to a thesis of cultural relativity on definitions of justice and morality.[7] He has observed that ideas of justice and morality vary from one social context to another, depending on the social organization. That is, ideas on justice and morality reflect the nature of person-to-person relationships that operate within a society and the manner in which responsibilities and benefits are distributed.

The western-liberal doctrine of human rights grew out of the European experience of feudalism and the associated belief in the inherent inequality of men. Concern with constitutionally guaranteed individual rights was in part a reaction to centralization and abuse of power. It reflected the need in western societies to protect the individual against the powers of the state and various forms of personal authority. The doctrine of individual rights gained additional relevance in western societies because individual initiative and competition were deemed essential for economic development. The capitalist market economy thrived on competitive individualism, and the doctrine of autonomous individualism served both as stimulus and as justification for the idea of inherent individual rights in western societies. The modern western capitalist polity and economy represent a society in which the individual is in need of protection against forces that threaten to overwhelm him. In this context, individualized rights have emerged as a response to existing objective conditions.

North American Indian tribes, by contrast, did not have the experience of feudalism. Moreover, unlike European states, the foundation of their social order was not based on hierarchical power wielded by a centralized political authority. Power and authority could not be claimed by or delegated to any individual or subset of the tribe; it was vested only in the tribe as a whole. The tribal community performed all governmental functions in an undifferentiated fashion. Although highly organized, the tribes did not undergo the separation of state and church from the community. Social order was based on spiritual solidarity derived from the moral integration that came from acquiescence to tribal customs. By unreservedly accepting customary authority as their legitimate guide in living and working together, Indians were freed from the need for coercive personal power, hierarchical authority relationships, and a separate ruling entity to maintain order. Because no state and no rulers existed, individuals had no need for protection from the authority of others. (See our paper elsewhere in this volume for a fuller discussion of power and authority relationships in tribal Indian societies.)

Custom not only offered a well-elaborated system of individual duties and responsibilities, but was designed to protect human dignity. If all members of the tribe obeyed the sacred customs, then as a logical outcome each member would be assured of equality, self-worth, personal autonomy, justice, and fraternity – that is, human dignity.[8] Dignity was protected by a system of unwritten, positively stated mutual duties rather than negatively stated individual legal rights. With the exception of his obligation to impersonal custom, the individual was unrestrained in his autonomy and freedom. Anything not proscribed by custom was 'permitted.' A. James Gregor quotes Franz Neumann: 'A political theory based upon individualistic philosophy must necessarily operate with a negative juridical concept of freedom, freedom as absence of restraint.'[9] In a society ruled by custom, the expression 'it is permitted' is often used, implying a positive concept of freedom. Because custom represented sacred and ultimate wisdom it was not construed as an infringement or threat to individual autonomy or freedom.

In tribal society all members participated in decision-making as a collectivity, for the common good. In such a society there is less potential for offences against the individual and less need for individual protection from the abuse of authority. Tribal Indians consequently came to define rights in terms of the common interest. Individual rights were perceived by Indians as working contrary to their common interest. Such rights were seen as jeopardizing the collectivity and, by logical extension, jeopardizing the individual member. Of what value, Indians today ask, are individual rights when they threaten collective and individual existence?

We want to stress here that in our discussion of traditional customs relating to group rights we do not propose that Indians are currently uniformly and consistently practising these traditions. However, contemporary Indians have embraced these traditions as their charter myth and as fundamental to their version of the 'good society,' much as western democratic societies have adopted equality and individual rights as their charter myth and version of the 'good society.' Largely as a result of federal government coercion, Canada's Indians have moved a long way in the direction of differentiated and segmentary institutions. This may mean that Indians will in future become 'modernized' within their own societies. That is, they may voluntarily choose impersonal, centralized, hierarchical political systems on their reserves. If and when this occurs, we can assume that individualized rights will take on greater relevance for them.

It should be emphasized that the concept of group rights does not imply any lack of respect and concern in Indian society for the individual member. Quite the contrary. Taking the governmental function as a case in point, Indian communities have engaged traditionally in an extensive consultation process in the selection of their leaders, and all decisions affecting the group required a consensus by members. Under the democratic representative electoral system imposed upon them by the Canadian government, however, leaders are generally elected by a minority of members, and the associated organization of delegated authority and hierarchical structures has relegated most members of the Indian community to the periphery of the decision-making process. Decisions are now made by Indian élites – elected and appointed.[10]

It is a matter of historical record that the enlightenment *philosophes* were influenced, if not inspired, by the North American Indians' practice of freedom of individual choice (liberty), denial of status differentials (equality), and rule by consensus (fraternity). Tribal communities conceived of social justice not as an abstract ideal or charter myth but in terms of actual social practice.[11]

Walter Miller, in his summary of the writings of traders, soldiers, and missionaries, proposes that the social organization of a society reflects that which exists in the pantheon. He suggests that whereas the representative European pantheon is vertically organized, the representative North American Indian pantheon was organized along egalitarian lines. 'Persons' of the other-than-human class existed in scores of manitus, each experiencing momentary advantage vis-à-vis other manitus; none was permanently supreme. Furthermore, the manitus' relationship to man was one of mutual obligation, not superiority. Power was equally available to 'persons' of all classes.[12]

The Charter and Tribal Traditions

The existence of the Indian community in Canada necessarily raises questions about the adequacy of western-liberal doctrines in dealing with their conception of rights. Native Indian leaders hold that the Canadian Charter of Rights and Freedoms, with its western-liberal principles of legal, social, political, and economic individualism, not only lacks relevance but threatens the destruction of their cosmocentric philosophy, their spiritual unity, and the customary precepts of their tribal society. In their brief to the parliamentary subcommittee on Indian women and the Indian Act, the Assembly of First Nations gave clear expression to their concern over the impact of the Charter's philosophy of individualism on their traditional way of life.

As Indian people we cannot afford to have individual rights override collective rights. Our societies have never been structured in that way, unlike yours, and that is where the clash comes ... If you isolate the individual rights from the collective rights, then you are heading down another path that is even more discriminatory. The Charter of Rights is based on equality. In other words, everybody is the same across the country ... so the Charter of Rights automatically is in conflict with our philosophy and culture and organization of collective rights. There would have to be changes. We could not accept the Charter of Rights as it is written because that would be contrary to our own system of existence and government.[13]

Indian leaders have identified several potentially critical consequences should the Charter apply to them. They fear that disgruntled members of their communities will exploit the Charter's provisions to their individual advantage, thereby undermining existing group norms. They believe that a series of judicial decisions in favour of individual rights versus group rights will result in a 'snowballing' of individualism.

The question of how the Canadian courts will interpret the provisions of the Charter in relation to the Indian Act is currently a subject of debate. In a case that is cited as a significant precedent (*R. v Drybones*, which dealt with the provisions of the Indian Act prohibiting off-reserve liquor sales to an Indian by a non-Indian), the Supreme Court held that the Indian Act provision in question represented discrimination based on race and therefore offended the Bill of Rights. The court gave effect to the Bill of Rights over the Indian Act provisions.[14]

The Charter as it now stands includes a provision (section 25) guaranteeing Indians that the rights and freedoms contained in the Charter 'shall not be construed so as to abrogate or derogate from any aboriginal, treaty or other rights or freedoms that pertain to the aboriginal peoples of Canada.' According to Kenneth Lysyk, this section preserves the status quo in that it guarantees that the rights and freedoms in the Charter are not to be read as subtracting from the rights and freedoms pertaining to aboriginal people.[15] What are these rights and freedoms that pertain to aboriginal people? Barsh and Henderson hold that these rights and freedoms exist at the discretion of Parliament to suspend or restrict them.[16] That is, the provision of section 25 is at bottom only a symbolic guarantee. When one takes this interpretation in the context of the government's liberal democratic orientation the future of collective rights and freedoms for Indians, as a special group, looks dismal indeed.

Indian leaders also perceive the Charter as potentially undermining their aboriginal right to self-government because it specifies that Canadian law will apply to the conduct of band members. Thus, Canadian courts will have jurisdiction to apply the law to Indians in accordance with procedures spelled out by Parliament. Furthermore, the Charter requires that Indian government be based on the western-liberal-democratic theory of individualism (one man, one vote), delegated authority, hierarchical structures, and so on. These provisions will not allow Indians to develop a social organization and government built on their traditional values.[17]

Indian leaders fear that the Charter's prohibition of racial discrimination, if applied to Indian bands, could be interpreted by the courts as a mandate to racially 'integrate' tribal administration and service staffs. On the same ground the courts could also rule out Indian ancestry as a tribal membership criterion, or disallow involvement by the tribal government in religious ceremonies. Such judicial decisions would fundamentally and irreversibly alter – and inevitably destroy – traditional Indian institutions, thereby facilitating the assimilation of Indians. Individual rights would be guaranteed by a judicial and political entity external to the Indian community, increasing the likelihood that assimilation will occur.

Indians have reason to distrust the Canadian government's stated good intentions in applying the Charter to them. Historically, Canadian Indian policy has consistently and rigidly been directed toward assimilation. Only the degree of coercion has varied. Before the Second World War Indian children were forcibly taken from their parents and placed in parochial residential schools, where traditional religious practices and languages were forcibly suppressed. In *Federalism and the French Canadians*, Canada's then Prime Minister Pierre Trudeau suggests that a state built on cultural and ethnic foundations cannot help but be autocratic, irrational, and repressive.[18] As a disciple of liberal-democratic doctrine, Trudeau idealizes neutral, universal principles. His 1969 White Paper policy, a master plan for assimilating Indians, similarly implies opposition to the concept of special status for Canada's Indians. Indians are convinced that the Canadian government seeks to achieve assimilation under the guise of human rights legislation.

Although Indians want constitutional protection from abuse by the larger society, they believe their security lies in laws protecting their collective rights, not their individual rights. They want to be protected as a group, not as individuals, from state violation of their human dignity and freedom.[19] They do not reject individualized conceptions of human rights on principle. Indeed, they accept the need for such guarantees in western societies. But they do assert that the doctrine of individualism and inherent inalienable rights, on which the Charter rests, is not part of their cultural heritage, serves no positive purpose for them, and threatens their integrity and survival as a unique people. By imposing highly individualistic conceptions of civil and political rights upon them, the Canadian government will destroy their collective community in the same way that the imposed democratic elective system of government effectively destroyed their traditional tribal political structures and practices.

Indians and other Canadians were recently given a preview of how the Charter's liberal-democratic definition of human rights can be used by the government to undermine the Indians' capacity to act in accord with their perceived collective self-interest. Sandra Lovelace, a Mic Mac Indian, lost her Indian status and band membership pursuant to section 12(1)(b) of the Indian Act, which stipulates that Indian women who marry non-Indian men lose their Indian status, band membership, and all associated special rights and privileges. Lovelace submitted a grievance to the United Nations Human Rights Commission. The commission found Canada in breach of article 27 (Rights of Minorities) of the International Covenant on Civil and Political Rights, which guarantees that persons belonging to ethnic, religious, or linguistic minorities 'shall not be denied the right, in community with the other members of their group, to enjoy their culture, to profess and practice their own religion, or to use their own language.'[20]

In short, the Canadian government was found guilty of denying 'Indian rights' to Indian women who had married non-Indians. Acutely embarrassed by this decision, the Canadian government moved promptly and cunningly to protect its international image as a champion of human rights. Government politicians recast the Lovelace affair as a simple case of sex discrimination and, with much fanfare, sought to invoke the Charter's provisions against sex discrimination to restore Lovelace's Indian status. Indian leaders resisted the Canadian government's initiative because they saw broader implications in the judicial subordination of the Indian Act to the Charter. They feared that such a precedent opened the door to judicial undercutting of their special status and could render all of their group rights inoperative on the ground of discrimination. Moreover, Indian leaders are, with good reason, apprehensive that the Canadian government will not provide a sufficient land base or sufficient funds to cope with the increased costs of supporting the reinstated Indian women and their families. Instead of dealing with these legitimate concerns, the Canadian government cynically portrayed Indian reticence as a case of opposition to female equality, and then blamed the whole situation on Indian male chauvinism. The Charter was exploited to create a public perception that Indian leaders are insensitive to human rights.

The reality is quite different. Since 1946 Indians have lobbied the government to remove the discriminatory sections of the Indian Act and allow individual bands to determine their own membership. In 1946 a special joint committee of the Senate and the House of Commons reviewed the Indian Act. Submissions were received from Indians across the country. Almost without exception, Indian bands and associations called for the abolition of involuntary loss of status, but the 1951 revision of the Indian Act continued the practice.

The Indian Act is a creation of the Canadian government, not of the Indian people. The offensive membership criterion that defines band membership eligibility on the basis of sex, and the provision that stipulates deregistration of Indian women who marry non-Indians, were not derived from Indian custom; they were derived from the general customs of patrilineal descent and patrilocal residence practised by the colonizers. They were designed to facilitate assimilation of Indians and to prune the number of Indian wards for whom the Canadian government would be obliged, under treaty, to take responsibility.

Discussion

The imposition of the Charter's provisions on Indians is being justified by the Canadian government as a means of enhancing their quality of life. The same justification was given for forcing Christianity on Indians; for enacting the racist provisions of the Indian Act; for imposing an elective system and a hierarchical structure of government; and for legislating a policy of assimilation. Implied in all of this is a deeply embedded ethnocentic assumption that Indian culture is inferior to European culture. Ethnocentrism is evident also in the government's contention that its version of human rights is the morally correct and best version for Indian people. To insist on imposing western-liberal conceptions of human rights on Indians is no less questionable than earlier initiatives to impose religious conformity to Christian beliefs.

Barsh and Henderson suggest that liberals who feel that protection of the special status of Indians violates their anti-racist ideals are confusing racial and political issues.[21] When the Canadian government enacted the Indian Act, giving Indians a special group status, they based that status on racial criteria. Thus, liberals see Indians as a deprived racial group and view their struggle to maintain their special status as an impermissible racist movement. But Indians do not seek protection for their racial characteristics, because being 'Indian' is for Indians a cultural and political identity, not a racial one. Indians seek protection for their identity as distinct nations of peoples, an identity that has its origins in their ancient history. Only in the eyes of the European colonizers were they seen as a racial group. By conceptualizing and legislating membership criteria in terms of racial attributes the colonizers redefined Indians as a racial community, and then proceeded to enshrine their racist conception in the Indian Act. Indians want to transform the negative racist philosophy of the Indian Act into a positive political-cultural guarantee, to be written into the constitution. If the movement were viewed as a struggle for political-cultural self-determination, then liberals could, in principle, accept special status for Indians as a valid objective.

Since the time of Hobbes and Locke political theorists have tended to conceive of rights in terms of individuals in relation to the state. Recently, however, Vernon Van Dyke advocated a more complex paradigm in which rights for groups, distinct from those of the persons composing it, would be recognized on the grounds that human needs exist at various levels and that the existence of needs, whether at the level of the individual or the level of the community, implies a right to meet such needs.[22] Van Dyke holds that most discriminatory practices are directed against individuals because of their membership in groups. Equality, individually defined, is of little value when the group of which the individual is a member is unable to assert his rights. This implies a right by the group to address such anti-group sanctions. Van Dyke goes on to say that his point is not to downplay the importance of individual rights, but to promote the view that ethnic communities also have just claims to human rights.

Advocates of liberal democratic doctrine oppose the recognition of group rights because they believe that group rights impact negatively on individual rights, that group rights are likely to prevail at the expense of individual rights. The Canadian Human Rights Commission takes the position that while individual and collective rights can coexist, individual rights must have priority over group rights. 'You cannot swallow up the rights of individuals in order to protect the collectivity ... The fundamental principle has to be that you cannot have group rights if you do not have individual rights; that is the foundation of everything ... The rights of Indian groups can only be enhanced by the protection of the rights of each Indian ...'[23]

Is there a necessary conflict between individual rights and the Indians' claim to group rights? Clearly, there is a potential risk in passing legislation extending group rights to Indians that such protective legislation may have negative implications from the standpoint of the individual members. However, a distinction must be made between negative implications for the individual member that derive from a violation of human rights and those that derive from the fact that the individual merely disagrees with the group's philosophy. If negative implications derive from an individual's dissatisfaction with the group's philosophy, this ought not to entitle one, on the ground of individual rights, to jeopardize the group's protected status and survival. The remaining group members, who want to retain their special group status and identity and who constitute the large majority of that group, merit a guarantee of their right to preserve their community. No society can please all its members, nor is it obliged to do so. Where irreconcilable conflict exists between an individual's rights and the group's right to survive, the individual can make a choice between leaving the group or submitting to it. Indians who wish to give priority to individual rights over group rights have a ready alternative – they can integrate with Canadian society. But if the Charter is imposed on all Indians, then those who want to express and practice their cultural values and customs will no longer have a space in which to do so.

Tension and conflict between group rights and individual rights are bound to occur when the criteria for one are developed in isolation from the other. And this is precisely the effect of imposing the Charter's liberal-democratic individual rights provisions on Indian groups. Individual rights as legally defined in the Charter by the Canadian government are inconsonant with group rights as culturally defined by Indians. To avert this conflict the definition of human rights that is to be applied to Indian communities should be allowed to grow out of Indian culture, politics, and goals.

Although United Nations declarations and covenants on human rights uniformly emphasize individual protection, the principle that certain collectivities have a right to preserve their culture and to survive as groups also appears in various contexts. The principle of collective rights finds support in resolutions of the General Conference of UNESCO, the United Nations Subcommission on Prevention of Discrimination and Protection of Minorities, the United Nations Committee on the Peaceful Uses of Outer Space, the World Conference to Combat Racism and Racial Discrimination, and the International Covenant of Human Rights.

The United Nations criteria for recognition of claims to group rights, though vague, generally imply the historical possession and present desire by a sufficient number of persons to preserve their cultural traditions. Under modern international law there is a consensus that an ethnic group that meets the criteria ought to have the right to preserve its culture. Canada acceded to the International Covenant of Human Rights on 19 May 1976, and has itself adopted various measures to protect its own cultural traditions (for example, regulations requiring Canadian content in broadcasting). Having taken such action, Canada ought to consider itself morally bound to respect and fulfil the terms of the covenant's provision for 'self-determination of peoples ... to enjoy their culture, to profess and practice their own religion, and to use their own language.' These are rights not of individuals but of peoples collectively, whether or not they are recognized as states.

Canada's Indians meet and, indeed, go beyond the criteria implied in the various United Nations declarations and covenants for rightful claim to cultural self-determination.[24] Most members of Indian tribes share a culture and a history; they have signed treaties with the Canadian government; they have a geographically and legally defined land base; they are treated as a distinct unit within Canada; they are bound by a separate law (the Indian Act); they are administered as a separate people; and they are treated differently from other Canadians with respect to political and civil rights and property rights. Furthermore, Indians do not see themselves as fully participating Canadian citizens and have shown little interest in such participation. They do not participate meaningfully in the legislative or bureaucratic aspects of any level of government other than their own tribal governments. The Canadian government does not derive and never has derived its power to govern Indians from the consent of Indian people.[25]

There is a contradiction between Canada's idealistic commitment to individual rights and the seeming disregard and lack of respect it shows for Indian group rights. The power to define rights and status within their communities is fundamental to the protection of Indian group norms and hence to their survival. The goals of justice and humanity are not served by imposing the Charter's liberal-individualistic provisions on Indian communities. Justice and humanity require that Indians be allowed to define human rights consistent with their philosophies and aspirations. This can be accomplished by entrenching in the Charter broad principles that would allow Indians to develop and enforce their own version of human rights and dignity. Indians will thus be guaranteed the human dignity and freedom that are appropriate to their cultures and the wishes of their people.

Our anaylsis of Indian rights in relation to liberal theory speaks to larger issues of human rights. Canadian Indians are not alone in rejecting the western-liberal human rights doctrine. Pollis and Schwab have shown that the majority of states of the world similarly reject the western-liberal doctrine, not because they have contempt for human dignity but because they lack a cultural heritage of individualism.[26] Pollis and Schwab infer from their findings the need for extensive empirical studies and theoretical reformulations aimed at achieving a doctrine of human rights that is more validly universal than the prevailing western-liberal tradition.

We argue that pursuing a formulation of universal human rights is not a practical goal. Human rights, if they are to be meaningful to the members of a society, must represent a natural evolution from indigenous cultural-philosophical principles, socio-economic and political structures, and developmental goals. The existing cultural-structural diversity among the world's communities implies a need for a corresponding diversity of human rights approaches. In some societies the implied need is to give priority to the individual; in others, to the group. Some societies feel a need to emphasize political and civil rights; others emphasize economic and social rights; still others emphasize the responsibilities of individuals rather than rights. If a trans-cultural approach to human rights is deemed a desirable goal, then let those nations with shared philosophic premises, social structures, and developmental goals co-operate voluntarily in developing such doctrines. There is no justification for using political and economic power as did the Carter administration in the United States, or moral pressure as is the case with the United Nations Universal Declaration, to impose western-liberal doctrines of human rights on resisting societies on the ground of ideological superiority.

Despite divergences in attitudes toward individualized human rights, virtually all societies have cultural and ideological systems that deem everyone to be entitled to human dignity. Virtually all societies seek to protect their citizens from various forms of indignity. Why not shift the emphasis from a universal doctrine protecting individualized human rights to a doctrine guaranteeing human dignity? The concept of human dignity, as Donnelly has stated, is more encompassing than that of human rights, and subsumes all of the humane objectives implied in the Universal Declaration. For example, individualized human rights do not represent the only pathway to equality of the sexes. Some native Indian tribes achieved the same objective through positively stated mutual obligations enshrined in sacred custom.

The pathway to implementing a universal doctrine of human dignity can be uniquely plotted by each society to fit its cultural history and contemporary situation. Some societies may emphasize the individual, others the collectivity. Some may seek to achieve the goal of human dignity through guarantees of individual rights, others through an emphasis on personal responsibilities. Such a 'home-grown' charter would have relevance for the citizens and their government and would be more realistic in terms of what a state is able to 'provide' in the way of human rights. The world community would expect each society to strive to implement its doctrine of human dignity. Provision could be made for the United Nations to hear and adjudicate cases of violation of an individual's human dignity.

Today, more societies violate than comply with the Universal Declaration's western-liberal principles of human rights. Our argument is not that a doctrine of human dignity and a culturally relative approach to implementing such a doctrine will guarantee human rights to all. But it will generate a more effective domestic and international moral-legal force for compliance with fundamental principles of human dignity and rights than is now the case with the current universalistic approach of the United Nations Declaration of Human Rights, which conflicts with the deeply held cultural values of many societies.

3 Historical and Contemporary Legal and Judicial Philosophies on Aboriginal Rights

ALTHOUGH RECENT EFFORTS BY ABORIGINAL PEOPLES to gain recognition for their definition of aboriginal rights have centred on the constitutional process, Indians in Canada have on a number of occasions sought such recognition in the courts. Some of the court decisions have been helpful to Indian claims, but overall the courts have not validated Indian definitions and interpretations of aboriginal rights.

The papers in this section provide historical and contemporary perspectives on the status of aboriginal rights in European and North American law. From the first colonial administrations to the present, the courts have consistently decided aboriginal-rights cases in the interest of the dominant society rather than on principles of justice. Motivated by racism, greed, and lust for land, colonial administrations deliberately transgressed the British and international laws that protected aboriginal rights. Once the colonial administrations gained legislative autonomy, the colonial governments (and their successors) proceeded to legalize retroactively the unlawful actions they had taken against the aboriginal peoples.

The Canadian courts, like those of New Zealand, Australia, and the United States, act as handmaidens of the government, consistently giving precedence to the legitimacy and validity of government power, policies, and actions at the expense of the basic principles of tort, restitution, contract, and property on which the western legal tradition stands. The courts made aboriginal rights subject to the self-interest of the dominant group; they subordinated fundamental principles of justice and human rights to the collective self-interest; and they legitimized the dominant group's use of political and legislative power to deprive the aboriginal peoples of their rights and self-government.

The papers in this section reveal the monstrous injustice suffered by aboriginal people and make a persuasive case that aboriginal peoples seeking justice in their claims to aboriginal rights should look elsewhere than to the courts of Canada. The issue of alternative strategies for achieving recognition of aboriginal claims is taken up in section 4.

JAMES YOUNGBLOOD HENDERSON

The Doctrine of
Aboriginal Rights in
Western Legal Tradition

The role of law in the development of the democratic state was created to guarantee the supreme goods of social life, order, and freedom to all people. Public laws were necessitated by the enmity of peoples competing for scarce resources and reinforced by the need for collaboration that marks social existence. Public rules placed limits on the pursuit of private ends, thereby ensuring that natural egoism and desires would not turn society into a free-for-all in which everyone and everything was endangered. This was called the principle of order. Public laws also facilitated mutual collaboration by granting the power to individuals to choose the ends and means of their striving without interfering with the strivings of others. This was called the principle of freedom.

Order and freedom were established in the modern liberal state by impersonal and neutral public rules. The impersonal public rules had to embody more than the values of any particular group. Any legislation that represented the interest of a single class of persons was held to destroy the freedom principle, since it constituted the dominion of some wills over the wills of others. Such partial legislation also left the order principle without any justification or support, for the oppressed seldom love the laws that limit their freedom.

The impersonal and neutral public rules of modern democratic states denied the positivist's command notion of law. Public rules were not the province of a political deity that stands above the contending private wills while at the same time representing them. The public rules of modern democratic states emerged from a felt need for standards or procedures capable of securing both order and freedom among diverse

Guidance has been provided by Ababinilli and Ma'heo'o; any errors of interpretation are mine.

interests in society. The democratic vision relied on intelligence to spell out a legitimate structure of relations between humans in society. It recognized that whenever humans want something they also want not to have it kept away from them, or taken away once it is already theirs. The democratic vision recognized too that when a person wants to carry out a particular course of action, he does not want to be stopped by others from executing his will. The legal system of the democratic state thus created, in my view, four fundamental principles of law which defined and structured the solution to human relations. These four fundamental principles are those of tort, restitution, contract, and property. These principles define the universal structure of human relations, and they also provide a standard for evaluating the performance of any legal system in dealing with aboriginal rights in North America.

The tort principle and the restitution principle committed public law to the maintenance of an individual's present system of rights and advantages by protecting him against involuntary losses. The tort principle holds that one who causes harm wrongfully should put the victim in as good a position as he would have been in had no harm been inflicted upon him. The restitution principle holds that when one person has been enriched unjustifiably at another's expense, the benefit should be restored based on the extent of the benefit to the person and not the extent of the harm inflicted.

The contract and property principles permit persons to make use of protected rights and advantages by enforcing voluntary dispositions between and across private spheres. The contract principle holds that persons should keep their promises, and if they do not the law should place the deceived beneficiaries of a promise in the position they would have been in had the promises been kept. The property principle defines the relationship that exists between animate persons and inanimate things and then applies the contract principle.

These four principles should have assured the integrity of tribal property from unconsented-to intrusions by the Europeans in Canadian law. The doctrines of treaty and aboriginal rights were firmly established in international law and the law of the British Empire, and protected by the four principles in the colonial law of British North America. The extent to which tribal wealth was left unprotected in Canadian law not only represents a failure in the uniform application of laws but also indicates that the benefits of the four principles are available only to members of a certain race. Canadian law is not impersonal but racially biased; its legitimacy is threatened if not destroyed by its denial of order and freedom to aboriginal people against non-Indians.

My discussion of the Canadian legal system's relationship to aboriginal rights will start by describing the statement of aboriginal rights in the laws of nations from the Holy Roman Empire to its secular beginnings. Next I will demonstrate how the common lawyers of England and the crown dealt with the international doctrine of aboriginal rights to create protected foreign jurisdictions in the law of the British Commonwealth. From this analysis I will proceed to illustrate the acceptance of British principles of aboriginal rights in the constitutional law of the United States. The paper will end with a discussion of how aboriginal ownership became confused with the fundamental title of the crown or state in the Anglo-American legal system and became racially biased against treaty and aboriginal rights in Canada.

Papal Entitlement and Aboriginal Ownership in International Law

The relationship between the European princes and the American nations was initially shaped under the legal structure of the Holy Roman Empire. The religious authority of the pope was considered naturally superior to the secular power of the various princes; the pope was deemed to be the source and standard of all ministerial and judicial jurisdiction and the final court of appeal in disputes between European princes.[1] In deciding a complex appeal involving jurisdictional limits in the New World, the pope held that Spain rather than Portugal should have jurisdiction because of Spain's efforts in initiating the discovery of the New World.[2] This decision came to be known as the papal donation or papal entitlement theory.

Juan Lopez de Palacious Rubios, one of the foremost jurists of that era, stated that the crown's jurisdiction did not rest on either the discovery of the new land or the conquest of the natives, but solely on a contractual notion, the papal grant of jurisdiction to Spain by Pope Alexander v, and the principle of restitution. Since this grant also limited exercise of jurisdiction over the aboriginal peoples, he urged that 'Indians' must be treated like tender new plants, worthy of the care and loving protection of the crown. Those subjects who used them as slaves or conquered people or otherwise mistreated them, he declared, must make due restitution to them (that is, restore to the Indians their freedom and properties based on the extent to which the subjects have unjustifiably been enriched). The sole right of the crown was to bring the Christian faith to the Indians, not to exploit them.[3]

The opinion of Palacious Rubios was limited to explaining the source and extent of Spanish jurisdiction in the New World. Spain asked

Franciscus de Vitoria for an expanded analysis of the nature of the interest of the aboriginal peoples in the New World under the concept of papal donation. In his official opinion as legal adviser on Indian affairs to the crown, Victoria recognized the national character of the Indian tribes, uniformly applied to those tribes the rights of the law of nations, and asserted their right to ownership of the land under their laws and customs, which antedated the papal grant to the crown.[4] Vitoria's perception of the fundamental equality of the rights of all human beings is now universally entrenched in the international covenants on human rights.

After discussing the nature of just conquest, and after rejecting the arguments that barbarians could not hold land by reason of their sin against Jesus, or their unbelief in the Catholic faith, or their 'unsoundness of mind,' Vitoria declared that 'the aborigines in question were true owners, before the Spaniard came among them, both from the public and private point of view.'[5] Neither discovery nor papal rights could convey any proprietary title to the crown.

Contractual grants created order among European nations in their quest to obtain the tribal lands of the New World. Stressing the distinction between jurisdiction and ownership, Vitoria established that exclusive jurisdiction *might* be acquired by the combination of discovery and papal grants 'because, if there was to be an indiscriminate inrush of Christians from other parts to the part in question, they might easily hinder one another and develop quarrels.'[6] But 'lordship in jurisdiction does not go so far as to warrant [the emperor] in converting provinces to his own use or in giving towns or even estates away at his pleasure.' Discovery and papal donation gave no 'right to occupy the lands of the indigenous population.' It could, however, suffice to bar other European nations from trading with the Indians.

Such contractual rights were limited by the tort and restitution principles. Even the Pope had no right by papal grant to partition the property of the American nations, Vitoria concluded. In the absence of a 'just war' to protect the aborigines' choice of religion, only the voluntary consent of the majority of the American nations could justify any annexation of their territory to the Spanish crown.

Once formulated, the doctrine of aboriginal rights (that is, the seminal doctrine of human rights) was quickly affirmed by the Roman Catholic Church and later by the Spanish crown. The church confirmed Vitoria's understanding of the inherent limitations of papal grants and aboriginal rights by affirming that the Indians were men rather than devils or beasts, and thus were governed by the standards of human conduct 'notwithstanding whatever may have been or may be said to the contrary, the said Indians and all other peoples who may be discovered by Christians, are by no means to be deprived of their property, even though they be outside the faith of Jesus Christ ... nor should they be in any way enslaved; should the contrary happen it shall be null and of no effect.'[8]

In 1550–1, at Valladolid, the Spanish crown requested a debate on the implications of the Vitorian model of aboriginal rights, and the papal confirmation of it, on the Spanish administration of the New World.[9] The Dominican friar Bartholomew de Las Casas argued that the Vitorian model of aboriginal rights was the most appropriate model for the administration of the New World. Although the actual results of the debate were not published, it appears from the many revisions in the *Recopilacion de Leyes de Las Indias* that the Vitorian model was accepted as the correct standard. Not only was the word 'conquest' eliminated from the laws, but the laws of the Indies required that restitution be made for encroachments of antecedent Indian property in Spanish grants.[10]

Book 4, title 12, law 9 of the *Recopilacion* commanded the Viceroy in 1551 'that the farms and lands which may be granted to Spaniards be so granted without prejudice to the Indians; and that such as may have been granted to their prejudice and injury be restored to whoever they of right shall belong.'[11] No provision of the Spanish law governing the New World made Indian rights dependent on a royal grant. The doctrine of aboriginal rights in Spanish law was firmly built on Vitoria's principles.

The doctrine of aboriginal rights enunciated by the legal opinion of Vitoria and codified by the church and the Spanish crown was based on a vision of universal rights and freedom in a world order. The doctrine was committed to the maintenance of the indigenous nations' existing system of rights and advantages through protection of their rights against involuntary loss. Although this doctrine protected aboriginal rights, the contractual and proprietary nature of aboriginal title also allowed for voluntary dispositions of protected rights by the indigenous nations to European nations. Clearly, the seminal ideas behind the principles of tort, restitution, contract, and property were essential to and inherent in the doctrine of aboriginal rights.

As the idea of a world state united by Christianity was transformed into the concept of the territorial sovereignty of the princes, the doctrine of aboriginal rights was accepted as legitimate in the law of nations. The adoption of the Vitorian principles of aboriginal rights by European jurists Gentilis, Grotius, and Pufendorf confirmed the vitality of the doctrine and created order. The European jurists' complete acceptance of Vitoria's doctrine of aboriginal rights was based on their acceptance of the natural rights principle: all rights precede rules and are the foundation of legitimate rules as law. The acceptance of aboriginal rights is evidenced most clearly in the European preoccupation with how to secure legitimately a jurisdiction in the New World. During the process of trying to find an acceptable principle for ordering European nations' rights of jurisdiction in the New World, the notions of papal entitlements, symbolic acts, letters patent, discovery, and prescriptive rights were all asserted. In the end, however, the contractual notion of discovery and voluntary disposition of aboriginal resources predominated as the guiding principle to regulate the rights of jurisdiction among European nations in tribal America.

Francis I of France initiated the discussion of legitimate jurisdiction in tribal America when he demanded that the pope show him the clause in the Bible which entitled only Spain and Portugal to divide the New World between themselves.[12] Elizabeth of England rejected discovery and papal entitlements as exclusive sources of jurisdiction. She held that other princes might trade with the countries of the New World without breaching the law of nations. Protesting any assertion of ownership derived from the fact that the Spaniards had 'arrived here and there, built Cottages, and given names to a River or a Cape,' Elizabeth held that such activities could not 'purchase any propriety' and asserted the contractual principle of voluntary disposition of aboriginal rights.[13]

Her views were derived mostly from the works of Alberico Gentilis. Gentilis, who is considered by many to be the founder of the science of international law, held in *De Jure Belli* (1588) that the jurisdiction of the Spanish crown could not be justified in law either by war or conquest. Such activities could only be justified if the natives refused to trade with the Spaniards, he wrote, but since he felt that the Spaniards fought for dominion rather than to enforce commercial rights they could not acquire any just jurisdiction or authority in America.[14]

Gentilis also adopted the Vitorian doctrine of aboriginal rights. Neither papal entitlement nor discovery or prescription, he wrote, would grant dominion over unknown lands inhabited by native governments. Only trading jurisdictions over the lands of the natives could be claimed by European nations, not the land itself. Proprietary interest in tribal lands or resources had to be obtained from the consent of the native governments.

The works of Hugo Grotius also confirmed and adopted the doctrine of aboriginal rights. Building on the distinction between 'title' (jurisdiction) and 'tenures' (property systems) in the law of nations, he argued that discovery of a new land can neither give a full title without actual possession, nor furnish a just cause for acquisition of territory by conquest.[15] The significance of his limited contribution to the discovery doctrine was that he was expressing the opinion of the princes of England, France, Holland, and other European principalities.[16] Ultimately, his opinions prevailed in the law of nations and provided the framework for the human rights covenants.

Aboriginal Rights in the British Common Law

The common lawyers of England were conceptually unprepared to confront the issues deriving from colonialization by the British crown. Struggling to develop a national law and preoccupied with the issue of where sovereignty resided within England, the common lawyers had little interest in the law of nations and no theory or doctrines of law. Instead, they believed in the history and experience of the ancient procedures and formulas of the common law. The common lawyers believed all political questions could be solved by reducing them to legal questions and deciding them on the basis of precedent. As an answer to the absolute monarchy and in support of parliamentary supremacy, the common lawyers offered an implicit conception of English history as a gradual and self-contained process of development over the centuries. The future would take care of itself so long as the traditions of the past were preserved by the law, since the law was sovereign.

The fragmented medieval thoughts of the common law, which regulated private disputes among British subjects in newly acquired territories, were gathered together in an opinion by Sir Edward Coke in 1607. Deriving insights from the experience of the common law of feudal England and its assumption that all lands were held in tenure by some higher authority (owned by a jurisdictional sovereign), Lord Coke held that if the inhabitants of a country conquered or purchased by England were civilized, their existing laws remained in force until altered by the sovereign or, after the Restoration, by Parliament. If they were savages or pagans it was presumed they had no law, and English law filled the vacuum at once. If the country was uninhabited 'desert,' Englishmen going abroad to occupy it took their law with them 'as their birthright.'

These historic principles guided judicial inquiries concerning the rights of British colonies or British subjects and the extension of the laws of England to other parts of the empire. Three principles vested existing rights of native governments in the British law of nations: the contractual principle of discovery, the proprietary principle of purchase of native lands, and the contractual principle of treaty commonwealth.

The Contractual Principle of Discovery

Faced with an international conflict over appropriate jurisdiction in the New World, the common lawyers originally asserted that the king's right to the soil could be founded on conquest. This proposition was rejected by other European jurists as inappropriate to the New World.[17] However, the international jurists were unaware of the domestic meaning of 'conquest' in English law. It did not mean military victory, as it did in the law of nations, but (as Littleton and Blackstone noted) implied the notion of voluntary purchase. Blackstone, in his *Commentaries on the Laws of England* (1765), defined the meaning of 'dominion of conquest':

What we call purchase, perquisitio, the feudalists called conquest, conquestus, or conquisitio ... though now, from our disuse of the feudal sense of the word, together with the reflections of [William the Norman's] forcible method of acquisition, we are apt to annex the idea of victory to this name of conquest or conquisition: a title which, however just with regard to the crown, the conqueror never pretended with regard to the realm of England; nor, in fact, ever had.[18]

Blackstone followed Littleton's definition of purchase: the possession of land and tenements which a man had by his own act or agreement, not by descent from any of his ancestors or kindred; but the acquisition of lands by way of bargain and sale, for money, or some other valuable consideration was also a purchase. Hence all consensual possession of land, not by inheritance, was by the 'dominion of conquest' to the English common lawyers.

   The English common lawyers and other European jurists eventually accepted the doctrine of discovery in the law of nations as sufficient to establish commerce privileges and later the prerequisite to acquire voluntary disposition of existing rights in the New World from the indigenous American nations. Blackstone summarized the British view of discovery when he discussed the applicability of the English common law in its settlements. The American plantations were obtained in the seventeenth century, he stated, 'either by the right of conquest and driving out the Natives (with what natural justice I shall not at present inquire) or by treaties.' Where plantations or colonies were gained by either treaties or conquest, the source of native and British rights is founded on the law of nature, or at least on the law of nations. The common law of England had no allowance or authority there – 'for such plantations are not part of the mother country, but distinct (though dependent) dominions.'[19] If the American nations had existing laws of their own, only the king could change those laws; but until he did actually change them by positive acts, the ancient laws of the country remained, 'unless such ... are against the law of God.'

The theory of discovery was compatible with the spirit of the feudal framework of the English common lawyers. It asserted a relative jurisdictional right against other European princes as a contractual convention among the noble families of Europe. The acquisition of tenure to the American lands by the crown was not by military victory (because of its inherent unstable nature) but rather by 'fair and honest' purchase from the native governments.

Discovery, however, was a limited right in international law. It gave a jurisdictional right to trade or to seek a voluntary disposition of existing rights and tenure from American nations. The rights of discovery, as understood by the common lawyers of England, was a concept needed only by one who was not in lawful possession of the land and who wished to claim it. It was similar to holding a pre-emptive right under English land law but never becoming scized of the estate itself. In that situation one could not make a grant, nor could descendants establish inheritance of a pre-emptive right; they must make themselves heirs of the ancestor from whom this right was derived.[20] By analogy and precedent, the common lawyers understood discovery to assert a 'perfectable entitlement' or 'pre-emptive' right. But only by a voluntary disposition from the American nations could one claim an estate or rights in the New World.

The Proprietary Principle of Purchase

Almost from the beginning of colonial expansion, British colonial governors in the New World had clear instructions to respect native land rights and to acquire territory only by purchase or treaty of purchase.[21] Although limited wars were fought against the American nations, conquest was never asserted as the legal justification for acquiring tenure from the natives. Conquest was used, however, to acquire discovery entitlement from other European princes. In the case of The Queen v Symonds (1847), Mr Justice Chapmen stated the legal position of the British crown:

The practice of extinguishing Native titles, is certainly more than two centuries old. It has long been adopted by the Government in our America colonies, and by that of the United States ... Whatever may be the opinion of jurists as to the strength or weakness of Native title ... it *cannot be too solemnly asserted that it is to be respected, and that it cannot be extinguished (at least in times of peace) otherwise than by the free consent of the Native occupiers.*[23]

The proprietary principle of purchase flourished among the British colonists in North America. By 1683, the New England Puritans considered that it was far more important to hold the land under a tribal deed by 'fair contract or just conquest' than under English law.[24] According to a surviving deed from the town of Salem in 1686, 'until the ensaling and delivery of these presents, they [the native governments] and their ancestors were the true, sole and lawful owners of all the aforebargained premises and were lawfully seized of and in the same and every part thereof in their own right.'[25] Some colonists in the dominion of the tribes without instrument of purchase were required by the colonial government to pay quit rents to the tribal government; similarly, the Lords of Trade instructed their commissioners to confirm all titles held under tribal deeds in Massachusetts in 1683.[26]

The first major legal test of indigenous tenure involved attempts by the colony of Connecticut to distribute lands located within its letters patent, but claimed by the Mohegan Indians under their seventeenth-century treaties with the crown. On application to the crown, the Mohegans requested the exercise of the exceptional jurisdiction of the Privy Council to establish a royal commission to adjudicate the controversy between the colony and the tribe.[27] It was determined that this was a proper exercise of the prerogative jurisdiction because the royal charter of Connecticut did not specifically include lands reserved for the tribe in the antecedent treaty and since a controversy existed between different jurisdictions under the crown.[28] Queen Anne declared the Mohegans to be her allies and the 'chief proprietors of all lands in those parts,' and appointed a special commission of inquiry.

In 1705, the commissioners ordered the removal of the colony's grantees. Connecticut evaded compliance with the order by unsuccessfully appealing the commission's decision on two grounds: whatever title the Mohegans may have enjoyed had been properly sold by their chiefs and, in any case, the trial of land rights within a colony was a matter for the colony's own local courts.[29]

Mohegan complaints led to the appointment of a second commission in 1737, but it was packed with Connecticut men and summarily dissolved the 1705 decision without permitting the Mohegans to appear. Because of the 'gross irregularities' in the proceedings, the Privy Council set aside the second commission's finding.[30] A third and final inquiry was conducted in 1743. On the issue of jurisdiction, a majority agreed with Commissioner Horsmanden that the Mohegans were still a foreign nation:

And it is plain, in my conception, that the Crown looks upon the Indians as having the property of the soil of these countries; and that their lands are not, by his majesty's grant of particular limits of them for a colony, thereby impropriated in his subjects till they have made fair and honest purchase of the Natives.

So that from hence I draw this consequence, that a matter of property in lands in disputes between the Indians a distinct people [for no act has been shewn whereby they became subjects] and the English subject cannot be determined by the laws of our land, but by a law equal to both parties, which is the law of nature and nations.[31]

Commissioner Colden was the only dissenter. He did not dispute the tenure of the natives, but argued that upon issuance of the letters patent to Connecticut they had become 'subjects of Great Britain, enjoying the benefit and protection of the English law, and all the privileges of British subjects,' and should be heard in an ordinary court.

Proceeding to the merits of the dispute, the court split more evenly. Colden and two other commissioners felt the letters patent had deprived the Mohegans of 'legal' (that is, transferable) title. Although they held an 'equitable right' to remain in possession, they had delegated this right to the colony by one or more treaties and deeds. Morris and Horsmanden dissented, arguing that the letters patent and treaties merely gave the colony 'the sole *right to purchase* these lands' from the Mohegans, or a right of 'pre-emption.' Subsequent deeds to the colony were meant to create a protective trusteeship only, not to give up the native use of the land altogether. Divided on both the precise nature of the Mohegan rights and the effect of the treaties and deeds made since 1640, the commission ordered some land returned to the colony and some reserved for the tribe. The Mohegans appealed, but their petition languished in procedural manoeuvres until 1772, when the Privy Council belatedly affirmed the 1743 commission decision without comment.[32]

The Contractual Principle of Treaty Commonwealth

However inconclusive the 1743 commission may have been, the Mohegans' argument that native lands could be acquired only by fair purchase, free of fraud or duress, clearly prevailed at Whitehall. In the interval between the original petition and the 1743 decision, Whitehall ordered the centralization of its relationship with American nations into treaty commonwealths and enacted limitations into prerogative instruments to prevent the 'mischief' of deed between the American nations and British subjects. These reforms resolved the inherent problems of the Mohegan Indians' case.

One of the predominant ideological forces behind these reforms was John Locke. The crown, seeking to reform the entire system of colonial administration, which was disintegrating into lawlessness, and acting under the threat of a take-over by Parliament, established a new committee of trade as a subcommittee of the Privy Council. Locke accepted a position on the new committee, and brought with him his political philosophy of consensual government and free association. In this capacity Locke introduced the reforms which eventually became the cornerstone of British law and policy toward American nations.

Through a different analytical process from that of Vitoria, Locke articulated the same doctrine of aboriginal rights – rights that existed distinct from the prerogatives of the crown. Starting from the analytical notion of the state of nature rather than the moral standards of the Bible, Locke postulated that the state of nature is the original condition of mankind. In the state of nature mankind lived without political superiors, and the relation of states to each other was one of independence. Independent states were equal in the sense that no one state had dominion or jurisdiction over another.[33]

Native governments of America were characterized by Locke as independent states under 'kings' or 'rulers.' Under this theory of the social contract, 'those who have the supreme power of making laws in England, France, or Holland are to the Indian but like the rest of the world – men without authority.'[34] This doctrine did not preclude American nations from entering into treaties with other European governments in order to create a more stable political environment, and it did not preclude England from entering into treaties in order to secure property rights from the natives. Locke called this 'treaty commonwealth' or 'treaty federalism.'

Treaty commonwealth was considered by Locke to be distinct from domestic consensual government. The major distinction between the two was that the former was a contractual alliance in the law of nations and hence was not a comprehensive subordination of will. The bonds of commonwealth were limited to the specific purposes expressed in the international treaty between the governments. Locke stated that it is not every compact

that puts an end to the state of nature between men, but only this one of agreeing together mutually to enter into one community, and make one body politic; other promises and compacts men may make one with another, and yet still be in the state of nature. The promises for truck between a Swiss and an Indian, in the woods of America, are binding to them, though they are perfectly in a state of nature in reference to one another. For truth and keeping the faith belong to men as men, and not as members of society.[35]

Since the treaties between the crown and the American nations provided clear evidence of the nature of an international political union of independent states, the colonial treaties and deeds created a troublesome issue in social-contract theory. When European immigrants purchased land by treaty or deeds from American nations, they theoretically became subjects of or citizens of the tribal society under Locke's theory of 'tacit' consent. Tacit consent is the corollary of the first duty of every government to protect property, whether in the narrow sense of possessions or in the wider sense of life, health, and liberty. The theory of tacit consent provided a solution to the problem of why any citizen who never actually expresses his consent to the formation of a consensual government is required to obey its laws. Governments established by social contract control land use and protect individual interests in the land from generation to generation; hence, one must obey the law to create continuity of ownership, security, and certainty in civil society.[36]

When the immigrants, individually or as a colonial government, purchased land from the American nations, they tacitly consented to be bound by the American nations' laws. If they or their heirs disliked those laws, they had the option of leaving. As long as they retained their privileges or benefits under a tribal authority, however, they consented to tribal authority. Since Locke never rejected the idea of subjectship and never discussed citizenship, he saw the holding of rights under native land tenure as the equivalent of accepting membership in tribal society.

Direct treaties between the crown and American nations were the sole cure for the mischief of the prior purchases of native lands. A prohibition against purchases by governors and subjects without expressed authority of the crown would resolve this problem in the future. Locke initially implemented these theories in the fundamental constitution for the government of Carolina,[37] and soon prerogative instruments reflected Locke's philosophy.

Acting under the recommendations of Indian Superintendent Edmond Atkins,[38] a circular instruction dated December 1761 went to the

governors of Virginia, the Carolinas, Georgia, New York, New Hamp-
shire, and Nova Scotia, demanding a 'just and faithful observance of
those treaties and compacts which have been heretofore solemnly
entered into' with the American nations.[39] The sovereign was 'determined to support and protect the said Indians in their just rights and
possessions and to keep inviolable the treaties and compacts which
have been entered into with them.' All governments were strictly
forbidden to grant lands 'claimed' by the tribes except those that had
been purchased, and were directed to remove all trespassers. With the
military conquest of the French in British North America two years
later, the prohibition was renewed and extended to the new provinces of
Quebec and Florida, as well as the western territories called 'Indian
Country' by the Royal Proclamation of 1763.[40] The framework of the
contractual notion of 'foreign jurisdictions' in the British commonwealth had been established. Although the prohibition against granting
lands claimed by natives to settlers was frequently ignored in the
colonies, in law they remained equivalent to constitutional limitations
on the power of colonial governments.

Treaty Commonwealth by Treaties of Protection

The contractual and proprietary principles codified in the treaties and
agreements with American nations and native governments created a
political confederation or a protectorate directly with the king. These
treaty confederations were accorded equal respect with the terms of
capitulation of a conquered state and the Acts of Union in the British
courts. The king's agreements with native peoples were no less sacred
and inviolable than his other agreements, since they were derived
from the same constitutional root – the prerogative powers in foreign
relations – in British law and international law.

When the monarchy, either by treaty or charter, agrees to confederate
or unite with or protect another government or group, the terms of the
agreement have the same force regardless of the race of the other party.
Race was not a distinguishing feature of subjectship in British law. The
express terms of the treaties or agreements controlled their interpretation. If His Majesty treated with a state, either civilized or uncivilized,
the royal courts strictly construed that section based on the existing
intent of the parties.

The protective prerogative powers of the king were first confirmed for
American nations by the Privy Council in the case of *Mohegan Indians*
v *Connecticut Colony*.[41] Attorney-General Northely determined that
the exercise of the Crown's exceptional jurisdiction in North American

colonies was proper, since the tribe was a different jurisdiction from the colony under the prerogative treaty, and the royal charter of Connecticut did not specifically include the lands reserved for the tribes within its territorial limits.[42] The jurisdiction of a commission of review was challenged by the tenants in possession of the controverted lands, but the commission of review overruled the plea in 1749, holding that the tribe was a distinct jurisdiction from the colony:

The Indians, though living amongst the king's subjects in these countries, are a separate and distinct people from them, they are treated with as such, they have a polity of their own, they make peace and war with any nation of Indians when they think fit, without control from the English.

It is apparent the crown looks upon them not as subjects, but as a distinct people, for they are mentioned as such throughout Queen Anne's and his present majesty's commission by which we now sit.

In the law of nations the status of protected states under another state was well defined. Writing in 1760, Emerich Vattel explained that protected states remained sovereign in the protector's territorial law.

We ought, therefore, to account as sovereign states those which unite themselves to another more powerful, by an unequal alliance, in which as Aristotle says, to the more powerful, is given the honor, and to the weaker, more assistance ... Consequently a weak state, which in order to provide for its safety places itself under the protection of a more powerful one, and engages, in return, to perform several offices equivalent to that protection, without however divesting itself of the right of government and sovereignty – that state, I say, does not, on this account, cease to rank among the sovereigns who acknowledge no other law than that of nation.[44]

Following Vattel and the principles of *Mohegan Indians* v *Connecticut Colony*, the Supreme Court of the United States applied these international principles to the treaties of protection between European sovereigns and the American nations. The principles also have been affirmed by the International Court of Justice.[45]

In 1832, the Supreme Court of the United States had to construe the meaning of treaties of protection signed between His Majesty and the Cherokee Nation in a conflict over jurisdiction between the tribe and a state.[46] Chief Justice Marshall found that the British sovereign had initiated the concept of treaty of protection with the Indian tribes in the eighteenth century; the tribes were bound to the British crown 'as a dependent ally, claiming the protection of a powerful friend and neighbour, and receiving the advantage of that protection, without involving a surrender of their national character.' In addition, 'the King never intruded into the interior of their affairs or interfered with their self-government so far as respecting themselves only.' Since the Treaty of Paris could not cede or delegate any authority over the Indians, the federal government of the United States had to enter into separate treaties with the native governments.[47]

Subsequently, in the case of *United States* v *Mitchell* (1835), the United States Supreme Court ruled that treaties between the Indian tribes and His Majesty 'waived all rights accruing by conquest or cession' from European powers.[48] Moreover, the treaties most 'solemnly acknowledged that the Indians had rights of property which they could cede or reserve, and that the boundaries of [His Majesty's] territorial and proprietary rights should be such, and such only, as were stipulated by the treaties.' The court then applied the principles of tort, restitution, contract, and property to the treaty rights. The unified concept in the modern law of protection is known as 'trust responsibility' in the federal law of the United States and as 'foreign jurisdiction' in the law of Great Britain.

The independence of native protectorates under prerogative treaties was held to apply to the native governments in India by the courts of the British Empire. In *Freeman* v. *Fairlie* (1828) the court held that the existing law of the native protectorates continued in their territory, except where limited by the terms of the treaty. In territory ceded to the crown by the native governments, the law of England applied so far as applicable to the circumstance of the territory.[49] Distinguishing between unpopulated territories and territories acquired by cession or conquest, James Stephen, the master in chancery, stated that since uninhabited territories discovered and settled by Englishmen have no existing civil institutions or laws, British settlers of necessity resort to the law of England. But in those territories acquired by cession or conquest the established existing law cannot conveniently be abrogated at once, since inhabitants are unfamiliar with English law and unprepared to receive it. In conclusion, he stated,

the course actually taken seems to have been, to treat the case, in a great measure, like that of a new-discovered country for the government of the Company's servants, and other British or Christian settlers using the laws of the mother country, as far as they were capable of being applied for that purpose, and leaving the Mahomedan and

Gentoo inhabitants to their own laws and customs, but with some particular exceptions that were called for by commercial policy, or the convenience of mutual intercourse.[50]

In *Advocate-General of Bengal* v *Ranee Surnomoye Dossee* (1863)[51] the Privy Council affirmed that English law governed both the British settlers and others assimilated in their settlements in populated countries; however, English law did not extend, by implication, to native inhabitants who retained an autonomous life in their territory under their customs. Cognizant that the British factories (settlements) in India utilized English law conditioned on the consent of the native sovereigns, Lord Kingsdown states: 'But the permission to use their own laws by European settlers does not extend those laws to Natives within the same limits, who remain to all intents and purposes subjects of their own Sovereign, and to whom European laws and usage are as little suited as the laws of the Mahometans and Hindos are suited to Europeans. These principles are too clear to require any authority to support them.'[52]

As a corollary to the principle that English law did not apply to Hindus at the time of the first settlement of the country, Lord Kingsdown held that the subsequent acquisition of sovereignty over the territory by His Majesty could not by itself change the pre-existing distinction between tribal and English jurisdictions. The sovereign might be able to alter the laws of the natives, but until they were clearly altered by positive laws the original distinction remained unchanged.

The British courts also held that treaties of protection with the natives were of the same legal force as other treaties. In *Secretary of State, India* v *Kamachee Baye Sahaba* (1859) treaties of protection with native states were given legal force. The prince retained absolute privilege of self-government under the treaties until the native state was formally annexed.[53] In the case of Calcutta, annexation occurred de facto, was acquiesced in by the natives over a period of years, but still required ratification by an act of Parliament which classified the territory specifically as a dominion of the crown.[54] Until annexation occurred, international sovereignty of the native governments continued intact under the state's treaty of protection with the crown.

In the Far East, the 'sovereignty of barbarous chieftains [was] recognized to as full an extent as that of sovereigns of what was formerly called "Christiandom."'[55] The basis of His Majesty's 'foreign jurisdiction' was treaty, although 'other lawful means' were also recognized as a sound foundation for the exercise of jurisdiction and were occasionally used, *treaty is resorted to whenever possible for its establishment. The due observance of these treaties is as much regarded by the Executive, and, if need be, enforceable by the Sovereign Prince. They are so concluded in virtue of the prerogative and independently of Parliament: hence the terms 'the King's foreign jurisdiction'.*

The rights which the King exercises in these countries are not his sovereign rights at all, but merely the delegated rights of the Sovereigns of the Country. Imperial Japanese Government v D.O. Co. [1875] AC 644; Secretary of State for Foreign Affairs v Charlesworth, Pilling & Co. [1901] AC 373.[56]

Moreover, Piggot states that 'such powers alone as are surrendered by the Sovereigns of the oriental country can be exercised by the Sovereign of the Treaty Power. All those powers which are not surrendered are retained; and to the exercise of such powers by the Sovereign of the oriental country, the subjects of the Treaty Power are bound to submit.' Piggot divided the treaties into two groups: in one type the oriental sovereign exercised jurisdiction over his own subjects; the other constituted 'a special relationship established between the two Sovereigns themselves *vis à vis* other Powers.' The latter type was described appositely as a treaty of protection.

The same principles were applied to the later colonial protectorates, by treaty, on the African continent. In *R. v Crews, ex parte Sekgome* (1910) it was held that until Her Majesty and the imperial Parliament and the tribal chiefs agreed to consensual annexation of territory protected by a treaty, the territory remained a foreign country to the surrounding dominions even though it was administered solely by servants of Her Majesty. Discussing the difference between annexation and protection in terms of British dominions, Kennedy LJ stated that 'what the idea of a protectorate excludes, and the idea of annexation on the other hand includes is the absolute ownership which was signified by the word "dominium" in Roman Law, and which, though perhaps not quite satisfactory, is sometimes described as a territorial sovereignty.'[58] Lord Chancellor Selborne summarized the distinction between annexation and protectorate in a similar manner:

Annexation is the direct assumption of territorial sovereignty. Protectorate is the recognition of the rights of the aboriginal or actual inhabitants of their own country, with no further assumption of territorial rights than is necessary to maintain the paramount authority and discharge the duties of the protecting power. In such a case, the measure of the protectorate, if assumed or asserted in general terms, would probably be the extent of territory occupied or inhabited by the races or tribes whom we have taken into our possession, from the coastline inland until some natural or tribal boundary was reached.[59]

The imperial Parliament clearly recognized the exclusive prerogative jurisdiction over native protectorates acquired through treaties and maintained directly under royal prerogative in the Foreign Jurisdiction Act, 1890.[60] The act provided for the continued exercise of Her Majesty's jurisdiction independent of the imperial Parliament, although exercise of prerogative powers in the foreign jurisdictions is limited in the same manner as acquisition of territories that were ceded or conquered (section 1). Furthermore, the act provides that every act done pursuant to this exclusive jurisdiction of Her Majesty in foreign countries shall be interpreted as valid (section 3). These foreign jurisdictions are distinct from dominions and colonies; they are derivative of delegations of authority from the native sovereigns and not inherent in the royal prerogative.[61]

The global treaties of protection eventually founded the independent nations of the British commonwealth, except in Canada. The Vienna Convention on the Law of Treaties consolidated the existing law of treaty and treaty protectorates and was adopted by the United Nations in 1969; the federal government of Canada acceded to and became bound by this convention in 1969. Yet neither the federal government nor the courts of Canada have construed the prerogative treaties of protection with native governments consistent with the law of Great Britain or applied the four fundamental legal principles of Canadian law to the natives of the land. There is no valid reason why these principles should not have been applied to the prerogative treaties of protection with the American nations of Canada. But neither the federal government under section 132 of the British North America Act (now the Constitution Act, 1867) nor the courts have accepted the imperial treaties of protection with American nations as equal to other sovereignty treaties or protectorate treaties. There is no valid reason for this failure to recognize the treaties with the American nations under the Vienna Convention on the Law of Treaties or the law of Great Britain.

Section 35 of the Constitution Act, 1982, may have resolved this problem or may have merely codified the past interpretation of Indian treaties by the courts. Section 35 provides that 'the existing aboriginal and treaty rights of the aboriginal peoples of Canada are hereby recognized and affirmed.'

Indian Tenure Affirmed in Anglo-American Law

The American Revolution created an artificial society, a constitutional representative democracy embodying the natural-rights theory of law. The United States assumed the divided jurisdiction over American nations held under the royal prerogatives. To implement the treaties the legislative body was given explicit power to regulate commerce between the Indian tribes. Consistent with the Royal Proclamation of 1763 and with Vitoria's doctrine of aboriginal rights and title, the first laws passed by Congress created a federal government pre-emptive power to acquire tribal land and prevented states and individuals from directly acquiring tribal land.[62]

The U.S. courts were the first to try to solve the problem of conflicting tenures. In liquidating their war debts, the states found it convenient to sell speculative grants of western lands not purchased by the federal government from the American nations. Faced with the question of a state's power to convey any interest in tribal land to an individual if it had never been purchased from the Indian tribes, the Supreme Court in *Fletcher* v *Peck* (1810)[63] was 'of the opinion that the nature of the Indian title, which is certainly to be respected by all courts, until it be legitimately extinguished,' nevertheless permitted the state to sell a legal interest burdened with the Indian title because, as Justice Johnson observed, such a sale of legal title amounted to nothing more than a 'mere possibility' that the Indian title would someday be relinquished.[64]

What would happen in the event the Indians decided to sell their land to the federal government without confirming the non-Indian estates within their tribal lands? This was the problem the Supreme Court faced in *Johnson* v *M'Intosh* (1823).[65] In 1773 and 1775 the Indian nations had conveyed land by deed poll to subjects of Great Britain and the colonies prior to the end of the American Revolution, pursuant to the Royal Proclamation of 1763. None of the purchasers had ever obtained or had taken possession of the land. While the purchasers were petitioning Congress for acknowledgment or confirmation of their title to the land, the United States acquired the land from the Indian tribes by treaties and then sold it to a man named M'Intosh under a federal patent. M'Intosh entered the lands and took possession of them. The tribal purchasers sued M'Intosh.

In the facts presented to the United States Supreme Court, both parties agreed that prior to discovery the land 'was held, occupied and possessed in full sovereignty by various and independent tribes or nations, who were the absolute owners and proprietaries of the soil.' They also agreed that after discovery the 'right of soil was previously obtained by purchase or conquest from the particular Indian tribes or nations by which the soil was claimed and held; or the consent of such tribe or nations was secured.' The parties further agreed that after the signing of the treaty of 1763 the Western Confederacy of Indians came under the protection of Great Britain 'as they had lived under that of France, but were free and independent, owing no allegiance to any foreign power whatever and holding their land in absolute property.'

Speaking for the court, Chief Justice Marshall applied the international convention of discovery and tribal tenure to domestic law. He stressed that all European nations had long ago agreed on an international convention for dividing up the New World, employing the 'pretense' of discovery. The European sovereign who first discovered an American nation had the exclusive right to acquire the land from the native tribes. But under this convention the Indian tribes 'were admitted to be the rightful occupants of the soil, with a legal as well as just claim to retain possession of it, and to use it according to their own discretion.' Marshall referred to the Indian tenure as a 'right of occupancy' to stress the fact of international recognition of tribal tenure and possession as distinguished from prescriptive European 'title,' that is, jurisdiction acquired by discovery.

In the context of the facts, the tribal cession of its land to the United States was necessary for the federal government to perfect its underlying title by discovery derived from Great Britain. According to this conceptualization, Europeans can acquire nothing as against their own government by dealing directly with the natives – although clearly they could acquire rights under the tenure of the tribe.[66] As long as tribal territory remained under tribal sovereignty and tribal law, the grantees of the tribe had an international claim to legitimate their land grant. But as soon as the territory passed to the United States by treaty, the tribal grantee had only such domestic rights as could be asserted by a U.S. citizen against the federal government – which, by act of Congress, were none. In short, discovery did not alter the native land tenure system until the natives relinquished their interests by cession.

Marshall amplified his views a decade later in *Worcester* v *Georgia* (1832)[67] in a dispute which involved, among other things, the power of the state of Georgia to grant lands lying within its letters patent, but not yet ceded by the natives to the United States. Marshall found that discovery, an international law convention, 'regulated the rights given by discovery among the European discoverers; but could not affect the rights of those already in possession, either by aboriginal occupants, or as occupants by virtue of a discovery made before the memory of man. It gave the exclusive right of purchase, but did not found the right upon a denial of the right of the possessor to sell.'[68] The Supreme Court admitted Georgia's future interest in the tribal lands, but denied the validity of state laws within the native protectorate, since the state laws conflicted with the tribal treaties.

Three years later, the Supreme Court confirmed the tenure of Indian land in *United States* v *Mitchell* (1835).[69] The court held that the one uniform international rule among European princes was that friendly Indians 'were protected in the possession of the lands they occupied and were considered as owning them by a perpetual right of possession vested in the tribe or nation inhabiting them as their common property.'

Indian possession or occupation was considered with reference to their habits and modes of life; their hunting grounds were as much in their actual possession as the cleared field of the whites; and their rights to its exclusive enjoyment in their own way and for their own purposes were as much respected, until they abandoned them, made a cession to the government, or an unauthorized sale to individuals. In either case their right became extinct, the land could be granted disencumbered of the right of occupancy, or enjoyed in full dominion by the purchasers from the Indians. Such was the tenure of Indian lands.[70]

Where a non-Indian claimed title under a recorded deed from the Creek Confederacy and under the authority of the King of England, and the United States claimed title under a treaty of cession with Spain (who in turn had acquired title in a treaty of cession from Great Britain), the court held that the tribal deed had to be respected by the United States. The court reasoned that neither the Spanish nor the British treaty had stipulated that pre-existing treaties with the Indians should be annulled or that tribal obligations were any less sacred than a European deed or treaty under international or domestic law. 'The Indian right to the land was not merely of possession,' the court stated; the right of 'alienation was concomitant; both [rights] were equally secured, protected and guaranteed by Great Britain and Spain.' The court ruled unanimously that

when inquiring into whether Indians within the United States had any other rights of soil or jurisdiction it is enough to consider it as a settled principle, that their right of occupancy is considered as sacred as the fee simple of the whites. 5 Pet. 48. The principles which had been established in the colonies were adopted by the King, in the proclamation of October 1763, and applied to the provinces acquired by the treaty of peace and the crown land in the royal provinces ... as the law which should govern the enjoyment and transmission of Indian and vacant lands.[71]

The crown's interest in the lands prior to alienation by the native government was characterized as a 'very remote contingent interest' or a 'remote ultimate fee.' Expressly relying on the British principle of continuity in *Campbell* v *Hall*, the court rejected the proposition that conquest over European nations in North America could be expanded to include aboriginal rights or tenure. Subsequent treaties with the American nations by the European sovereigns, moreover, 'waived all rights occurring by conquest and cession' from other European sovereigns. The validity of Indian treaties

did not depend on the motives which lead to their adoption; [they] bound [the crown's] faith and when approved by [the crown] became the law of provinces, by the authority of royal orders, which were supreme and bound both King and Indians, as contracting parties, in this respect, as nations on a footing of equality of right and power. [Indians] became entitled by the law of nations and of the provinces, on the same footing as other inhabitants which, in every dominion, equally affect and protect all persons and all property within its limits, as the rule of decision, for all questions which arise there.[72]

Moreover, the treaties 'most solemnly acknowledged that the Indian had rights of property which they could cede or reserve, and that the boundaries of [the crown's] territorial and proprietary rights should be such, and such only as were stipulated in these treaties.'

In 1856 the Supreme Court determined the states' future interest in tribal land, a question it had avoided in the early decisions. In *Fellows* v *Blacksmith*[73] the court held that only the national government had authority to execute a treaty and to decide when ceded lands were available for resettlement, effectively ending the states' claimed interest in tribal land.

In the first century of its existence the United States Supreme Court incorporated the international doctrine of treaty and aboriginal rights into federal law consistent with the basic principles of tort, restitution, contract, and property law. Aboriginal rights were not unique to a people who proclaimed in their Declaration of Independence that all men are endowed by their Creator with inherent and inalienable rights.

Indian Tenure and the Assumptions of the Radical Title of the Crown

In his general discussion of property, Blackstone noted a truth about the British mind in relation to dominion or property rights. Admitting that there is nothing which strikes the imagination and engages the affection of mankind so much as the right of property, he observed that *there are very few, that will give themselves the trouble to consider the origin and foundation of this right. Pleased as we are with the possession, we seem afraid to look back to the means by which it was acquired, as if fearful of some defect in our title; or at best, we rest satisfied with the decision of the laws in our favour, without examining the reason or authority upon which those laws have been built. We think it enough that our title is derived by the grant of the former proprietor, by descent from our ancestor, or by the last will and testament of the dying owner; not caring to reflect that (accurately and strictly speaking) there is no foundation in nature, or in natural law, why a set of words upon parchment should convey the dominion of land ... These inquiries, it must be owned, would be useless and even troublesome in common life. It is well, if the mass of mankind will obey the laws, when made, without scrutinizing too closely into the reasons of making them.*[74]

The habitual acceptance of the colonial laws and the failure of colonial lawyers to challenge them led colonial officers to attempt to subvert the incorporation of the doctrine of aboriginal tenure and purchase in the Royal Proclamation of 1763 by issuing licences or 'tickets of location' or by allowing a settler to possess protected tribal properties and later convert them into legal title under some colonial statute. This is no different from the speculative grants of the United States and is common to English land law, which devises estates in land through time to different people. But speculative grants to immigrants by colonial officers, without a treaty of cession and agreement as required by the Royal Proclamation of 1763, could not justify confiscation of treaty rights or aboriginal rights in British North America according to the precedents of the U.S. courts.

The protection of Indian tenure in the radical title of the crown by treaties solved the problem of the seventeenth-century settlements in British North America. In order to secure redress of an alleged wrong by colonial government, the American nations had to petition the crown in the manner of *Mohegan Indians* v *Colony of Connecticut*. Only through the petitions of right to recover property from the crown or to remedy a breach of contract could the king, in his discretion, refer the cause to one of the ordinary courts to be tried; no crown liability in tort or restitution was recognized in British courts until 1947. The denial of direct access to the royal courts deprived the American nations of equal protection under the law and made them vulnerable to involuntary loss of their rights and advantages in the colonies. It gave the colonial officers judicial carte blanche over tribal rights and lands.

An example of the problems of royal protection of Indian tenure occurred in the coastal settlements of the colonies of Nova Scotia and New Brunswick after 1820. The basic components of constitutional law in Nova Scotia and New Brunswick were the instruments of the prerogatives, which included the public Royal Instruction of 1761 and the Royal Proclamation of 1763 prohibiting violations of eighteenth-century treaties and compacts between the crown and the Indian nations which guaranteed legal recourse to the royal courts. The governments were also strictly forbidden to grant lands claimed by the tribes except such as had been purchased with direct royal authority. As well, their own charters limited any grants to immigrants until the government had 'settled and agreed with Inhabitants of our Province for Such Lands, Tenements and Hereditaments as now are or hereafter shall be in our power to dispose.'[75] Yet when faced with accelerated migration and the need to minimize friction between the Micmacs and the Nova Scotia government, the colonial officials, without the authority or approval of the crown, occasionally identified areas frequented by Micmac clans and families and reserved them from settlement, and allowed settlers to take the rest.

This practice was standardized in 1820 by an order-in-council directing the survey of 'reservations' in each country.[76] No effort was made, however, to force the Micmacs to move to the areas reserved from settlement or to prevent their use of other areas. The evident failure of colonial administrators to moderate the dispossession of Indian tenure throughout the Empire led a select committee of the British House of Commons to recommend strict central control over Indian affairs.[77] The committee urged the universal application of the Royal Proclamation of 1763: that no colonial legislation affecting native peoples should take effect without the express sanction of the queen, and no colonial administrator should presume to interfere with native lands except in accordance with the express direction of Parliament.

So far as the lands of the Aborigines are within the territories over which the dominion of the Crown extends, the acquisition of them by Her Majesty's Subjects, upon any title of purchase, grant or otherwise, from their present proprietors, should be declared illegal and void. This prohibition might also be extended to lands situated within territories which, though not forming a part of the Queen's dominions, are yet in immediate contiguity to them. Your committee recommends that it should be made known to all governors in Her Majesty's Colonies, that they are forbidden by Her Majesty to acquire in her name any accession

*of territory, either in sovereignty or in property, without the previous
sanctions of an Act of Parliament[.]*

Persons already occupying native lands without express imperial
sanction should have no legal protection.[78] This proscription applied to
lands actually used and occupied by native peoples, however, and not to
truly 'vacant' tracts.

Since Gladstone was one of the authors of the recommendation, its
influence on the Colonial Office was considerable. When the Colonial
Office received a petition of right from Micmac leaders in 1841,
complaining of displacement under 'the ticket of location' system in
Nova Scotia, Lord Russell immediately ordered Lord Falkland to
investigate. The provincial authority, reported Lord Falkland, had no
intention of providing for native rights. He suggested a more extensive
reservation system as a remedy. Unappeased, the Colonial Office
observed that the Micmacs had 'an undeniable Claim to the Protection
of the Government as British Subjects' and were entitled 'to be compensated for the loss of the lands.' To satisfy the Colonial Office, the Nova
Scotia legislative assembly passed legislation organizing Indian reservations under the direction of a special commissioner, but did nothing to
prevent further settlements.[79]

Recognizing the lawless nature of the settlers in Nova Scotia, the
special commissioner told the legislative assembly that 'under present
circumstances, no adequate protection can be obtained for Indian
property. It would be in vain to seek a verdict from any jury in this Island
against the trespassers on the Reserves; nor perhaps would a member of
the Bar be found willingly and effectually to advocate the cause of the
Indians, inasmuch as he would thereby injure his own prospects, by
damaging his popularity.'[80]

Faced with the failure of provincial courts, the legislature, instead of
acting to protect Indian property, authorized the commissioner of
Indian affairs to sell lands reserved to the Micmacs to the trespassers,
with the proceeds to be held in trust for the Indians. In 1860 the
Micmacs petitioned the representative of the crown in Nova Scotia for
redress, bitterly condemning the settlers' 'lawless and unrestrained
aggression' and the province's intention 'to deprive [the Micmacs] of
their rights by entering into a compromise with the violators of them.'[81]
Nothing was done; both Halifax and Whitehall were preoccupied with
proposals for a Canadian confederation. Lawlessness prevailed over
the legal protection of the Micmac people. They have never been
compensated for the violations of their treaty and aboriginal rights.

A similar situation developed in Australia. The royal instructions of

1787 protected the 'several occupations' of the natives from wanton destruction or unnecessary interruption. The governors interpreted this to mean that settlement without purchase was not prohibited; the instructions merely proscribed physical cruelty. In 1825 and 1834 the governors were given authority over native affairs and commanded to 'especially take care to protect them in their persons, and in the free enjoyment of their possession.' Nevertheless, the natives were dispossessed of their land and no reserve system was established.

After the select committee's report in 1848, Lord Gray warned the Australian government that 'unless suitable reserves are immediately formed for [the aborigines'] benefit, every acre of native soil will shortly be leased out and occupied as to leave them, in a legal view, no place for the sole of their feet.'[82] Again lawlessness prevailed; no reserves were established. Compensation is now being proposed by the Australian government.

The select committee's recommendations had considerable impact on subsequent British expansion into western Canada and New Zealand. The Canadian experience is dealt with elsewhere in this book, and the prairie treaties speak unambiguously to that subject; therefore I will focus on New Zealand to illustrate the failure of British law to maintain prerogative protections of native lands.

In New Zealand the Maoris' aboriginal rights were recognized from the start under the Vitorian international principles of aboriginal title and Locke's prerogative treaties. The Maoris were recognized as both the owners and sovereigns of the island, and the 1840 Treaty of Waitangi represented the most explicit attempt thus far to settle questions of property by consensual agreement in advance of colonization.[83] By the terms of the treaty the Maori chief and headmen delegated their sovereignty to the crown, reserving the 'full, exclusive and undisturbed possession of their lands and states, forest, fisheries and other properties,' subject only to the exclusive right to accept future land cessions, in the crown. They were guaranteed all the rights of British subjects, including recourse to the courts for the protection of their territory.

Lord Russell of the Colonial Office praised the crown's representative in New Zealand, reaffirming that 'Her Majesty ... has distinctly established the general principle that the territorial right of the Natives, as owners of the soil, must be recognized and respected.'[84] But again the British courts failed the natives. Pressure from immigration and unrestrained greed soon led local officials to look the other way, and in 1844 a parliamentary select committee suggested that the Maori rights be recognized only to the extent of their actual use and occupation, notwithstanding the clear language of the treaty.

As friction between the Maoris and the colonists grew, a new governor was dispatched to try to reconcile the situation. The Colonial Office made it plain that aboriginal rights would be protected, but only within prescribed limits. Lord Gray understood the law to provide that

the aboriginal inhabitants of any country are the proprietors of every part of the soil of which they have been accustomed to make any use, or to which they have been accustomed to assert any title. This claim is represented as sacred, however ignorant such Natives may be of the art of habits of civilized life, however small the numbers of their tribes, however unsettled their abodes and however imperfect the uses they make of the land.[86]

This meant that the Maoris were entitled to 'that portion of the soil, whatever it might be, that they really occupied'; but it would be 'unjust' and inconsistent with 'the grounds upon which the right of property in land is founded' to permit them to claim lands never 'subdued to the purposes of man' by labour. This restriction on Maori rights enraged a number of prominent colonists, and was withdrawn within a year.[87] Meanwhile, Lord Gray tested the nature of the crown's pre-emptive land right in the colony's courts. In *The Queen* v *Symonds* (1847) the New Zealand Supreme Court agreed that the crown's exclusive right to acquire native lands was necessary to protect the aborigines from unscrupulous settlers. But this gave the crown only a 'technical seisin against all the world except the Natives' themselves, who remained free to use the property and trade it among themselves as they pleased.[88] Native title was to be respected by the courts and could not be extinguished other than with the free consent of the native occupiers.[89] The Native Rights Act of 1865 generally incorporated this contractual and proprietary view of native rights.

Despite the entrenchment of native rights by prerogative treaty, colonial legislation, and judicial decision, those rights did not remain secure. The insecurity was created by the colonial courts – the guardians of the law. The Bishop of Wellington accepted a specific grant of land from Maori leaders in 1848, and in 1851 secured a crown grant for the same tract for the purpose of establishing a school. The school was never built. When the Maoris sought to regain possession, the New Zealand Supreme Court rejected their lawful efforts, reasoning that the crown's grant was irrebuttable evidence that their aboriginal interest had been properly extinguished.[90] Whether the native owners had relinquished their rights permanently was a matter of the prerogative, not a matter of judicial review. The native right of occupation was not immune from unilateral crown disposition because the natives had no land tenure system 'capable of being understood and administered by the courts of a civilized country.' The crown, 'as the supreme protector of the aborigines,' had the right to determine the extent of its rights to Maori land in the exercise of its unreviewable prerogative discretion. Despite the entrenchment of international rights in a domestic statute and the principles of contract and property in British law, racism prevailed over legal doctrine and statute; the colour of the plaintiff's skin influenced the application of British and New Zealand law. The New Zealand Supreme Court casually ignored the explicit terms of the Native Rights Act of 1865, which had entrenched native rights in land according to 'the Ancient Custom and Usage of the Maori people so far as the same can be ascertained.' This section meant nothing, the court explained, because 'a phrase in a statute cannot call what is non-existent into being,' that is, a system of invisible native land tenure.[91]

The Judicial Committee of the Privy Council demolished some of the conceptual underpinnings of *Wi Parata* in *Nireaha Tamaki* v *Baker* (1901),[92] reasoning that colonial officials cannot constitutionally alienate or extinguish native title except in accordance with some express legislative sanction. The crown's grant was not irrebuttable if inconsistent with a statute, nor was it an act of state since a lawsuit against crown officials for repossession of native title was not a lawsuit against the crown. Courts were to construe Maori 'custom and usage as far as they could be ascertained by evidence.' However, 'the native title of possession not being inconsistent with the seisin in fee of the Crown, ... by asserting his Native title [Tamaki] implied, asserts and relies on the radical title of the Crown as the basis of his own title of occupancy and possession,'[93] and his claim was compatible with, not adverse to, the crown's interest. In seeking relief in British courts the natives had implicitly extinguished their right to consensual and voluntary dispositions of native title.

When the Maori claimants tried to relitigate *Wi Parata* under the construction laid down by the Judicial Committee in *Nireaha Tamaki*, the New Zealand Supreme Court refused to abandon its former view that 'the issue of a Crown grant implies a declaration by the Crown that the Native title had been extinguished.'[94] Nor was native title protected by law until confirmed by expressed legislation. Hence, the bishop's crown grant was good because it preceded the Native Rights Act.[95] In 1913, the New Zealand Supreme Court upheld Maori rights to a lake but divided on whether their title had been created or merely confirmed by legislation.

Current opinion appears to be that 'the right of the Maoris to their tribal land depended wholly on the grace and favour of Her Majesty Queen Victoria, who had,' at least until 1865, 'an absolute right to disregard the Native title to any land in New Zealand.'[96] Dogma has replaced historical facts. Within one hundred years natives went from ownership of the soil to dependency on the grace and favour of the queen. This was a journey into the dark side of law – a failure of the rule of law in British society.

This abrogation of the legal rights of native people was not limited to New Zealand. It also happened in Canada, the United States, India, Africa, and Australia, in a manner that could have been predicted from Blackstone's comment about the nature of property in the British mind. It eventually led to the creation of specialized land claims commissions and a sham generosity that concealed the extent of the frauds and breaches of duty committed by the government, and the instability of titles paid for by the immigrants and taxed by the government. The land claims commissions' remedies were not consistent with either the tort principle or the restitution principle of the rule of law. They sought only to justify the past violations of the principles of contract and property. The wrongdoer was allowed to determine the remedies for his violations of established rights of native people. Greed and racism prevailed over the application of law.

The Constitution Act, 1982: Remedies

There is a time in the political life of every country when certain fundamental questions must be asked. These questions evoke passions of history, identity, and purpose. Since they challenge the assumed world of political myths and the commonsense world of daily life, the answers are always vague to some, clear to others, and bewildering to most. The character of a political society, however, is forged by its answers.

Canada arrived at this crucial moment of truth in its political life with the passage of the Constitution Act, 1982. The various peoples of Canada were asking themselves: Who are we? What sort of society do we live in? How did we arrive at this place? Who can correct the evils of our past progress in reaching this place? How can we fulfil our obligations to our man-made society? The future was pregnant with the answers.

The Parliament of Canada in the Constitution Act, 1982, sought to correct prior Canadian judicial decisions that had either failed to recognize treaties with the American nations and aboriginal rights, or considered them inferior to the legislative enactments of Parliament. In section 35 of the act, Parliament proclaimed that 'the existing aboriginal and treaty rights of the aboriginal peoples of Canada are hereby recognized and affirmed.' In addition, Parliament declared that the rights of aboriginal peoples constrain the requirement of legal generality in the Canadian Charter of Rights and Freedoms: the Charter 'shall not be construed so as to abrogate or derogate from any aboriginal, treaty or other rights or freedoms that pertain to the aboriginal peoples of Canada including (a) any rights or freedoms that have been recognized by the Royal Proclamation of October 7, 1763; and (b) any rights or freedoms that may be acquired by the aboriginal peoples of Canada by way of land claims settlement.' The value expressed through these constitutional provisions is consistent with the international status of treaties and human rights. The act seeks to prevent any Canadian government from establishing or reinforcing, through legislation or law, the historical collective disadvantage or inferiority of the rights of aboriginal peoples.

The act attempts to untangle the enigma of outdated provisions of the British North America Act and Canadian law. It overrules the precedential value of a tangle of contradictory judicial decisions dealing with the legislative right of Parliament and provincial legislatures to abrogate aboriginal rights and treaty rights. In the past, the construction of aboriginal rights and treaties depended more on race, political perspectives, and class than on concepts of law.

Moreover, the act's provisions seek to end the historical distinctions between human rights and aboriginal rights. This is consistent with United Nations declarations, since the fundamental rights and freedoms in the doctrine of aboriginal rights have been universally accepted by all nations and extended to all peoples under human rights convenants. Aboriginal rights are, after all, the basic human rights of native peoples which protect their society and wealth from confiscation by emigré Canadian governments organized under colonial charters by the crown. The concept of British treaties of protection and treaty commonwealth are firmly grounded on aboriginal rights in international law. The modern human rights covenants codify and supplement the older doctrines of aboriginal rights and treaties of protection. That is the positive side of the aboriginal rights provisions in the act; however, there is a negative side.

The history of aboriginal rights and treaties in the British Empire illustrates that authoritative legal documents have never been sufficient to overcome institutional racism. Based on the poverty created by the judicial and administrative construction of prerogative treaties with the American nations in the Canadian quest for responsible government, can there be any historical foundation of Canadian law of aboriginal and treaty rights other than 'might makes right' and its corollary, 'equality means nothing more to lose'?

Equalization of the unjust enrichment of Canadian governments with the victimized tribal nations is demanded by the constitutional affirmation of treaty and aboriginal rights, as well as by the application of the tort and restitution principles of Canadian law to the historic governmental and private violations of the contractual and proprietary rights of aboriginal peoples under aboriginal rights and treaties. Equally important is whether fundamental lessons have been learned by Canadian society by the denial of the rule of law to one segment of the population. The federal government's willingness to equalize the involuntary losses of the aboriginal peoples and to attempt to make restitution will be the litmus test of the recognition of aboriginal and treaty rights in the Canadian constitution.

Another limitation involves the political representation of treaty Indians in Parliament and provincial legislatures in order to assure a legitimate check on the future abuse of aboriginal and treaty rights by Canadian governments. Is treaty commonwealth to be respected in the framework of Canadian federalism?

The Constitution Act, 1982, recognizes and affirms aboriginal rights and treaty rights to a constitutional status, but it does so without compensation for historical wrongs. The historic failure of the Canadian governments and courts to protect the aboriginal and treaty rights of the American nations has created emigré wealth and rights in British North America. The act does not use the principles of tort, restitution, contract, or property to compensate the aboriginal peoples for the loss of their wealth. Under section 36 of the act, the wealth of aboriginal peoples taken or taxed by Canadian governments in the past three hundred years is shared only between Parliament and the provincial governments. The act is silent about promoting equal opportunities for the well-being of aboriginal peoples, furthering economic development to reduce the disparity in opportunity, or providing equalization payments for Indian reserves. This continues a historical wrong.

Although the act's provisions respecting the rights of aboriginal people place a constraint on governmental action, its provisions are subject to amendment under section 38. The act can be abolished at any time by the non-Indian majority in Canada, even over the objections of the remaining minority of aboriginal peoples who have survived the dehumanizing experience of genocide, despair, and poverty. The power of amendment vests in Parliament and the provincial legislative assemblies, which gives the authority to one segment of Canadian society to bring the rights of aboriginal people permanently under the heel of the majority's interest and opinions through the democratic process.

The Constitution Amendment Proclamation, 1983, seeks to prevent this situation by stating (in section 37.2) that only the agreement of the aboriginal peoples, the provinces, and the federal government can alter the aboriginal peoples' constitutional rights. This concept is not new in constitutional law; it is merely the restatement of the requirement of tribal consent recognized in the Royal Proclamation of 1763. The Constitution Amendment Proclamation, 1983, was necessary because the collective inferiority of aboriginal people cannot be avoided or corrected by the normal devices of electoral politics in Canada. The historic exclusion of aboriginal peoples from meaningful participation in Canadian politics, because of the segregation of treaty-commonwealth aboriginal peoples from the immigrants' colonial governments and the ordinary operation of racism, has politically isolated the aboriginal peoples. Legal protections for aboriginal peoples have not been respected by the Canadian institutions of government, and aboriginal peoples have been denied the right of self-determination through tribal representation in Canadian governments and the rights accruing to British subjects and Canadian citizens.

Both the Constitution Act, 1982, and the first Constitution Amendment Proclamation, 1983, are agonizingly vague as to the proper guardians of the constitutional rights of aboriginal people in an era of multiple, federally funded Indian organizations. The nagging and persistent problem of who is properly entitled to represent and protect those constitutional rights illustrates a central shortcoming in the constitutional framework and accords. The lack of method of political representation of treaty Indians in Parliament and provincial assemblies still jeopardizes the legitimacy of the entire constitutional framework and social order of Canada.

There is growing evidence that the existing bias within the legal profession in Canada respecting native rights will remain an obstacle to the task of remedying the wrongs. The symbol of the controversy is the use of the phrase 'existing aboriginal treaty rights.' The government's interpretation of section 35 is that it does not recognize or revive or affirm aboriginal or treaty rights that have ceased to exist because of their having been superseded by legislation prior to the act.[97] This construction reflects the New Zealand model of aboriginal and treaty rights discussed above and serves but one purpose: apologetics. If this construction is adopted by the Canadian courts, the provisions of the Constitution Act, 1982, will perpetrate a constitutional fraud on aboriginal peoples.

Similar restrictive constructions were urged by the legal profession in the United States when Congress reorganized tribal governments in the Indian Reorganization Act of 1934. The crucial phrase in section 16 of that act provided that 'the powers which may be exercised by an Indian tribe or tribal council include all powers which may be exercised by such tribe or tribal council at the present time.' Both counsel for the Department of the Interior[98] and the federal courts rejected that restrictive interpretation of tribal powers 'at the present time' in favour of the restorative theory of 'inherent tribal sovereignty' based on the British theory of continuity found in *Campbell* v *Hall.*[99] The past violations of aboriginal and treaty rights by the federal or state governments were recognized, and the original rights were revived by the legislative reorganization.

If sections 25 and 35 of the Constitution Act, 1982, are interpreted as having merely preserved the unjust confiscation of aboriginal wealth by emigré Canada and the systematic discrimination and oppression of the aboriginal peoples, then the aboriginal peoples have few, if any, 'existing' rights under the Constitution Act, 1982. The constitutional protections of these sections will be without substance; Canada can merely shrug its shoulders at the historic violations of aboriginal rights and treaties by its governments. This situation is unacceptable under international standards of human rights and by virtue of the rule of law. The remedy becomes as unjust as the past oppression of the aboriginal people.

In the patriation debates, the Trudeau government opted for a particular theory of Canadian government under the Constitution Act, 1982: a commitment to a democratic republic based on a legal theory of popular consensus or acquiescence rather than the Austinian command theory. The theory of popular consensus, an essential concomitant of liberalism, establishes the rule of law as the foundation for freedom and order in Canadian society. The shift in legal theories underscores the past failure of the judicial theories of formalism and objectivism to protect either aboriginal or treaty rights from the greed and desires of emigré Canada and unites it with the contemporary construction urged on the Constitution Act's protections for aboriginal people by the legal profession. The rule of law cannot cure aboriginal injuries if it is itself the disease.

By the judicial theory of formalism I mean a commitment to and a related belief in the possibility of a method of legal justification that can be clearly contrasted to other open-ended disputes about the basic terms of social life – disputes people call ideological, philosophical, or visionary. Formalism characteristically invokes, first, impersonal purposes, policies, and principles as the indispensable components of legal reasoning; and second, a restrained, relatively apolitical method of analysis of legal doctrine. Formalism as a legal theory is held together by a belief that lawmaking and the applications of law differ fundamentally and check any abuse of governmental power.

By the judicial theory of objectivism I mean the belief in authoritative legal materials; for example, a system of written treaties and statutes. Decided cases embody and sustain the written defensible scheme of human associations and display, though always imperfectly, either an intelligible moral order or the results of practical public constraints on private ends in society. When taken together with constant human desires, these authoritative legal materials have a normative force. Law is justified as more than merely the outcome of contingent power struggles or of practical pressures lacking in rightful authority.

The failure of these judicial theories for aboriginal peoples has created dehumanization and an unjust social order. The denial of equal application of the rule of law to native peoples in Canada repudiates both formalism and objectivism as modes of legal justification. It reflects an unacceptable order in a democratic state in Anglo-American law. The denial also illustrates a failure of social theory. The security of contractual and aboriginal rights of native peoples of North America has fallen hostage to strategic legislative jostling, racism, and self-interest.

What is left of the concept of impersonal law that moderates the desires of men in society when judged from the modern position of aboriginal rights in the courts of Anglo-American law? The Anglo-American experience underscores the pernicious nature of reasoning, of power, and the problem with instrumental use of legal practice and legal doctrine to advance the aims of non-aborigines over aborigines. It shows how legal reasoning can become a collection of makeshift apologies tainted with racism and strictly materialistic concepts of human existence once that reasoning departs from the fundamental principles of the legal system.

Even when the courts uphold the doctrine of aboriginal rights or title (as in Spain, Britain, and the United States) subsequent purposive theories of adjudication are quick to rationalize and vindicate de facto exercises of absolute power to displace native groups. The purposive theory of adjudication states that to apply the laws correctly and uniformly the judges must consider the purposes or policies the law serves. However, as long as governments restrained themselves their courts explained this restraint as law; and when governments began to take action adverse to native interest, their courts called the new policy 'law' and the past restraint 'policy.' Law-maker and law-applier become participants in a collaborative endeavour. The judge uses his judicial power to promote the legislator's power even if the natives are not represented in the legislature.

Anglo-American decisions on aboriginal rights share three main themes. First, there is legal acceptance of the doctrine of aboriginal rights and treaties existing in the law of nature and nations, with contractual principles ordering the jurisdiction of European nations and the American nations. Second, the law recognizes the necessity of uniting American nations in a political commonwealth by international treaties of protection, so that they can be protected by the ultimate sovereign against his subjects and other sovereigns. The third theme, the dark theme, is that once within the colonizer's legal system, each protecting government is mystically given by its courts the unlimited power to extinguish Indian treaty and aboriginal rights for the good of the rest of the society. Moreover, the courts fail to question the legitimacy or validity of the governmental actions under a command theory of law, and the basic contractual nature of political power in international law and political theory is ignored.

Neither of the last two themes destroys the legal effect of the doctrine of aboriginal rights or treaties; they merely mask the doctrine. Courts focus only on the side of government's power; usually they quibble about their power to hear the issues. Suffering from the paralysing sense of the magnitude of the injustice, and caught between devotion to the higher demands of law (the belief in truth and justice) on the one hand and the potential loss of peer approval on the other, most judges are content to apply bureaucratic law rather than the principles of justice.

Instead of facing the role of law in society, weak judges rely on legal precedents and the history of imperial racism. The courts became caretakers of the racism of the late nineteenth and twentieth centuries. Such coward-ice incurs an enormous cost. When governments act in a disorderly and lawless way, their courts save face by classifying oppression as justice or confiscation as a political question. Either way, they remove the cause of action from their jurisdiction. Their decisions do not pretend to have any generality or stability, nor can they sensibly speak of fixed entitlements and duties. As a result, aboriginal people are deprived of the rule of law.

The historical fascination of Anglo-American society with terror – combined with the systematic use of violence unlimited by law as a device of social control – has laid the foundation for the destruction of all political and property rights in modern society. In its approach to the rights of native peoples the law becomes tyranny at worst and an ineffective apologist at best. The Canadian governments may call it law, but it is racism. It is not found-ed on the principles that recognize the supremacy of God and the rule of law.

WILLIAM B. HENDERSON

Canadian Legal and Judicial Philosophies on the Doctrine of Aboriginal Rights

The doctrine of aboriginal rights is fairly well established in the United States, but not in Canada. Aboriginal rights can be defined in terms of political, social, or constitutional theory. Unfortunately, Canadian law has no complete theory of aboriginal rights. Canadian courts have not recognized the rights of any aboriginal group in this country, nor have they expressed much interest in defining aboriginal rights. The new constitution recognizes and affirms 'existing' aboriginal and treaty rights, yet neither the government nor aboriginal groups are able to say precisely what those words mean. Whether that inability is an imperfection, an immaturity, or simply a failure of our legal system is a question that deserves to be studied.

The foundation of aboriginal rights, in legal theory, is not so much common-law as it is commonsense. There were functioning sovereign entities on this continent long before anyone in Europe suspected their existence. The commonsense approach was set out early in American judicial decisions. In the case of *Worcester* v *Georgia*, it was expressed by Chief Justice Marshall:

America is separated from Europe by a wide ocean, was inhabited by a distinct people, divided into separate nations independent of each other and of the rest of the world, having institutions of their own, and governing themselves by their own laws. It is difficult to comprehend the proposition that the inhabitants of either corner of the globe could have rightful original claims of dominion over the inhabitants of the other. Or that the discovery of either, by the other, should give the discoverer rights in the country discovered which annulled the pre-existing right of its ancient possessors.

The chief justice said that under the prevailing laws of nations no act by a sovereign European state could have any legal, practical, or other effect on the sovereign nations of North America.

'Aboriginal' is a European term that refers to those people who were here before the Europeans came. 'Aboriginal rights' refers to the rights of the first inhabitants. The term implies that their rights are distinct from whatever rights Europeans had. The issue of aboriginal rights first surfaced when the European nations began to encroach on the sovereign nations of North America. Initially, the doctrine of aboriginal rights was used to allocate jurisdiction among Europeans. It provided ground rules by which European governments could settle who would exercise dominion over which territories and which people without interfering with the established rights of those people. It represented an attempt to reconcile competing European claims to land without impairing the vested rights of the first nations.

The law has had great difficulty dealing with the doctrine of aboriginal rights. Whereas lawyers and the courts tend to view aboriginal rights as a question of law, native people view the issue as one of justice, having to do with what is right, fair, reasonable, or equitable. Canadian judges do not like to make the broad statements about justice that are necessary to deal fairly and equitably with aboriginal rights. The law is an imperfect device for dealing with questions of justice; but St Augustine wrote many centuries ago that without justice the state is nothing but a robber band. Most people who have not gone to law school would be surprised to learn how little the law is actually concerned with justice. The law is primarily concerned with problem-solving. This is particularly true of common law, which seeks to resolve practical problems between people.

Legal philosophy is called jurisprudence, and those who practise it look at law as a system, not simply as a set of rules. There are three major schools of jurisprudence. The natural-law school believes that there are some immutable principles inherent in human societies that cannot be ignored by any law; that any law which runs counter to those immutable principles is automatically invalid. The concept of natural law is still accepted under the designation of canon law within the Catholic church, but not by the judicial system as such. There are obvious problems in identifying immutable principles common to all humanity; for example, 'Thou shalt not kill' is generally deemed to be a desirable moral principle even though many of the peoples of the world accept capital punishment and wage 'just' wars.

The positivist school views the law as a closed system. The true positivist does not care whether a law is good or bad; he will simply look at the formality of its enactment to ascertain whether or not it is a law. The difference between the positivist school and the natural-law school is illustrated by the traditional Iroquois belief that the world is an island resting on the back of a turtle. The positivist will never look beneath the turtle to see what the turtle is standing on; the natural lawyer is interested in little else.

The realist school is most prevalent in the United States. A realist takes the approach that justice may be blind but judges aren't. He acknowledges the idealistic aspirations and goals of the legal system as desirable, but recognizes that judges are fallible humans with their own unique backgrounds and predispositions, their own particular training, their good and bad days, and their friends and enemies. As fallible humans they will be less than perfect in applying the law.

In resolving a legal dispute or determining a legal question, a judge is always engaged in a common-law problem-solving exercise. The judge is sometimes in the position of a person doing a crossword puzzle who, lacking the right answer at the end of the puzzle, settles for a word that seems to fit. The judge settles on the interpretation of the law that seems to fit, which is not necessarily the right interpretation. In many cases, the Canadian courts have treated aboriginal rights in this fashion; in others, they have simply left the last squares blank.

Among the three schools of jurisprudence the positivist school is predominant in Canada. The judges in this country will look to see if they can find an applicable law and, regardless of their feelings about the merits of that law, will apply it. In numerous native law cases – some dealing with aboriginal rights, others with treaty rights – judges have said at some length that though the applicable law is totally immoral and unfair, the law is the law and they have no choice but to apply it.[2] This predominance of the positivist approach among Canadian judges holds negative implications for future judicial recognition of aboriginal rights. Our legal tradition does not include the kinds of judgments Chief Justice Marshall was making in the United States 150 years ago. If it did, aboriginal rights today would be a very different study.

The Canadian legal system also is flawed in its *process* of dealing with aboriginal rights. All litigation is treated as an adversarial process. An example of what happens in court under the adversarial system can be found in the recent Federal Court of Appeal decision in the *Musqueam* case.[4] That case dealt with a lease to the Shaughnessy Golf Course of extremely valuable Indian reserve land situated in the City of Vancouver. This lease had been made by the Department of Indian Affairs, on behalf of the Musqueam band, on terms the band had not approved and which turned out to be quite improvident. The lower court allowed the band to recover $10 million from the federal government on the ground of breach of trust. The federal government appealed. The Federal Court of Appeal reversed the lower court, holding that no trust existed which the band could enforce in the courts.

There is reason to be concerned about a legal process that allows this to happen. I doubt that anyone in the federal government, especially those charged with responsibility for administering reserve lands, would seriously argue that the federal government did not hold those lands on some form of trust. Yet in the *Musqueam* case the federal government successfully argued that no trust was created. While the adversarial process didn't compel the federal government to make such an argument, it certainly encouraged it to do so.

The government argued that the Musqueam interest in their reserve lands was not a proprietary interest. The government pointed out that courts have always held aboriginal rights or title to land not to be property. The legal underpinnings for that position come from the *St Catherine's Milling* case,[4] decided almost a century ago. This case emerged as a constitutional fight between the federal government and the government of Ontario. The federal government argued that the terms of Treaty 3 gave it control over certain lands in the province of Ontario. Ontario contested that claim. The dispute found its way to the Judicial Committee of the Privy Council, which ruled that under the Royal Proclamation of 1763 the aboriginal interest in the land, covered by Treaty 3, existed only at the pleasure of the crown: in the words of the proclamation, 'Until our further pleasure be known.' Their lordships decided that this meant that the king or his ministers could annul the aboriginal interest at any time. If aboriginal title can be annulled at any time, it cannot be regarded as a proprietary interest. Similarly, in the *Baker Lake* case,[5] the court held that under the proclamation 'aboriginal rights to land are not property.' In my opinion, the proclamation argument should have disappeared with the *Calder* case.[6] In that case, the Supreme Court of Canada held that aboriginal title comes from previous occupation by an organized society and does not depend on the arcane wording of the proclamation.

If in future the courts should decide that aboriginal rights to land are property, serious problems will be created. Such a decision would have far-reaching implications for unresolved constitutional issues between the federal government and the provinces. Ironically, most of the cases dealing with aboriginal title that have been argued in court so far are constitutional cases in which the federal government has been fighting with a province over jurisdictional matters. Notable examples are the *St Catherine's Milling* case, the *Star Chrome* case,[7] and *Ontario Mining*

Company v *Seybold.*[8] None of these constitutional fights involved the Indians, whose interests were most at stake. They were not represented by counsel and they had no chance to make submissions. Unkind things were sometimes said about them to justify the cavalier treatment of their rights.

If aboriginal title is recognized as property, then these earlier decisions will no longer be binding. In law, when title to property or a proprietary interest comes before the court, everyone who has or might have an interest in that property has to be in court; they are necessary parties. The old cases may be defective, since the Indians whose interests were being litigated were not before the court, although the federal government will argue that it was representing the Indian interests.

Indians and aboriginal groups have themselves forced cases dealing with aboriginal title into court, but these are very few.[9] All of these have been initiated in the last fifteen years, and two of them are still before the courts. I am pessimistic that the courts in future will acknowledge aboriginal title as property, and it is unclear whether the Constitution Act, 1982, will compel them to do so.

A lesser obstacle to the recognition of aboriginal title as property has its origins in the law schools of Canada. Until about twenty years ago, legal education did not include any instruction on native or aboriginal rights. The topic of aboriginal rights is still treated in law schools as though it were some kind of strange, exotic flower. Aboriginal rights are not dealt with in constitutional, international, environmental, resource, mineral, or property law courses, nor are they dealt with in contract law courses. Because aboriginal rights is an issue set off by itself and not made relevant to these other areas, anyone who doesn't take a special course on aboriginal rights doesn't know what is involved and doesn't see its relevance to other areas of the law. Many lawyers consider aboriginal rights to be unimportant on the assumption that if they were important they would have been dealt with in mainstream courses. Happily, this obstacle is slowly being overcome, partly because of the recent prominence of native issues and partly because of the increasing numbers of native law students.

The courts in this country regard Parliament and other constitutional legislatures as being supreme. This attitude of our courts derives partly from Lord Coke's disputes with the Stuart kings, but primarily from the works of Professor Dicey, a British legal scholar. Dicey held very strongly to the doctrine of parliamentary supremacy: the principle that Parliament can do anything, however unfair or oppressive its laws may appear. Even though the constitution has been patriated, I predict the courts will continue to say that there is nothing that either Parliament or a provincial legislature, or both, working together, cannot do. Either Parliament or a legislature will be deemed by the courts to have legislative authority or jurisdiction over every possible matter.

On the question of parliamentary supremacy, there is a fundamental difference between our constitutional theory and the constitutional theory of the United States. In the United States certain constitutional rights, such as those contained in the Bill of Rights, are expressly reserved to the people of the country, and no government, state or federal, can interfere with those rights. That is not the way the Canadian legal system has dealt with human rights. Unlike United States legal decisions, constitutional debates in Canada rarely deal with the merits of a particular law. The argument in this country is almost always over who can pass the law, Parliament or the provinces. Courts never enquire whether it is just that anyone should be able to pass such a law.

The doctrine of parliamentary supremacy has implications for the treatment of aboriginal rights in our courts. The American doctrine of aboriginal rights places severe restrictions on the courts' powers to find that aboriginal title or aboriginal rights are extinguished. However, if one accepts the doctrine that Parliament is supreme in its legislative jurisdiction over Indians and lands reserved for the Indians, and that it can withdraw aboriginal rights at any time, then theoretically there is no limit to how far Parliament can go in eliminating (with or without compensation, negotiation, or consent) aboriginal rights. This is precisely what the federal government had in mind when it brought forward the White Paper in 1969. Aboriginal rights were difficult, if not impossible, to deal with, so they were to be done away with. In order to make sure that those rights would be completely eliminated, the government was also going to do away with the concept of 'Indian' at the same time. Treaty rights were regarded as historical anomalies, and they too were to be extinguished. In constitutional conferences, native groups sit across the table from people who firmly believe in parliamentary supremacy and who are uncomfortable with the new constitutional rule that they cannot eliminate the rights of aboriginal peoples.[10]

What are the possibilities of bringing international law, the law of nations, to this country and having it applied in a meaningful way to the determination of aboriginal rights? Legal theory in this country tends to view international law as a kind of international morality rather than as law. For the positivists, the existence of a penalty is the traditional indicator of the existence of a law. If the government can fine you, jail you, or otherwise punish you for having infringed a law, then that suggests the existence of a law.

International-law penalties are ambiguous and there is no enforcement power short of war. Napoleon obviously grasped this fact when,
informed that the Pope opposed his excursions into another country,
he asked how many troops the Pope had at his disposal. The lack of
enforcement power is a continuing shortcoming of international law; it
is only binding in any country to the degree that legislators and judges
are willing to accept it as binding.[11] The Canadian public, parliamentarians, and lawyers have shown little inclination to support the idea that
our treatment of aboriginal rights must meet the standards of international morality.

Social theory also has implications for aboriginal rights. There is, of
course, no single social theory; rather, there are several important social
theories that have influenced the legal process and judicial attitudes in
this country. One of the foremost was derived from the work of Jeremy
Bentham. Bentham reacted violently to Blackstone, who wrote commentaries on the English law and who had been one of Bentham's law
professors. Bentham spent most of his life trying to develop alternative
legal moralities and drafting constitutions. He established the utilitarian school of social theory, which holds that laws must reflect the
greatest good for the greatest number. This theory has become very
closely linked, in lawyers' minds at least, to the positivist school of legal
philosophy. The difficulty with utilitarianism, as John Stuart Mill
described it, is that it leads very quickly to a tyranny of the majority.
A government that bases its policies exclusively on the greatest good
for the greatest number will inevitably undervalue minority rights.
Utilitarianism has found its way from social theory into legal theory
in this country and has had negative consequences for the treatment
of aboriginal rights: the 1969 White Paper was a classic treatise of
utilitarian thought.

The issue of communal versus individual rights also holds implications for the doctrine of aboriginal rights. Communal rights are contentious in this country: the law has wrestled interminably with the
legal status of associations, trade unions, and fraternal lodges. Indian
bands encounter similar problems under current legislation. The lawyer
involved with an Indian band will be puzzled as to how to sue on its
behalf. Current legislation simply does not recognize the band as a
collectivity. It is not clear whether bands can sue or be sued, how they
can assert various rights, or whether, under the Indian Act, bands have
any rights or any powers other than the few expressly assigned to them.

The absurdity of this situation found its way into the Federal Court of
Appeal when teachers on the St Regis Indian reserve decided to form a
bargaining unit. The band objected and took the teachers to court; the

band leaders contended that the band could not be an employer because a band is not a legal entity under the Indian Act. Two judges of the Federal Court of Appeal accepted that argument. The third judge took a more commonsense approach. He said that the situation was clearly one of employment: there were people doing a job; their functions were clear; they went to work; they put in the time; they got their salary; they received direction from the school committee; and the whole thing was organized by the band council. If that isn't employment, what is? How can you have employment without an employer? On appeal, the Supreme Court agreed with the third judge.

Another dimension of communal rights that particularly affects natives is a fundamental problem of jurisdiction. Assuming that under our new constitution some aspects of aboriginal and treaty rights have been placed beyond the ordinary legislative powers of Parliament, the question arises whether these rights are within the communal control of the aboriginal groups who retain or bargained for them. Stated another way, the issue is this: if an aboriginal person can assert his special rights against other Canadians, is he none the less subject to the control of the aboriginal group to which he belongs? If so, then aboriginal groups have a hitherto unrecognized 'legislative' jurisdiction; if not, then there is a gap in the doctrine of parliamentary supremacy that can only be filled by constitutional amendment.

The idea of communal versus individual rights is not satisfactorily dealt with by any of the three schools of jurisprudence. Sir Henry Maine once commented, 'The march of the common law is the march from status to contract.' Under the feudal system in England, the concept of status existed in the prevailing customary laws and practices of local communal groups all over the country. Status determined what laws applied and what courts had jurisdiction. But these communal laws and practices disappeared under the umbrella of the common law, which eliminated the various local customs and practices.

Today, the common law of Canada denies to aboriginal peoples their traditional communal status and rights, and this reflects a typically Canadian view that there should be one law for everyone. As a political goal, that ideal has never been achieved, but the White Paper represented a major initiative in what many regarded as the right direction. Native peoples disagreed, and now the constitution partly reflects the native claim to communal status and rights.

There are many other areas in which Canadian law does not supply any kind of satisfactory answer to the injustices experienced by native people. There is little hope that law, left to its own devices, is going to solve these deficiencies in future. Recently, a u.s. judge said that aboriginal title is a problem that should be resolved in the political forum; but if it is not resolved in the political forum, they can bring it to the courts, which provide relief. That is not a sentiment that occurs in Canadian law.[12] Canadian law regards the question of aboriginal rights as one that must be resolved in a political forum. The courts have indicated time and again that they are not prepared to recognize aboriginal rights until they are virtually certain of the consequences. The constitutional conferences do offer a political forum to address those issues, and it is unlikely that the courts will do anything dramatic until the politicians complete their work.

The challenge and the opportunity exist today to instruct our lawyers and our judges in how to do justice in respect of the aboriginal rights of our native peoples. Now, as never before, international tribunals stand ready to assist.[13]

THOMAS FLANAGAN

Metis Aboriginal Rights: Some Historical and Contemporary Problems

After long and bitter controversy, amendments to the Canadian constitution approved in 1982 have entrenched the aboriginal status of the Metis. The relevant sections are 25 and 35:

25 The guarantee in this Charter of certain rights and freedoms shall not be construed so as to abrogate or derogate from any aboriginal, treaty or other rights or freedoms that pertain to the aboriginal peoples of Canada including
  (a) any rights or freedoms that have been recognized by the Royal Proclamation of October 7, 1763; and
  (b) any rights or freedoms that may be acquired by the aboriginal peoples of Canada by way of land claims settlement.

35 (1) The existing aboriginal and treaty rights of the aboriginal peoples of Canada are hereby recognized and affirmed.
  (2) In this Act, 'aboriginal peoples of Canada' includes the Indian, Inuit and Metis peoples of Canada.

There are many difficulties in categorizing the Metis as an aboriginal people. These difficulties are partly historical and logical questions about the rightness of regarding the Metis as aboriginal, and partly practical problems arising from any attempt to give legal substance to this concept. I raise these problems now because I saw no evidence that they were seriously considered when the constitutional amendments

This paper is a somewhat altered version of 'The Case against Metis Aboriginal Rights' 9 *Canadian Public Policy/Analyse de Politiques* (1983) 314–25. Thanks are due to the editors of that journal for permission to rework the material published there.

were adopted. Perhaps reflection on these points may save us from future blunders injurious to the Metis themselves as well as to the public interest.

The Dubious Origin of Metis Aboriginal Rights

Prior to the acquisition of Rupert's Land in 1869–70, people of mixed Indian-white ancestry were not dealt with as a separate group. In some cases they were treated as Indians, in others as whites, but not as a legal category sui generis. These approaches to dealing with mixed-bloods conflicted with a large half-breed population which was socially distinct from the Indian tribes and which saw itself as a 'new nation,' neither white nor Indian. At least since the clash with the Hudson's Bay Company and the Battle of Seven Oaks in 1816, many Metis thought of themselves as in some sense the owners of the land they inhabited. However, it was not inevitable that the Metis would emerge as a distinct aboriginal people under Canadian law. That this happened was an unintended consequence of the Red River insurrection of 1869–70; it had been desired neither by the government nor by the Metis themselves.

Manifestos and lists of rights were produced by the Metis; these documents affirmed that the Metis were civilized men, part of the community of Red River, who possessed exactly the same rights as the white inhabitants. There was never a demand for special treatment of the Metis as a group. It was assumed that as equal members of a self-governing community they would look after their own interests in a locally elected legislature in which they would constitute a majority. Their consistent demand was not for a land grant to extinguish their aboriginal title but for local control of public lands.

When the Reverend N.J. Ritchot went to Ottawa on behalf of the Metis in the spring of 1870 to negotiate the entry of Rupert's Land into Canada, he carried a list of demands which specified that 'the Local Legislature of the Province of Assiniboia shall have full control over all the public lands of the province.'[1] Father Ritchot was not officially instructed to negotiate the extinguishment of Metis aboriginal title or to request a land grant. His private instructions from Louis Riel imply that there were other aspects of the land question under consideration; but to the extent that they emerge from the text, they seem to involve French-English ethnicity rather than specific Metis rights. Riel wrote:

Exigez que le pays se divise en deux pour que cette coutume des deux populations vivant séparément soit maintenue pour la sauvegarde de nos droits les plus menacés.

Cette mesure, je n'en doute pas, va faire bien dés grimaces, mais pour que la grimace soit plus complète, ayez la bonté d'exiger encore que cette division du pays soit faite par l'autorité de la Législature seulement.[2]

The emphasis was on provincial control of public lands through the legislature.

This position was bound to be unacceptable to Sir John A. Macdonald, for it would have impeded his plans for nation-building. He wanted surveying, settlement, land distribution, and railway construction to be under the control of the federal government. Father Ritchot discovered this in April 1870, when he negotiated with Macdonald and Cartier the entry of Manitoba into Confederation. As a compromise, Ritchot suggested that the federal government could retain control of public lands if it would guarantee to the old settlers title to the lands on which they were now living and if it would reserve a quantity of lands for distribution to future generations of Metis. The Metis, it appears, became an aboriginal people at Ritchot's initiative, although he may have been articulating views that already existed among them.

The entries in Ritchot's diary permit the emergence of Metis aboriginal rights to be traced in detail. On 26 April Macdonald and Cartier presented to Ritchot and his colleague a draft of the Manitoba Act, which reserved control of all public lands in the new province to the federal government. Ritchot argued stoutly for provincial control of public lands; when he realized that was impossible, he conceded, 'We cannot renounce control of lands unless we have compensation or conditions which, for the present population, would be the equivalent of control of the lands of their province.'[3] The government offered all inhabitants free possession of lands on which they were settled; this offer was accepted and the arrangement was codified in section 32 of the Manitoba Act.

Ritchot then raised the question of special Metis rights. At first the ministers resisted, saying that 'the inhabitants of the North-West, claiming and having obtained a form of government suited to civilized men, ought not to claim the privileges accorded to the Indians.' Ritchot insisted that the Metis, in claiming the same rights as other Canadians, had no intention 'of losing the rights which they can have as descendants of Indians.'[4] Here arose for the first time the idea that aboriginal title could be transmitted through racial inheritance even though the descendants' way of life might differ radically from that of their ancestors.

Ritchot did not record whether the ministers were persuaded by the logic of his position; but at this point they began to bargain, offering to set aside 100,000 acres for distribution to the children of the Metis. Ritchot, dismissing this offer, countered with a demand of 200 acres of land for each adult Metis, male and female, and a like amount for all children as they reached maturity, this process to be extended for several generations (the diary cannot be deciphered at this point, so it is unclear how many generations Ritchot had in mind). The ministers would not accept such a far-reaching scheme, but they did grudgingly increase their own offer in stages, until an acceptable compromise was reached at 1,400,000 acres.

Ritchot thought it had been agreed to allow the Manitoba legislature to supervise the half-breed land grant. However, the draft of the Manitoba Act, which received first reading on 2 May, reserved all details of the land grant to the governor-general-in-council.[5] The ministers at first claimed this made no practical difference. When Ritchot protested, he was told that it would not have been possible to pass the bill in the desired form. To assuage Ritchot, the ministers promised to appoint through an order-in-council persons nominated by the delegation to supervise the land grant – a promise that was never kept.[6] In the end, the federal government succeeded in keeping the half-breed land grant entirely under its own control, thus negating much of Ritchot's victory at the bargaining table. The land grant would not have its ostensible effect of consolidating the Metis as a land-owning class in Manitoba.

The diary contains no evidence that Macdonald and Cartier, who were at first opposed to any special consideration for the Metis, accepted Ritchot's theory of a Metis aboriginal title inherited from Indian ancestors. The ministers obviously wished to concede the minimum required to get Manitoba into Confederation. They would worry later about the rationale of their concessions.

The Manitoba Act, drafted while negotiations were in progress, bore some traces of Ritchot's inheritance theory:

31 And whereas, it is expedient, towards the extinguishment of the Indian Title to the lands in the Province, to appropriate a portion of such ungranted lands, to the extent of one million four hundred thousand acres thereof, for the benefit of the families of the half-breed residents ...[7]

It is hard to say exactly what these words meant. They linked the land grant to the extinguishment of Indian title but did not specify the nature of the Metis share in this title. Were the Metis a distinct aboriginal people, like the Indians? Or had they, as Ritchot maintained, inherited a share of Indian title? The only link between the Metis and aboriginal title was the unhelpful word 'towards.'

In the House of Commons Macdonald was a little clearer. On 2 May 1870 he claimed that the grant of 1,400,000 acres was 'for the purpose of extinguishing the Indian title.'[8] Two days later he added, 'Those half-breeds had a strong claim to the lands, in consequence of their extraction, as well as from being settlers.'[9] The Liberals retorted that it was strange to give a land grant to people who had never asked for it, but they lacked the votes to obstruct Macdonald.

Later events showed that the notion of a Metis share of Indian title had not been clearly thought through. In 1874, Parliament created an additional land grant for the white Selkirk settlers and their descendants.[10] This was done for political considerations, so that all old settlers of Red River might be treated more or less in the same way. There was no pretence that the Scots deserved the land grant as a right; it was purely a matter of policy. In the end, all old settlers of Red River received approximately the same thing: title to land on which they lived and an extra allotment to be sold or retained as they pleased. Metis aboriginal title was tenuously vindicated in the Manitoba Act, but in practice was merged into a wider policy toward old settlers of all races (excluding Indians, who were considered by all parties to be in a separate category).

Fifteen years later, in 1885, Macdonald declared to the House of Commons that the land grant had been a matter of policy, not of right:

In that Act [the Manitoba Act] it is provided that in order to secure the extinguishment of the Indian title 1,400,000 acres of land should be settled upon the families of the half-breeds living within the limits of the then Province. Whether they had any right to those lands or not was not so much the question as it was a question of policy to make an arrangement with the inhabitants of the Province ... 1,400,000 acres would be quite sufficient for the purpose of compensating these men for what was called the extinguishment of the Indian title. That phrase was an incorrect one, for the half-breeds did not allow themselves to be Indians.[11]

But the clock could not be turned back. The Manitoba Act was still in force, and its language had been imitated in the Dominion Lands Act of 1879, which provided for a half-breed land grant in the North-West: 'To satisfy any claims existing in connection with the extinguishment of the Indian title, preferred by half-breeds resident in the North-West Territories.'[12] In January 1885 the government had decided to go ahead with the distribution authorized in the Dominion Lands Act. It was now predictable that Metis claims based on aboriginal title would have to be satisfied whenever new parts of Rupert's Land were opened to settlement. From 1885 until 1923, each time a new part of the prairie provinces or the Mackenzie Valley was ceded by Indians in a treaty, persons of mixed blood who chose not to adhere to the treaty were allocated scrip redeemable in dominion lands.[13]

Contemporary spokesmen for Metis aboriginal rights now ground their claims on this sequence of precedents. Harry Daniels writes on behalf of the Native Council of Canada:

The paramount issue, after 1870, was that of aboriginal title. Among its other purposes the Manitoba Act sought to extinguish Metis title by means of special land grants. This measure was obviously predicated on a recognition of the aboriginal nature of Metis rights and identity. Similarly, the land rights of the resident half-breeds in the North-West Territories were recognized in the Dominion Lands Act of 1879 in connection with 'extinguishment of Indian title.'[14]

But what does the existence of precedent prove? Is government always bound by what it has done in the past? Ivor Jennings, writing about the conventions of the British constitution, argues that the mere existence of precedents, no matter how numerous, does not create a binding constitutional convention. Although the analogy with repetition of policy decisions is imperfect, it suggests the considerations that arise when government is urged to maintain continuity with the past: 'We have to ask ourselves three questions: first, what are the precedents; secondly, did the actors in the precedents believe that they were bound by a rule; and thirdly, is there a reason for the rule? A single precedent with a good reason may be enough to establish the rule. A whole string of precedents without such a reason will be of no avail.'[15]

The same three questions can be posed about Metis aboriginal title. What are the precedents? Clearly, there is a train of precedents recognizing a Metis share of aboriginal title to be extinguished in a way other than by simply allowing persons of mixed blood to become treaty Indians. Did the actors in the precedents believe they were bound by a rule? John A. Macdonald was the most important actor, since he was responsible for the Manitoba Act, the Dominion Lands Act of 1879, and the decision to grant scrip. It is likely that to him the half-breed land grants were a matter of policy, not satisfaction of a right. Is there a reason for the rule? In answering this question the notion of the Metis as a distinct aboriginal people encounters the most trouble. Ideally, one wants to demonstrate that the Metis would be logically entitled to aboriginal rights under normal definitions. According to the leading Canadian textbook, 'Aboriginal rights are those rights which native people retain as a result of their original possession of the soil. We have defined aboriginal rights as those property rights which inure to native peoples by virtue of their occupation upon certain lands from time immemorial.'[16]

Can one reasonably construe the Metis as having 'original possession of the soil' or as having 'occupation upon certain lands from time immemorial'? By definition, there could have been no Metis until the commencement of contact between Indians and whites. Thus, their possession of the soil could not have been original in the usual sense of pre-dating European contact. The Metis of Rupert's Land did not become a distinct social group until the end of the eighteenth century or the beginning of the nineteenth century. They dramatically signalled their existence to the outside world in 1816 in the battle of Seven Oaks. They were very much, as they called themselves, a 'new nation.' The relatively short duration of their occupancy may not be an insuperable problem in itself, for the United States Supreme Court has held that fifty years of possession was sufficient to secure the aboriginal title of the Seminole Indians to part of Florida.[17] But the Metis presence was so obviously a result of white intrusion that it challenges credibility to call it original possession.

The difficulties are even greater if we consider the recent decision of Justice Mahoney in the *Baker Lake* case. Regarding Inuit claims to barren lands in the eastern Arctic, Mahoney held:

The elements which the plaintiffs must prove to establish an aboriginal title cognizable at common law are:
1 *That they and their ancestors were members of an organized society.*
2 *That the organized society occupied the specific territory over which they assert the aboriginal title.*
3 *That the occupation was to the exclusion of other organized societies.*
4 *That the occupation was an established fact at the time sovereignty was asserted by England.*[18]

The Metis seem to be disqualified on all four counts. They were certainly members of an organized society, but they did not constitute a distinct society to themselves, which is what Mahoney's dictum means in context. The Metis came into existence through contacts between white fur traders and Indian. In the nineteenth century the Metis (particularly the French-speaking element) began to develop a distinct national identity, but they never constituted a separate society in the classic sociological sense of a self-sufficient group of people living under common rules of conduct. They were never self-sufficient demographically, economically, or culturally.

The Metis had no exclusive territory over which they roamed. Most were in quasi-permanent residence around Fort Garry or other trading posts; in this respect they differed little from white pioneers, such as the Selkirk settlers. Lands were conveyed to the Metis, as to other occupants, by section 32 of the Manitoba Act. Beyond that, the Metis did not hunt and gather food in a specific territory marked perhaps by rivers or mountain ranges. Rather, they travelled for commercial purposes over much of North America, from the Oregon territory to the Mackenzie Valley, from the Dakotas to Hudson Bay, from Minnesota to Montreal. They repelled by force of arms any Indian who tried to interfere with their cart-trains or hunting expeditions, but they did not interdict specific areas to Indian tribes, as the Indians tried to do with respect to each other. The Metis claimed the right to go anywhere they chose. Recognizing this, Louis Riel asserted Metis aboriginal title to the whole of Rupert's Land, which he estimated to comprise 1,100,000 square miles.[19] This, as Riel explicitly stated, required recognition of a double aboriginal title for all land – one held by the Metis, the other by the local Indian tribes. Such a requirement differs from Mahoney's conception of aboriginal title based on exclusive use and occupancy.

Finally, it is obvious that the Metis cannot claim to have been in possession of Rupert's Land 'at the time sovereignty was asserted by England.' Assuming this date to be as late as 1670, when the Hudson's Bay Company Charter was emitted, it would be absurd to speak of Metis possession. English half-breeds did not exist because their white fathers had not yet arrived. A French Metis population was arising as a consequence of the Canadian fur trade, but the majority of these people would have been in the St Lawrence drainage, the Great Lakes basin, or the Mississippi Valley.[20] French penetration of Rupert's Land, and particularly of the west, did not come until the next century.

All these difficulties point to a deeper problem. In my view, the doctrine of aboriginal title evolved in British law to cover the situation where British sovereignty was imposed upon nomadic, hunting, food-gathering peoples. The underlying theory was that the introduction of European methods of agriculture, which would increase the productivity of the soil and enlarge the population, justified the sovereigns' requiring the natives to surrender their right to live off the land and to settle down in a way compatible with European-style agriculture.

Where, As in India, the British encountered a dense agricultural population, they left the local structure of property rights intact and did not impose land-surrender treaties on the inhabitants. The logic of aboriginal rights, extinguishment, and compensation was irrelevant to that situation. It was relevant in British North America because the Indians would have to renounce their right to roam at will over the land before agricultural civilization could develop. A formal surrender with compensation was one way of obtaining the land for purposes of civilization without resorting to brute force.

Aboriginal title makes no sense unless the imperial power recognizes a distinction between agricultural and nomadic existence. Conquest of agricultural peoples calls for retention of their property rights as part of the successor-state doctrine of the law of nations. The less individualistic property rights of uncivilized peoples are protected through the devices of aboriginal title, extinguishment, and compensation. A.H. Snow wrote in 1919 in a summary of European practice at that time: 'Aborigines are the members of uncivilized tribes which inhabit a region at the time a civilized State extends its sovereignty over the region, and which have so inhabited from time immemorial; and also the uncivilized descendants of such persons dwelling in the region.'[21] In other words, aboriginal rights are not merely, or even chiefly, a question of who was there first; they arise as an adjustment in the contact between agricultural and nomadic peoples.

The Metis of Rupert's Land were vastly different from the Indians. They did not exist in a natural economy of hunting, fishing, and food-gathering. They were part of the colonial fur-trade economy. Some were long-term employees of the fur-trading companies. Others worked intermittently on the cart-trains and boat bridges. Many hunted buffalo, but not in a subsistence fashion. Their hunts were highly organized affairs that resulted in a sale of pemmican and robes to the trading companies. Some, particularly in the Red River settlement, were self-employed as free traders or craftsmen. Finally, almost all halfbreeds engaged in some agriculture, using the same methods as white pioneers in the area.

Although the Metis travelled a great deal in the course of their hunting and trading, they were not nomads. Many were commercial people accustomed to money, contracts, business dealings, and the division of labour. For most the way of life was much closer to that of their white ancestors than to that of their Indian ancestors. Their religion was Protestant or Catholic Christianity. Many were familiar with white political institutions such as written law, courts, magistrates, elections, representative assemblies, and committees. Their families were essentially monogamous, although Metis men, like white fur traders, often practised serial monogamy as they moved from one location to another. They all spoke some English or French, sometimes both, although many also spoke one or more Indian languages. Their food, clothing, housing, and other artefacts were largely derived from European models, modified by Indian influences, as was true for many white settlers. The Metis were mostly illiterate, but this did not seriously differentiate them from whites in an age when formal education was not universal. A substantial minority of half-breeds, especially those of English or Scottish background, could read and write to some degree; and some were well-educated merchants, lawyers, doctors, or surveyors.

Some mixed-blood men had Indian wives, lived with Indian bands, and were scarcely distinguishable from Indians. But they could be, and usually were, allowed to adhere to treaty as part of the bands with whom they lived. To the extent that the Metis led a truly aboriginal life, they were not distinct from the Indians; to the extent that they were distinct from the Indians, their way of life was not aboriginal.

Perhaps recognizing the difficulty of showing that the Metis are a distinct aboriginal people, proponents of Metis aboriginal rights, from Ritchot and Macdonald in 1870 to the Native Council of Canada today, have resorted to the notion of inheritance. The Metis allegedly have aboriginal rights because their Indian ancestors had them. As the Lands Commission of the Manitoba Metis Federation said in 1978, 'Let us start with the premise that the governments of England and Canada recognized that the Metis of Manitoba in 1870 had aboriginal rights by virtue of their Indian blood.'[22] But this argument poses difficulties. Indians have been endowed with aboriginal rights under British law because of their level of social development. If they had been as advanced as the peoples of the Indian subcontinent, the British would not have invented the concept of aboriginal status for them. Aboriginal title is not a racial characteristic to be passed along, such as dark eyes or straight hair. It is a legal formula for reconciling nomadic peoples to the demands of European civilization through the devices of treaty, extinguishment, and compensation. It is inheritable as long as the aboriginal people retain their way of life, so that those born into the people participate in the same community. But mere racial extraction ought to be irrelevant. An Indian child kidnapped by British explorers and raised in London among white men would have no need of aboriginal rights; a white child kidnapped and brought up among Sioux or Cree Indians would quite properly have been allowed to adhere to treaty.

To speak of aboriginal title being passed on to the Metis through inheritance from the Indians, even though the Metis way of life was very different from that of the Indian, is a racist misunderstanding of aboriginal title. It would be as logical (and as absurd) to argue that Metis, because they are descended from whites, could never enjoy aboriginal rights. That also contradicts common sense, as shown by the sensible practice of admitting to treaty Metis who lived with and like Indians. The determining criterion should always have been way of life, not racial extraction.

This analysis suggests that the case for Metis aboriginal rights is weak at the level of first principles.[23] The historical precedents are not compelling because they lack internal rationale. The notion that the Metis were a distinct aboriginal people with rights different from those of either whites or Indians was accepted by the government for reasons of short-term expediency. It should not be allowed to dominate our thinking indefinitely.

Contemporary Problems

Of the many contemporary problems that could be raised, I will discuss three. The first two are somewhat technical in nature and can conceivably be solved by appropriate legislation or judicial decision. The third is more fundamental and probably has no solution, for it stems from the permanent conflict between any sort of special status and the principles of liberal democracy.

First, who are the Metis? In historical usage the term refers to the mixed-blood population of Rupert's Land, the children of the fur trade, who had become a cohesive social group long before Rupert's Land was acquired by Canada in 1870. These were the people who received the land grants and scrip mentioned above. But in contemporary usage 'Metis' also refers to any person in Canada of part-Indian descent who is not a legal Indian under the Indian Act. 'Metis' in the popular sense means about the same as 'non-status Indian'; there are considerable populations of native persons in all provinces and territories who refer to themselves, and are identified by others, as Metis, even though they have no connection to the historic Metis of Rupert's Land.

For the purpose of assigning aboriginal rights any definition would have to be a legal one – one that established objective criteria under which courts and administrative agencies could operate according to the rule of law. The only such definition of the term now in existence is in the Alberta Metis Population Betterment Act. In the original version of the act (1938), 'Metis' was defined as 'a person of mixed white and

Indian blood, but [the term] does not include either an Indian or a non-treaty Indian as defined in *The Indian Act*.'[24] In 1940, the qualification was added that Metis must have no less than one-quarter of Indian blood.[25]

What 'Metis' means in the new constitution is completely unknown. Will the term be limited to the traditional Metis of Rupert's Land, or will it include non-status Indians? In a recent discussion of the question, Kenneth M. Lysyk declares, without offering evidence, 'It seems likely that the term was intended to be understood in this broad sense for purposes of the Constitution Act'; but he stresses that a more precise legal definition will be necessary if Metis status is to carry tangible benefits.[26] The solution to this problem could be vitally important. If non-status Indians are to be included, the number of legal Metis may increase greatly from generation to generation as a result of racial mixing. The difference between Metis and non-status Indians could be conveniently ignored as long as both groups were politically represented by the Native Council of Canada; but now that the prairie Metis have split off to form the Metis National Council, the difference is out in the open for all to see.

Second, what is meant by the word 'existing' in section 35(1), which was inserted at the last minute to assuage the opposition of Premier Lougheed of Alberta? This is a question of great import for aboriginal rights in general, but it is particularly pertinent to the Metis.

A decade ago, it was generally assumed that whatever aboriginal rights the Metis might once have possessed had been effectively extinguished through the series of land grants and scrip distributions that took place between 1870 and 1923. The second edition of *Native Rights in Canada* (1972) stated somewhat tentatively that 'those Metis who received scrip or land may ... have had their aboriginal rights extinguished.'[27] It thus seemed that while a few Metis living outside the three prairie provinces or the Mackenzie Valley might be able to mount a claim, the vast majority of Metis had been dealt with. But the various Metis organizations now claim, in the words of the Metis lawyer Clem Chartier, that 'our aboriginal title remains unextinguished.'[28] It is held that the land grants and scrip allotments were so poorly designed and administered as to constitute an exercise of bad faith. So little benefit came to the Metis that they did not effectively receive the compensation required to extinguish their title to the land. According to the Metis Association of Alberta, 'the government was guilty of a breach of trust. The government had the responsibility of dealing fairly with the native people in their land settlements. In dealing with Treaty Indians, the government extended itself to protect the Indians' lands by making them inalienable. The government made only half-hearted attempts at providing any similar protection to the Half-breeds.'[29]

The land grants and scrip allotments are criticized on several counts. It is alleged that many instances of fraud took place in which grant or scrip documents were delivered not to Metis claimants but to white speculators. Beyond this, it is argued that both the land grant and scrip programs were designed in such a way as to facilitate quick sale by the Metis recipients. Scrip was payable to bearer, parents were allowed to sell children's entitlements, and so on. In fact, the various half-breed commissions were physically accompanied by agents representing major speculators. The recipients usually sold their scrip to these agents on the same day they received it, usually at a discount of about 50 per cent of the nominal value.

The contemporary position of Metis spokesmen is that the scrip payment program was so transitory that it was not a realistic compensation for the value of the land surrendered, and hence did not extinguish aboriginal title. The argument is persuasive in some respects, but it suffers seriously from anachronism. At the time these distributions took place, the Metis insisted on receiving their entitlements in as liquid a form as possible. For example, in an attempt to curb speculation, the minister of the interior instructed the half-breed claims commission of 1899 to issue scrip that would require a legal assignment of title. The Metis of Lesser Slave Lake refused to accept such scrip until it was made payable to bearer.[30]

Another argument, applying only to Manitoba, has been developed by the historian D.N. Sprague.[31] In Manitoba, land and scrip were distributed under section 31 of the Manitoba Act, a statute which is listed as part of the constitution of Canada in the schedule to the Constitution Act, 1982.[32] In section 6 of the Constitution Act, 1871, the imperial Parliament expressly prohibited the Canadian Parliament from amending the Manitoba Act. According to Sprague, eleven statutes passed by the federal government between 1873 and 1884 were in effect amendments to the Manitoba Act, even though they were given other titles. It is now contended that most of these were ultra vires of the Parliament of Canada, and that the land grant that took place was accordingly illegal.

Litigation has now begun in the case of *Manitoba Metis Federation and Native Council of Canada* v *Attorney-General of Canada and Attorney-General of Manitoba*. A statement of claim filed by the two native organizations in the Court of Queen's Bench of Manitoba on 15 April 1981 maintains exactly what Sprague has contended in the learned journals:

The Plaintiffs contend that all of these purported alterations and elaborations by the Parliament of Canada and the Legislature of Manitoba of the rights conferred by sections 31 and 32 of the Manitoba Act were, by reason of section 6 of the British North America Act, 1871 (34 & 35 Vict., c.28) beyond the constitutional competence of both Parliament and the Legislature and were therefore invalid and of no effect.[33]

The Manitoba Metis are seeking only a declaratory judgment that the government acted unconstitutionally; they are not seeking redress or compensation from the courts. A decision in their favour would nullify the government's claim that whatever share of aboriginal title their ancestors may have had was extinguished, but it would not establish what that title consisted of. The case is better seen as a step in a political campaign to force the government to make negotiated concessions than as a definitive judicial test of Metis aboriginal rights.

The underlying issue is of cardinal importance. Since 1870 government policy toward the Metis has rested on the assumption that whatever aboriginal rights the Metis may have possessed had been extinguished by the land grant and scrip programs. The current views of Metis spokesmen would overturn this old understanding, creating a need for many practical measures to right the wrongs of a century of neglect.

Third, current Metis proposals involve a fundamental shift in thinking about the Metis. The campaign on behalf of Metis aboriginal rights superficially takes the form of recovering what should rightfully have come to the Metis in the first place: since they did not receive their promised compensation for extinguishment of aboriginal title, they should receive the equivalent now. The substance of the claim is quite different, however. The original land and scrip programs involved grants to individuals as individuals; they did not purport to set up the Metis as a continuing corporate entity. In that respect, the extinguishment of the aboriginal rights first ascribed to the Metis by the Manitoba Act was very different from the extinguishment of Indian title. If it can now be shown that some Metis did not receive their entitlement, the logical consequence would be to compensate their individual descendants. However, contemporary Metis spokesmen realize that the lapse of time has made such a solution impractical. It would be impossible to determine with certainty which Metis were defrauded of land or scrip, who sold it to speculators, and who retained it, let alone to identify their descendants. The current Metis proposal is not for a repetition of land or scrip schemes, but for new programs that will establish the Metis as a continuing corporate entity.

Native People and the Constitution of Canada, a report prepared by the Native Council of Canada in 1981, is the most complete statement of Metis objectives. It proposes the creation of separate institutions for the Metis in almost all aspects of life. For example, a Metis National Council, elected by the Metis themselves, would administer government services such as employment or welfare programs. Politically, the Metis would be represented in Parliament by special native members and senators. Metis cultural, educational, and communications institutions would be publicly encouraged and supported. Above all, Metis land rights would be recognized through compensation for the failure of previous land grant and scrip programs as well as through conferring control on the Metis of crown lands where they now live.[34]

In my opinion, these proposals represent a disturbing challenge to one of the most fundamental principles of liberal democracy – equality before the law. They would set the Metis systematically apart from other citizens of the polity, encapsulating them as a society within society. Even if done for benevolent motives, such a division is still a racial segmentation of society. A group of people distinguished fundamentally by ancestry is marked off for far-reaching special status under the law. A century of such an arrangement for Canada's Indians has been so notoriously unsuccessful that we should be leery of putting the Metis in a similar position even if they request it.

If the Metis were a prosperous, economically dynamic minority like, say, the Chinese in Malaysia, legal segmentation might not interfere with their self-sufficiency. But in fact the Metis are one of the poorest, least-skilled groups in Canadian society. Segmentation will inevitably increase their dependence on government transfers of resources. It is utterly unrealistic to think that government would wish to, or would be able to, make such a large initial transfer of land and capital to the Metis that they would be self-sufficient thereafter. Segmentation will make the Metis more than ever clients of the government, destined to plead for an endless series of inadequate programs, benefits, and transfers. The energies of their ablest leaders will be channelled into conflict with political authorities over the allocation of resources rather than into economic and professional advancement. This may lead to stimulating careers for Metis lawyers and political leaders, but it is unlikely to do much for the general standard of living of the Metis people. What the black economist Thomas Sowell has written of the United States is equally true of Canada:

Political success is not only relatively unrelated to economic advance, those minorities that have pinned their hopes on political action – the Irish and the Negroes, for example – have made some of the slower economic advances. This is in sharp contrast to the Japanese-Americans, whose political powerlessness may have been a blessing in disguise, by preventing the expenditure of much energy in that direction. Perhaps the minority that has depended most on trying to secure justice through political or legal processes has been the American Indian, whose claims for justice are among the most obvious and most readily documented ... In the American context, at least, emphasis on promoting economic advancement has produced far more progress than attempts to redress past wrongs, even when those historic wrongs have been obvious, massive, and indisputable.[35]

Metis aboriginal rights are a kind of word-magic. They conferred no lasting benefit on the Metis when they were invoked in the nineteenth century, nor will they be of any real help today. Indeed, they will be harmful to the extent that they obscure the reality of the situation. The Metis are an economically marginal, incohesive assortment of heterogeneous groups, widely dispersed across Canada. They lack internal unity, political power, and social influence. Their prosperity and self-respect will depend on their learning how to advance themselves within the liberal society, the capitalist economy, and the democratic polity of Canada. Conjuring with the magical formulae of aboriginal rights may produce a temporary sense of self-esteem, but it will not serve their long-term interests.

4 Negotiated and Supranational Approaches to Securing Aboriginal Rights

THE PAPERS IN SECTION 2 provided an overview of the almost incomprehensible complexity associated with efforts to achieve meaningful recognition for aboriginal rights through the constitutional process. In section 3 the writers gave us a pessimistic analysis of the prospects for achieving recognition of aboriginal claims through court action. In this section, alternative approaches to achieving aboriginal rights are considered and evaluated.

Gurston Dacks, Billy Diamond, and Leon Mitchell propose that aboriginal leaders should shift their goal from seeking to enshrine the principles of aboriginal rights in the constitution and in law to negotiating for the substance of aboriginal rights, such as land claims settlements, self-government, education, and health care. Their thesis is that negotiation and mediation allow a much broader set of issues and solutions to be considered than a court or the constitutional process; thus, the day-to-day needs of aboriginal people can be better addressed. Moreover, the implications of entrenching vague but sweeping principles in the constitution or in law are impossible to assess. As a consequence, legislators and judges are intimidated by the unknown potential cost of recognizing aboriginal rights. Negotiation and mediation on the substance of aboriginal rights would permit the two sides to come to a mutually agreeable and affordable settlement.

The application of supranational legal initiatives was raised briefly in section 3 by W.B. Henderson. He made the point that international laws, because they tend to have no enforceable penalties attached to them, have come to be viewed as standards of morality rather than as laws in the conventional sense. By petitioning the British crown and Parliament, aboriginal groups embarrassed the Canadian government into hearing their arguments for entrenching aboriginal rights in the constitution. In this section Douglas Sanders explores the effectiveness of supranational strategies in the aboriginal peoples' historic quest for recognition of their claims. Rudolph Ryser reviews the strategies used by indigenous peoples in various parts of the globe as they seek to reclaim their homelands and national identity. The methods used in these confrontations range from political and economic sanctions to armed combat.

GURSTON DACKS

The Politics of Native Claims
in Northern Canada

The native claims settlement process north of sixty degrees is glacial: it advances very slowly and, like the glaciers, will leave a profound social, economic, and political mark on the North for generations to come. Until the claims are settled, it will be difficult for northern political institutions to develop. Native people have stated that their claims must be settled either before or as part of any process of institutional development in the North. Significant devolution of power to the territorial governments will be resisted by native people who interpret such moves as undermining their claims. If Ottawa disregards this position it will jeopardize the legitimacy of northern governmental institutions in the minds of native people, whose support for these institutions is essential to their viability.

Until the claims are settled, the future of the renewable-resources economy in the North, based primarily on hunting, fishing, and trapping by native people, cannot be planned, and native people cannot begin to use powers sought through the claims process to safeguard and promote this economy. And, until the claims are settled, the non-renewable-resources industries of the North (most notably the oil and gas industry) face native opposition to their proposed projects. Finally, the basic social contract between natives and non-natives defining their respective rights cannot be drawn up until the claims are settled. In the absence of a claims settlement, neither group will feel comfortable about its status in the North and the process of building positive relationships between them will be severely hampered. If the North is to

The author acknowledges with gratitude the financial assistance of the Boreal Institute for Northern Studies of the University of Alberta, which supported the research upon which this chapter is based.

avoid such problems and emerge from its political, economic, and social ice-age, native claims must be settled soon.

The Logic of the Claims

Canada's native peoples are increasingly defining themselves as nations. They are unreservedly Canadian, but they want the right to endure and evolve as distinct peoples and the right of nationhood to exercise control over that evolution. Only in the North do these claims have much hope of being realized. North of sixty degrees, native people comprise a much larger proportion of the total population than in any of the provinces. Moreover, their claims are technically termed 'comprehensive' – that is, unlimited by the content of earlier treaties.[1] The goal of northern native groups is not simply to engage in a real estate transaction by which a diffuse claim to a large amount of territory is traded for cash and a recognized title to a fraction of the original area is claimed. Northern natives have sought to establish social contracts by which they will be guaranteed the means to formulate their own choices about their futures.

Natives are determined to preserve their traditional way of life, their culture. Culture depends on many factors, and guaranteeing cultures into the distant future requires complex claims and settlements. As their first priority in protecting their traditional ways the northern native groups claim the right to harvest wildlife over all the lands covered by their claim. This position has led them to take three initiatives. The first has been to claim legal title to large areas of land to ensure that those members who wish to pursue a traditional hunting and fishing life-style can do so. But for the land to retain its cultural symbolism and economic benefit to native people, mere ownership of the surface of the land is not enough; it does not give them power to prevent activities on the land that are incompatible with native uses. For this reason, the native groups have sought subsurface ownership rights on lands adjacent to or near their communities. In this way, they seek to remove the possibility that resource developers might gain exploration rights near native communities and initiate activities that run counter to native wishes. The second initiative has been to insist on special hunting rights on lands outside the claimed territories: if resource development on the lands damages wildlife stocks on which natives depend for a livelihood, then compensation must be paid. The third initiative has been to seek the power to determine policies of wildlife management and land use, particularly on the native peoples' own lands.

A second priority for native claims groups in the North is the inclusion of cash grants in the settlement of their claims. They argue that they are entitled to a portion of the wealth earned by others from past extraction of minerals on their lands. They seek compensation for the social and cultural damage caused by these activities and by the actions of governments and others, which have degraded native life and which require expensive remedial programs. In addition to the lump-sum settlement, they also seek a guarantee from the federal government of continuous funding. They fear that the federal government will argue that the lump-sum settlement is intended to replace present ongoing program funding. Finally, the natives seek a share of future resource revenue on the grounds that they own the resources and that the process of extracting them will incur a continuing social cost. In effect, the claims represent a one-time opportunity for native people to obtain the capital they need to secure their traditional life-styles and to finance their entry into the modern economy.

Northern native groups also seek a share in governmental power. They want a meaningful say in programs that affect the learning of cultural values – education, social assistance, child welfare, broadcasting, and specifically cultural programs. However, they appreciate that projected developments will impose difficult cultural choices upon them. For example, resource extraction megaprojects often impose patterns of worker rotation on and off the job that upset accustomed family patterns or disrupt the cycle of life on the land. Megaprojects may damage the land and the wildlife on which native people depend. Such possibilities lead native groups to argue that special provisions must be made to give native people a strong voice in deciding whether such projects, or the exploration activities leading up to them, will be permitted and under what conditions.

The Response of the Government of Canada

The government of Canada has historically viewed the North as a colony, and the basic thrust of its northern policy has been that the North must serve the strategic and economic needs of southern Canada. Northern megaprojects create southern jobs, investment opportunities, markets for Canadian manufacturers, mineral exports, and much-needed tax and royalty revenues, not to mention political and economic leverage in dealing with obstinate resource-producing provinces. To achieve these benefits, the federal government must remove the uncertainties posed by possible legal actions based on native claims. Court rulings have made aboriginal title a potential threat to the federal government's economic ambitions in the North. The Northern Pipeline Act demonstrated that the federal government can deny megaproject opponents access to the courts; but this denial of normal rights – which would have to be legislated, possibly on an individual project-by-project basis – would be contentious, and might invite an appeal on constitutional grounds. The federal government would prefer a comprehensive resolution of the legal problems that native claims pose for development. But as long as the government has available to it a legislative escape-hatch, the price it is prepared to pay for an agreement is limited.

The federal government also wants native claims to be resolved in order to address the legal anomaly of native peoples within the Canadian state. This consideration weighs particularly heavily because the entrenchment, without clear definition, of 'aboriginal rights' in the Constitution Act, 1982, has greatly increased the credibility, if not the legal significance, of native claims to aboriginal rights. At the same time, the government wants to break out of its unsuccessful and expensive native policies of the past. For all of these reasons the government is anxious to find a way of settling the claims at an acceptable cost or, failing that, to neutralize the claims.

The federal government's policy on comprehensive claims settlements is outlined in the 1981 Department of Indian Affairs and Northern Development (DIAND) publication *In All Fairness*.[2] The purpose of this very brief and vague document is to dampen claimant groups' expectations and to downplay the liability of the federal government. For example, in *In All Fairness* the government asserts that while it will negotiate native claims, it does not admit to any obligation in law to do so. In this document the government rules out issues of constitutional development and native self-determination as topics for negotiation and defines native claims significantly more narrowly than the comprehensive social contract natives seek. The government thereby requires native groups to negotiate these issues in forums where they lack the bargaining strength that the concept of aboriginal title gives to them in the claims-negotiating forum.

In *In All Fairness* the government insists that all settlements must be final and that monetary compensation must be 'specific and finite.' The government not only seeks to limit the immediate price it will pay for claims settlements, but also insists on a stipulation of what it will pay in the future. This requirement ignores the fact that the future needs of northern native peoples cannot be predicted. If, as expressed in *In All Fairness*, payments and their timing should be tailored to 'meet the needs of various native groups,' flexible arrangements are required. In practical terms, this issue becomes one of resource revenue sharing, an approach to settlements that the federal government has not ruled out of negotiations but has strongly resisted.

The government proposes to limit claims settlements by requiring that natives accept, as given, existing rights of non-native Canadians, including 'rights of access such as transportation routes within and through a settlement area; rights of way for necessary government purposes; rights of access to holders of subsurface rights for exploration, development and production of resources.' In addition, 'native people should only select settlement lands which they currently use and occupy.' This policy can work against the interests of native people if the federal government applies a restrictive definition of current use and occupancy.

In summary, the position of the government of Canada is that it desires a comprehensive claims settlement, but it is determined to limit the price it will pay. In pursuit of this position, a process for negotiating claims has been established. The focus of this process is the Office of Native Claims, established in 1974 within DIAND. It researches and develops policy, co-ordinates the participation of a wide variety of federal government departments whose mandates are affected by claims negotiations, and supports the work of the federal teams actually undertaking negotiations.

Since 1980, the federal negotiating teams have been led by government negotiators who are appointed from outside the public service. This innovation was welcomed by native peoples in the expectation that outside negotiators might be more responsive to native claims than civil servants. However, problems arose when these external negotiators found themselves unable to persuade the minister, the Office of Native Claims, or other federal departments holding a veto over certain aspects of settlements to accept agreements reached during negotiations. It is difficult to judge whether this is because the negotiators lack the credibility with government that an in-house negotiator might have, or because the negotiated agreements are simply deemed to be too costly.

The Claims Settlement Process

The process for reaching a comprehensive claims settlement involves several stages. First, a native group presents a basic statement of its claim to DIAND, which determines whether it will accept the claim as negotiable. Second, if DIAND views the claim as historically and legally well-founded, the claimant group researches its claim further, elaborates it, and begins to negotiate. Successful negotiations will lead to agreements in principle, which will then be submitted to the beneficiaries of the claim and to the federal cabinet for ratification. The third step is to flesh out the agreement in principle, which will then be legislated. The third step offers much opportunity for frustration; the process of defining details may reveal misunderstandings that were not apparent in the preparation of a briefer and more conceptual agreement in principle. To reduce the potential for misunderstanding, the agreements in principle in the second step of the process are specified in substantial detail, thus making the third stage in a final settlement less contentious.

A significant aspect of the claims settlement process is the manner of its funding. Only for the first stage, the preparation of the basic statement of claim, does the federal government pay for the costs incurred. The second stage is financed by interest-free loans to native claimants, and the third stage by interest-bearing loans. Thus, while federal government support for the preparation of native claims north of sixty degrees totalled $28.73 million to 13 March 1983, $27.1 million of that is recoverable as a first charge against claims settlements.[3] This arrangement places pressure on native people to settle, particularly in the third stage when the cost of negotiation affects the claimant group's finances most directly.

The Role of the Territorial Governments

Legally, the governments of the two northern territories are not entitled to take part in the claims settlement process. Claims are being presented to the federal government because Ottawa is constitutionally responsible for native people and owns the land in question. If it wished, Ottawa could legally proceed on its own to settle claims north of sixty degrees. It is also constitutionally empowered to impose any settlement on unwilling territorial governments. However, because the claims settlements will affect so profoundly the future of all segments of northern society, not just the native people, the federal government does not wish to exclude the territorial governments; accordingly, they are invited to participate not as equal partners but as part of the federal negotiating team.

The extent to which non-native northerners view the claims settlements as fair will affect interracial harmony in the North. If an interracial consensus comes out of the claims settlement process, the prospects for moderate and harmonious politics are greatly enhanced. This would make the federal government feel more comfortable about transferring more power, in the form of self-government and (ultimately) provincial status, to the North. In the shorter term, many aspects of the claims settlement process affect the goals and programs of the territorial governments. For example, the government of the Yukon Territory places great importance on gaining control over large portions of land, but Ottawa has said this transfer of power will not occur until after native claims in the Yukon are settled.[4] Similarly, the government of the Northwest Territories endorses the principle of dividing the territories into two political units, but the minister of Indian affairs and northern development has stated that substantial progress must first be made in settling native claims in the territories.[5] These and other factors make it appropriate that the territorial governments sit at the claims tables. There they can consider the full implications of any claims settlement for their territories and can suggest modifications to minimize disruption of territorial programs. Moreover, the territorial governments' presence at the negotiations can facilitate prompt legislation on those aspects of the claims settlement which fall under territorial jurisdiction.

The two territorial governments have performed very differently in their role as participants in the claims negotiation process. The Yukon government has generally resisted native claims and has sought to use the claims process as a vehicle for gaining jurisdiction, currently held by the federal government, over surface lands in the Yukon. Indeed, from December 1982 to June 1983 the Yukon government boycotted the claims negotiations in an attempt to wring concessions on this point from Ottawa.[6] It has also attempted to set as a condition of its support for the claims process that native people will have no special status in discussions of Yukon's constitutional future.[7]

By contrast, the government of the Northwest Territories has, since the election of the Ninth Legislative Assembly in 1979, strongly supported native claims. In the words of James Wah-Shee, minister for aboriginal rights and constitutional development, 'In essence, the position of the GNWT is that it supports an early and satisfactory settlement of aboriginal claims and that no initiative on its part should prejudice the outcome of settlement negotiations currently underway. To this end ... native organizations [should] be fully involved in the process of political and constitutional development in the North.'[8]

Consistent with its position of support for native claims, the government of the Northwest Territories supported a court action by which the hamlet of Baker Lake attempted to use the concept of aboriginal rights as a means of opposing unwanted mineral exploration. It also supported native people in their struggle to have aboriginal rights entrenched in the Constitution Act, 1982. More recently, it has worked jointly with native groups to create the Constitutional Alliance of the Northwest Territories, by means of which the people of the territories are developing proposals for their own constitutional future. In view of the preponderance of native people in the territorial electorate, and because the majority of its members are natives, the Tenth Legislative Assembly of the Northwest Territories will undoubtedly continue policies in support of native claims.

Individual Claims

To most southern Canadians, the North is all of a piece, characterized more by its vastness, coldness, and sparse population than by the contrasts in its different regions and peoples. However, these differences exercise a particular significance for native claims; each reflects a unique history, degree of development pressure, and set of native goals. It is useful to elaborate on the generalizations offered to this point with a brief consideration of each of the claims and the state of their negotiations.

The Council of Yukon Indians

The Council of Yukon Indians (CYI) was created in 1974 to negotiate a joint claim, entitled *Together Today for Our Children Tomorrow*, presented to the federal government by both status and non-status Indians in 1973. Little progress was made until 1979, when CYI submitted a revised statement of claim, entitled *Proposal for a Yukon Indian Settlement*. This proposal sought to create a separate Yukon Indian government that would control areas of jurisdiction of particular interest for the approximately 5,500 native people CYI represents. These areas of jurisdiction included education, taxation, the administration of justice, and aspects of health care and social programs. The proposal also sought significant Indian participation in decisions on land use, wildlife management, and resource development, as well as a cash and land settlement. The proposal was also noteworthy in that it sought entrenchment rather than extinguishment of the aboriginal rights of Yukon Indians.

Since 1979, the claim has been negotiated actively. The door to negotiations was opened when CYI withdrew from its proposal the requirement of a separate government by and for natives in the Yukon. Instead, CYI opted to work within a single government for all people in the Yukon, and agreed to remove discussions about that government from claims negotiations.

In 1981, an agreement in principle was signed providing for the advance payment of certain benefits to Yukon Indian elders, whose advanced age made it unlikely that they would live long enough to share in any benefits flowing from a final claims settlement. Agreement has been reached on most of the issues under negotiation, including 'Yukon Indian rights to wildlife harvesting, the provision, delivery and funding of programs to beneficiaries, economic and corporate structures, financial compensation and settlement land selection, and local government matters [for most of the native communities].'[9] Few items remained to be settled, but three major issues – taxation, Ottawa's pursuit of extinguishment rather than entrenchment, and rights to subsurface resources – proved extremely contentious.

For its part, CYI, having come so far, appeared quite eager to achieve a settlement. The Yukon Indian people have been heavily and adversely affected by contact with non-native society. They form a minority of the electorate of the Yukon and feel threatened by its government; they view a claims settlement as the only possible remedy for their problems. The conventional wisdom that a Progressive Conservative government in Ottawa would deal less generously with native people than the Liberal government[10] and the presumption that a federal election would lead to a Conservative victory in 1984 placed great pressure on CYI to settle the few remaining issues quickly. For example, the native community of Old Crow voted to ratify an incomplete and to them not fully satisfactory agreement in principle largely because, as one local leader put it, 'the consequences of waiting will be too grave. Our relations with the Yukon Conservative government are not a bed of roses. A national Conservative government would be worse.' Largely as a result of these pressures, a draft agreement in principle was initialled early in 1984 by the negotiators for Ottawa, the Yukon territorial government, and CYI. The agreement required that ten of the twelve native communities in the Yukon ratify it by 31 December 1984 or the agreement would be considered void. Largely because the draft agreement stipulated the extinguishment of aboriginal rights in the Yukon, several of the communities balked at ratifying it. Although the new Progressive Conservative government could have extended the deadline for ratification, it declared the agreement lapsed and the negotiation process suspended. The new government went out of its way to apply pressure on CYI. It announced that CYI would receive no new funding from Ottawa. Moreover, it relaxed the land freeze that the previous Liberal government had put in place to prevent the transfer of lands, sought by the Yukon native communities as part of the settlement, from crown ownership to private hands.[11] This draconian response may have been merely a device to accelerate the settlement process, but it seems more consistent with the thesis that the Conservative government will respond less sympathetically to native claims groups than did the Liberals. In any case, it appears that more than a decade of work in pursuit of a settlement may go for naught. With it may go the Yukon Indians' hope for a better life.

Committee for Original Peoples Entitlement

Pressure to achieve a prompt settlement has weighed most heavily on the Committee for Original Peoples Entitlement (COPE), which represents approximately 2,500 Inuvialuit of the western Arctic. COPE must deal with the social and environmental dislocation brought about by the massive Beaufort Sea hydrocarbon exploration activities and the prospect of other major development projects in the future. The Inuvialuit look to a settlement of their claim to define their rights to the land; to empower them to protect the land and water; to give them the means to develop programs to cushion the social impacts of development; and to prepare their people to reap the benefits development can provide. Clearly, COPE's strategy was to settle its claim while resource development is still a high priority for the federal government, thus inclining the government to negotiate more flexibly.

COPE also hopes to settle its claim quickly because of the frustration it has encountered in its negotiations with Ottawa. The initial stages proceeded well enough; an agreement in principle was signed in October 1978, less than eighteen months after the claim was originally submitted. The agreement in principle was notable in that it provided for the extinguishment of Inuvialuit rights. This appeared to set a precedent that conflicted with the goal of constitutional entrenchment of rights, which the other northern native groups hold to be of vital importance. Extinguishment of native rights is also at odds with section 35 of the Constitution Act, 1982.

The agreement in principle identified Inuvialuit ownership and subsurface rights to 95,830 square kilometres of land and surface rights to an additional 12,950 square kilometres. In addition, the Inuvialuit were to receive a sum equal to $45 million in 1978 dollars. The agreement provided for the establishment of Inuvialuit investment, development, and land corporations, and a social development program. It included provisions guaranteeing certain wildlife-harvesting rights to the Inuvialuit and their participation in advisory bodies overseeing land use and planning.[12]

The 1979 and 1980 federal elections interrupted the negotiation process, however. After the 1980 elections the federal government introduced a new set of guidelines for the final agreement. COPE interpreted this move as a repudiation of the agreement in principle that had been signed two years earlier. Negotiations broke off in December 1980 and were not resumed again until the spring of 1982. In December 1983 a new agreement in principle was initialled by the negotiators for COPE and the federal government. A final agreement was legislated in June 1984, shortly before the dissolution of Parliament.

The settlement provides the Inuvialuit with surface and subsurface rights to approximately 1,800 square kilometres of land adjacent to each of their six communities, and with surface title and rights to sand and gravel but not to other subsurface resources on an additional 78,000 square kilometres of land. Two thousand square kilometres of land in Cape Bathurst have been designated a protected area in which no development is to occur. Inuvialuit wildlife-harvesting rights are entrenched in the settlement. Further, the settlement gives the Inuvialuit $45 million in 1977 dollars plus an additional $7.5 million social development fund. These benefits will be administered by Inuvialuit corporations established as part of the settlement. Finally, the Inuvialuit will participate in, but not control, boards and committees responsible for environmental screening and reviewing; determining compensation in the event of damage to wildlife populations; and wildlife management. In general, this settlement has been favourably received. Although it does not necessarily provide a blueprint for the other northern claims, it is most significant as a reference point for them; Ottawa may offer different terms to other claimants, but it is highly unlikely to offer them better terms. In this way, the COPE settlement cannot help but influence the expectations all parties will bring to future northern claims negotiations.

Claims in the Mackenzie Valley

The claims negotiation process in the Mackenzie Valley has been complicated by the presence of two claimant groups representing, together, approximately 13,000 native people. The Dene Nation, whose predecessor, the Indian Brotherhood of the Northwest Territories, submitted a claim in 1976, represents those native people, status and non-status, who choose to affiliate with it. The other claimant group, the Metis Association, submitted its claim in 1977. It represents a significantly smaller number of native people – those who are not status Indians and who have decided not to join the Dene Nation. Ottawa has stipulated that there can only be one settlement over any piece of territory, and therefore the two groups must present a single claim. This requirement has posed great difficulties, for the two groups differ in philosophy. The Metis are oriented toward enhancing their participation in the wage economy, while the Dene prefer to emphasize issues of cultural survival and political self-determination. The groups also differ on questions of membership eligibility. The Metis Association favours enrolling relatively recent native arrivals to the region whom the Dene consider ineligible. With the election of new leaders for both groups in 1983 and the appointment of a single negotiator to represent both groups, the prospects for unity in negotiating significantly improved. Early evidence of progress was the ratification in the summer of 1984 of a comprehensive claims negotiating package, a milestone in the history of the claim.

Still, the negotiations have a great distance to go. In order to facilitate negotiations the Dene have agreed to remove issues of self-determination from the claims process and to pursue them through the overall constitutional development process in the Northwest Territories. This step removed an obstacle that had stalled claims negotiations for several years. Beyond that, however, the parties to the negotiations have as yet agreed only on a statement of basic principles. Everything else remains to be negotiated. The main item on the agenda, aside from the overlapping territorial claims between the Dene / Metis group and others, is the matter of benefits native people will derive from the expansion of the Norman Wells oil field and the construction of a pipeline to carry the oil to the South. While this may seem a narrow issue, its resolution may significantly influence other important provisions of the overall settlement. The lengthy agenda and the fact that the Dene do not seem to feel intimidated by a change of government in Ottawa suggest that the Dene / Metis claim will take a long time to negotiate.

The Tungavik Federation of Nunavut

After an erratic early history, the claim of the approximately 13,500 Inuit of the central and eastern Arctic appears to be making headway, but it still faces formidable obstacles. The claim was first presented by the Inuit Tapirisat of Canada (ITC) in 1976.[13] At the time the ITC encompassed the western Arctic Inuvialuit who are now represented by COPE. The claim sought the creation north of the treeline of an Inuit territory to be called Nunavut, and anticipated eventual provincial status for it. In addition, the claim sought surface rights to land, resource-royalty sharing, and participation in land-use planning.

The period from 1976 to 1981 was marked by a series of interruptions in the claims process. At one point, the ITC withdrew its claim in order to consult more fully with the Inuit whom it represented but whose support it could not claim with certainty. The claims process was disrupted several times when the ITC revised the structures through which it negotiated its claim. Negotiations were disrupted further by the change of federal governments in 1979 and 1980. During this period additional documents were published elaborating on the concept of Nunavut.[14] Against the background of these events negotiations were resumed in 1980.

In 1981 an agreement entitled 'Wildlife Provisions of an Agreement-in-Principle' was initialled by the ITC and the federal negotiator. The heart of this agreement was the creation of a joint Inuit / federal government wildlife management board with equal representation from the two sides. The board would be empowered to act, not merely to advise the government. However, the agreement gave ultimate authority to the minister of Indian affairs and northern development to overturn decisions of the board.

Possibly because they doubt that DIAND will safeguard adequately their own northern policies, several departments of the federal government challenged the agreement in principle. This rebuff has dismayed the Inuit, particularly because the wildlife agreement is consistent with the logic of their positions on land use and non-renewable resource management. Still, the Inuit remain committed to the claims process. They anticipate that future economic development in the North will affect them even more than it has in the past, and they want joint development management agencies created before development pressure intensifies. Like CYI and COPE, they wish to have in place social and other programs to manage the potential disruption caused by the new developments.

Given the federal government's position that division of the Northwest Territories must wait until native claims are settled or at least close to being settled, the Tungavik Federation of Nunavut (TFN), which was created in 1982 and now represents the Inuit, views a speedy resolution of their claim as accelerating the creation of Nunavut. Negotiations with TFN have been proceeding. Reports on the negotiations are optimistic.[15] However, crucial issues involving the sharing of powers currently held by the federal government have not as yet been addressed. Until they are, a settlement of this claim is not imminent.

Conclusion

This review should make it apparent that the Liberal government was not so eager to settle comprehensive claims in the North that it made significant compromises to achieve settlements. It can be expected that the only northern settlements likely to take place under the Conservative government are those in which the native claimants have substantially accepted Ottawa's bargaining position, particularly its insistence that claims will not shape the constitutional future of the North or involve a transfer of powers from the federal government. Joint decision-making bodies may result from claims settlements, but in all cases the minister in Ottawa will retain veto power over the decisions of such bodies.

Even more discouraging for northern native claimants is the possibility that the comprehensive review of the claims process ordered by David Crombie, the new minister of Indian affairs and northern development, may terminate the claims negotiating process entirely. His letter to CYI suggested that the claims process may have been 'overtaken by events,' specifically, the entrenchment of aboriginal rights in the Constitution Act, 1982, and all-party support in Parliament for Indian self-government.[16] The benefits native people are likely to receive from these two events is uncertain; in particular, the constitutional provision is not promising. It is too early to tell whether the claims process will resume in tandem with these policy initiatives or whether it will be superseded by them. To the extent that the northern claims process is replaced by the vague and partial Indian policies currently evolving for all of Canada, the bargaining position of the northern native claimants will be diminished, and so will the benefits that they are likely to receive.

For COPE, the change of government may well affect the implementation of the settlements. The claims-settlement implementation process will no doubt bring to the surface areas of vagueness in the settlements and introduce unanticipated problems. This will necessitate further negotiation and modifications to the original documents. The claims-settlement implementation process – as distinct from the claims negotiation process – will take a long time to complete. The native groups will have to work with the Conservative government and may find that the goodwill essential for success is in short supply. However, the Conservative factor should not be overstated. The Liberals have proved far from open-handed in dealing with northern native claims, and the public servants who have developed existing claims policy will for the most part remain in place. Still, to the extent that a change of government can make a difference, the Conservative government undoubtedly is a change for the worse for northern native groups.

BILLY DIAMOND

Aboriginal Rights: The James Bay Experience

Aboriginal and treaty rights of the aboriginal peoples of Canada are recognized and affirmed by the Constitution Act, 1982. A series of conferences on constitutional matters directly affecting the aboriginal peoples of Canada is under way. Thus, the definition of aboriginal rights, their extent, and how they are to be dealt with are part of an ongoing process. I propose to present a short history of some of the principal factors relating to aboriginal rights that were involved in the complex James Bay settlement.

The James Bay Area and the Crees of Quebec

The area traditionally occupied by my people, the James Bay Crees, consists of over 150,000 square miles in northern Quebec. It stretches approximately from the forty-ninth to above the fifty-fifth parallels of latitude, and is bounded by the Ontario-Quebec border, James Bay, and Hudson Bay on the west. The eastern boundary follows approximately the height of land and at certain points stretches several hundred miles inland as far as the Labrador border.

This territory has been inhabited by Cree bands from time immemorial. Archaeological data have shown that Crees occupied the area for thousands of years prior to the arrival of the white man. With the coming of the white man, our traditional territory supposedly became part of Rupert's Land or the Hudson's Bay Company territory. From Confederation until the passage of the Quebec Boundaries Extension Acts, this area was part of the Northwest Territories. The southern portion of this area became part of Quebec in 1898, and it was not until

I wish to acknowledge the assistance of Mr James O'Reilly in the legal aspects of this paper.

1912 that the northern portion of our traditional area became part of the province of Quebec. This was accomplished by the boundaries extension legislation enacted by Parliament and the Quebec legislature, and was adopted in 1898 and in 1912 pursuant to the Constitution Act, 1871.

Several major rivers flowing into James Bay and Hudson Bay were traditionally used by my people as transportation routes. The territory was inhabited almost exclusively by the Cree people, and for centuries has been quite isolated.

When the James Bay project began in 1971, our people were heavily dependent upon hunting, fishing, trapping, and the harvesting of the natural resources of the land for our livelihood. We were divided into eight Cree bands, four of which had settlements along the James Bay coast, one of which had a settlement on Hudson Bay in the same general location as the Inuit, and three of which were settled inland. The total registered Cree population was 5,638 persons. The Crees shared a common language, common traditions, and a distinct culture.

In summary, at the time of the announcement of the James Bay project we, like our forefathers, occupied and used all of our traditional territory and the resources of that territory. We hunted, fished, and trapped as a way of life and were heavily dependent on the land and the wildlife for our food and subsistence. The Cree peole were able to live off the land despite the fragility of the northern environment. When the James Bay project began, our land was still seen by the white man as a frontier. But we believed that we were still the owners of our traditional lands and that we would not be disturbed in the possession of our lands without our permission.

Announcement of the James Bay Project

When the government of Quebec announced the development of the James Bay territory and, in particular, the James Bay hydroelectric project in the spring of 1971, we were astounded. The subsequent creation of the James Bay Development Corporation to develop all the natural resources of the territory caught us by complete surprise. We were concerned about the devastating impact that this project would have on our way of life, and we were convinced that we were not prepared for development. We were also astounded that our rights and claim to our lands could be so blatantly ignored.

It was clear to us that the government of Quebec intended to proceed with the project regardless of our position. The plans for this massive project demonstrated to us beyond any doubt that the government of

Quebec believed that we had no aboriginal rights and even if such rights did exist they were subordinate to the province's right to develop our traditional lands and territory, even without our consent.

In the spring of 1972, the government of Quebec announced its decision to develop the La Grande hydroelectric complex in the northern portion of our traditional territory. The project involved the generation of over 8,000 megawatts of electric power, the construction of four dams along the La Grande River, the creation of four huge reservoirs and other forebays, the diversion of three major rivers, the flooding of over 3,400 square miles of land, and large increases in the flow of certain rivers. The issue for us was not merely a land claim settlement: It was a fight for our survival as a people and the survival of our way of life.

Opposition of the James Bay Cree

The Crees across northern Quebec organized themselves to fight the project vigorously. In June 1971 we met in Mistassini and passed a resolution asking the minister of Indian affairs and northern development to intervene on our behalf as the trustee of the Indian people. We informed the federal government of our view that we had aboriginal rights to the territory and that the province could not develop our traditional area without our consent. We contended that our way of life was threatened by the project, and we asked the government of Canada to take our side and to act on our behalf. At the same time we made our opposition known to the government of Quebec and to the public. Unfortunately, the Quebec government held firmly to its position that we had no aboriginal rights, and the efforts of the federal government to persuade the government of Quebec to deal with us were unsuccessful.

In April 1972 having exhausted all other recourses, we decided to take the government of Quebec and its agencies to court. We were joined in that decision by the Inuit of Quebec. In May 1972 proceedings were initiated in the Superior Court of Quebec in two separate actions. The first action, against the government of Quebec and Hydro-Quebec, sought a declaration that the provincial James Bay Region Development Act was unconstitutional. The second, against the James Bay Development Corporation and its contractors, requested a permanent injunction to stop the James Bay project.

When first launched in May 1972, both actions reserved native arguments based on personal and usufructuary rights; they were based primarily on constitutional and environmental grounds. In the fall of

1972 we amended our action to allege an infringement of the personal and usufructuary rights of the Crees and Inuit; this issue became the focal point of our battle.

Before describing the James Bay court proceedings, I will set out the positions of the two levels of government on aboriginal rights and give a brief resumé of what transpired in Quebec from 1967 until the announcement of the James Bay project.

The Quebec and Federal Governments

I have already briefly sketched the basic position of the government of Quebec in 1971 on the question of aboriginal rights: in Quebec the Indians did not have an aboriginal right to the exclusive use of land that had been occupied by their forefathers and that was now occupied by them.

Prior to 1971, several meetings had been held between the government of Quebec and representatives of the Indians of Quebec Association (IQA) which represented all the Indian nations of Quebec, including the James Bay Crees. These meetings focused on the aboriginal rights claimed by the Indian people, including hunting, fishing, and trapping rights. At this time the government of Quebec asked the Dorion Commission, (named after its chairman, Mr Henri Dorion), which had been established to review the territorial integrity of Quebec, to study the particular question of Indian rights. The Quebec government recognized that in northern Quebec section 2(C) of the 1912 Quebec Boundaries Extension Act implied a recognition of Indian rights, but it held that those rights were essentially limited to the right to hunt, fish, and trap. It did not accept the argument that the several Indian bands in Quebec still retained aboriginal rights over different parts of the province.

The Dorion Commission came to the conclusion that the Indians had some rights in different areas of Quebec, including northern Quebec. But the commission was also of the opinion that these rights were restricted to hunting, fishing, and trapping rights. The total value of all Indian and Eskimo rights for all of Quebec was estimated by the Dorion Commission to be a maximum of $34 million, from which would be deducted the value of the services rendered to the Indians by the province of Quebec. Lawyers for the provincial government later argued in the James Bay court proceedings that the Cree and Inuit had *no* rights in northern Quebec.

To assess properly the strength of our claim based on aboriginal rights, it must be recalled that in 1971 the official position of the federal government was that aboriginal rights would not be recognized; the Supreme Court of Canada would not hear the *Calder* case until 1973.[1] At the time that we initiated our court proceedings, the British Columbia Court of Appeal had ruled against the Nishga's claim to aboriginal title. Thus, even though we felt strongly that our aboriginal rights were reinforced by the provisions of the 1912 Quebec Boundaries Extension Acts, neither the government of Quebec nor the government of Canada even recognized our aboriginal rights. Moreover, no court in Canada had ever granted an injunction based on a violation of aboriginal rights. The federal government, though sympathetic to our position, considered that it had to maintain an official position of informed neutrality. It agreed to assist us in financing our case, but we received no political support or legal assistance. In October 1972, after we were told by Premier Bourassa that the project was non-negotiable and would proceed, we decided to fight the battle in the courtroom. Our fate now depended on the judicial process.

The James Bay Court Proceedings

It is difficult to summarize the complex legal proceedings of the *James Bay* case. In November 1971 we amended our action and asked for an interlocutory injunction to stop the project immediately. We argued that there had been a violation of Indian title or aboriginal rights, and cited precedents relating to Indian rights in law. The James Bay Energy Corporation, which was to carry out the hydroelectric project, was added as a defendant.

The lawyers for the Quebec government attempted to have our application for an interlocutory injunction dismissed immediately on the ground that we had no aboriginal rights and that it was therefore useless to go into a long hearing. This proved to be a turning-point, since Mr Justice Albert Malouf of the Superior Court of Quebec, who had been assigned to hear the petition, would now have to rule on whether there existed any *apparent* rights on which we could base our case.

The legal arguments lasted over three days. On 8 December 1972, almost two months before the Supreme Court of Canada judgment in the Calder case, Justice Malouf held that the Crees and the Inuit had some apparent rights in the territory; the hearing was allowed to begin. In support of his decision Mr Justice Malouf referred to the 1870 order-in-council admitting Rupert's Land into the union, and particularly section 14 thereof, the 1872 Dominion Lands Act, the Quebec Boundaries Extension Acts of 1912, various orders-in-council relating thereto, and *R. v Sikyea*.[2] He then stated:

The terms used in these various documents, namely: Claims to compensation for lands, Indian title to territory, Indian claims, cessation of their title in the lands, their rights and title to the territory, rights of the Indian inhabitants in the territory, show without doubt that the government of Canada recognized that Indians were entitled to exercise rights in the territory described. To say less than this would render these words meaningless. The position of the government of Canada is also clearly shown in the numerous treaties entered into with the Indians. The Province of Quebec by the Act of April 3, 1912 agrees to recognize the rights of the Indian inhabitants in the territory, and by Bill 50 provided that the rights of Indian communities living in the territory would be respected.[3]

One of the longest interlocutory injunction hearings in Canadian legal history then began. The hearing lasted nearly three months, and over 150 witnesses were heard. Mr Justice Malouf's deliberations lasted almost five months. He considered lengthy legal submissions based on aboriginal rights and the other rights of the Cree and Inuit in northern Quebec, and substantial evidence relating to Cree and Inuit use of and dependence on the land, birth records, the description of the James Bay hydroelectric project, the ecology of northern Quebec, the effect of the project on the environment and on wildlife, and the balance of convenience – the impact of the project on the way of life of the Crees and the Inuit, the demand for energy, and the effect on Hydro-Quebec of halting the project.

In a ruling of over 170 pages rendered on 15 November 1973, Mr Justice Malouf ordered Hyrdo-Quebec, the James Bay Energy Corporation, and the James Bay Development Corporation and their contractors and subcontractors to take the following action:

1 *To immediately cease, desist and refrain from carrying out works, operations and projects in the territory described in the schedule of Bill 50 including the building of roads, dams, dykes, bridges and connected works;*
2 *To cease, desist and refrain from interfering in any way with the rights of the Cree and Inuit petitioners, from trespassing in the said territory, and from causing damage to the environment and the natural resources of the said territory.*[4]

The decision shocked the Quebec Government and the principal developers, Hydro-Quebec, the James Bay Energy Corporation, and the James Bay Development Corporation. With limited exceptions, Mr

Justice Malouf effectively shut down all development in our traditional area. The effect of his judgment was that development by governments and those authorized by them could not proceed in an area that was still subject to outstanding claims of aboriginal rights, even though such development had already begun. Unfortunately, the significance of this judgment was subsequently overshadowed when, a week later, the Quebec Court of Appeal suspended the injunction; because of subsequent legal events, which I will shortly describe, it never became operative again. The suspension was made by virtue of a provision in the Quebec Code of Civil Procedure which allowed the Court of Appeal to suspend provisionally any injunction, even without a hearing. The practical effect of Mr Justice Malouf's judgment, however, was that the corporations building the James Bay project immediately shut down all activities and sent hundreds of workers home while awaiting the final outcome of the legal proceedings.

The Crees consider that Mr Justice Malouf's decision represents one of the most significant judgments on aboriginal rights in modern times. In terms of its practical effects it easily compares to the *Calder*, *Paulette*,[5] and *Baker Lake*[6] decisions, and has had a stronger practical result than either the *Paulette* or *Baker Lake* decisions. In making these remarks I do not intend in any way to underemphasize the consequences of the *Calder* case, which had very favourable consequences for the aboriginal rights claims of native peoples. Nor do I wish to minimize the impact of the *Paulette* and *Baker Lake* decisions. I simply wish to suggest that the Malouf decision does not seem to the Crees to have been assigned the significance it deserves for advancing the claim to aboriginal rights; nor has the significant role the Crees played in advocating the cause of aboriginal rights through the James Bay court proceedings and later through the James Bay and Northern Quebec Agreement been adequately acknowledged.

Although the Quebec Court of Appeal reversed Mr Justice Malouf's decision, the Supreme Court of Canada gave the Crees and the Inuit permission to appeal from the Court of Appeal judgment. However, the case was settled out of court. I will provide some details of this settlement later in this paper. Moreover, the Crees considered it highly unlikely that after its decision suspending the injunction granted by Mr Justice Malouf the Quebec Court of Appeal would uphold his decision on the interlocutory injunction itself. From a practical point of view, doing so would have virtually required a reversal by the Quebec Court of Appeal of a judgment of three of its judges. We were proved right in our speculation, as I shall describe later.

In any event, the judgment of Mr Justice Malouf was the key to the

James Bay and Northern Quebec Agreement. Had we lost that judgment it is highly improbable that the Crees would have obtained anything near what we did through that agreement. The Crees hold today that the agreement is based on the rights found to exist by Mr Justice Malouf. Because of its significance I propose to highlight parts of his decision, spurred on by the realization that there has been relatively little commentary on this judgment to date. The Crees and their advisers have often wondered whether this lack of commentary is in part due to the fact that Mr Justice Malouf's judgment was never reported in English. The French version appeared in the Quebec Practice Reports and was reproduced in its entirety in *La Baie James Indienne*, published by Les Editions du Jour.

It should be noted that by the time of the judgment Mr Justice Malouf had before him the decision of the Supreme Court of Canada in *Calder*. Mr Justice Malouf discussed the *Calder* case, but he was of the opinion that that judgment was not decisive of the issues raised in the James Bay proceedings:

The case of Frank Calder et al. vs. The Attorney-General of British Columbia is the last decision rendered by the Supreme Court of Canada on Indian title. The judgment was pronounced January 31, 1973. Of the seven judges who heard the appeal, three held that the Nishga Tribe of Indians in British Columbia had a right to possess the lands therein described and the right to enjoy the fruits of the soil, of the forest, and of the rivers and streams within the boundaries of the said lands, and that their rights thereto had not been extinguished. Three decided that they had no such rights and therefore were not entitled to a declaratory judgment stating that their rights had never been extinguished, and the seventh judge did not pronounce himself on the merits of the case but simply stated that for a procedural reason the action had to fail. Consequently this decision is not decisive on the issues raised in the judgment.

Mr Justice Malouf pointed out that Mr Justice Judson of the Supreme Court does not say that the Nishga tribe never had any title to the land, but simply that whatever title it did have was extinguished when the government decided to exercise complete dominion over the lands in question. Mr Justice Malouf then gave a summary of the reasons of Mr Justice Hall, and went on to say:

The Calder case is distinguishable from the present case. The Supreme Court was not dealing with any statutory provision which could benefit the Indians. I refer to the statutory provision contained in the

Law of 1912 by virtue of which the Province of Quebec undertook to recognize the rights of the Indian inhabitants to the same extent and obtain surrenders of such rights in the same manner as the government of Canada had previously recognized such rights and obtained surrender thereof. Secondly, I refer to the statement of Judson J. who stated that the sovereign authority in the Calder case elected to exercise complete dominion over the lands in question. In the present case the sovereign authority has never elected to exercise such complete dominion over the lands in question. On the contrary it decided to recognize the rights of the Indians in the manner stated above.

Mr Justice Malouf dealt with the question of the title of the Crees and Indians. He characterized his task as follows:

Petitioners allege that they have a real right in the land, an interest that includes a usufructuary or possessory title. They do not dispute the sovereignty of the Federal Parliament and admit that their rights cannot be alienated except to the Crown. However, they allege that the Province of Quebec cannot develop these lands until a surrender of the Indian rights has been obtained. In order to determine the nature and extent of the Indian title, the court will examine the legislation by virtue of which the Province of Quebec assumed a certain obligation towards the Indians, the historical events prior and subsequent to Confederation, the treaties entered into with the Indians, and the Jurisprudence.

Quoting from *In re Southern Rhodesia,*[7] Mr Justice Malouf said: 'On the other hand, there are indigenous peoples whose legal conceptions, though differently developed, are hardly less precise than our own. When once they have been studied and understood they are no less enforceable than rights arising under English law.' He referred to an important provision in the 1912 Quebec Boundaries Extension Act that covered the area where the James Bay hydroelectric project was to be built. The same provision was in both the federal and provincial statutes that extended the boundaries of Quebec to include not only the northern portion of our traditional area but also the remainder of northern Quebec. He pointed out that in the Act of 1912 the extension of the province was made subject to, inter alia, the condition contained in section 2(C):

That the Province of Quebec will recognize the rights of the Indian inhabitants in the territory above described to the same extent, and will obtain surrenders of such rights in the same manner, as the government of Canada has heretofore recognized such rights and has obtained surrender thereof, and the said province shall bear and satisfy all charges and expenditure in connection with or arising out of such surrenders.

Mr Justice Malouf quoted two federal orders-in-council issued in 1910, which indicated that what the federal government had in mind in enacting section 2(C) of the Quebec Boundaries Extension Act was a treaty along the lines of Treaty 9 in Ontario. He held that it was for the court to decide what those rights were and in what manner the government of Canada obtained surrender thereof. At the time of the Hudson's Bay Company Charter, both the French and the English authorities were concerned about the original inhabitants of this country. It was their desire to recognize the rights of Indians to hunt, fish, and trap on all unoccupied lands. They did not wish to disturb this right except in areas where land was required for the settlement of the white inhabitants, and in such cases treaties were entered into by virtue of which the Indians gave up all or part of the rights they had in those lands. It was the policy of the imperial crown to enter into agreements with the Indians when lands were required for settlement by the white colonists. The Hudson's Bay Company gave effect to this policy by entering into such agreements with the Indians. Mr Justice Malouf cited the cases of *R v White and Bob* in support of that proposition. He then stated that the history of the origin of the Indian title is treated in great detail in the *Calder* case and in the *Wesley* case, and mentioned the instructions to Governor Murray in 1763, the Royal Proclamation of 1763, and various pre-Confederation treaties. He concluded that 'it is clear therefore that prior to Confederation, the right of Indians to hunt and fish on unoccupied Crown lands had always been recognized in Canada (*R. vs. Sikyea*). We will see later that the recognition of the Indian title to the land continued up to the present day.'

Mr Justice Malouf dealt with the post-Confederation period and outlined various constitutional documents, including the imperial order-in-council of 23 June 1870, the Manitoba Act, the Dominion Lands Act, 1872, and the Ontario Boundaries Extension Acts.

The orders-in-council, resolutions, addresses and legislation referred to, all clearly show that the authorities therein mentioned recognized that the Indians had a right and title to the land. When the Imperial Crown transferred Rupert's Land to Canada, the Canadian Government undertook to settle the claims of Indian tribes to compensation for lands required for the purposes of settlement in conformity with equitable principles. In order to give effect to this undertaking, the government of Canada entered into treaties with the Indians whenever it desired to obtain lands for purposes of settlement. When the Canadian Government decided to extend the boundaries of the Provinces of Quebec and Ontario to include additional portions of Rupert's Land it obliged the Provinces of Quebec and Ontario to assume similar obligations towards the Indians. Subsequent to the Law of 1905 the Ontario Government, when it desired to open up certain lands for settlement, entered into treaties with the Indians in accordance with its obligation under the said legislation ... The Province of Quebec has not yet entered into any treaties with the Indians.

He then reviewed pre-Confederation and post-Confederation treaties, and stated 'It is clear, therefore, that the Crown before Confederation and the Canadian Government after Confederation treated all the Indians throughout Canada as having an interest in the land that required a treaty to effect its surrender.' Mr Justice Malouf analysed certain provisions of various treaties and observed that

there is no doubt, therefore, that the government of Canada recognized that the Indians had certain rights and title to the land which were greater than simply the right to hunt and fish therein. In some treaties an absolute right of ownership appears to have been recognized whereas in all the others with the exception of the last two, the government of Canada recognized their rights as being more than simply the right to hunt and fish. In order to pen up the land for settlement or otherwise make use of the land the government of Canada recognized that it was necessary to obtain the consent of the Indians and this consent was obtained through treaties. How else can these treaties be interpreted? If the Indians had no title to the land, why were all these treaties with the various tribes concerning territory in various areas of the country entered into? It is quite clear that in order to extinguish the Indian right, title and interest in the land, the Canadian Government found it necessary to enter into treaties with the Indians and furthermore that their title to the land was at the very least a personal and usufructuary one including rights of hunting, fishing and trapping.

Mr Justice Malouf dealt summarily with the case law relating to Indian title, quoting extracts from the reasons of Ritchie cj and Strong j in the Supreme Court of Canada in *St Catherine's Milling and Lumber Co.* v *The Queen*[8] in relation to Indian title. He cited a part of the 1889 Privy Council decision on the same case,[9] particularly the statement of Lord Watson to the effect that under the Royal Proclamation of 1763 the tenure of the Indians was a personal and usufructuary right dependent on the goodwill of the sovereign. He then cited the case of *R.* v *Wesley*:[10]

Whatever the rights of the Stoney and other Indians were under the Hudson's Bay regime, it is clear that at the time of the making of the treaty to which I shall next allude, the Indian inhabitants of these western plains were deemed to have or at least treated by the Crown as having rights, titles and privileges of the same kind and character as those enjoyed by those Indians whose rights were considered in the St Catherine's Milling Case because it is a matter of common knowledge that the Dominion has made treaties with all of the Indian tribes of the Northwest within the fertile belt in each of which they have given recognition to and provided for the surrender of the Indian title.

Mr Justice Malouf referred to the Supreme Court of Canada and the Northwest Territories Court of Appeal decisions in *R* v *Sikyea* to the effect that the right of Indians to hunt and fish for food on unoccupied crown lands was recognized in Canada in the early days as an incident of ownership of the land and later by the treaties through which the Indians gave up their ownership right in those lands.

Mr Justice Malouf also mentioned the argument as to whether or not the Royal Proclamation applied to the Hudson's Bay Company lands and the statement in *R.* v *Sikyea* that that fact was not important because the government of Canada treated all Indians across Canada, including those living on lands claimed by the Hudson's Bay Company, as having an interest in the lands that necessitated a treaty to effect its surrender.

In his conclusions respecting the nature and extent of the Indian title in the James Bay area Mr Justice Malouf made the following statement:

Since the application presently before me is for an interlocutory order of injunction, it is unnecessary to define the exact nature and extent of the Indian title to the land. Suffice it to say that the material examined in this part clearly shows that at the very least the Cree Indian and Eskimo have been exercising personal usufructuary rights over the territory and the lands adjacent thereto. They have been in possession and occupation of these lands and exercising fishing, hunting and trapping rights therein since time immemorial. It has been shown that the government of Canada entered into treaties with Indians whenever it desired to obtain lands for the purposes of settlement or otherwise. In view of the obligation assumed by the Province of Quebec in the Legislation of 1912 it appears that the Province of Quebec cannot develop or otherwise open up these lands for settlement without acting in the same manner, that is, without the prior agreement of the Indians and Eskimo.

One week later, after only one day of argument, three justices of the Quebec Court of Appeal, in a decision of a few pages, suspended the effect of Mr Justice Malouf's injunction. They held that the works that were the object of the injunction were carried out under a provincial law, which should apply until it had been declared unconstitutional or unless there were absolutely exceptional circumstances. The Court of Appeal stated that the intent of the Quebec legislature in passing that law was to safeguard Quebec interests. The interest of all the people of Quebec must be weighed against the interest of approximately 2,000 of its inhabitants. The court felt that at this stage of the proceedings the balance of interests clearly lay with the defendant corporations who were developing the territory. It therefore granted a suspension of the interlocutory injunction. This judgment meant that work on the James Bay project could proceed.

We knew it would be several months before the Quebec Court of Appeal would rule on the merits of the interlocutory injunction application and that it was highly unlikely it would give us a favourable judgment. We also knew it was doubtful the Supreme Court of Canada would agree to hear an appeal from the judgment of the Court of Appeal. None the less, we felt that we had no choice but to try to appeal to the Supreme Court.

Time was on the side of the developers. The longer the judicial proceedings took, the farther the work would advance, making it more and more unlikely that a court would ever stop the project again. We therefore asked the Supreme Court of Canada for permission to appeal the judgment of the Quebec Court of Appeal. The argument lasted two full days before the five senior judges of the Supreme Court of Canada. In a three-to-two decision, the Supreme Court refused permission to appeal, holding that suspension of the injunction was within the discretion of the Quebec Court of Appeal.[11] Justices Martland and Ritchie, dissenting, felt that there were material issues involved which warranted a determination by the court.

This brings me to the judgment of the Quebec Court of Appeal on the merits of the interlocutory injunction application. The hearing was held in June 1974, and the judgment rendered on 21 November 1974.[12] In passing, I should mention that the Supreme Court judgment had convinced our people and our legal advisers that it was extremely doubtful that we would win in the Quebec Court of Appeal. Furthermore, given what would then be the advanced stage of the project, and the refusal of the Supreme Court of Canada to get involved in the first round, we felt it was doubtful that the Supreme Court would uphold Mr Justice Malouf's judgment, at least in regard to the balance-of-convenience issue. Thus, by the time the Quebec Court of Appeal rendered its judgment we had entered into an agreement in principle in respect to the James Bay project. I will say more about the agreement in principle shortly.

It is interesting to dwell on certain aspects of the Quebec Court of Appeal judgment. The judgment was a unanimous decision of the five-man court. The two principal sets of reasons were delivered by Owen JA and Turgeon JA. In essence, Owen JA was of the opinion that the rights invoked by the Crees and Inuit were not clear and that there was serious doubt about the existence of any right or title of the Cree or Inuit applicants. Owen JA said that it was doubtful, to say the least, whether the Indians or Eskimos had had any rights in the territory since the Hudson's Bay Company Charter of 1670; however, in any event the question of rights or titles would be determined by final judgment. He went on to say that the balance of convenience necessary to obtain an interlocutory injunction favoured the defendant corporations who were developing the territory.

The judgment of Turgeon JA followed very closely the factum of the defendant corporations. He was of the view that the Indians and the Inuit had abandoned the way of life of their ancestors and had adopted the way of life of the white people. He stated further that he had serious doubts about the rights of the Crees and the Inuit and was of the view that the Hudson's Bay Company Charter of 1670 had extinguished any rights the Crees and Inuit had in the territory. He admitted that the 1912 Quebec Boundaries Extension Acts raised difficult and complex questions, but he doubted that the Crees and Inuit had the rights they claimed to have. He also stated that the Indian right is a very fragile right and that, basically, the Crees and Inuit could not have recourse to an injunction, but merely had an action in damages as a result of the works. Turgeon JA also came to a completely different conclusion from Mr Justice Malouf as to the effect of the evidence, and went so far as to say that there was no positive proof that there would not be beneficial ecological changes which would result from the James Bay project. Lajoie JA, Crete JA, and Kauffman JA also agreed that there was serious doubt about the existence of the rights claimed by the Crees and Inuit. Kauffman JA noted, however, that he did not suggest that certain damage to the environment had not already been done, or that more would not occur as time went on, but he was of the view that inundations of large tracts of land were still four years away and he hoped that the basic issues would by then have been decided on their merits.

Leave to appeal from the judgment of the Quebec Court of Appeal was granted by the Supreme Court of Canada on 13 February 1975. However, because the James Bay and Northern Quebec Agreement settled the James Bay court proceedings, there was no final pronouncement on the aboriginal rights of the Crees and the Inuit in the James Bay territory.

James Bay Negotiations

Immediately after Mr Justice Malouf's judgment of 15 November 1973, the Quebec government made an offer of settlement to the Crees and the Inuit. We did not feel that it was a good offer, although it contained some interesting points. In any event, our people remained bitterly opposed to the development project. The decision of the Supreme Court of Canada in December 1973 not to give us permission to appeal the judgment of suspension was a turning-point. We undertook an intensive consultation process with our people and informed them of the offer the Quebec government had made. We also discussed with all the bands the likely outcome of the legal proceedings, the advantages and disadvantages of relying entirely on the courts, and the strengths and weaknesses of our case. Our people decided, reluctantly, to see what could be achieved through negotiation.

The decision to negotiate was based on our conviction that we would lose the case in the Quebec Court of Appeal and probably in the Supreme Court of Canada. We were also worried that a reversal of Mr Justice Malouf's judgment on the merits might seriously undermine our strong negotiating position. Moreover, as the work on the project progressed, our chances of obtaining essential changes to the project decreased. Significantly, despite its financial assistance, the federal government had refused to support our position in court and was urging us in no uncertain terms to negotiate. We feared that if we did not negotiate, even if we should win in the courts, Parliament would respond to political pressures from the Quebec government and would eventually pass a law extinguishing our aboriginal rights.

We were also worried about the lack of definition in the courts' discussion of aboriginal title. The three judges who formed part of the majority in the *Calder* case had refused to pronounce on the content of aboriginal rights, and we could not get around the fact that *Calder*, though a great victory for the Indians, was still a judicial loss. With the changing composition of the court, our lawyers felt that the reasoning of Hall J. would not be followed in the future by the Supreme Court of Canada. In addition, because of the wording of the statutory obligation in the 1912 Quebec Boundaries Extension Act, there was a real possibility that the Supreme Court of Canada would ultimately hold that the rights being contemplated for the Indians and the Inuit were essentially the rights in the numbered treaties. For these reasons the basic decision was to negotiate while at the same time pursuing the legal proceedings as expeditiously as possible. If we could arrive at an acceptable settlement through negotiation, we could then consider whether to terminate the legal proceedings. If negotiations did not produce a satisfactory result, then we would once more rely entirely on the courts. The Inuit agreed with this strategy.

Intensive negotiations led to an agreement in principle. It was clear to us that the agreement in principle was effectively based on Mr Justice Malouf's judgment. Even if we had proceeded with the court proceedings and won, it is doubtful that we could have obtained much more. Our people were consulted for weeks prior to the signing of the agreement in principle, and they determined that it contained the elements of an acceptable settlement.

The fundamental points we felt we had to achieve were the preservation and protection of our traditional way of life; certain modifications to the project to minimize the negative ecological effects; suitable land, hunting, fishing, and trapping rights; control of our own institutions; adequate monetary compensation; and participation in the development of the territory. We felt that the agreement in principle reflected our minimum requirements in these areas and went much further in certain areas. Obviously, there were painful compromises that we had to make. On the whole, however, the agreement in principle, if translated into a final agreement, would guarantee our survival as a people and give us a strong base for the future.

In so far as aboriginal rights were concerned, we agreed that we would surrender all our general claims, rights, titles, and interests in and to land in Quebec in return for specific and defined rights, privileges, and benefits which would be confirmed by federal and provincial legislation. Without question, these were not easy decisions to make. Now, more than eight years after the agreement in principle was signed, we are more than ever convinced that we made the right decision.

The James Bay and Northern Quebec Agreement

The James Bay and Northern Quebec Agreement was signed on 11 November 1975 between the Grand Council of the Crees (of Quebec), the Cree Bands of Quebec, the James Bay Crees, the Northern Quebec Inuit Association, the Inuit of Quebec, and the Inuit of Port Burwell on the one hand and the government of Quebec, the James Bay Energy Corporation, the James Bay Development Corporation, Hydro-Quebec, and the government of Canada on the other. The agreement terminated the James Bay court proceedings.

The James Bay and Northern Quebec Agreement is a lengthy and complicated document. At our insistence technical and legalistic language was used to ensure precision in defining our rights. Claiming rights is one thing; having them recognized is quite another. We were determined that our rights would be written down with as much precision as possible.

In my view the James Bay and Northern Quebec Agreement does not represent an abandonment of aboriginal rights. To the contrary, the agreement recognizes specific and precise claims regarding the land which could have no source other than aboriginal rights. In effect, the agreement says what the various parties mean and accept in so far as Cree aboriginal rights are concerned. The agreement recognizes exclusive native hunting, fishing, and trapping rights over virtually all of our traditional territory. It establishes the right to hunt, fish, and trap all species of animals, fish, and birds everywhere and at all times, with limited exceptions having to do with conservation and public safety. The agreement gives us exclusive hunting and fishing rights in an area of 17,000 square miles, and further imposes specific restrictions and controls on hunting and fishing by non-native people.

Moreover, special hunting, fishing, and trapping rights are given to the Cree over the remainder of their traditional territory. Although these lands are subject to development, they can only be used in a restricted manner by non-Crees, and any lands used for development must be replaced. Furthermore, if there is development in the remainder of the territory, such development will be subject to a special environmental and social protection regime which takes into account the use of the land by the Crees. The Crees also are assured participation in the management of the wildlife of the territory.

The agreement also establishes a system of Cree and Inuit local government and a Cree school board, giving us substantial control over the education of our children; it establishes a Cree regional board of health and social services; it provides for Cree police forces and extensive control over the administration of justice; it provides for various economic and social development measures and for monetary compensation for the Crees from the governments of Quebec and Canada as well as special corporations to manage the compensation. The benefits and provisions of the agreement are in addition to any existing federal and provincial programs and funding that apply to the Crees. Under the agreement, the so-called non-status Crees are treated as Crees.

The foregoing sketch of rights, privileges, and benefits does not do full justice to the benefits that accrue to my people as a result of the James Bay and Northern Quebec Agreement. It may be useful to summarize briefly some of these rights and benefits.

1 The agreement has retained many of the traditional rights and given specific recognition to them.
2 The agreement provides particular mechanisms for the application, enforcement, and protection of those rights.
3 The agreement sets out a system for dealing with future development and a system to minimize future conflicts with the Quebec government and developers.
4 The agreement provides for substantial control by the Crees of education, health, policing, and justice.
5 The agreement provides for an extensive system of Cree local government.
6 The agreement provides for specific economic and social measures as well as a substantial financial base to implement them.

The agreement secures the traditional way of life while allowing those Crees who wish to pursue a new way of life to do so. It also allows for a mixture of the two.

The agreement contains amendment procedures. Six amending agreements have been signed to date, and two separate agreements have emerged as a spin-off of the James Bay and Northern Quebec Agreement. These are the Chisasibi Agreement, which provided for the construction of a new village for the Fort George people, valued at over $50 million, and the Sakami Lake Agreement, which provides for a contribution of over $25 million for the improvement of another Cree community. The monies obtained under these last two agreements are in addition to the monies paid under the James Bay and Northern Quebec Agreement. The James Bay and Northern Quebec Agreement has effected a recognition of aboriginal rights and an exchange of part of those rights for specified other rights. In many respects the agreement represents a definition of the content of the aboriginal rights of the Crees.

As I indicated earlier, the James Bay and Northern Quebec Agreement, consistent with the agreement in principle, effected a cession and surrender of all the native claims, rights, titles, and interests of the Crees in and to land in Quebec. What exactly was surrendered, and what exactly was the nature of the native claim to the land, however, is a matter of future controversy. Further, the federal legislation extinguishing Inuit and native claims, rights, title, and interests in and to the James Bay and northern Quebec territory may also not have effected the extinguishment of aboriginal title, which is a broader concept involving the right to self-government. In any event, even if such aboriginal title has been surrendered or extinguished, it was done in consideration of the two levels of governments and other parties giving, granting, recognizing, and providing to the James Bay Crees and the Inuit of Quebec the rights, privileges, and benefits specified in the agreement.

The agreement as it relates to aboriginal rights, therefore, can be looked upon from a number of viewpoints. Obviously, if the Quebec Court of Appeal's decision had reflected the actual situation, the Cree people gave up nonexistent rights for substantial existing rights. Likewise, if the aboriginal right is merely a right to hunt, fish, and trap, as the *Baker Lake* case seems to indicate, then the James Bay and Northern Quebec Agreement gives the Cree people much more. If the aboriginal right of the Crees amounted to a full and exclusive benefit and right, in all respects, to the land, then it is possible that the agreement does not represent as much as the Crees might otherwise have been able to obtain.

It is arguable that without a negotiated settlement the Crees would not have been able to obtain a comprehensive disposition and gain control of their own government and institutions. It is also arguable that even if the Supreme Court of Canada would have decided that the Crees had aboriginal rights to the full use and benefit of the land in all respects, the Crees still might not have obtained any more than they did under the James Bay and Northern Quebec Agreement. Such a decision might have called forth federal legislation extinguishing such rights in exchange for compensation, and compensation under such legislation might have been less generous than that achieved by the Crees through the James Bay and Northern Quebec Agreement.

In any event, the Supreme Court of Canada has not yet made any substantial pronouncement on aboriginal title since the *Calder* decision. The provincial and federal governments have not yet recognized aboriginal rights as meaning the right to the full use and benefit of the land to the exclusion of all others. The Lubicon Lake Band legal proceedings in Alberta are an example of non-recognition of aboriginal rights by the provincial and federal governments.

I hope the courts will interpret broadly section 35 of the Constitution Act, 1982, but like many other Indian leaders I am worried about the use of the term 'existing' given the uncertain status of the content of aboriginal rights at the time the Constitution Act, 1982, was adopted. At the very least, however, I suggest that the James Bay and Northern Quebec Agreement is a major precedent in support of the view that aboriginal rights are substantial.

Legislative Protection

The James Bay and Northern Quebec Agreement was given effect by parallel federal and provincial legislation – the James Bay and Northern Quebec Native Claims Settlement Act[13] and The Act Approving the Agreement Concerning James Bay and Northern Quebec.[14] Section 3 of the federal statute provides that upon the extinguishment of the native claims, rights, title, and interests the Cree and Inuit beneficiaries under the James Bay and Northern Quebec Agreement shall have the rights, privileges, and benefits set out in the agreement. The provincial legislation contains a similar recognition of such rights. Finally, both the federal and provincial statutes validating the settlement prevail over all other legislation applicable to the territory. In our view this legislation has made the rights, privileges, and benefits under the agreement not only contractual but statutory.

The Test of Time

On the whole, the Crees consider that the James Bay and Northern Quebec Agreement has so far passed the test of time. Despite certain problems of implementation (which have led to some major court cases against the federal and provincial governments) many provisions of the agreement are working well. In the last eight years the Cree people have enjoyed greater financial security and substantially improved living conditions. The traditional way of life continues and actually has been enhanced for many of our people. There has been a dramatic reduction in government interference in our affairs, especially in the areas of hunting, fishing, and trapping. The agreement is an evolving document, and we acknowledge that we must be vigilant in ensuring that our rights under the settlement are properly respected.

Based on our experience, there is no question that when it comes to dealing with the two levels of government it has been easier for us to argue from the basis of the James Bay and Northern Quebec Agreement than it was to argue from the concept of aboriginal rights. The agreement is not perfect. Significant implementation problems must still be solved. We are constantly seeking ways to improve our rights and the general welfare of our people under the settlement. None the less, the advantages of the agreement have to date heavily outweighed the disadvantages of not having the agreement.

Constitutional Protection

At the outset of this paper I mentioned the Constitution Act, 1982. In the opinion of the Crees, the James Bay and Northern Quebec Agreement, although it goes far beyond the 'classical' treaties, is a treaty within the meaning of section 35 of the Constitution Act, 1982. Consequently, in our view, the rights of the Crees under the James Bay and Northern Quebec Agreement are recognized and affirmed by section 35. We may argue in the future that we still retain 'existing aboriginal rights.'

Conclusion

It is my hope that this summary of the history of the James Bay legal proceedings, the James Bay negotiations, and the James Bay settlement will not only help in the understanding of the nature and the content of aboriginal rights but will assist in understanding the practical considerations that must be assessed and applied in dealing with questions of aboriginal rights. Our experience is that it demonstrates the link between the way in which our rights are interpreted and the everyday welfare of our people. It appears to me that the Constitution Act, 1982, even though recognizing existing aboriginal and treaty rights, leaves many problems unsolved. This is undoubtedly one reason that the native peoples across the country, including the Crees of Quebec, are pushing for further constitutional reform.

As a member of a native group that has had to fight for its survival, I can assure you that there is no easy way to achieve success. But I can also assure you that success is attainable. When we look back over ten short years, it is evident that the Crees and other native people have progressed remarkably in their quest for recognition and just implementation of their aboriginal and treaty rights. Although it will be a continuous and most difficult struggle, I think the native people of Canada are moving closer to the day when they will finally receive the special treatment they deserve as the aboriginal occupants of this country.

LEON MITCHELL

Using Mediation
to Resolve Disputes
over Aboriginal Rights:
A Case Study

In 1976 I was appointed mediator in a dispute between a group of five Indian bands from northern Manitoba on the one side and Manitoba Hydro, the Manitoba government, and the federal government on the other. The dispute arose out of the proposed diversion of waters from the Churchill River to the Rat River, the Burntwood River, and the Nelson River. The diversion was to enable Manitoba Hydro to build hydroelectric generating stations. The consequences of this diversion for the Indian bands were serious: hundreds of thousands of square miles of traditional fishing and hunting territory, which constituted their main economic resource, would be damaged to an unknown extent. It was that threatened damage to their subsistence that caused the five Indian bands to come together and form the Northern Flood Committee. Their goal was to stop the project and thus preserve their ability to earn their livelihood in accordance with the traditional Indian life-style and culture.

The area that was to be flooded included some Indian reserve land, which gave the Indian people some bargaining power. According to section 35 of the Indian Act, only the federal government can expropriate Indian lands. When Manitoba Hydro and the Manitoba government demanded that the federal government expropriate this land to enable the generating facilities to be constructed as quickly as possible, the federal government took the position that it would not exercise its expropriation power unless it had the consent of the bands affected. The bands refused to give their consent, and the project was halted.

One of the reasons for the bands' refusal to give their consent was, as I have already mentioned, the potential damage to their lands and livelihood. Another important reason for their refusal was a difference of opinion with the provincial government over rights. The Indian bands maintained that before they would allow the province to damage their property the province must negotiate with them in good faith and come forward with some plan for compensation that would allow them to continue to pursue an independent living. The provincial government took the position that the land was needed for a public purpose, to serve the interest of the majority of the people of Manitoba, and no one group could be allowed to thwart or frustrate the duty and authority of government to serve that interest.

The Manitoba government held that Indians ought not to have greater rights than any other citizens. If the land in question had been the property of an ordinary private owner, the Manitoba government, pursuant to provincial statute, would have had the right to expropriate the land. The government would be obliged to attempt to negotiate an agreement, but if a settlement could not be reached the matter would be referred to arbitration for a final decision. Expropriation proceedings could begin even before the arbitration hearing was held. But the Churchill River project involved Indian bands, a treaty, the Indian Act, and owners over whom the Manitoba government had no authority.

The impasse placed the federal government in an odd conflict-of-interest situation. In the 1960s the government of Canada negotiated an agreement with the province of Manitoba. Under this agreement the province was given permission to divert the Churchill River for the purpose of generating power, and was authorized to construct the necessary hydroelectric generating facilities. Indeed, the federal government had advanced money to the province to enable it to build the requisite transmission lines. In other words, the federal government was a party to the project; yet, when it came to the issue of flooding Indian reserve land, this same federal government, in its role as trustee of Indian lands, said: 'We need the consent of the band before we can authorize you to flood it.'

Lawyers for the Northern Flood Committee reached an agreement with lawyers for the opposing parties to have the matter referred to an arbitrator. The arbitrator, a person acceptable to both sides, would be given full authority to determine the matter of compensation and other issues. When the bands' lawyers presented the agreement to settle by binding arbitration the Indians refused to accept it. They said, in effect, 'We had better get another lawyer because we're not going to allow an arbitrator, particularly a non-Indian arbitrator, to determine our rights to our land or our hunting and fishing rights.'

The bands retained a new lawyer, who had to find a negotiating arrangement that would be acceptable to the Indians – an instrument that would not allow an unacceptable settlement to be imposed on them. The new lawyer sought my advice, and I recommended the use of a form of non-binding mediation. Mediation in this form, in essence, has the parties agreeing to conduct a joint search for a mutually acceptable resolution of the dispute.

I suggest that in a dispute with Indians involving rights, land claims, and treaties, neither arbitration nor the court is an appropriate instrument for resolution of the dispute. There is a vast cultural chasm between Indian people and the dominant majority in this society. That chasm cannot be bridged without effective communication and a willingness on the part of both parties to understand the cultural interests affected by the dispute. Mediation represents an effective instrument for such communication.

Through mediation the Indian bands and the Manitoba government were able to resolve matters that no court or arbitrator would have had the authority or the means to enforce. They arrived at an agreement in December 1977, after twenty-two months of intermittent negotiation. The agreement included significant items that would not normally have been considered by either an arbitrator or a court. One of these items was a reverse-onus provision in damage claims. If an Indian resident claimed damages resulting from the hydroelectric project, it would be up to Manitoba Hydro to prove that it was not responsible for the damages; normally the onus would have been on the Indian claimant to prove that Manitoba Hydro was responsible. This is a major departure from the traditional approach to determining the right to damages.

Another unique term included in the settlement was that the remedy to be given to a claimant (an Indian person, group, or band, which may have a claim as a collectivity) could be in the form of remedial or mitigatory measures rather than in monetary compensation. For example, instead of accepting monetary compensation in settlement of a claim the band could request a remedial measure, such as having a recreation hall built, to improve amenities on the reserve. Another special provision included in the agreement was that Indian people were to be trained and employed as conservation officers by the Manitoba government.

The agreement also provided that the Indians were to have effective representation on a wildlife management advisory committee. The Indians insisted on this provision because they believe no one is in a better position than they are to know what is needed to ensure the conservation of wildlife. Their position was graphically explained to me during one of the mediation meetings on the reserve: 'You white men consider yourselves secure when you have lots of money in the bank; but our security lies in the quantity of wildlife that is available in the hinterland. We don't want you to do things that will diminish our sense of security, like killing our wildlife, wantonly, for sport; we need it for food. Apart from the fact that we don't like sardines, a tin of sardines costs more than we can afford.'

This successful experience with mediation leads me to conclude that in a dispute between Indian people and governments which requires effective communication and which has as it premise that the resolution must be mutually acceptable to all of the parties, mediation is preferable to such other alternatives as reference to a third-party tribunal. An arbitrator or a court would impose a solution to the problem and would have less discretion in the matters that could be included in a solution.

Indian leaders can achieve the greatest gains for their people when they address pragmatic issues rather than legal principles. I will illustrate this point by describing an experience with the Canadian Indian Rights Commission (CIRC). CIRC was established as a forum for the purpose of trying to persuade the federal government to recognize the special rights of Indian people with respect to exemption from taxation, hunting and fishing, free health services, and free education at all levels. I attended a joint meeting of CIRC and a committee of cabinet. Present were senior cabinet ministers, the presidents of provincial Indian organizations, and the president of the National Indian Brotherhood (NIB).

During the course of the meeting the presidents of the provincial Indian organizations and the president of the NIB presented, in a very persuasive manner, the grounds on which they based their claim that treaty Indians are entitled to free education at all levels. Allan MacEachen, one of the cabinet members present, said that it would be impolitic for the federal government to recognize, for all time, this special right for Indian people. The government was prepared, however, to offer maximum access to free education, at all levels. The Indian representatives noted that the purpose of CIRC was to get rights recognized, not to negotiate compromises of rights. Furthermore, they feared that if they accepted any compromise it would be taken as a precedent indicating that Indian people had abandoned their firm belief in their absolute right to free education. After the Indian leaders had expressed this view, Marc Lalonde asked the Indian representatives if they could accept a government proposal of maximum access to free education with a proviso that this would in no way affect the continued assertion of their right to free education, at all levels, as a matter of treaty rights. The offer was not accepted.

In terms of the day-to-day needs of the Indian people, the offer of the federal government was a generous one. It would have contributed substantially to meet those needs. However, in terms of aboriginal rights, acceptance of the federal government's offer would have qualified the Indian claim no matter what proviso was inserted. So this question arises: what is possible for Indians in attaining rights from a dominant society that is non-Indian; from politicians who, in order to retain power, must retain the support of the electorate? The net result of the joint meetings with the cabinet ministers was frustration on the part of the National Indian Brotherhood. When it became clear that no progress would be made in obtaining recognition of Indian rights the NIB withdrew, and the commission was dissolved.

From the ashes of the Canadian Indian Rights Commission rose the Indian Commission of Ontario, composed of representatives from the four Ontario Indian organizations, the government of Ontario, and the federal government. This tripartite instrument was established for the purpose of addressing issues of mutual concern to all three parties. The commission agreed to discuss hunting and fishing, reserve policing, services to bands, lands and resources, wild-rice harvesting and Indian land claims, of which there were no fewer than six hundred. What has the commission accomplished since its formation? Admittedly, no Indian land claim has been settled, but important practical issues have been addressed and agreements have been negotiated. An agreement on policing Indian reserves and establishing an Indian Police Commission in Ontario was signed by all parties. Another agreement, reached after several years of dispute, resulted in an amendment to Ontario fishing regulations which confers some special rights on Indians.

An attempt by the Indian Commission of Ontario to establish a viable wild-rice industry has not succeeded. When discussions on this topic began the Indian representatives indicated that they had an absolute and exclusive right to harvest wild rice. The federal government representatives refused to accept that position. Thereupon the Indian representatives, through the Indian Commission of Ontario, delivered to the federal government an official copy of Treaty 3; in that treaty words affirming the right to 'ricing' appeared. Inexplicably, in the Treaty 3 documents of the Canadian government, the word 'ricing' does not appear. When this information was forwarded to the minister of Indian affairs, John Munro, he sent a letter in August 1980 to the government of Ontario informing them that in the light of the new information the federal government was obliged to take a different view from that taken until then regarding Indian rights to ricing. For over one hundred years the federal government had based its policy on Indian rights to ricing on a questionable document.

Despite its modest achievements, the experience of the Indian Commission of Ontario is encouraging. It has demonstrated that when practical issues are addressed, progress can be made in meeting some of the needs of Indian people. If we insist on the position that we must first agree on the principles underlying aboriginal rights before we address the practical issues, then it will be difficult if not impossible to obtain a consensus between the non-Indian and Indian points of view. The Indian people know what aboriginal rights are; non-Indian people do not. I am concerned about how aboriginal rights will come to be defined in a constitution written by non-Indian politicians, in English, to be interpreted by non-Indian judges. It may be wiser for Indians to establish their aboriginal rights through discussion and negotiation rather than through the courts, and by implementing pragmatic policies rather than by litigating principles and constitutional definitions.

DOUGLAS SANDERS

Aboriginal Rights: The Search for Recognition in International Law

Indigenous people have repeatedly sought support for their aboriginal rights beyond the borders of the nation-state within which they live. The appeals of Canadian Indians to the United Kingdom and to international bodies over the constitutional reform issues is one of the most remarkable examples of the use of this strategy.[1]

A supranational strategy for recognition of rights is not normally available to minority groups. International interest cannot be assumed, because international concern for minorities has an uneven history. Traditionally, minority-rights questions were seen as 'domestic' issues and therefore beyond the reach of international law. This has never been wholly true, but it has been a major theme in traditional international law. Minority-rights questions were a major concern of the League of Nations, but the only concrete action taken was the protection of specific minorities in the European peace treaties that were signed after the First World War. Even this limited incursion into the protection of minorities was not fruitful. The league efforts were seen as a failure. Minority-rights concerns were effectively discredited by the international community of nations for over two decades.[2]

Indigenous minorities have certain advantages in pursuing a supranational strategy. First, the 'noble red man' has a strong and enduring image outside the Americas. The Indians were the first indigenous population to be encountered by European colonizers, and came to play a unique role in European romanticism. Second, indigenous minority populations have the strongest moral claims to unique status and special rights of any definable population grouping. Their lands were taken, and their economies were often destroyed. Europeans created new nation-states and relegated the indigenous population to the lowest economic and social levels. Even in the western industrial democracies indigenous people often lead marginal existences, and in parts of South America they are still subject to cultural annihilation and genocide. Third, indigenous populations have certain legal and political arguments not available to other minority populations. Indigenous populations became minorities as a result of colonial expansion. A major period of decolonization of overseas territories is now coming to an end, and indigenous populations are arguing for an extension of decolonization principles to themselves. This would result in the formalization of systems of local autonomy rather than the achievement of full independence. While the international-law materials recite the proposition that the principle of 'self-determination of peoples' does not apply to minorities, indigenous minorities can argue that they are not simply minorities but victims of colonialism.

The supranational activity of Canadian Indians can be somewhat arbitrarily divided into appeals within the imperial structures of the British empire and appeals to international institutions such as the League of Nations and the United Nations. Both strategies have been followed by indigenous populations in Australia, New Zealand, and Canada.

Appeals within Imperial Structures

Canadian Indians have been given strong doses of British monarchical culture. Alexander Morris, the primary negotiator of the western treaties, was a devoted son of empire. He unblushingly praised the Great White Mother who lived across the seas. When the Indian leader Kamooses asked Morris if his child would be troubled by the queen, he was told that the 'Queen's power will be around him.'[3] Instruction in the Anglican mission school on the Blood reserve in southern Alberta stressed the British tradition:

Every week, S.H. instructed the advanced students for half an hour on 'the duties of British citizenship' and strongly encouraged patriotism among the Bloods. Portraits of King George v and Queen Mary were hung in the school's big dining room, and the Union Jack was flown every Sunday. S.H. even taught his students to eat as they did in the 'Old Country.' 'Stay with your British teaching,' he told them. 'The fork is a left-hand instrument.'[4]

The British praise of the crown as the font of justice logically led the Indians to petition the crown for protection against the actions of the local settler population. In 1906 three important chiefs from British

Columbia went to England to meet Edward VII. A second British Columbia delegation visited the king in 1909, after an attempt had been made to dispossess some Indians near Prince Rupert. The Nishga tribe had a London law firm draw up a petition to serve as a basis for a hearing before the Judicial Committee of the Privy Council (the body which served as the final court of appeal for the countries of the British empire). The petition was forwarded to the Canadian government in 1913 and to English authorities in 1918. The strategy of the tribes of British Columbia, down to the special joint committee hearing on their claims in 1927, was to seek a judicial hearing in England.[5]

An unknown number of written petitions were submitted by Indians to the crown. Here is the text of one petition presented to the king in 1907:

To: The King's Excellent Majesty
  Most Gracious Sovereign

We your local subjects of the western portion of your Empire do hereby appear again before His Majesty personally wish to express to your Majesty our strong allegiance to your Crown and Dignity. That we your children have a grievance which cannot be settled by your Majesty's Dominion Government.

Many years ago the late Sir James Douglas came to our country when the Province of British Columbia was under Crown Government and have granted to us small plots of land to all the various tribes in British Columbia.

Now all these are nearly entirely taken away from us but very small portions remaining.

Which we really regret for our lands have been taken away from us. And praying that your Majesty may be graciously pleased to take the petition into consideration and to signify your Royal pleasure as to grant us and appoint where we settle the affair if it is the Dominion Government at Ottawa.

New Westminister, British Columbia
May 27, 1907.   *[three signatures]*

Such a petition could not be effective. The Department of Indian Affairs reported to the Canadian cabinet that no lands had been taken from the Indians in British Columbia. The king was informed that if the Indians presented specific grievances to the Department of Indian Affairs, those grievances would be dealt with and given 'due consideration.'

The idea that there could be imperial intervention in indigenous policy in Canada was no Indian invention. The Royal Proclamation of 1763 represented imperial recognition of Indian political and territorial rights against local 'frauds and abuses.' The Select Committee of the British House of Commons on Aborigines (British Settlements), which reported in 1837, urged that jurisdiction over indigenous policy be kept out of the hands of local settlers in order to protect indigenous populations. The order-in-council admitting Rupert's Land and the Northwest Territory to Canada in 1870 specified that Indian claims were to be dealt with by Canada 'in communication with the Imperial Government.' British colonial officials cautioned local British Columbia officials that mistreatment of the Indians would cause political problems in Britain (for the Aborigines Protection Society was active there as a humanitarian lobbying organization).[6] The 1871 terms of union of British Columbia and Canada provided that any disagreement between Canada and British Columbia in relation to Indian reserve lands could be arbitrated by the British secretary of state for the colonies.

The early petitions were forgotten and the Indian confidence in the crown came to be seen as naïve. The Indians had accepted the major symbol of British political culture and clung to it through decades of ill treatment by Canadian society. The granting of an honorary Kainai chieftainship to the Prince of Wales in 1919 can be understood as part of the surge of patriotism that followed the First World War; but the pattern was continued. Honorary chieftainships were granted to governors-general in 1931, 1936, 1951, 1952, and 1970. Lieutenant-governors of Alberta were inducted in 1951, 1967, and 1976. The Prince of Wales was inducted in 1977. Other honorary chieftainships have been granted to the queen's representatives: Viscount Alexander was made Chief Nakupunkim in a 1946 ceremony in Vancouver witnessed by thousands of people.[7] The Indian devotion to the crown has continued, though few Canadians now take the monarchy seriously. Canadian Indians attended the coronation of Elizabeth II in 1953. Chief William Scow, representing the Native Brotherhood of British Columbia, was seated in full regalia in Westminister Abbey for the ceremony.[8] Indians travelled to England on the centennial of Treaties 6 and 7 in 1976:

Six Alberta Indian chiefs and their wives, in full traditional dress, went to Buckingham Palace ... for an audience with the Queen. The Queen, in jolly mood, entertained them in a groundfloor reception room overlooking the sweeping palace gardens. The chiefs conveyed greetings on the 100th anniversary of two important Indian treaties signed with Queen Victoria, 'The Great White Mother'. The Indian party was accompanied to the palace by Canadian High Commissioner, Paul Martin. The party was led by Lt. Gov. Ralph Steinhauer of Alberta, a Cree Indian chief.[9]

These actions seem non-political, even reactionary. But they kept alive the possibility of petitioning the crown by reaffirming a special link to the monarchy.

In the 1950s a dispute arose over membership in the Samson Band in Alberta. The government alleged that certain individuals were not entitled to Indian status because their fathers or grandfathers had accepted half-breed scrip. One of them voiced the feeling that if only the queen knew what was happening, she would not allow them to be stripped of their rights. This statement prompted their lawyer to communicate with the queen. A letter was forwarded to the governor-general who, on instructions from the government of Canada, did not forward it to England. John Diefenbaker, then the leader of the opposition, raised the matter in the House of Commons and denounced the government for interfering with a citizen's communication with the queen. The story now seems just an amusing anecdote, but it was part of a political strategy of publicizing the dispute.

It is standard practice during every royal visit to Canada to show off some Indians. Gradually, Indian leaders began to use these occasions as a forum for political statements. In 1970 the queen presented commemorative medals to four chiefs at The Pas, Manitoba. Following the presentation, David Courchene, the head of the Manitoba Indian Brotherhood, spoke:

It is with sorrow we note that the promises of peace and harmony, of social advancement and equality of opportunity have not been realized by Indian people ... we would ask that you see for yourself the results of a century of deprivation and ask that you advocate on our behalf to your loyal ministers, the need for greater understanding on their part, the need to provide for greater participation of Indian people in the decision making process of our society and the need for tolerant understanding in our negotiations.[10]

In 1973 the queen again visited Canada. In Regina Chief David Ahenakew, head of the Federation of Saskatchewan Indians, gave a speech in her presence. The pattern was repeated in Calgary by Harold Cardinal, the head of the Indian Association of Alberta. The queen replied, reading a text prepared jointly by the federal government and the Indian Association of Alberta. The queen acknowledged that many Indian people had been left to live in 'poverty and distress,' and added:

You may be confident of the continued cooperation of my government which represents your people as it represents all the people of Canada. You may be assured that my government of Canada recognizes the importance of full compliance with the spirit and terms of your treaties.

I am deeply impressed with the pride of heritage which has sustained you through so many dramatic changes and difficulties. I hope this very sense of identity will help you find on your own a truly Indian place in the modern world.[11]

In 1975 the Prince of Wales visited the Northwest Territories. Chief Frank T'Seleie attempted to give the prince a petition dealing with Dene land claims, but was prevented from doing so by the commissioner of the Northwest Territories. The commissioner's action proved controversial, and the petition, in the end, was sent by mail to the prince.[12]

In 1978 the National Indian Brotherhood (NIB) sought involvement in the constitutional revision process. In August the NIB announced that if it did not get recognition in Canada, a delegation of chiefs and elders would go to England and petition the queen directly. They would urge her to block patriation and amendment of the Canadian constitution until Indian rights were recognized in a new constitutional document.

The NIB was invited, as an observer, to the first ministers' conference in October 1978. The next first ministers' conference, in a closed meeting in February 1979, added 'Canada's native peoples and the constitution' to a dozen other constitutional agenda items. The NIB, denied involvement at the level of the first ministers' conference went ahead with the planned trip to England. The Conservative government of Prime Minister Joe Clark had to deal with the issue in its first cabinet meeting. The prime minister asked the queen not to meet with the Canadian Indian delegation. Editorial comment in Canada criticized the government's decision to block the meeting. In the end, some two hundred Indians made the trip. They met with the leader of the opposition, members of the House of Commons and the House of Lords, various high commissioners, and a senior official in the Foreign Office.[13]

Alberta Indians, remembering the side-show treatment given them by the London press in 1976, did not make the trip to England in 1979. Instead, they met with the queen's representative in Canada, the governor-general. This alternative had been put forward by the government in its only serious effort to divert the Indians from the London

298   Douglas Sanders

strategy. Alberta Indians met with Governor-General Edward Schreyer at the Alexander Reserve near Edmonton on 19 July 1979. The Indians made lengthy, detailed presentations. The governor-general stated that he could not participate in political discussions, but noted that there was a lot of 'unfinished business' between the Indians and the federal government. He was given a head-dress and the name 'Eagle Chief.'[14]

The last stages of Indian lobbying in England with respect to the patriation and reform of the Canadian constitution involved direct dealings with members of Parliament and litigation in the courts. The treaty link with the queen was emphasized in these arguments in order to establish that residual crown obligations rested with Britain as the imperial power. The strategy of petitioning the crown was the preliminary stage in a complex lobbying effort which delayed patriation and led to Indian questions dominating the final debates in the British House of Commons and House of Lords.

International Appeals

No minority-rights provisions were written into the Covenant of the League of Nations because Australia and New Zealand wished to avoid any international scrutiny of their treatment of aborigines and Maoris.[15] Nevertheless, attempts were made by Indians and Maoris to gain access to the League to protest their treatment by national governments. Dr René Claparede, the head of an international support group, the International Bureau for the Defence of Indigenous Peoples, recounted the origins of the bureau:

Before the foundation of this International Bureau, there were already in several countries societies for the protection of native races of which the Anti-Slavery and Aborigines Protection Society of London is the oldest, the most active and the best known.

A League was founded in Switzerland in 1908, in order to inform our public on the atrocities committed in the Congo of Leopold II. This and other isolated Leagues, without any connection with each other, could only have a feeble and insufficient scope of action, but in 1913 the visit of a noble woman, Mrs. Harris, who had passed several years in the Congo, and who had since then undertaken an extensive journey of enquiry in Africa, came to stir up in our country public opinion that had become asleep, and to make us understand the importance of those questions ... Unfortunately, the war broke out shortly afterwards and paralyzed the work at its very beginning. After the termination of hostilities by the various peace treaties ... a large committee was

formed, comprising among its members some eminent jurists, and the
Bureau was given its present designation – Bureau International pour la
Défense des Indigènes (B.I.D.I.).

  The exploitation of natives in Africa, in South America, in Asia and
Australasia takes different forms, from the ancient form of classical
slavery to the more modern forms of disguised slavery, such as
indentured labour, compulsory public work and peonage (or slavery for
debts). Examples abound and it would be easy to give a whole list but
that would unnecessarily lengthen this letter.

  It is important that such a Bureau should exist at Geneva which is
not merely the seat of the League of Nations but also the seat of many
other international institutions, such as the Red Cross.[16]

The existence of such support groups is important in any supranational
strategy. BIDI played a significant support role in the visit to Geneva of
Deskaheh, a leader of the Six Nations Iroquois Confederacy. Much later,
the English organization Survival International was important in
facilitating the Canadian Indians' constitutional lobby in London.

  The Iroquois Confederacy, whose people live in parts of the United
States and Canada, has pioneered much of the international activity of
indigenous peoples. In the early colonial history of North America, the
Iroquois Confederacy was a major regional power. The Confederacy was
an ally of colonial powers and insisted on the political independence
signified by that relationship. After the Revolutionary War, a major part
of the Iroquois population emigrated to Canada. Because they had been
allies of the British, they were rewarded with land grants in Canada.
Canada treated them as coming under Canadian sovereignty and
classified their lands as Indian reserves under the Canadian Indian
Act. The Iroquois Confederacy did not accept that definition of their
situation.

  In 1922 Deskaheh presented a petition to the Dutch ambassador to
the United States, asking that it be forwarded to the League of Nations.
Deskaheh spent much of 1923 and 1924 in Geneva meeting diplomats
and arguing the Iroquois case. The governments of the United Kingdom
and Canada went to some lengths to prevent the questions from being
discussed within the League. The Netherlands did forward the petition
to the secretary-general, asking that it be communicated to the council
of the League. When that initiative had been successfully stalled, four
League members (Ireland, Panama, Persia, and Estonia) revived the
question by writing to the president of the League's assembly asking
that the petition be communicated to the assembly and asking for an
advisory opinion from the Permanent Court of International Justice as

to whether the Iroquois Confederacy was a state. In December 1923 the Persian member of the League's council asked that the matter be put on the agenda of the council. Each of these three attempts to have the petition considered was stopped by diplomatic intervention. The government of Canada prepared a reply to the Iroquois allegations, which was published in the official journal of the League.

While Deskaheh was still in Europe, the Canadian government dissolved the traditional council at the Six Nations Reserve and established a new elected band-council system. Since the confederacy supporters refused to participate in the new system, this had the effect of depriving Deskaheh of his right to speak for the confederacy, at least according to Canadian law. The fight was not abandoned. Confederacy representatives continued to attend international meetings and sent a delegation to San Francisco at the time of the founding of the United Nations in 1945.[17]

The United Nations, unlike the League of Nations, was committed by its charter to the promotion of human rights and fundamental freedoms. No minority-rights provisions appear in the charter or in the 1949 Universal Declaration of Human Rights. The Human Rights Commission established pursuant to the charter is an organ of the Economic and Social Council; the commission early ruled that it did not have the authority to hear or consider complaints of denials of human rights coming from private individuals rather than from member states of the United Nations. Lists of such petitions were kept, and the documents in the John Humphrey Human Rights Collection at McGill University show that complaints from Indian individuals or groups in North America were regularly received. Three Indians representing the North American Indian Brotherhood, a regional organization in British Columbia, took a petition to the United Nations in 1953. John Humphrey, a Canadian and the head of the Human Rights Division, advised them that they would have to deal directly with the government of Canada.

The opening for indigenous peoples in post-war international law proved to be in the fight against racial discrimination. Racial discrimination is condemned in the United Nations charter and in the Universal Declaration of Human Rights. In 1963 the general assembly adopted the Declaration on the Elimination of All Forms of Racial Discrimination, and in 1965 it approved the text of the International Convention on the Elimination of All Forms of Racial Discrimination, which came into force in 1969. More than a hundred states are signatories to the racial-discrimination convention. The Subcommission on the Prevention of Discrimination and the Protection of Minorities (established under the Human Rights Commission) initiated a study of racial discrimination in a number of countries. A 1970 draft of the report identified the need for a 'complete and comprehensive study' of discrimination against indigenous peoples. In 1971 the Economic and Social Council authorized the subcommission to initiate that study. The work has proceeded slowly and the text is not yet complete, though draft sections have circulated for a number of years.

In 1978 the United Nations Conference on Racism, held in Geneva, considered the plight of indigenous peoples, primarily at the initiative of the Norwegian delegation. The final statement approved by the conference included the following passage:

8 *The Conference urges States to recognize the following rights of indigenous peoples:*

(a) To call themselves by their proper name and to express freely their ethnic, cultural and other characteristics;

(b) To have an official status and to form their own representative organizations;

(c) To carry on within their areas of settlement their traditional structure of economy and way of life; this should in no way affect their right to participate freely on an equal basis in the economic, social and political development of the country.

(d) To maintain and use their own language, wherever possible, for administration and education;

(e) To receive education and information in their own language, with due regard to their needs as expressed by themselves, and to disseminate: regarding their needs and problems.

This statement, together with other resolutions of the conference, was adopted by the general assembly in the fall of 1978. The topic of indigenous populations was raised in at least one regional United Nations conference on racism and in the second Geneva conference in August 1983. In 1982 the Subcommission on the Prevention of Discrimination and the Protection of Minorities established a working group on indigenous populations. The working group, whose members are drawn from the subcommission, will meet every summer in Geneva in advance of the meetings of the subcommission.

These slow institutional developments have occurred in a period of increasing domestic and international support for minority rights, and in a period in which indigenous people have developed more broadly based international patterns of activity. In 1974 the American Indian Movement established the International Indian Treaty Council. In 1975 the World Council of Indigenous Peoples was formed, with the sponsorship of the National Indian Brotherhood. The Inuit Circumpolar Conference first met in 1977 and was formally established in 1980. The organization of Non-governmental Organizations (bodies accredited by the Economic and Social Council of the United Nations) held two human rights conferences in Geneva in 1977 and 1981, led by members of the International Indian Treaty Council. The legal group that did work for these conferences developed into the Indian Law Resource Centre. Five bodies now have non-governmental organization status at the United Nations: the World Council of Indigenous Peoples, the International Indian Treaty Council, the Indian Law Resource Centre, the Inuit Circumpolar Conference, and a newer group representing four Indian groups in the United States and Canada, the Four Directions Council. These organizations participate in a continuing forum at the annual meetings of the working group on indigenous populations. After two or three years of discussion, the Canadian government has now established an 'indigenous desk' in the Department of External Affairs.

A Forum or a Process?

It is common wisdom that the queen and the United Nations are powerless. Is the goal of supranational strategies simply 'political theatre' – the search for an international forum in which the nation-state can be embarrassed? Clive Linklater, the primary organizer of the 1979 chiefs' trip to London, has said that the chiefs went to England in order to get a hearing in Canada. But as the London lobby developed, it appeared possible that a coalition of British members of Parliament who supported the Indians or the provinces (along with a few others who thought Prime Minister Pierre Trudeau was a communist) could lead to the defeat of the Canada Act. We now know that Prime Minister Margaret Thatcher warned Prime Minister Trudeau that the Canada Act could be in trouble in the British Parliament if the Canadian government pressed ahead against the strong domestic opposition that existed in 1980–1. The 'Indian sections' in the final constitutional package without question made the Canada Act easier to sell in the British Parliament. In retrospect, the Indian lobby in London was designed to influence both Canada and Britain.

A similarly complex state of affairs exists internationally. Autralian aborigines appeared before the Human Rights Commission in 1980 to denounce the mining of sacred sites at Nookanbah; the Australian government was embarrassed, even though it was clear that the commission could and would do nothing. The tactic of international accusations serves both the short-term goal of applying pressure on the nation-state and the long-term goal of developing international standards.

Indigenous populations persist in the belief that their rights are not simply a matter for domestic law. Well-meaning advisers have in the past often tried to steer them away from petitions to the crown or appeals at the international level. But the expert's vision of what is possible has proved faulty. Only by ignoring advice and persisting in their beliefs have indigenous peoples initiated changes in the Canadian constitution and in international law.

RUDOLPH RYSER

Fourth World Wars: Indigenous Nationalism and the Emerging New International Political Order

The descendants of ancient nations exist in the shadows of the massive, modern states that surround them and exploit them. In fulfilment of ancient prophecies uttered by Hopi, Naga, Basque, Cree, Saami, and Kanak thinkers, fourth-world indigenous nations are re-emerging as independent states in their own right. A new international political order, based on concepts of diversity and decentralization, is evolving under the influence of a global political movement led by indigenous populations. Modern states are slowly, reluctantly, yielding to the increasing demands of indigenous populations who seek to regain their natural place in the family of nations.

The desire of indigenous peoples to reclaim their nations as separate and distinct from neighbouring peoples has begun to shake the stability of many states. Some nationalist movements of indigenous peoples threaten to dismember the large artificial states that surround them, thus giving rise to the formation of many small states.

Through political activism and violent revolution, indigenous peoples have come into direct confrontation with states on every continent to challenge their expanding economic, social, military, and political power. Such confrontations, combined with increasing evidence that large states can no longer manage and control their domains, promise to alter boundaries, eliminate existing states, and change, once again, the structure of global human organization.

In the sweep of time, human history has seen the rise and fall of great states. The empires of Maya, Egypt, Rome, Inca, Ottoman, and Britain grew and then declined. Each in its time came to surround and control vastly diverse peoples. Yet despite the establishment of extensive political networks and complicated methods for controlling the empire, these massive systems of human organization were destined to collapse into simpler forms of social organization. The organization that endures best among human beings is the small group ranging in size from perhaps four hundred individuals to not more than a few hundred thousand. Diverse, adaptable, flexible, and strongly supportive of the human spirit, the most successful unit of human organization has been, and continues to be, the small community or nation.

Peoples who make up small nations, and the customs they practise, are often regarded by larger societies and empires as primitive, barbaric, and savage. Small nations have been dominated, rearranged, dismembered, eliminated, and otherwise destroyed by large states. Yet despite these acts of brutality, human beings continue to group themselves into small societies in unconscious recognition that small nations are the most comfortable and efficient form of human organization.

Unlike the large artificial states created as a consequence of colonization (most of which were created only during the last two hundred to five hundred years), indigenous peoples make up natural nations descended from the ancient beginnings of humankind. Artificial states such as France, Great Britain, Canada, the United States of America, and the Union of Soviet Socialist Republics have been superimposed like a global patchwork quilt, over the ancient world of original nations. These large states have imposed their will on indigenous nations and claimed world supremacy in the same spirit as earlier empires.

The French state was imposed on the smaller nations of Alsatians, Basques, Bretons, Normans, Kanaks, Polynesians, and Catalans. In what is now called Great Britain we find the smaller nations of the English, Scots, Irish, Cornish, Welsh, Manx, and many others colonized by Britain. Canada and the United States of America were superimposed over the ancient nations of Bella Coola, Shuswap, Cree, Hopi, Dene, Chippewa, Lakota, Aleute, Cheyenne, and Seminol. Other states, such as Peru (imposed on part of the Quecheua and Aymara nations) and Nicaragua and Honduras (imposed on the Miskito, Sumo, and Rama nations), were established on top of ancient nations that had existed in their territories thousands of years before the idea of these states was conceived.

Of the indigenous nations present on each continent, many are now engaged in political or violent conflict with the state that surrounds them. They seek to regain their national identity as autonomous or independent nations. Their struggle to be free from the dominating influence and control of a state has begun to tear apart the patchwork quilt and to add to the instability of large states.

In the Middle East, Lebanon is split into warring factions of indigenous groups. The Kurds, who share territory and boundaries with the

Soviet Union, Iran, Iraq, Syria, and Turkey, continue to challenge those states' political authority within Kurdish territory. The indigenous Basques seek to separate their homelands from Spanish control, and their sometimes violent challenges to Spain's authority continue to destabilize that state.

Since the end of the Second World War, indigenous nations have engaged in political and military confrontations with no fewer than one hundred of the world's artificially established states. Engaged in 'cold wars' and 'hot wars', indigenous nations are a major factor affecting the future of states and the future of peaceful international relations.

Indigenous nationalism became increasingly manifest during the active United Nations–sponsored decolonization period that began in 1960. During this period colonial Africa and South Asia saw the creation of many new states. The boundaries and governmental systems of those new states were often the same as those that existed during the colonial period. The imposition of the new artificial states stirred rather than stilled indigenous nationalist passions.

Indigenous nationalist movements were rekindled. They took several forms: some were separatist or independence movements; others began as movements for increased regional autonomy within an existing state; still others are irredentist – they seek to change state borders and political authority to accommodate their traditional indigenous cultural boundaries. In all cases, indigenous nationalism was largely motivated by the need to reassert land or territorial rights, and to reclaim a national identity, often expressed as cultural identity. Whether characterized as separatist/independent, regional autonomy, or irredentist, each indigenous group uses political or military confrontation (or a combination of both) to secure its nationalist goals.

Indigenous Hot Wars

Indigenous nations are involved in many of the regional hot wars that have flared up around the world since the end of the Second World War. During 1982, indigenous nations were involved in twenty of the forty-five wars raging in the world. In Europe, Central and South Asia, the Middle East, Africa, the western Pacific Ocean, and central and South America, and along the borders of the Soviet Union, indigenous peoples waged wars with states. Some of the competing forces in these confrontations are shown in table 1.

In 1983, the Center for Defense Information in Washington reported that during the thirty-eight years following the end of the Second World War, more than 16 million people had been killed in civil wars and wars between states. The magnitude of human killing during this period of 'peace' exceeds that of the First World War, when an estimated 10 million people lost their lives. The total loss of life during little more than three decades represents more than one-third of the total loss of life during the Second World War. Indeed, the post–Second World War generation of 'peace' has been as costly as any world war in terms of human misery.

TABLE 1
States and indigenous nations at war

States	Indigenous nations
Nicaragua and Honduras	Miskito, Sumo, and Rama
El Salvador	Pipil
Guatemala and Mexico	Mayan, Zapotec, and Mixe
Indonesia	Timorese, Papuans, and Moluccans
Philippines	Kalinga, Bontoc, Morazan, and Sabah
India	Naga, Sikhs, Misoram, and Kachins
Sri Lanka	Tamil
Brazil	Yananomu
Malaysia	Sarawak and Sabah
Lebanon	Maronites, Palestinians
South Africa	Ovimbundu, Harrah (Namibia), and Bantu
Syria, Iraq, Iran, Turkey, and Russia	Kurds
Spain	Basques
Italy	Corsicans and Sardinians
Israel	Palestinians
Iran and Pakistan	Baluchis
Turkey	Armenians
Afganistan and Pakistan	Pathans
Afganistan and Russia	Pathans, Tadziks, and Turkmen
Burma and Thailand	Karens
Ethiopia	Eritrea, Tigre, Somalis, Hara, and Wollo
Morocco and Mauritania	POLISARIO, a political movement (West Sahara)

The weight of human misery has fallen especially hard on indigenous nations since the beginning of the 1960s. In the twenty hot wars in which indigenous nations are participants, they are either direct combatants against a state or targeted non-combatants in wars where organized rebel forces seek to overthrow the governing authorities of a state. From 1960 to 1983 more than four million indigenous people were killed. The grim reality of this figure is that indigenous population deaths represent more than 25 per cent of the deaths from all wars since the end of the Second World War. The number of human lives lost among indigenous nations equals the devastation suffered by indigenous peoples in an earlier period when Christian European states colonized and exploited vast territories. John Bodley has written, 'It might be conservatively estimated that during the 150 years between 1780 and 1930 world tribal populations were reduced by at least 30 million ... A less conservative and probably more realistic estimate would place the figure at perhaps 50 million.'[1]

The intrusion of states into indigenous national territories constitutes a new wave of colonialism comparable in magnitude to the old form of colonialism. The brutal killing of over four million indigenous people in twenty-three years assumes greater immediacy when it is noted that during an eight-year period (from 1975 to 1983) more than 100,000 Timorese in East Timor were killed by Indonesian military forces, a loss of about one-third of the total Timorese population. And in a period of just five years (between 1979 and 1983) the El Salvadoran government and various rebel forces and death squads killed thirty thousand Pipil Indians, or about 10 per cent of that indigenous nation's population.

As a reaction to indigenous nationalist movements, and to satisfy their expansionist ambitions, many state governments and non-indigenous rebel forces have undertaken the deliberate liquidation of indigenous nations to preserve the power of the state. The curse of colonial expansion, world-wide, into indigenous national territories during the earlier centuries has now changed into a state-by-state subjection if not elimination of indigenous territories, peoples, and cultures. Under the guise of civil wars, anti-communist and anti-capitalist insurgencies, and wars of liberation, state governments and rebel forces have targeted indigenous nations for obliteration.

Cold-War Confrontations

While many indigenous nations are engaged in hot wars to reclaim their homelands and national identity, many more are engaged in cold war confrontations with states (see table 2). Although it is difficult to measure the number of lives lost in these conflicts, the political and social disruption of indigenous nations is as destructive as that caused by hot wars. The impact of indigenous nations on the state is destabilizing, but not destructive. Cold-war confrontations are fought with political and economic weapons, although sporadic physical violence will erupt in isolation. As with hot wars, indigenous nations engage in cold wars to reclaim their territory and national identity.

TABLE 2
States and indigenous nations engaged in cold wars

States	Indigenous nations
Canada	Micmac, Cree, Lakota, Shuswap, and Bella Coola
United States	Quinalt, Hope, Lakota, Iroquois, Inuit, and Aleute
Norway, Sweden, and Finland	Saami
China	Tibetans and Taiwanese
Italy	Corsicans and Sardinians
Yugoslavia	Croatians, Bosnians, and Slovenes
Denmark	Inuits of Greenland
Mexico	Zapotec, Mixe, and Mayans
Costa Rica	Baruca, Cabecares, and Bribris
Chile	Mapuche
New Zealand	Moari
Australia	Pitjantjatjara, Yirikala, Gurintji, Warlpiri, and Wombaya
Nigeria	Yoruba, Ibo, and Ibibo
Zaire	Shaba and Luba Kasai
Bangladesh	Chakmas
Thailand	Meo
India	Tripura, Mizorma, Manipur, and Meghalaya
Japan	Ainu

Indigenous nations engaged in cold wars are commonly under rigid administrative control of state government officials. The United States, Canada, New Zealand, and the Scandinavian states have each established complicated governmental bureaucracies designed to manage and control indigenous populations, their lands, and their economic livelihood. An extensive body of domestic law controls the behaviour of individual citizens of indigenous nations.

The United States practises the most extensive governmental control of indigenous nations. India has also instituted extensive governmental control over indigenous peoples and their territories. India has been less successful than the United States in controlling indigenous populations through bureaucracy and domestic law; as a result, India has resorted to the use of police and militia. Only on rare occasions in this century has the United States sought to enforce its will by using force; during the eighteenth and nineteenth centuries, of course, the United States conducted full-scale wars against indigenous nations.

Canada, Australia, and Mexico have instituted indigenous control agencies, but these have not developed to the extent achieved in the United States. Their political, economic, and social control over indigenous nations is consequently less effective. In these states, and particularly in Canada, indigenous peoples are less inhibited in their pursuit of nationalist goals.

With some exceptions, indigenous nations seek political independence; however, they often consider forms of autonomy or irredentism within a state more achievable. Despite this tendency, indigenous nations engaged in cold wars persist in their efforts to remain separate from the state society. Civil disobedience, domestic legal confrontation, and political activism in opposition to official state government policies are the preferred means for achieving nationalist goals.

Small Nations into States

The struggle to reclaim national identity is a preoccupation of indigenous nations, often consuming the energies and resources of many people for generations. As the twentieth century comes to a close, it is becoming more apparent that this persistence is producing results. Many indigenous nations formerly under the control of a colonial state have achieved the political status of free and independent states. Tanzania, Papua New Guinea, Vanuatu, Kiribati, Qatar, the Solomon Islands, and Nauru are examples.

The 'proliferation of mini-states,' as leaders of large states disdainfully describe the changing status of small nations, has altered the political balance of international institutions. The voting power necessary to control decisions of the United Nations General Assembly has significantly shifted away from large states, and small states increasingly hold sway in opposition to large state interests.

Most of the small states that have achieved independence since 1960 occupy territories outside the boundaries of the original colonizing state. Their new political status has been achieved as part of a world-wide decolonization process that encouraged large states to disengage colonial control over peoples and territories outside state boundaries. The League of Nations took the position that non-self-governing peoples should determine their own political future. The large states were fearful of being dismembered, however, and the decolonization process did not extend to indigenous nations surrounded by larger states.

To ensure that decolonization would not extend to indigenous nations within established states, those states with indigenous populations decided among themselves in the early 1960s that decolonization, or the right of self-determination, did not necessarily apply to indigenous nations if their exercise of self-determination meant the 'dismemberment of an existing state.' The conventional wisdom has been that indigenous nations located within an existing state must be granted the status of a 'minority population' under the jurisdiction of the state. By this process of denying 'enclave' indigenous nations the right to choose their own national political future, the large states hope to maintain their position of hegemony.

Despite the prohibition against the decolonizing indigenous nations, the urge to re-establish indigenous national identity continues to spawn nationalist movements against large states. The hot and cold wars in which indigenous nations are involved are testimony to the drive to dismember large states to form many small indigenous states.

Indigenous nations in upper North America have been engaged in a cold war with Canada since 1876, when the British Parliament established the Dominion of Canada in the indigenous peoples' territories. As a part of extensive decolonization of Great Britain's holdings throughout the world, Canada was granted increasing control over her internal and external affairs by a series of parliamentary acts. The Canadian decolonization process was completed in 1982 when the British Parliament enacted the Canada Act, which effectively granted Canada the status of an independent state.

Two important political changes resulted from the British Parliament's enactment of the Canada Act, 1982. First, Canada was granted full political independence from Great Britain. Second, the long-standing trustee relationship between the United Kingdom and upper North American indigenous nations was unilaterally dissolved. All responsibilities and obligations of trusteeship assumed by the United Kingdom (under treaties, the Royal Proclamation of 1763, and other instruments of agreement with indigenous nations) were abrogated and rendered null and void. By virtue of this single legislative action, the British government formally withdrew from its political responsibilities for the Dominion of Canada and all of the indigenous nations therein. Britain's less-than-perfect statesmanship left upper North America with two separate and distinct political groups of peoples – which share neither common origins nor common aspirations – contending for political power. The political status and future of the indigenous nations were left undefined and unsettled.

Indigenous nations are now vulnerable to Canadian political and economic exploitation. In recognition of this new circumstance, indigenous nations such as the Micmac, Cree, Bella Coola, and Shuswap initiated political actions to strengthen their defences against an unfettered Canadian government. These and other indigenous nations discovered that the change in Canada's political status placed their own political future in jeopardy. It became clear to indigenous leaders that their nations were not now, nor had they ever been, a part of Canada. Indeed, whether indigenous nations would coexist or be absorbed into Canada became the central question.

The failure to resolve the question of indigenous national political status created a situation where Canada claimed sovereignty over all territory within its asserted boundaries. Many indigenous nations claimed independent sovereignty over enclave territories scattered throughout Canada. These competing claims of sovereignty served as the basis for political confrontation and laid the foundation for potential violent conflict.

Since 17 April 1982, indigenous nations in Canada have been without a political status as distinct peoples. They have suffered the unilateral abrogation of their treaties and agreements with Great Britain and have begun to experience increasing interference from Canada in their internal affairs. Britain's withdrawal and the unsettled status of indigenous nations have created a political vacuum which threatens the stability of Canada and the future of scores of indigenous nations.

The political vacuum into which indigenous nations in Canada have been thrust is analogous to the conditions experienced by the Timorese peoples when Portugal withdrew from East Timor in the 1970s after a long period of colonial occupation. Once Portugal withdrew from the island country, the Indonesian government quickly moved to fill the resulting void by forcibly asserting its sovereignty over Timorese territory and peoples. Though the Timorese did not invite or accept Indonesian authority over them, Indonesia claimed and enforced its authority over East Timor and occupied Timorese lands.

When Great Britain withdrew from India in 1947, many indigenous nations, including the Nagas and the tribal populations of Assam, Meghalaya, Mizoram, Pripura, and Manipu (now including an indigenous population of twenty-five million), were cut off and left to be recolonized by the newly independent Indian state. Despite objections from indigenous nations, the new state of India extended its sovereignty over indigenous territories and imposed its rule. Once promised their independence by Mahatma Gandhi, indigenous nations of the Indian subcontinent found themselves being absorbed against their will into a larger state. After years of political cold war with India, the Nagas and other indigenous nations began to fight a hot war, which continues today. The indigenous nations of northeast India seek to establish their own rule over their own states; they are working to achieve the repeal of 'black laws' which they regard as repressive measures aimed at indigenous populations. They also seek to achieve the removal of Indian military and paramilitary forces from indigenous territories. India's response to indigenous appeals has been to promote the influx of foreign nationals from Nepal and indigenous nationals from Bangladesh into indigenous national territories. The war of words has slowly become a war of guns.

The decolonization and recolonization process was repeated in 1980 when Britain withdrew colonial administration over British Honduras – then the new state of Belize was granted independence. Britain's departure placed the Kekchi people (a branch of Mayan-speaking people who number about twelve thousand) in a political void which was quickly dominated by the newly independent Belizian government against the Kekchis' will. The Kekchi nation and its territory are now also threatened with absorption by Guatemala as a result of an unsettled border dispute with British Honduras. The Kekchi nation is not part of Belize or of Guatemala, but neither state is willing to accept Kekchi nationalism.

The unsettled political status of indigenous nations in Canada is functionally the same situation as that which exists inside many other states. Canada is attempting to repeat the apparent success of the United States by enacting domestic legislation designed to control indigenous nations through bureaucracy. India and Indonesia are attempting to achieve the same goal by imposing political and military control over their indigenous nations. The political or military suppression of indigenous nationalism by state governments is not unique to a particular form of government or ideology. Socialist, capitalist, communist, and fascist governments respond to indigenous nationalism in the same ways. The Soviet Union, China, Yugoslavia, and Nicaragua have all acted decisively to suppress indigenous nationalist movements.

Following its revolution in 1917, the Soviet Union immediately occupied indigenous homelands in Latvia and Saamiland in the west. The revolutionary government occupied Armenian, Turkmen, Tadzhik, Kirghiz, Usbek, and Georgian territories to the south and east. Just as the Chinese imposed central government control over the Tibetans and claimed Taiwan, the Soviet Union imposed its neocolonial control over indigenous nations.

The Miskito, Sumo, and Rama nations have been struggling since 1974 to stabilize their territorial frontiers in eastern Nicaragua and Honduras. What began as a political struggle over land rights and political autonomy has since 1981 become a full revolt against state control. With a permanent population of about 300,000 people (including Miskito, Sumo, Rama, and Creoles, and a small population of Mestizos), and a claimed territory of about 35,000 square miles, an indigenous organization, Misurasata, is moving to establish a new indigenous government. 'Aisuban Tasbya' (a Miskito phrase meaning 'our land' or 'homeland') may become the name of a new state bordering on Honduras and Nicaragua, neither of which is eager to see a new indigenous state established on their eastern borders.

The pattern of Nicaraguan government behaviour toward the indigenous and Creole peoples of Aisuban Tasbya is similar to the patterns of behaviour exhibited by other states. Like Canada, the Soviet Union, the United States, Indonesia, and India, Nicaragua's Revolutionary Government of National Reconstruction (the Sandinistas) expanded its governmental authority over indigenous territories. On 12 August 1981 the government issued a declaration of principles regarding indigenous communities in the Atlantic coastal region. The provisions of the declaration reflect the same intolerance of indigenous nations as the domestic laws of Canada and other states. The Sandinista declaration states that there is but one nation within the boundaries of the state; territorially and politically, it cannot be dismembered, divided, or deprived of its sovereignty and independence. The natural resources of the territory are the property of the Nicaraguan people. Each of these principles denies the national integrity and separateness of Aisuban Tasbya, rejects its territorial and political distinctiveness, and advances the right of the Nicaraguan government to confiscate indigenous natural resources. Nicaragua seeks to extend its sovereignty over indigenous territories and peoples through political means and, if necessary, by force.

The peoples of Aisuban Tasbya have never agreed to become a part of Nicaragua under the terms set out in the Sandinista declaration. Despite the declaration and despite Nicaraguan efforts to control Aisuban Tasbya, the Miskito, Sumo, and Rama peoples continue to struggle against the annexation of their homelands. They have organized their own provisional government and established a force of more than eighteen thousand warriors to defend their homelands against external forces. With few allies and virtually no external support, Misurasata vigorously advanced Aisuban Tasbyan self-determination, political autonomy, and the right to independent governance. What began as an irredentist movement in the early 1970s became an effort aimed at total independence in the 1980s. Nicaragua is now faced with the prospect of having to deal with Aisuban Tasbya as a political equal.

Small States and the New Order

As the indigenous nationalist movements demonstrate, more small states are in the process of emerging. The natural order of small nations is again challenging large artificial empires to rearrange the global political landscape. The large states were born not as a product of nature but as a product of the forced consolidation of central power over unwilling subjects. Under other circumstances, the world would be made up of hundreds of small natural states of approximately equal size. The natural diversity of peoples would be reflected in the multiplicity of small states. The capacity of any state to wage global war or enforce its dominance over others would be minimized. The balance of terror between massive states like the United States and the Soviet Union would not exist.

Today a renewed will is giving rise to a new international political order. Massive states are being dismembered by the weight of their own inability to manage and control their own bigness and the inexorable movements of small nations to reclaim their place among the family of nations. One need only note that of the fifty or more new states formed since the beginning of 1960 about forty have populations of fewer than one million people. Twelve of these new states were formed by indigenous nations. From the island states of Tuvalu (7,000 people and a territory of ten square miles) and Nauru (8,000 people and a territory of eight square miles) to the indigenous states of the United Arab Emirates (871,000 people and 32,000 square miles), Swaziland, Guinea-Bissau, and Gabon (637,000 people and over 102,000 square miles), the proliferation of mini-states continues.

The irony of the emerging new international political order is that it is regarded by many as a source of greater global instability; in fact, it is the large, artificial states that create global instability and do the greatest violence to humanity. The preservation of global diversity and human adaptability is the promise of small nations. Global peace and the renewal of the human spirit through the restoration of the natural order of nations is the promise of indigenous nationalist movements.

5 Aboriginal Rights and Indian Government

THE CONCEPTS OF ABORIGINAL RIGHTS and sovereign Indian self-government are considered by most Indian leaders to be virtually synonymous. That is, sovereign self-government is held to be an aboriginal right, and without sovereign self-government aboriginal rights are rendered meaningless. Canadian government policy, however, makes a sharp distinction between the two concepts. The federal and provincial governments reject all notions of sovereign Indian government as an inherent aboriginal right. However, they are ready and willing to negotiate a more limited form of self-government for Indians on the understanding that such self-government will be granted as a constitutional or legislative act. Even this represents a significant shift from earlier policies of cultural and political subordination and assimilation.

The papers in this section approach the relationship between aboriginal rights and Indian self-government from different perspectives. Paul Tennant analyses this relationship from a contemporary political-legislative perspective; Boldt and Long analyse it from a social-cultural perspective. Both agree that the movement to Indian self-government faces numerous obstacles, and that it is loaded with cultural, political, and structural complexities that carry profound implications for the future survival of Indians as distinct tribal societies.

PAUL TENNANT

Aboriginal Rights and the Penner Report on Indian Self-Government

Concepts of aboriginal rights and of Indian self-government have evolved rapidly in Canada in recent years and have become fused with each other. Indian self-government is now advocated as an aboriginal right by Indian spokesmen and a variety of aboriginal rights are advanced as aspects of Indian self-government. Both ways of using the concepts seem appropriate. Indian self-government may well come to be considered the pre-eminent, overarching, collective aboriginal right, subsuming whatever other more particular aboriginal rights may be advanced. In any case, Indian self-government is now the major policy item on the agendas of both Indians and government, even though the two sides differ on whether Indian self-government is an aboriginal right.

An examination of the origin and substance of the major Indian self-government proposals is relevant to an understanding of both Indian and government views of aboriginal rights in Canada. Such an examination must include, first, a consideration of Canadian Indian policy since Confederation; second, an analysis of the path-breaking 1983 proposals of the House of Commons Special Committee on Indian Self-Government (the Penner Committee); third, an analysis of the stillborn proposals developed subsequently within the Ministry of Indian Affairs and Northern Development; and fourth, an examination of the proposals embodied in Bill C-52 of June 1984. These proposals will be examined in terms of the source, purpose, powers, autonomy, base, and structures of the particular type of government envisioned.

The term 'Indian self-government' rather than 'aboriginal self-government' will be used here. While any general expression of aboriginal rights must apply equally to Indians, Metis, and Inuit, self-government for these three groups will differ in regard to the six aspects listed above. The Metis, for example, lack the economic, religious, and cultural diversity of the Indians, and Inuit self-government will be greatly affected by the potential Inuit majority in an eventual province of the Eastern Arctic. Moreover, only the Indians have been subjected to the system of land reservations and the social control inherent in such a system. Consequently, for Indians more than for Metis or Inuit, self-government is a means of escape from federal government control. Finally, the development among Indians of notions of self-government has occurred with little if any reference to Metis or Inuit. The federal government has similarly dealt with Indian self-government as a distinct policy area. This is not to say, however, that the Metis and the Inuit are not constrained by concepts and precedents relating to Indian self-government. As minorities within the larger aboriginal group they will probably be subject to the concepts of aboriginal rights and to limitations on such concepts, which are derived from Indian policy.

The context of Indian policy-making in Canada is fashioned, first, by the respective basic beliefs, structures, and decision-making processes of Indians and non-Indians and, second, by the manner of interaction of the two sides. Until the last decade, the making of Indian policy in Canada was shaped by a consensus within the dominant Canadian society that Indians should be assimilated. This consensus was an outgrowth of the post-seventeenth-century western European philosophy in which the self-directed, self-interested, individual person was seen as the primary unit in economic and property matters as well as in politics and religion. At its charitable best the dominant society regarded continuation of traditional Indian ways, which emphasized 'community,' as an impediment to the individual Indian's health, welfare, and happiness, which could be fully attained only through assimilation. At its self-interested worst the dominant society adopted these views in order to justify its colonial occupation of North America. By defining Indians as nomads without social order, without property, and without political structures and processes to govern their own affairs and property relations, the European colonizers legitimized their takeover of Indian lands. Indians were expected to be grateful for the opportunity to assimilate into the 'superior' European culture and society.

Closely related to these views and values, and just as questionable, was the dominant society's view of what made an Indian an Indian. Racial characteristics and traditional cultural elements such as language, religion, weapons, tools, transport, and clothing were the criteria adopted. Aboriginal people and culture were taken to have existed in a pure form before contact, but to have been 'diluted' through interbreeding and acculturation. This erosion of Indian race and culture was used to discredit contemporary Indian claims to aboriginal rights on the ground that the claimants had ceased to be Indians.

Before the 1970s Indian peoples were in no position to present their own philosophies and interpretations of their history, or even to advance their own views on who was an 'Indian' and why. Except in a few regions, notably British Columbia, there were no Indian political organizations or political communications beyond the band or tribal level, and no pan-Indian consensus or political strategy existed. No policy alliance between Canadian Indians and government was present or possible. Indian policy was determined entirely by the dominant society through the federal government. Some other interest groups such as churches, railways, resource industries, and the provinces exercised some influence, but Indians were excluded from the policy-making process.

In this context emerged the four major elements that have been evident in Canadian Indian policy since Confederation. The first of these was the conversion of Indians to Christianity. The second was the signing of treaties with the Indians and, south of the sixtieth parallel, the confining of Indians to reservations. Implementation of these two policy elements was largely completed by the turn of the century, except in British Columbia, where the establishment of reservations was not completed until the 1920s, and where the province, through its ownership and control of land, was able to prevent the signing of any treaties. The third policy element was compulsory schooling of Indian children in government-financed religious residential schools. The fourth element was the inducement of Indian peoples to adopt government structures and processes derived from British and American models. These latter two elements, like the first two, had as their explicit purpose the destruction of traditional Indian society and the preparation of Indians for assimilation into the larger society.

The last two elements have remained the major factors in federal Indian policy during this century. Education policy, however, has changed greatly in recent decades, with the phasing-out of parochial residential schools and the acceptance of using education to preserve some Indian traditions. The insistence on imposing an elective form of government on Indians has been the most consistent, though least evident, element in federal Indian policy since Confederation. The practice of Christianizing Indians and imposing the reservation system and segregated schools provoked considerable controversy in the dominant society, but the issue of Indian government seems to have been ignored or not comprehended.

The philosophy underlying aboriginal societies emphasized community; to accord primacy to the self-directed, self-interested individual would have been to destroy the very basis of that community. The Indian philosophy was and is collective or corporate: the individual is seen as attaining his place and meaning within the traditions of the community and through performance of communal obligations. Community decision-making and social control structures and processes – that is, government – took a distinct and specialized form only where populations were substantial and concentrated; even then, 'government' included all other aspects of community. Although aboriginal styles of government varied greatly, in general each government was both territorial and communal. This is not to say that the two aspects could in practice have been separated.

Since the time of European occupation Indian spokesmen in all parts of Canada have expressed the view that Indians cannot rightfully be deprived of the use and occupation of their traditional lands. They also claim the right of community decision-making in regard to their land and people. The Nishga of British Columbia provide a particularly unambiguous example of such claims to land and to continuing Indian government over it.[1] Such historical claims are still not widely accepted by the dominant society.

In keeping with aboriginal philosophy, Indian claims are invariably advanced on behalf of the community. Indians take the position that their claims to land and self-government do not depend on racial criteria or particular cultural elements, but rather on the existence of their communities from time immemorial. The origin and continuing existence of the communal or corporate identity are decisive for their claims. The individual Indian's claim to aboriginal rights is derived from membership in the aboriginal community. The notion of communal primacy and integrity implies that the community must be allowed to evolve and adapt according to its own contemporary will.

Aboriginal origin means only incidentally that contemporary members of the community have indigenous pre-contact ancestry. More important, it means that the community was established and functioned in a particular place prior to and apart from any external or externally derived authority. Indeed, the only way in which an aboriginal community could, of its own accord, cease to exit – that is, forsake its aboriginal rights – would be by knowingly giving up its claim to its particular place.

'Place' is the key element; it implies and includes the claim to continued functioning of the community in that place, and self-government is a key feature of this functioning. Aboriginal title to land is the demonstration of aboriginal government. To hold aboriginal title to the land is to hold the aboriginal right to communal self-government on that land. Whether and how title was or could be transferred from Indian jurisdiction to the Canadian government is the critical historical and ethical question pertaining to Indian self-government in Canada.

The federal government's policy on Indian government has been substantially at variance with Indian traditions and views.[2] The source of the authority exercised by Indian governments established under the federal government's policy was the British–Canadian legal system. Each Indian government was created by federal officials under parliamentary authority. Title to land was claimed for the crown and aboriginal title was flatly denied. The federal government's purpose in establishing Indian governments was to destroy traditional Indian political structures and practices that were based on a belief in the collective aboriginal community. The federal government also intended to undermine the authority and prestige of aboriginal leaders, thereby facilitating control over Indian communities by the agents of the dominant society. No allowance was made for traditional Indian social organization or any other organization of Indian choosing.

The powers granted to Indian governments were both delegated and limited in scope, and the exercise of those powers was subject to the control of the federal government. Indians could never expect to achieve the full range of powers they had exercised in their communities before contact with the colonizers. Indian government was limited to the individual band, whose membership was defined and assigned under parliamentary authority. Autonomy was non-existent because Indian communities were totally financially dependent on the federal government.

The structures of band government were copied from the municipal model. A chief and a council, equivalent to a mayor and aldermen, were to be elected by adult suffrage. Each adult was to have the right to seek elective office. Political equality, elections, and access to public office are central tenets of individualistic philosophies. When applied to the aboriginal communal setting, these ideas undermined traditions of individual obligation and accountability to the community and subverted the notion that political power is best exercised by elders having exceptional wisdom and experience. Moreover, in the aboriginal communal setting the elective system promoted factionalism in the population, instability in leadership, and inconsistency in public policy.

The federal government policy met strong, and in some cases continuing, opposition from Indians. In response to this opposition the Indian-government policy was modified to allow bands to use some customary methods of choosing leaders rather than the elective system. Nevertheless, the system of band government had far-reaching effects on all aspects of Indian life. For a century Indian political activity was of necessity largely oppositional and limited to the band levels.

During the 1960s new personnel in the Department of Indian and Northern Affairs modified certain policies. One significant change was the decision to consult Indians on matters affecting them and to encourage community-development initiatives. A White Paper was introduced in 1969, and with it came the sudden emergence of Indian political organizations at the provincial and national levels. These organizations undertook much research on Indian government. Not surprisingly, given the youthfulness that characterized the new organizations, many of the initial ideas about Indian government contained a mixture of assumptions, concepts, and values adopted from the dominant society.

A notion frequently advanced by the new Indian organizations was that the constituency of Indian government should be defined regionally – that is, in terms of Indian populations within the various provinces and territories rather than in band or tribal terms. Concurrent with this, a common early assumption was that the powers and responsibilities of the Indian Affairs Department would be quickly transferred to the emerging regionally based Indian organizations. Toward this end leaders of the Indian organizations modelled their organizational structures after those of the department. Before long, band and tribal leaders who saw the emerging 'brown' bureaucracy as no more compatible with Indian values and traditions than the white bureaucracy challenged these organizational models. The critics proceeded to develop a counter-model, in which the base of Indian government was the autonomous traditional community (the band or tribal group) independent of centralized bureaucracies of whatever shade. Because this model stressed uniqueness and diversity among Indian communities, its advocates faced a difficult task in creating a united political front, let alone a common strategy leading to its adoption.

Within the Indian organizations and among Indians generally there was no clear consensus on whether Indian government should exist only at the traditional community level. Some organizational spokesmen and some hired consultants continued to advocate provincial or even national Indian government as the best model. By the late 1970s terms such as 'Indian government,' 'self-government,' 'Indian nation,' 'autonomy,' and 'sovereignty' were being used freely, but more often than not without specifying the level of political organization to which they would apply. Similarly, details of government structure were given little attention.

Indian leaders, however, managed to achieve a consensus on some significant aspects of Indian government. It was agreed that the purpose of Indian government, whatever its base, must be to advance the collective Indian interest; in order to do this it must have significant powers and substantial autonomy. It was also agreed that the authority base for Indian government must derive from aboriginal title to the land, not from Parliament or any other external source of authority. The intensity of Indian feeling and sentiment on this point was not and is not sufficiently appreciated in the dominant society. Non-Indians do not understand that for Indians autonomous Indian government is an aboriginal right. In this formulation the existence of autonomous Indian government is necessary, but not sufficient; the essential requirement is that the aboriginal source of such government must be acknowledged by the dominant society.

During the 1970s, under pressure from Indian political organizations, the Indian Affairs Department developed new proposals for band government. The department was now willing to depart from its policy of the past century on a number of areas. A policy proposal was developed that would allow each band to decide on its own government structures and to exercise some increased powers. But the policy did not recognize the aboriginal source of authority for Indian government, and it was deemed unacceptable by Indian leaders. Nevertheless, the government's policy development process provoked discussion and a better understanding among Indians about self-government. Indeed, it was in this process that the phrase 'Indian self-government' emerged.

Meanwhile, Prime Minister Trudeau's proposals for a new constitution for Canada brought the matter of aboriginal rights into some prominence. Much of the Indian response to the prime minister's constitutional initiative dealt with principle rather than detail; once the notion of a first ministers' constitutional conference on aboriginal rights was accepted, however, it was clear that such a conference could not avoid the question of Indian self-government. The federal cabinet called on the House of Commons to form a special committee, with Keith Penner as chairman, 'to act as a Parliamentary Task Force on Indian Self-Government, to review all legal and related institutional factors affecting the status, development and responsibilities of Band Governments on Indian reserves.'[3]

A word needs to be said about the composition of the special committee. By the mid-1970s the Indian right to vote (granted in 1960) had resulted in the election of a small group of MPs from ridings with substantial numbers of Indian voters. These MPs were relatively knowledgeable about Indian issues; never before had such a group existed in Parliament. Because Indians had not formed a national voting bloc, the group of MPs cut across political party lines. The special committee members – one New Democrat, three Conservatives, and four Liberals – were drawn from this group of MPs. Had the committee members *not* been drawn from this group, it is doubtful that it would have proceeded as it did or produced the policy proposals that it did.

Unlike any previous parliamentary committee on Indian affairs, the special committee appointed Indians seconded from Indian organizations to important staff positions. Additionally, it appointed representatives from Indian organizations as non-voting but fully participating members of the committee. In effect, the committee established a policy alliance with Indian interests; that is, it allowed full access for Indian views and insisted that those views be taken into account in drafting policy proposals. As Sally Weaver has said, 'the committee became a vehicle to secure Indian co-operation and to organize and articulate Indian demands.'[4] The committee's research and cross-country hearings provided the most thorough examination ever given to an Indian issue.

In its unanimous report[5] the committee made fifty-eight recommendations, all of which flowed from Indian views and demands presented in the hearings. In Weaver's words, 'The spirit and intent of the *Penner Report* lies in its values which echo the basic policy paradigm of Indians.'[6] The committee proposed that Indian government should exist at the level of the 'Indian First Nations.' By allowing for tribal-level self-government the committee exceeded its terms of reference, which originally had limited it to a consideration of band government. The committee also went beyond its mandate by tying Indian self-government to land-claim settlements.

The most notable recommendation made by the committee was that Indian self-government should be recognized as an aboriginal right and that this right should be 'explicitly stated and entrenched in the constitution of Canada.'[7] The governments of Indian first nations would derive their legitimacy not from Parliament and not even from the constitution itself, for the constitution would simply acknowledge or 'recognize' the pre-existing right of aboriginal peoples to self-government. If this recommendation was implemented, Indian first nation governments would 'form a distinct order of government in Canada.'

The committee did not base its expectations for implementation exclusively on constitutional amendment. Stating at one point that the amendment should come 'eventually,' the committee devoted most of its recommendations to the steps Parliament and the government should take under the existing constitutional provisions. Among the recommended steps were abandoning the alternative band-government legislative proposals, reducing departmental authority over Indians, and phasing out the department as its functions were assumed by Indian governments or by new agencies proposed by the committee.

The committee's major recommendation was the immediate passage of its proposed legislation that would (1) require the federal government to recognize Indian governments accountable to their own people; (2) authorize bilateral federal-Indian agreements as to jurisdiction; and (3) 'under authority of Section 91(24) of the *Constitution Act, 1867* ... occupy all areas of competence required to allow Indian First Nations to govern themselves effectively and ... ensure that provincial laws would not apply on Indian lands' except with Indian consent.

There are two essential observations to be made for a full appreciation of these recommendations. First, the committee interpreted section 91(24) to allow Parliament to enact laws in *all* fields (including those reserved by section 92 to the provinces), in so far as such laws pertain to 'Indians, and Lands reserved for the Indians.' The Indian Act already deals with some provincial fields. The committee thus recommended that Parliament 'exercise its jurisdiction [under section 91(24)] in all fields, particularly where the absence of federal legislation has resulted in the extension of provincial jurisdiction to Indian lands and peoples.' Parliament should then proceed to 'vacate these areas of jurisdiction to recognized Indian governments.' As a result, 'virtually the entire range of law-making, policy, program delivery, law enforcement and adjudication powers would be available to an Indian First Nation government within its territory.'

Second, the recommended bilateral Indian-federal mechanism for establishing Indian first nation governments would continue to operate even if the constitution was amended to recognize the rights of aboriginal peoples to self-government. In no sense did the committee imply or recommend that constitutional entrenchment would in itself amount to recognition of Indian governments. The committee proposed that a new ministry of state be responsible for such recognition.

Substantively, then, the committee endorsed self-government not only as an aboriginal right but also as a communal right, with the major purpose of enhancing the survival of Indian communities. At the same time, by providing that the actual powers, autonomy, and structures of each Indian government would be uniquely devised, the committee recognized the diversity of Indian communities. The Penner Committee's achievement was to flesh out each of the six aspects of government (source, purpose, power, autonomy, base, and structure) and to assemble them in a coherent and authoritative design for Indian self-government. The committee's design was readily comprehensible to anyone with knowledge of Indian policy. Overnight the committee's design became accepted as the standard for the discussion of Indian self-government.

The Indian Affairs Department, in consultation with the executive of the Assembly of First Nations, responded quickly to the Penner Report by assigning senior officials to draft policy proposals for new legislation.[8] The proposals, completed in December 1983, resulted in the draft Indian Nations Recognition and Validating Act, which went even further than the recommendations of the Penner Report by reducing the discretion of government officials in recognizing an Indian first nation. Moreover, the draft proposals provided that the traditional laws of each nation would be validated to the extent that they did not conflict with laws of Parliament. Each nation would have all powers under section 91(24) except those withdrawn by Parliament. From the Indian view, this remedied a weakness in the Penner Report, which recommended that acquisition of powers by Indian communities be accomplished through delegation from the federal government. The draft proposals pushed the federal government's prerogatives under section 91(24) to the limit, to produce in Canada a system of internally sovereign Indian nations. In early 1984 the legislation went to the cabinet, where it was promptly killed. For Indians, the draft act remains the high point in federal–Indian self-government proposals.

Just prior to the first ministers' conference of March 1984, the minister of Indian affairs, John Munro, gave the federal government's public response to the Penner Report. The minister declined to endorse self-government as an aboriginal right and rejected the notion of pushing section 91(24) to its limits. But he did promise to drop the band-government legislation and to pursue the 'primary thrust' of the report in new legislation, to be termed 'general framework legislation.'

The first ministers' conference generated only one surprise: Prime Minister Trudeau proposed that the constitution be amended to recognize in principle an aboriginal 'right to self-governing institutions.' Although the premiers did not reject the proposal, only the premiers of Manitoba, Ontario, and New Brunswick – those already used to dealing with non-assimilated minorities – supported the prime minister's proposal.

A group from the constitutional unit of the Indian Affairs Department and the public-law unit of the Ministry of Justice were by this time drafting new legislation. The group sought to have Parliament approve what the Penner Committee had recommended. The draft was rejected by the priorities and planning committee of cabinet, which gave firm instructions that Indian government powers were to be limited, and delegated, by Parliament. The cabinet committee also rejected a number of specific recommendations of the Penner Committee, including that of creating a new ministry of state for first nations. Officials from the Prime Minister's Office and the Ministry of State for Social Development were added to the initial group. The new group's draft legislation, entitled Bill C-52, was introduced in the House of Commons by the honourable John Munro, minister of Indian Affairs, on 27 June 1984. The executive of the Assembly of First Nations had been consulted continuously during the drafting process, by both the initial and the expanded drafting group.

Bill C-52 was little more than the old band-government legislative approach decked out in a bit of verbal finery borrowed from the Indians and the Penner Report. The bill was entitled 'An Act Relating to Self-Government for Indian Nations' (the term 'first nation' had been ruled out). The bill did, however, follow Penner by defining an Indian nation to be one or more bands or a tribal group. An Indian nation, having drawn up its own constitution and having received official recognition from a federally appointed panel, would possess delegated powers comparable to those normally held by Canadian municipal councils. With specific cabinet approval in each case, additional and broader powers not unlike those envisioned in comprehensive land-claim settlements could be delegated. Under Bill C-52 an Indian nation's constitution could be amended only through an order of the panel. However, the federal cabinet could disallow any law enacted by the Indian nation. As for the application of provincial laws, the bill merely restated the present reality: such laws would apply to Indians and Indian lands unless in conflict with a treaty or act of Parliament.

Response to Bill C-52 was muted as a consequence of the circumstances in which it was introduced (including the simultaneous introduction of a bill restoring Indian status to non-status Indian women). Parliament was about to be dissolved and an election held, and there was no chance that the bill would even be considered. The most charitable explanation for Bill C-52 is that the minister was using this device to serve notice to Indians as to the maximum concessions his cabinet colleagues were prepared to make in regard to aboriginal rights and Indian self-government.

Clearly, the federal Liberal government and the Assembly of First Nations executive proved unwilling and unable to continue the sort of policy alliance that formed the foundation of the Penner Report. The legacy of that alliance will likely persist, however, because the federal government's old Indian policies are dead. The new policy consensus among Indians in regard to autonomous nations is unlikely to disappear. Indian self-government has gained major allies within Parliament and within the Indian Affairs Department, and there is now at least some awareness on the part of the dominant society about Indian intentions and aspirations. Indian self-government is to be based on traditional band and tribal communities, not on provincial or federal constituencies; as this concept becomes more widely disseminated, it is possible that the dominant society's opposition to recognizing Indian self-government as an aboriginal right will continue to decrease. As a dispersed and diverse minority, weak in social, political, and economic terms, Indians are able to effect policy gains only to the degree that they are able to form policy alliances with groups within the dominant society, in particular with officials or groups within government. This may be the most critical factor affecting any policy gains on Indian self-government.

MENNO BOLDT AND J. ANTHONY LONG

Tribal Traditions and European-Western Political Ideologies: The Dilemma of Canada's Native Indians

In their quest for political and cultural self-determination, Indian leaders in Canada have adopted the concept of sovereignty as the cornerstone of their aspirations. They advance claims to inherent sovereignty in order to establish the legal, moral, and political authority that will allow them to nurture and develop their traditional tribal customs, values, institutions, and social organization. The concept of sovereignty represents for the current generation of Indian leaders a means to an end rather than an end in itself.

Recently, Indian leaders have taken their claim to inherent sovereignty into the international arena in an attempt to bring external political pressure to bear on the Canadian government. They feel that the more enlightened norms of international law and the United Nations covenants on political and cultural self-determination will bolster their case for sovereignty and will serve to counteract the negative treatment their claims have received at the hands of Canadian judges and policy-makers.

In this paper we address ourselves to the question of how the European-western idea of 'sovereignty' fits into traditional tribal Indian customs, values, institutions, and social organizations. This question implies more than a linguistic or semantic analysis; it goes to the very heart of Indian culture. We will first examine the implications and pitfalls of sovereignty for traditional Indian customs, values, and institutions, and we will then explore alternative ideas for achieving political and cultural self-determination.

This paper appeared previously in a slightly more expanded form in 17 *Canadian Journal of Political Science* (1984) 537–54.

Before we proceed with our discussion, however, three important points need to be made. First, our statements about traditional Indian society refer to the period prior to European-influenced change. However, our analysis has relevance for contemporary Indian society because many traditional values have persisted even in the face of systematic and coercive measures taken by European colonizers and their successors to eliminate these values. More important, there is a strong cultural nationalist movement among Indians today that has as its objective the reinstitution of many traditional values and customs.

Second, we use the term 'tribe' to refer to a type of social organization, not to a level of political jurisdiction. Historically, Indian tribes were autonomous and self-sufficient social groupings. The Indian Act organized Indians into legal entities called bands. But Indian people today still recognize the concept of 'tribe,' just as they still recognize the concept of 'Indian nation.' In our usage both 'bands' and 'nations' qualify as tribal societies.

Finally, although we use the term 'Indian,' we do not intend to imply that Canada's indigenous tribes constitute a single people in any socio-cultural or political sense. Great diversity exists among tribes in language, political styles, cultural heritage, and so on. However, today, as in the past, many cultural traits and values are shared by most Indian tribes: the reaching of decisions by consensus, institutionalized sharing, respect for personal autonomy, and a preference for impersonal controls and behaviour.[1]

Tribal Traditions and the Concept of Sovereignty

Youngblood Henderson has noted that for Indians sovereignty is 'a matter of the heart' – an emotional not an intellectual concept.[2] This probably helps us to understand why their conceptions of how sovereignty would function in a tribal context are still embryonic and inchoate. In fact, much of the emotional appeal that sovereignty holds for Indians stems from its vagueness. It allows them to project onto it a promise of most of their political, socio-cultural, and economic aspirations without a rigorous analysis of the adequacy of their resources and instrumentalities for achieving it. The ambiguity of the concept also averts factionalism within Indian society, as each group is free to infer its preferred meanings and objectives.

Indian leaders, in their discussion of sovereignty, focus their attention almost exclusively on its instrumentality for checking the intrusion of external authority and power into their social and political structures, and territory; sovereignty is narrowly conceived of as a strategy to free themselves from external intrusions into their society. In their preoccupation with the goal of self-determination they overlook almost entirely the potential significance of sovereignty for ordering internal tribal authority and power relationships. Indian leaders have ignored the latent peril that the idea of sovereignty may hold for their traditional tribal customs, values, institutions, and social organization. If they are going to advocate sovereignty as the foundation of their contemporary and future goals, they must consider its implications for the central values of their tribal traditions – the very values they seek to protect. These values will not be preserved if the concept of sovereignty is inconsistent with their cultural legacy.

The potential consequences of sovereignty for Indian tribal traditions must be evaluated in the context of some key ideas contained in European-western doctrines of sovereignty, namely, the concepts of authority, hierarchy, and a ruling entity and the notions of statehood and territoriality.

Authority, Hierarchy, and a Ruling Entity

The concept of 'authority' is critical to any analysis of how the European-western doctrine of sovereignty can function in the context of indigenous North American forms of the 'band,' 'tribe,' or 'nation.' Bodin and Hobbes wrote of sovereignty as if it were equivalent to absolute and perpetual authority derived from either God or the people. For Locke and Rousseau sovereignty arose from absolute authority derived from the voluntary agreement of independent wills (contract of association) delegating their authority to the government, the fiduciary sovereign. Common to both of these conceptions of sovereignty, and generally implied in all European-western concepts of sovereignty, is a principle of authority defined as the supreme, if not the absolute and inalienable, power of the ruling entity to make decisions and to enforce them, if necessary, through sanctions or coercion.

Invariably linked with this principle of authority is the idea of a hierarchy of power relationships. This association between hierarchy and authority is exemplified in Haller's theory that authority is the base of sovereignty and that sovereignty arises from the natural superiority of one over another.[3] Haller reasons that equals will not obey equals; hence, sovereignty can only be exercised in a state of inequality where the stronger rules. For Haller this represented a universal law of nature – even among the birds of the air and the beasts of the forest the stronger always ruled. This assumption of a hierarchy of authority relationships is not only general in traditional European doctrines of sovereignty, but is also evident in contemporary conceptions of 'popular sovereignty.'

The European-western assumption of hierarchical authority relationships implies a ruling entity, that is, a particular locus for sovereign authority. In European society this precept found expression in the authority of rulers. In fact, much of the philosophical debate about sovereignty has focused on the appropriate locus for sovereign authority, whether in the monarch, his assembly, the people, the parliament, or judicial institutions. Even in the ideal sense of popular sovereignty – that is, where authority is derived from the people – this authority, once it is delegated by the people, must be lodged somewhere. Thus, terms such as 'political rulers,' 'decision-makers,' and 'governments' are used to distinguish those who exercise authority from the rest of society. These terms imply that an identifiable subset of the members of the total society have the power of authority in their hands.

How do these three key ideas – authority, hierarchy, and a ruling entity – contained in European-western concepts of sovereignty fit into traditional Indian society? In examining the question we want to reiterate that our discussion of authority, hierarchy, and government in traditional Indian society has reference to the basic political culture of most tribes. We are not suggesting that everywhere, without exceptions, North American Indians adopted the same model.

Taking the idea of authority first, the history and experience of North American tribal societies was very different from that of European societies. The European-western notion of a sovereign authority had its origin in the system of feudalism and the associated belief in the inherent inequality of men. The indigenous peoples of North America, however, never experienced feudalism, and most believed in the equality of men. In the Hobbesian doctrine of sovereignty, authority was deemed necessary to protect society against rampant individual self-interest. But in Indian tribal society individual self-interest was inextricably intertwined with tribal interests; that is, the general good and the individual good were virtually identical. Laslett's 'onion-skin' analogy aptly illustrates the mythical quality of individuality in traditional Indian society. To apprehend the individual in tribal Indian society, he says, we would have to peel off a succession of group-oriented and derived attitudes. The individual turns out to be metaphorical layers of group attributes, at the bottom of which nothing remains.

Indians traditionally defined themselves communally, based on a spiritual compact rather than a social contract. The tribal will constituted a vital spiritual principle which for most tribes gained expression in sharing and co-operation rather than private property and competition.

This obviated the need for sovereign authority to sustain the integrity of the society against the centrifugal forces of individual self-interest. The political and social experiences that would allow Indians to conceive of authority in European-western terms simply did not exist, nor can sovereign authority be reconciled with the traditional beliefs and values that they want to retain.

The idea of hierarchical power relationships contained in European-western concepts of sovereignty is likewise irreconciliable with Indian history and experiences. In European thought the Enlightenment concept of egalitarianism emerged as a reaction and response to excesses resulting from the hierarchical doctrine of sovereignty. Egalitarianism was imposed on the hierarchical concept of sovereign authority to produce more humane political structures. In traditional Indian society, however, the idea of egalitarianism did not emerge as a reaction to excesses of hierarchical authority. Equality was derived from the Creator's founding prescription. The creation myth held that from the beginning all members of the tribe shared and participated equally in all privileges and responsibilities. In their dealings with the British crown Indian representatives used equality imagery – 'links in a chain' or 'going down the road together.'[4] Neither the members of the tribe nor the outsiders who studied them found images of hierarchical political authority. The exercise of hierarchical authority would have been viewed as a device to deprive the people of equality.

Traditional Indian beliefs and values also clash with the concept of a ruling entity – that is, a dichotomy of ruler(s) and the ruled. In Europe, even after the Enlightenment era, it was not authority per se that came under question, but rather who should exercise authority. New, more humane arrangements for exercising authority were devised, including election and delegation. Most Indian tribes, however, did not accept that any man or agency had the inherent or transferred right to govern others, even in the service of the tribal good. The people ruled collectively, exercising authority as one body with undivided power, performing all functions of government. The tribe was not the result of a contract among individuals or between ruler(s) and ruled, but of a divine creation. No human being was deemed to have control over the life of another. Therefore, the authority to rule could not be delegated to any one member or subset of members of the tribal group. This denial of personal authority extended even to the notion of transferring the right to govern within specified fixed limits. Any arrangement that would separate the people from their fundamental, natural, and inalienable right to govern themselves directly was deemed illegitimate.

In place of personal authority, hierarchical power relationships, and a ruling entity, the organizing and regulating forces for group order and endeavour in traditional Indian society were custom and tradition. Put another way, Indians invested their customs and traditions with the authority and power to govern their behaviour. In the traditional myths custom had a source and sanction outside the individual and tribe. Customs were derived from the Creator. They had withstood the test of time and represented the Creator's sacred blueprint for survival of the tribe. By implication, therefore, everyone must be subject to custom; everyone was equal under the same impersonal customary authority. By unreservedly accepting custom as their legitimate guide in living and working together they alleviated the need for personal authority, a hierarchical power structure, and a separate ruling entity to maintain order. Customary authority protected individuals from self-serving, capricious, and coercive exercise of power by their peers. Since customs are not readily changed or new ones quickly created, authority was not easily or expediently expanded.

Conformity to custom was a matter of religious obedience that accorded with the generally accepted moral standards of the tribe, and it was not deemed necessary to appoint agents with authority to enforce custom. Custom carries authority of a 'moral kind';[5] that is, it obliges individuals, by conscience, to obey. This is quite different from law that is a dictum accompanied by an effective sanction. Rule by custom, without a separate agency of enforcement, was possible in traditional Indian society because a face-to-face society can maintain order with a few broad rules known to everyone. When large gatherings of diverse bands occurred (for example, during the Sun Dance) it was customary to invest one of the Indian societies with a temporary peace-keeping role.

Rituals confirmed customs by linking them to a sacred beginning. Through consecrated rituals the testimony of the ancestors, who first had witnessed the sacred founding of custom, was passed from one generation to the next. Arendt has identified a similar concept of order in the Roman image of the pyramid, which reached non-hierarchically into the past – a past that was sanctified.[6]

The absence of personal authority, hierarchical relationships, and a separate ruling entity carried profound implications for the exercise of leadership in Indian society. For example, elders performed an essential and highly valued function by transmitting the Creator's founding prescriptions, customs, and traditions. But they had no authority; they merely gave information and advice, and never in the form of a command or coercion. The elders were revered not because of their power or authority but because of their knowledge of the customs, traditions, and rituals and because of their ancestral links with the sacred beginning. Chiefs, like elders, led without authority. Their personality or skills as warriors and hunters would gain them a following, but the chief was on the same level as the follower – personal domination over others did not exist. In fact, most tribes had a multiplicity of chiefs at any one time, each without any sanctioning powers beyond his personal charisma and proved ability. Even in the heat of battle a warrior could choose to participate, or not, without prejudice. Self-direction (autonomy), an aristocratic prerogative in European society, was everyone's right in Indian society.

An interesting model of non-authoritarian leadership is contained in Paul-Louis Carrier's 'coach-driver' analogy.[7] In his analogy Carrier proposes that in a liberal state of affairs the government is like a coach-driver, hired and paid by those he drives. The coach-driver conveys his patrons to the destination and by the route they choose. To an uninformed outsider the coach-driver may appear to be the master, but this is an illusion. Carrier's model of non-authoritarian leadership only approximates the traditional Indian conception of leadership. In tribal Indian society leadership was more aptly symbolized by the relationship of a military drummer to his company. The drummer can establish a cadence but he has no authority to require individuals in the company to march to it. That authority comes from an external source. For Indians this external source was always to be found in their sacred customs. Unlike Carrier's coach-driver, who is subordinate to his patrons, the Indian leader, like the drummer, is not subordinate to the dictates of those who march to his beat. Like them, he is responsible only to the external authority – the sacred tribal customs and traditions.

Government without rulers requires special procedures. The mechanism used in traditional Indian society was direct participatory democracy and rule by consensus. This implies an adequate level of agreement among all who share in the exercise of authority. Custom provided the mechanism to ensure that order did not break down through failure to achieve consensus. This is possible only in a face-to-face society like the Indian tribes.

Statehood and Territoriality

In addition to the concepts of authority, hierarchy, and a separate ruling entity, the European-western doctrine of sovereignty subsumes two more ideas with special implications for Indian tribal traditions: the notions of statehood and territoriality. Merriam points out that while an unresolved debate exists among scholars as to whether sovereignty is an essential characteristic of the state, all theorists of sovereignty implicitly, if not explicitly, assume that statehood is an essential and indispensable requirement for sovereignty.[8] F.F. Hinsley has asserted that the emergence of the state as a form of rule is by definition a necessary condition for the exercise of sovereignty.[9]

Prior to colonization, Indian tribes held an independent self-governing status best defined as 'nationhood,' not 'statehood.' In place of the 'myth of a state,' they had a 'myth of the nation.' As nations of people they regulated their internal and external relations. But unlike that of states, their foundation of social order was not based on hierarchical authority wielded by a distinct central political entity. The state represents a structure of hierarchical political authority imposed upon the community; the tribes, though highly organized, had not undergone the separation of authority from the community. They lacked separate state forms and government institutions. It is a mistake, however, to view traditional Indian nations as though they were at some primitive stage of statehood undergoing a transition to full statehood. As we said earlier, in tribal Indian society authority and order rested on custom and the directly spoken consensus of the community. Indian nations had no need for statehood and the condition of hierarchical authority that statehood implies. Their community performed all of the necessary political functions: it kept the peace, preserved individual life, and protected its members from injustice, abuse, and arbitrary actions by any of their number.

The concept of territoriality also is fundamental to European-western doctrines of sovereignty and statehood. Brierly expresses this as follows: 'At the basis of international law lies the notion that a state occupies a definite part of the surface of the earth, within which it normally exercises ... jurisidiction over persons and things to the exclusion of other states. When a state exercises an authority of this kind ... it is popularly said to have sovereignty over the territory.'[10] Although Indian leaders today place great emphasis on land claims and their irrevocable rights to reservation lands, this emphasis represents a concession to European-western political-legal influence. Traditionally, Indian notions of territoriality were not conceived of in terms of precisely fixed territorial boundaries. Tribes existed as spiritual associations that transcended narrow issues of territory. The basis for nationhood was their community, not a fixed territory or geographically defined citizenship. Most tribes had no concept of private or collective land ownership. They believed all land belonged to the Creator, who had made the land for all life forms to use in harmony. This belief imposed certain restraints on tribes in their territorial claims and in their relationship to each other.

The lack of precisely delineated and recognized territorial borders occasionally produced conflicts over hunting privileges, but tribes fought mainly over access to game in the territories, not over the territories themselves. Even when they were at war with each other Indian tribes displayed an abiding respect for each other's autonomy and community. As Ahenakew points out, 'It was unknown among the First Nations that one nation could by force deprive another nation of its right to self-determination and to sufficient lands and resources to maintain the lives of its people.'[11] Because the notion of territoriality did not have primacy for them, victorious tribes did not colonize vanquished tribes in the way that European states did. In short, whereas the European-western concept of sovereignty was based on authority by the state over a piece of territory, clearly demarcated by boundaries, Indians traditionally based their concept of nationhood on their social community.

Implication of Aspirations to Sovereignty for Indian Culture

Indians in Canada are opting for sovereignty because they view it as the most promising doctrine for protecting their ancestral heritage from encroaching external influences and powers. They want sovereignty not to justify internal authority within their communities, but to exclude the sovereign authority of the Canadian government.

As part of their political-legal justification for sovereignty and to convince the Canadian government and the international community that their claim to sovereignty is legitimate, contemporary Indian leaders are reconstructing and reinterpreting their tribal history and traditional culture to conform to the essential political and legal paradigms and symbols contained in the European-western concept of sovereign statehood. They are creating the fiction that Indian societies, prior to European contact, had hierarchically structured governments that exercised authority through a ruling entity and that were in possession of lands clearly defined by political and territorial boundaries. To rationalize their claim to sovereignty, some Indian leaders are resorting to unsupportable and selective assumptions about the traditional exercise of authority by tribal groups, assumptions that contradict the images Indians hold of their traditional aboriginal reality when they are not specifically making a political-legal case for tribal sovereignty. As we have documented, sovereignty was not relevant to their internal or external relationships. Furthermore, all claims to inherent tribal sovereignty, as distinct from claims to nationhood, are necessarily hypothetical since, historically, the European conception of sovereignty was not in the cultural apparatus of Indians. It should be emphasized that this fiction does not represent a cynical manipulation of political concepts so much as a misguided reinterpretation of traditional aboriginality.

By resorting to the expedient claim of inherent sovereign statehood Indian leaders are legitimizing European-western–type philosophies and structures of authority and decision-making within contemporary Indian communities. Most Indian communities initially opposed the imposition of European-western models of elected democratic government and the associated bureaucratic administrative structures. They protested the hierarchical authority structures that relegated most tribal members to the periphery of decision-making. Yet, by adopting the European-western ideology of sovereignty, the current generation of Indian leaders is buttressing the imposed alien authority structures within their communities and legitimizing the associated hierarchy composed of indigenous political and bureaucratic élites. This endorsement of hierarchical authority and a ruling entity constitutes a complete break with traditional indigenous principles. It undermines fundamental and substantial distinctions between traditional Indian and European political and cultural values. The legal-political struggle for sovereignty could prove to be a Trojan horse for traditional Indian culture by playing into the hands of the Canadian government's long-standing policy of assimilation.

An Exploration of Alternative Models of Self-Determination

The Canadian government and native Indians must find a way of coexisting that will allow each to preserve that which it deems essential to its survival and identity. The Canadian government has made clear that it will not accept sovereignty for Canada's Indians. For most Indians, assimilation into Canadian culture is repugnant and unacceptable. Thus, the acceptable model for a relationship between the federal government and Canada's Indians lies somewhere between assimilation and sovereignty.

Most Indian peoples are committed to a separate social system with corresponding networks of social institutions that are congruent with their historical tribal arrangements and that are based on their traditional identity, language, religion, philosophy, and customs. The Canadian government is ready to accept Indian self-government. The challenge for Indian leaders is to develop a model of self-government that is acceptable to the Canadian government and that gives Indians internal self-determination without compromising fundamental traditional values. The option of pluralism suggests itself.

In his analysis of pluralism, Kenneth McRae identifies three uses of that term: (1) that of the British political pluralists (J.N. Figgis, Harold Laski, and G.D.H. Cole), who viewed pluralism primarily in terms of alternative foci of citizen loyalties vis-à-vis the sovereign state; (2) that put forward by the American writers (A.F. Bentley, David Truman, Robert Dahl, and others), which contains the central idea of countervailing but overlapping interest groups competing in policy formation; and (3) that expressed in the literature on colonial and post-colonial societies (J.S. Furnival, M.G. Smith, Leo Kuper, and Pierre van den Berghe), which posits two or more social systems and associated constitutional networks within one political system.[12] This latter use of pluralism, which allows for the presence of several nations within one sovereign state, is evident in the 'consociational school' (notably Arend Lijphart, Gerard Lehmbruch, Hans Doalder, Jurg Steiner, and Val Lorwin). A consociational arrangement is a significant step short of separation and sovereignty. Theoretically, it could accommodate the essential political requisites of both the Indians and the Canadian government, but it is unacceptable to Indians because of its emphasis on rule by élites.

A more promising political model can be found in the works of Vernon Van Dyke.[13] Briefly stated, Van Dyke challenges the two-level theory of rights. He proposes that rights are not simply a question of the individual and the state, and that ethnic communities meeting certain criteria should be considered as unities (corporate bodies) with moral rights and legal status accorded them as groups rather than as individuals. He proposes that ethnic communities, not only states, are entitled to be regarded as right-and-duty–bearing entities. Traditional European-western concepts of sovereignty provide no place for groups in the state, only individuals. European philosophers like Hobbes and Locke emphasized the right of the individual in his relationship to the sovereign state. Western liberal political theorists have continued that emphasis on the relationship between individual and state. Robert Nisbet identifies this as the most influential philosophy of freedom in modern Western society.[14]

Van Dyke advocates a more complex paradigm, one that would permit both group and individual rights, legal and moral, to exist side by side. The objective is not to downplay equal treatment for individuals but to extend to groups equal rights to preserve their integrity. This model implies the principle that a nation of people has an intrinsic and unalienable collective right to self-determination. This principle, as Van Dyke points out, had legitimate status in the League of Nations Charter and now enjoys the same status in the United Nations Charter, where the moral if not the legal right to self-determination by nations of people is upheld. Wendell Bell has proposed that the nation state is one possible outcome of an exercise in self-determination, but other models are possible.[15] The ultimate choice will be based on the perceived efficacy of the model in achieving constituents' aspirations to liberty, equality, and fraternity. Puerto Rico, for example, has chosen common-wealth status.

How does Van Dyke's model fit the historical and contemporary status of Indian tribes? Prior to colonization Indian tribes operated as independent stateless nations in their own right – not a derived, delegated, or transferred right, but one that came into existence with the group itself. Under the Indian Act and by historical convention Indian tribes in Canada have retained their special group-based status and rights.

Nationhood

Using social-science criteria Walker Connor defines the essence of a nation as 'a psychological bond that joins a people and differentiates it, in the subconscious conviction of its members, from all other people in a most vital way.'[16] He adds in another context that 'national conscious-ness is therefore accompanied by a growing aversion to being ruled by those deemed aliens.'[17] Other social scientists have defined a nation as 'a social group which shares a common ideology, common institutions and customs and a sense of homogeneity.'[18] Clearly, Indian tribes meet the social-science criteria of nationhood.

The very high level of cultural uniqueness and homogeneity of Indian tribal groups not only strengthens their political integration as nations but also acts as a barrier to political integration into Canadian society. The fact that Indian cultural uniqueness has become politicized has created an additional serious obstacle to integration into the larger society.

Van Dyke's paradigm provides a framework within which Indians and the Canadian government may be able to negotiate internal self-determination that will provide Indians with the opportunity to retain their group differences. The component unit representing native people would be the 'nation' based on traditional cultural and linguistic communities. The Indian nations would function in a constitutionally defined and guaranteed relationship with the provincial and central governments. Both the Canadian state and the Indian nations would be subject to domestic arrangements specified by general rules or particu-lar treaty agreements regulating the relationship between them.

Indian peoples would be subject to Canadian sovereignty and control over their external affairs, but there would be constitutionally defined limits to Canadian control over Indian internal affairs. Although the Canadian government, pursuant to agreements, would continue to exercise some indirect control over individual Indians (for example, in the area of criminal law), in those matters not covered by agreement or treaty Indian nations would be paramount in setting policies over their own territories and people within their territories. They would exercise jurisdiction over their legal, political, social, and economic institutions.

The Canadian federal system provides an institutional framework for accommodating Van Dyke's paradigm. That paradigm could be acceptable to the Canadian government because Indian nationhood does not require sovereignty, statehood, or separation. It does not threaten the territorial integrity or impair the sovereignty of the Canadian state. The Indian minority would not be seen in competitive terms because it would not have equal weight with the majority. Negotiated limits would place Indians in a position so that they could not significantly change the existing distribution of power. In fact, most Indians would shy away from exercising reciprocal authority over the non-Indian political community. Their basic desire is for self-government and control over their own affairs, not for participation in the governing of the rest of Canada through representation in Parliament, the Senate, or the provincial legislatures.

Resolution of common problems or conflicts between the Canadian government and Indian nations could occur through political and administrative mechanisms involving consultative negotiations. Such a model, imbedded as a constitutionally guaranteed principle, would allow Indians the freedom they need to build the types of communities they desire. Furthermore, by avoiding the issue of sovereign statehood this model conforms approximately to the United Nations ambiguous strictures on self-determination of peoples. This gives it greater legal, political, and moral validity.

Conclusion

The most critical political and legal objections of the Canadian government are directed at Indian claims to European-western–style sovereign statehood, not at the principle of self-government. In a struggle to achieve sovereign statehood Indian people could well provoke a full-scale power struggle with the Canadian government. Such a struggle would consume their limited human, political, and economic resources in a futile exercise and could create a backlash in which the nationhood option might be eliminated. Furthermore, whereas the Indian condition of economic dependence is a serious constraint on aspirations to sovereign statehood, there is no necessary incompatibility between the current economic dependent status of Canadian Indians and a claim to nationhood. Perhaps more important for Indians than the political-economic feasibility of autonomous nationhood is its compatibility with their traditional beliefs. Autonomous nationhood, unlike sovereign statehood, would allow Indians to preserve traditional beliefs, values, customs, and institutions and to integrate these with emergent group interests.

The Canadian government is confronted with two choices. It can continue its thinly disguised, much despised policy of assimilation, or it can adopt a policy of meaningful self-determination for Indian tribes. The Canadian government has a moral if not a legal obligation to deal justly and humanely with the Indian people. If it denies their historical and legitimate claim to nationhood through political or legal stratagems, the Indian sense of injustice will persist. That sense will inhibit meaningful improvement in Indians' economic, social, and political condition. If this situation is allowed to fester it could erupt in extralegal actions culminating in violence.[19] If, however, Indians are accorded 'nation' status within the Canadian federation, and if they are dealt with fairly and honourably, such an arrangement could foster a sense of mutual trust, depoliticize cultural divergency, and, in the long term, ease cultural co-operation with Canadian society. Native Indian loyalties might, over time, be voluntarily transferred to Canadian society.

Epilogue

To understand the present and future problems in resolving the aboriginal rights issue, we need to understand the broader Canadian political agenda within which those issues exist. The same controversies that beset most social and economic policy-making in Canada also plague aboriginal policy-making. At the core of any attempt to deal with aboriginal peoples is the conflict of federal and provincial interests and jurisdictions. This was evident during the second and third constitutional conferences. When Prime Minister Pierre Trudeau proposed a constitutional amendment at the second constitutional conference to entrench the principle of aboriginal self-government and to commit the governments of Canada to negotiating the implementation of aboriginal self-governing institutions, six of the ten provinces refused to support it. At the third constitutional conference there appeared to be greater support among the provinces for Prime Minister Mulroney's proposed constitutional amendment regarding aboriginal self-government, but Alberta and British Columbia remained adamantly opposed. The provincial premiers justified their dissent on the ground that they did not understand the full meaning and implications of the proposed amendment. However, their opposition can also be understood as an expression of the persistent mistrust felt by the provinces about the federal government's intentions with respect to provincial interests and jurisdictions.

Federal and provincial conflicts regarding aboriginal peoples centre on three important issues: land claims, self-government, and financial liability. In regard to land claims, the provinces have a stake in both specific and comprehensive claims. Because most provinces fall under one or more of the numbered treaties (1–11), they are required to co-operate with the federal government in the settlement of specific claims – that is, grievances with respect to unfulfilled treaty obligations and the maladministration of Indian lands and other such assets under government control. The three prairie provinces, for example, are bound by legal agreement to surrender unoccupied crown lands, as needed, to settle unfulfilled treaty obligations. Provincial governments, however, encounter considerable pressure from non-Indian interest groups such as ranchers, oil companies, and sportsmen opposing settlements that would increase the amount of land given to Indians. Moreover, provinces know that the surrender of lands will affect their future sources of revenue, especially if mineral resources must be ceded along with the land. Because of these conflicting interests, the few land settlements that have been concluded have usually entailed a protracted negotiation process. The provinces subject every land claim to a time-consuming examination. The report of the Treaty Land Entitlement Commission created by the province of Manitoba to study Indian claims exemplifies this drawn-out process.

Comprehensive claims – those claims deriving from aboriginal peoples' traditional use and occupancy of land – pose additional problems for the provinces. Not only are the land boundaries in such claims ill-defined, but the range of negotiable items included in such claims is very broad and can include economic benefits and self-government, among other things. Examples of this kind of claim settlement are the James Bay and Northern Quebec Agreement of 1975 and the Supplementary Northeastern Quebec Agreement of 1978. These claim settlements were the product of trilateral negotiations between aboriginal peoples, the federal government, and the Quebec government. Although this agreement is held up as a model by the Quebec government and many Cree Indian leaders in Quebec, it has been roundly denounced by Indian leaders elsewhere in Canada as a sell-out of the principle of aboriginal title. As a consequence, comprehensive claims now under negotiation by the Nishgas in British Columbia and by the Naskapis-Montagnais Indians in Labrador have become politically sensitive and face a rocky road to resolution.

Provincial interest in the land issue takes on another form in the case of the Metis. The Metis claim a land base as an integral part of their quest for self-governing status. To bolster their land claims, the Metis seek to be identified with Indians; they hope to achieve this aim by lobbying to come under federal jurisdiction within the meaning of section 91(24) of the Constitution Act, 1867. Regardless of whether they achieve this status or remain under the jurisdiction of the provinces, the Metis, in order to acquire a land base, will require not only provincial consent but also provincial land. This is the case in the prairies, where the federal government owns very little land. Because the provinces have no legal obligations to provide the Metis with land, they can be expected to mount considerable resistance to Metis claims for a land base.

The second issue, aboriginal self-government, more than any other aspect of aboriginal rights spills over into the larger field of federal-provincial relations. Depending upon which aboriginal group is being considered, federal and provincial governments hold varying positions on aboriginal self-government. Since the mid-1970s the federal government has been committed to a policy of increased self-government for Indians. This commitment has been expressed in three ways. First, the Department of Indian Affairs has attempted to transfer program-delivery functions to band governments through a policy of devolution of powers and bloc funding. Second, the federal government has sought on several occasions to increase Indian autonomy by enacting special band government legislation as an alternative to the restrictive Indian Act provisions. The latest manifestation of this approach was Bill C-52, the Liberal government's legislative response to the report of the Special Committee on Indian Self-Government in Canada (the Penner Committee). In essence, the proposed legislation would have allowed broadening of powers for those Indian first nations (band or tribal councils) that developed internal constitutions specifying political and financial accountability criteria and protection of individual and collective rights. Any first nation that fulfilled these criteria would have been recognized under the act; once recognized, its delegated legislative powers would have been broadened and it would have been eligible to enter into short-term and long-term bloc-funding arrangements with the federal government.

A third approach to increased Indian self-government was taken at the last two constitutional conferences when federal officials proposed amendments to entrench the principle of self-government for aboriginal peoples, along with a negotiating process leading to its definition and entrenchment in the constitution. Questions have been raised about whether the federal government's constitutional initiatives represent sincere policy initiatives. Some view them as part of a political strategy to deflect Indian frustrations at the lack of progress on aboriginal issues from the federal government to the provinces.

Although the provinces share some of the same goals as the federal government in regard to Indian self-government, their preference is for a more slowly paced, cautious, and conservative approach on the issue of autonomy for Indians. The federal government has shown a willingness to accept Indian government as a third order of government – that is, territorial enclaves with province-like powers. But provincial governments insist that Indian government must take a political and administrative form inferior to the provinces.

Federal policy toward self-government of the Inuit (with the exception of those Inuit residing within provincial boundaries) has been linked tightly to the settlement of Inuit land claims and the evolution of territorial government. The federal strategy ostensibly has been to respond positively to Inuit demands for greater participation in decisions that touch on their traditional way of life, such as wildlife-harvesting and control of environmental conditions, and on revenue-sharing from natural resource exploitation in their territories.

In regard to Metis self-government, the federal policy position seems to be one of providing ad hoc assistance through various programs housed in several different government departments while waiting to see what may emerge from constitutional or other political negotiations. Understandably, the federal government is reluctant to accept responsibility for Metis. Unknown financial costs, jurisdictional uncertainty, and administrative complexity make it extremely difficult for federal officials to chart a clear policy with respect to the Metis.

All federal policies on aboriginal self-government, whether administratively, legislatively, or constitutionally based, flatly reject aboriginal claims to inherent sovereignty. This position was clearly stated by Prime Minister Trudeau during the first constitutional conference and has been reaffirmed in subsequent negotiations with aboriginal leaders.

The provinces do not present a united front on aboriginal self-government. At the second constitutional conference differences emerged among the provinces on matters of process as well as of principle. British Columbia, Alberta, Saskatchewan, Nova Scotia, Prince Edward Island, and Newfoundland insisted that the structures of aboriginal government must be clarified and the jurisdictional and financial aspects be agreed upon prior to constitutional entrenchment, if entrenchment is deemed necessary. Ontario, Manitoba, and New Brunswick appeared willing to support entrenchment of the principle of aboriginal government and to negotiate the details later. Although there appeared to be less disagreement among the provinces at the 1985 constitutional conference on increased aboriginal self-government, the consensus necessary for a constitutional amendment was not present. The Lévesque government in Quebec has not yet recognized the validity of the Constitution Act, and has refused to participate in any amending process. Indeed, the Parti Québécois government proposes to deal with aboriginal peoples residing within its borders on a bilateral basis outside the constitutional discussions.

Provincial governments in general insist that Indians are and should continue to be a federal responsibility under section 91(24) of the Constitution Act, 1867. Within this framework they are generally supportive of federal efforts to devolve federal powers to band and tribal governments, providing provincial jurisdiction is not altered or diminished. Moreover, it appears that the provinces are prepared to continue to accept responsibility for the Metis and non-status Indian groups and to provide some support to the Metis for a limited measure of self-government equal to that provided to municipalities. Alberta and Quebec government support for the Metis, however, will be offered only within the parameters of provincial jurisdiction. Should the Metis insist on coming under the provisions of section 91(24), these provinces may alter their policies and take a hands-off approach to the question of Metis self-government.

The Inuit, who have made the most moderate demands for self-government, are most harmed by provincial intransigence on aboriginal self-government. Even though provincial relationships with the Inuit are restricted to only two provinces, Quebec and Newfoundland, provincial opposition to entrenchment of aboriginal self-government has the effect of denying constitutional recognition to Inuit self-government in the North.

The third key issue in federal-provincial jurisdictional conflicts, financial liability for aboriginal peoples, must be placed in the context of a larger federal–provincial conflict over fiscal responsibilities. The past two decades have witnessed an attempt by the federal government to transfer an increasing share of the financial burden for social services to the provinces. One effect of this federal policy thrust has been to shift responsibility for providing some social services to Indians to provincial governments. For example, some provinces now extend health, education, and social-welfare services to Indians living on reserves as well as those living off reserves. The provinces are also becoming involved in economic development for Indians, especially in the areas of small-business development and agricultural assistance. Many of the provincial programs for Indians are based on trilateral or bilateral agreements, and involve some form of federal–provincial cost-sharing.

To perform their expanding role in delivering services to aboriginal peoples, most provinces have established special policy-making and program-delivery structures. These structures may include cabinet portfolios with limited bureaucratic structures, as in Alberta; Indian and native affairs secretariats, as in Saskatchewan; and tripartite councils that include representatives from the province, the federal government, and the aboriginal peoples, as in Ontario.

A good deal of provincial apprehension over federal initiatives to extend increased self-government to Indian peoples derives from their suspicion that such a move is a disguised scheme to shift social responsibility and the attendant costs for all aboriginal peoples to the provinces. Indian peoples are in a position not unlike that of developing nations; they are in need of administrative and technical assistance in addition to extensive financial support. Despite the federal government's assurances that it will provide adequate levels of funding for Indian self-government, the provinces worry that they will be required to put up increasing amounts of fiscal and other forms of support to underwrite the cost of emerging aboriginal self-government.

The expanding role of the provinces in service delivery to Indian bands is forcing Indian leaders to make a difficult choice. Indian leaders fear that by accepting financial and program assistance from the provinces they will undermine their traditional trust relationship with the federal government under section 91(24), thereby forfeiting their aboriginal and treaty rights. Their fear has been heightened by the negative experiences of Indian leaders in their dealings with the provinces during the constitutional conferences. Many band governments, however, recognize that provincial assistance is essential if they hope to alleviate the intolerable economic and social conditions that exist on their reserves. For the approximately 30 per cent of Indians that live off reserves, this issue is no longer a matter of dispute. For them, provincial agencies already are the main if not the only providers of social and economic assistance.

For Indians leaders, who are agonizing over what the nature of their relationship with the provinces should be, the key question is how the principles of Indian nationhood and aboriginal rights can be reconciled with accepting assistance from the provinces. In dealing with this question, Indian leaders are confronted with a dilemma. On the one hand, if they choose to deal with provincial governments, thereby compromising the principles of nationhood and aboriginal rights, they will lose the support of their constituents. On the other hand, if they insist on entrenching these principles in law and the constitution they will encounter continuing provincial government intransigence and lack of progress. Provincial governments, however, have shown a willingness to negotiate on specific practical issues, and such negotiations have in the past produced incremental gains. The challenge facing Indian leaders is how to reconcile their own constituents' insistence on entrenching basic principles with the provincial governments' insistence on limiting negotiations to specific practical issues.

The dilemma of principle versus pragmatism is causing conflicts in all aboriginal political organizations over leadership stances. Some of these conflicts have degenerated from policy conflicts to conflicts of personality. Such disputes impede the capacity of aboriginal political associations to present unified, coherent policy positions in negotiations with governments. If the conflicts persist, the inclination of governments to bargain seriously with aboriginal political associations will be undermined, particularly as provincial governments turn their attention to other pressing matters.

The dilemma of principle versus pragmatism may become more sharply focused as younger, university-educated, aboriginal élites move into leadership positions. These new élites are likely to take a pragmatic approach regarding what can be accomplished within the Canadian federal system. Such a development holds a potential for intergenerational conflicts between older leaders arguing from principle and younger leaders who develop their policy stances based upon a calculation of what they deem possible.

The Penner Report, which stands as the most exhaustive parliamentary study of Indians in more than three decades, recommends that the federal government deal with Indians as nations. The Liberal government gave some legitimacy to this notion in its proposed legislation for Indian self-government. But the proposed legislation (Bill C-52) did not provide the degree of political autonomy that nationhood implies, nor did it satisfy most Indian leaders' expectations. Moreover, the provinces view Indian nationhood status as a threat to their jurisdiction and powers within Confederation and are not ready to accept such a status.

Since the beginning of Confederation, aboriginal peoples have been treated as inferiors in their negotiations with governments in Canada. Because their people historically were self-governing, aboriginal leaders insist on equality in their negotiations with the dominant society. Throughout their long contact with European civilizations they have consistently adhered to the 'going-down-the-road-together' philosophy that holds the white man to be their equal. They expect a reciprocal attitude from the dominant society.

Above all, aboriginal peoples seek justice. Canadians should be forewarned that a sense of injustice can dwell in the hearts of a people for generations. There it breeds feelings of hopelessness and desperation and a festering hate; these feelings can erupt in acts of violence. Precedents abound – the Irish, the Basques, the Sikhs, the Armenians, the Palestinians. The potential human costs of meting out injustice to aboriginal peoples are immeasurable and the long-term consequences for the Canadian self-concept debilitating. Is this the legacy we want to hand down to future generations of Canadians?

Appendices

A/Royal Proclamation of 1763 (excerpt)

And whereas it is just and reasonable, and essential to our Interests, and the Security of our Colonies, that the several Nations or Tribes of Indians with whom We are connected, and who live under our Protection, should not be molested or disturbed in the Possession of such Parts of our Dominions and Territories as not having been ceded to or purchased by Us, are reserved to them, or any of them, as their Hunting Grounds. — We do therefore, with the Advice of our Privy Council, declare it to be our Royal Will and Pleasure, that no Governor or Commander in Chief in any of our Colonies of Quebec, East Florida, or West Florida, do presume, upon any Pretence whatever, to grant Warrants of Survey, or pass any Patents for Lands beyond the Bounds of their respective Governments, as described in their Commissions; as also that no Governor, or Commander in Chief in any of our other Colonies or Plantations in America do presume for the present, and until our further Pleasure be known, to grant Warrants of Survey, or pass Patents for any Lands beyond the Heads or Sources of any of the Rivers which fall into the Atlantic Ocean from the West and North West, or upon any Lands whatever, which, not having been ceded to or purchased by Us as aforesaid, are reserved to the said Indians, or any of them.

And We do further declare it to be Our Royal Will and Pleasure, for the present as aforesaid, to reserve under our Sovereignty, Protection and Dominion, for the use of the said Indians, all the Lands and Territories not included within the Limits of Our said Three new Governments or within the Limits of the Territory granted to the Hudson's Bay Company, as also all the Lands and Territories lying to the Westward of the Sources of the Rivers which fall into the Sea from the West and North West as aforesaid.

And We do hereby strictly forbid, on Pain of our Displeasure, all our loving Subjects from making any Purchases or Settlements whatever, or taking Possession of any of the Lands above reserved, without our especial leave and Licence for that purpose first obtained.

And We do Further strictly enjoin and require all Persons whatever who have either wilfully or inadvertently seated themselves upon any Lands within the Countries above described, or upon any other Lands which, not having been ceded to or purchased by Us, are still reserved to the said Indians as aforesaid, forthwith to remove themselves from such settlements.

And whereas great Frauds and Abuses have been committed in purchasing Lands of the Indians to the great Prejudice of our Interests and to the great Dissatisfaction of the said Indians; in order therefore to prevent such Irregularities for the future, and to the end that the Indians may be convinced of our Justice and determined Resolution to remove all reasonable Cause of Discontent, We do, with the Advice of our Privy Council, strictly enjoin and require, that no private Person do presume to make any Purchase from the said Indians of any Lands reserved to the said Indians, within those parts of our Colonies where We have thought proper to allow Settlement; but that if at any Time any of the said Indians should be inclined to dispose of the said Lands, the same shall be Purchased only for Us in our Name, at some public Meeting or Assembly of the said Indians, to be held for that Purpose by the Governor or Commander in Chief of our Colony respectively within which they shall lie; and in case they shall lie within the limits of any Proprietary Government, they shall be purchased only for the Use and in the name of such Proprietaries, conformable to such Directions and Instructions as we or they shall think proper to give for that Purpose; and we do, by the Advice of our Privy Council, declare and enjoin that the Trade with the said Indians shall be free and open to all other Subjects whatever, provided that every Person who may incline to Trade with the said Indians do take out a Licence for carrying on such Trade from the Governor or the Commander in Chief of any of Our Colonies respectively where such Person shall reside, and also give Security to observe such Regulations as We shall at any Time think fit, by ourselves or by our Commissaries to be appointed for this Purpose, to direct and appoint for the Benefit of the said Trade.

And we do hereby authorize, enjoin, and require the Governors and Commanders in Chief of all our Colonies respectively, as well those under Our immediate Government as those under the Government and Direction of Proprietaries, to grant such Licences without Fee or Reward, taking especial Care to insert therein a Condition, that such Licence shall be void, and the Security forfeited in case the Person to whom the same is granted shall refuse or neglect to observe such Regulations as We shall think proper to prescribe as aforesaid.

And we do further expressly enjoin and require all Officers whatever, as well Military as those Employed in the Management and Direction of Indian Affairs, within the Territories reserved as aforesaid for the use of the said Indians, to seize and apprehend all Persons whatever, who standing charged with Treason, Misprisions of Treason, Murders, or other Felonies or Misdemeanors, shall fly from Justice and take Refuge in the said Territory, and to send them under a proper guard to the Colony where the Crime was committed of which they stand accused, in order to take their Trial for the same.

Given at our Court of St James', the 7th Day of October, 1763, in the Third Year of our Reign.

GOD SAVE THE KING

B / A Declaration of the First Nations (1981)

We the Original Peoples of this Land know the Creator put us here.

The Creator gave us Laws that govern all our relationships to live in harmony with nature and mankind.

The Laws of the Creator defined our rights and responsibilities.

The Creator gave us our spiritual beliefs, our Language, our culture, and a place on Mother Earth which provided us with all our needs.

We have maintained our freedom, our Languages, and our traditions from time immemorial.

We continue to exercise the rights and fulfill the responsibilities and obligations given to us by the Creator for the Land upon which we were placed.

The Creator has given us the right to govern ourselves and the right to self-determination.

The rights and responsibilities given to us by the Creator cannot be altered or taken away by any other Nation.

TREATY AND ABORIGINAL RIGHTS PRINCIPLES

1 The aboriginal title, aboriginal rights and treaty rights of the aboriginal peoples of Canada, including:
   a all rights recognized by the Royal Proclamation of October 7th, 1763;
   b all rights recognized in treaties between the Crown and nations or tribes of Indians in Canada ensuring the Spiritual concept of Treaties;
   c all rights acquired by aboriginal peoples in settlements or agreements with the Crown on aboriginal rights and title;
   are hereby recognized, confirmed, ratified and sanctioned.
2 'Aboriginal people' means the First Nations or Tribes of Indians in Canada and each Nation having the right to define its own Citizenship.

3 Those parts of the Royal Proclamation of October 7th, 1763, providing for the rights of the Nations or tribes of Indians are legally and politically binding on the Canadian and British Parliaments.

4 No Law of Canada or of the Provinces, including the Charter of Rights and Freedoms in the Constitution of Canada, shall hereafter be construed or applied so as to abrogate, abridge or diminish the rights specified in Sections 1 and 3 of this Part.

5 a The Parliament and Government of Canada shall be committed to the negotiation of the full realization and implementation of the rights specified in Sections 1 and 3 of this Part.

  b Such negotiations shall be internationally supervised, if the aboriginal peoples parties to those negotiations so request.

  c Such negotiations, and any agreements concluded thereby, shall be with the full participation and the full consent of the aboriginal peoples affected.

6 Any amendments to the Constitution of Canada in relation to any constitutional matters which affect the aboriginal peoples, including the identification or definition of the rights of any of those peoples, shall be made only with the consent of the governing Council, Grand Council or Assembly of the aboriginal peoples affected by such amendment, identification or definition.

7 A Treaty and Aboriginal Rights Protection Office shall be established.

8 A declaration that Indian Governmental powers and responsibilities exist as a permanent, integral fact in the Canadian polity.

9 All pre-confederation, post-confederation treaties and treaties executed outside the present boundaries of Canada but which apply to the Indian Nations of Canada are international treaty agreements between sovereign nations. Any changes to the treaties requires the consent of the two parties to the treaties, who are the Indian Governments representing Indian Nations and the Crown represented by the British Government. The Canadian Government is only a third party and cannot initiate any changes.

JOINT COUNCIL OF THE NATIONAL INDIAN BROTHERHOOD
18 November 1981

C/Metis Declaration of Rights

DECLARATION OF RIGHTS, NATIVE COUNCIL OF CANADA, 1979

We the Metis and Non-Status Indians, descendants of the 'Original People' of this country declare:

That Metis nationalism is Canadian nationalism. We embody the true spirit of Canada and are the source of Canadian identity.

That we have the right to self-determination and shall continue – in the tradition of Louis Riel – to express this right as equal partners in confederation.

That all Native people must be included in each step of the process leading to changes in the constitution of Canada.

That we have the right to guaranteed representation in all Legislative Assemblies.

That we have the inalienable right to the land and the natural resources of that land.

That we have the right to determine how and when the land and resources are to be developed for the benefit of our people and in partnership with other Canadians for the benefit of Canada as a whole.

That we have the right to preserve our identity and to flourish as a distinct people with a rich cultural heritage.

That we have the right to educate our children in our Native languages, customs, beliefs, music and other art forms.

That we are a people with a right to special status in confederation.

D/First Ministers' Accord Pertaining to Aboriginal Peoples in the Constitution, November 1981 (excerpt)

25 The guarantee in this Charter of certain rights and freedoms shall not be construed so as to abrogate or derogate from any aboriginal, treaty or other rights or freedoms that pertain to the aboriginal peoples of Canada including

(a) any rights or freedoms that have been recognized by the Royal Proclamation of October 7, 1763; and

(b) any rights or freedoms that may be acquired by the aboriginal peoples of Canada by way of land claims settlement.

34 (1) The aboriginal and treaty rights of the aboriginal peoples of Canada are hereby recognized and affirmed.

(2) In this Act, 'aboriginal peoples of Canada' includes the Indian, Inuit and Metis peoples of Canada.

36 (1) Until Part VI comes into force, a constitutional conference composed of the Prime Minister of Canada and the first ministers of the provinces shall be convened by the Prime Minister of Canada at least once in every year.

(2) A conference convened under subsection (1) shall have included in its agenda an item respecting constitutional matters that directly affect the aboriginal peoples of Canada, including the identification and definition of the rights of those peoples to be included in the Constitution of Canada, and the Prime Minister of Canada shall invite representatives of those peoples to participate in the discussions on that item.

E / Sections of the Constitution Act, 1982, Pertaining to Aboriginal Peoples

25 The guarantee in this Charter of certain rights and freedoms shall not be construed so as to abrogate or derogate from any aboriginal, treaty or other rights or freedoms that pertain to the aboriginal peoples of Canada including

(a) any rights or freedoms that have been recognized by the Royal Proclamation of October 7, 1963; and

(b) any rights or freedoms that may be acquired by the aboriginal peoples of Canada by way of land claims settlement.

35 (1) The existing aboriginal and treaty rights of the aboriginal peoples of Canada are hereby recognized and affirmed.

(2) In this Act, 'aboriginal peoples of Canada' includes the Indian, Inuit and Metis peoples of Canada.

37 (1) A constitutional conference composed of the Prime Minister of Canada and the first ministers of the provinces shall be convened by the Prime Minister of Canada within one year after this Part comes into force.

(2) The conference convened under subsection (1) shall have included in its agenda and item respecting constitutional matters that directly affect the aboriginal peoples of Canada, including the identification and definition of the rights of those peoples to be included in the Constitution of Canada, and the Prime Minister of Canada shall invite representatives of those peoples to participate in the discussions on that item.

(3) The Prime Minister of Canada shall invite elected representatives of the governments of the Yukon Territory and the Northwest Territories to participate in the discussions on any item on the agenda of the conference convened under subsection (1) that, in the opinion of the Prime Minister, directly affects the Yukon Territory and the Northwest Territories.

F / Resolution to Amend the Constitution Act, 1982 (1983)

Whereas the *Constitution Act, 1982* provides that an amendment to the Constitution of Canada may be made by proclamation issued by the Governor General under the Great Seal of Canada where so authorized by resolutions of the Senate and House of Commons and resolutions of the legislative assemblies as provided for in Section 38 thereof:

And Whereas the Constitution of Canada, reflecting the country and Canadian society, continues to develop and strengthen the rights and freedoms that it guarantees;

And Whereas after a gradual transition of Canada from colonial status to the status of an independent and sovereign state, Canadians have, as of April 17, 1982, full authority to amend their Constitution in Canada;

And Whereas historically and equitably it is fitting that the early exercise of that full authority should relate to the rights and freedoms of the first inhabitants of Canada, the aboriginal peoples;

Now Therefore the [Senate] [House of Commons] [Legislative Assembly] resolves that His Excellency the Governor-General be authorized to issue a proclamation under the Great Seal of Canada amending the Constitution of Canada as follows:

PROCLAMATION AMENDING THE CONSTITUTION OF CANADA

1 Paragraph 25(b) of the *Constitution Act, 1982* is repealed and the following substituted therefore:
  '(b) any rights or freedoms that now exist by way of land claims agreements or may be so acquired.'
2 Section 35 of the *Constitution Act, 1982* is amended by adding thereto the following subsections:
  '(3) For greater certainty, in subsection (1) "treaty rights" includes rights that now exist by way of land claims agreements or may be so acquired.
  (4) Notwithstanding any other provision of this Act, the aboriginal and

treaty rights referred to in subsection (1) are guaranteed equally to male and female persons.'

3 The said Act is further amended by adding thereto, immediately after Section 35 thereof, the following section:

'35.1 The government of Canada and the provincial governments are committed to the principle that, before any amendment is made to Class 2, Section 91 of the *Constitution Act, 1867*, to Section 25 of this Act or to this Part,

(a) a constitutional conference that includes in its agenda an item relating to the proposed amendment, composed of the Prime Minister of Canada and the first ministers of the provinces, will be convened by the Prime Minister of Canada; and

(b) the Prime Minister of Canada will invite representatives of the aboriginal peoples of Canada to participate in the discussions on that item.'

4 The said Act is further amended by adding thereto, immediately after Section 37 thereof, the following Part:

'PART IV.1
CONSTITUTIONAL CONFERENCES

37.1 (1) In addition to the conference convened in March 1983, at least two constitutional conferences composed of the Prime Minister of Canada and the first ministers of the provinces shall be convened by the Prime Minister of Canada, the first within three years after April 17, 1982 and the second within five years after that date.

(2) Each conference convened under subsection (1) shall have included in its agenda constitutional matters that directly affect the aboriginal peoples of Canada, and the Prime Minister of Canada shall invite representatives of those peoples to participate in the discussions on those matters.

(3) The Prime Minister of Canada shall invite elected representatives of the governments of the Yukon Territory and the Northwest Territories to participate in the discussions on any item on the agenda of a conference convened under subsection (1) that, in the opinion of the Prime Minister, directly affects the Yukon Territory and the Northwest Territories.

(4) Nothing in this section shall be construed so as to derogate from subsection 35(1).'

5 The said Act is further amended by adding thereto, immediately after Section 54 thereof, the following section:

'54.1 Part IV.1 and this section are repealed on April 18, 1987.'

6 The said Act is further amended by adding thereto the following section:

'61 A reference to the *Constitution Act 1867 to 1982* shall be deemed to include a reference to the *Constitution Amendment Proclamation 1983*.'

7 This Proclamation may be cited as the *Constitution Amendment Proclamation, 1983*.

G/Proposed Constitutional Accord on the Rights of the Aboriginal Peoples of Canada (1984)

WHEREAS pursuant to the 1983 Constitutional Accord on Aboriginal Rights a constitutional conference composed of the Prime Minister of Canada and the first ministers of the provinces was held on March 8 and 9, 1984, to which representatives of the aboriginal peoples of Canada and elected representatives of the governments of the Yukon Territory and the Northwest Territories were invited:

AND WHEREAS it was agreed at that conference that certain amendments to the Constitution Act, 1982 would be sought in accordance with section 38 of that Act;

AND WHEREAS that conference had included in its agenda the following matters that directly affect the aboriginal peoples of Canada:

– Equality Rights
– Aboriginal Title, Aboriginal Rights, Treaties and Treaty Rights
– Land and Resources
– Aboriginal or Self Government

AND WHEREAS it was agreed in the 1983 Constitutional Accord on Aboriginal Rights that future conferences be held at which constitutional matters that directly affect the aboriginal peoples of Canada will be discussed;

AND WHEREAS the Senate and House of Commons of Canada and the legislatures of nine provinces that have, in the aggregate, more than fifty per cent of the population of all the provinces have passed resolutions supporting changes to the Constitution of Canada that were the subject of the 1983 Constitutional Accord on Aboriginal Rights;

NOW THEREFORE the government of Canada and the provincial governments hereby agree as follows:

1 The Prime Minister of Canada will lay or cause to be laid before the Senate and House of Commons, and the first ministers of the provinces will lay or cause to be laid before their legislative assemblies, prior to December 31, 1984, a resolution in the form set out in the Schedule to authorize a proclamation to be issued by the Governor General under the Great Seal of Canada to amend the Constitution Act, 1982.

2 The government of Canada and the provincial governments are committed to negotiating with representatives of the aboriginal peoples of Canada to identify and define the nature, jurisdiction and powers of self-governing institutions that will meet the needs of their communities, as well as the financing arrangements relating to those institutions, and to presenting to Parliament and the provincial legislatures legislation to give effect to the agreements resulting from the negotiations.

3 The government of Canada and the provincial governments, in consultation with representatives of the aboriginal peoples of Canada and representatives of the governments of the Yukon Territory and the Northwest Territories, shall review all aspects of social, cultural and economic programs for and services to the aboriginal peoples of Canada, with the following objectives:

(a) clarification of federal and provincial responsibilities for programs and services provided to the aboriginal peoples of Canada, having regard to the existing and potential roles of aboriginal governments;

(b) enhanced participation of the aboriginal peoples of Canada in the area of programs and services, including their increased involvement in the design and delivery of programs and services, taking into account the special social, cultural and economic needs of the aboriginal peoples of Canada;

(c) assessment of financial provisions, including consideration of existing arrangements between the government of Canada and the provincial governments;

(d) examination of eligibility requirements of programs and services for the aboriginal peoples of Canada, including residency requirements; and

(e) examination of programs and services to the aboriginal peoples of Canada, including the degree to which they are comparable with services received by other Canadians residing in similar communities.

4 The government of Canada and the provincial governments shall report on the findings of the review referred to in article 3 to the first constitutional conference held pursuant to the proposed section 37.1 of the Constitution Act, 1982, as agreed to in the 1983 Constitutional Accord on Aboriginal Rights.

5 In preparation for the constitutional conferences contemplated by the changes to the Constitution of Canada that were the subject of the 1983 Constitutional Accord on Aboriginal Rights, meetings composed of ministers of the government of Canada and the provincial governments, together with representatives of the aboriginal peoples of Canada and representatives of the governments of the Yukon Territory and the Northwest Territories, shall be convened at least annually by the government of Canada.

6 Nothing in this Accord is intended to preclude, or substitute for, any bilateral or other discussions or agreements between governments and the various aboriginal peoples and, in particular, having regard to the authority of Parliament under Class 24 of section 91 of the Constitution Act, 1867, and to the special relationship that has existed and continues to exist between the Parliament and government of Canada and the peoples referred

to in that Class, this Accord is made without prejudice to any bilateral process that has been or may be established between the government of Canada and those peoples.

7 Nothing in this accord shall be construed so as to affect the interpretation of the Constitution of Canada.

SCHEDULE

Motion for a Resolution to authorize His Excellency the Governor-General to issue a proclamation respecting amendments to the Constitution of Canada.

WHEREAS the Constitution Act, 1982 provides that an amendment to the Constitution of Canada may be made by proclamation issued by the Governor-General under the Great Seal of Canada where so authorized by resolutions of the Senate and House of Commons and resolutions of the legislative assemblies as provided for in section 38 thereof;

AND WHEREAS the Constitution of Canada, reflecting the country and Canadian society, continues to develop and strengthen the rights and freedoms that it guarantees;

AND WHEREAS it is fitting that the government of Canada and the provincial governments work with the representatives of the aboriginal peoples of Canada to develop their special place in Canadian society through the strengthening of self-governing institutions and the preservation of their cultural heritage.

NOW THEREFORE the [Senate] [House of Commons] [Legislative Assembly] resolves that His Excellency the Governor General be authorized to issue a proclamation under the Great Seal of Canada amending the Constitution of Canada as follows:

Proclamation Amending the Constitution of Canada

1 (1) Section 25 of the Constitution Act, 1982 is renumbered as subsection 25(1).
(2) Section 25 of the said Act is further amended by adding thereto the following subsection:
'(2) Nothing in this section abrogates or derogates from the guarantees of equality with respect to male and female persons under section 28 of this Charter.'

2 The said Act is further amended by adding thereto, immediately after Part II thereof, the following Part:

'PART II.1
Commitments Relating to Aboriginal Peoples of Canada

35.2 Without altering the legislative authority of Parliament or of the provincial legislatures, or the rights of any of them with respect to the exercise of their legislative authority,

(a) Parliament and the legislatures, together with the government of Canada and the provincial governments, are committed to

(i) preserving and enhancing the cultural heritage of the aboriginal peoples of Canada, and

(ii) respecting the freedom of the aboriginal peoples of Canada to live within their heritage and to educate their children in their own languages, as well as in either or both of the official languages of Canada;

(b) the aboriginal peoples of Canada have the right to self-governing institutions that will meet the needs of their communities, subject to the nature, jurisdiction and powers of those institutions, and to the financing arrangements defined through negotiations with the government of Canada and the provincial governments; and

(c) the government of Canada and the provincial governments are committed to participating in the negotiations referred to in paragraph (b) and to presenting to Parliament and the provincial legislatures legislation to give effect to the agreements resulting from the negotiations.'

H/Indian Treaty Areas

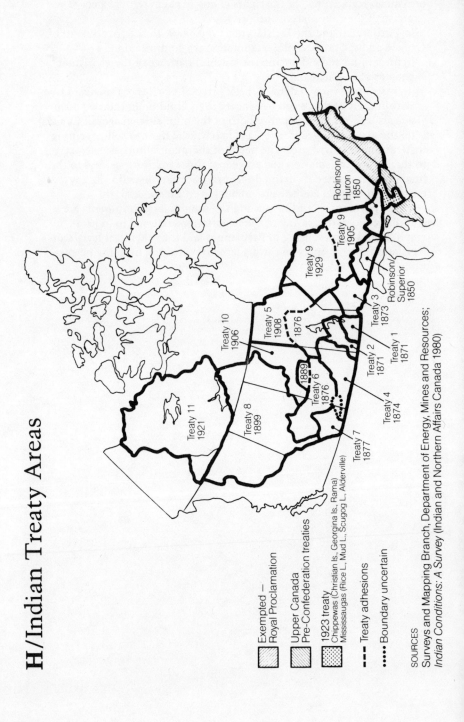

Robinson/
Huron
1850

Treaty 9
1905

Robinson/
Superior
1850

Treaty 9
1929

Treaty 3
1873

Treaty 5
1908

1876

Treaty 1
1871

Treaty 10
1906

Treaty 2
1871

1889

Treaty 6
1876

Treaty 11
1921

Treaty 8
1899

Treaty 4
1874

Treaty 7
1877

Exempted —
Royal Proclamation

Upper Canada
Pre-Confederation treaties

1923 treaty
Chippewas (Christian Is., Georgina Is., Rama)
Mississaugas (Rice L., Mud L., Scugog L., Alderville)

— — — Treaty adhesions

• • • • • Boundary uncertain

SOURCES
Surveys and Mapping Branch, Department of Energy, Mines and Resources;
Indian Conditions: A Survey (Indian and Northern Affairs Canada 1980)

I / First Ministers' Conference on Aboriginal Constitutional Matters: Proposed Accord Relating to the Aboriginal Peoples of Canada (1985)

WHEREAS the aboriginal peoples of Canada, being descendants of the first inhabitants of Canada, are unique peoples in Canada enjoying the rights that flow from their status as aboriginal peoples, from treaties and from land claims agreements, as well as rights flowing from Canadian citizenship, and it is fitting that

(a) there be protection of rights of aboriginal peoples in the Constitution of Canada,

(b) they have the opportunity to have self-government arrangements to meet their special circumstances as well as the opportunity to exercise their full rights as citizens of Canada and residents of the provinces and territories, and

(c) they have the freedom to live in accordance with their own cultural heritage and to use and maintain their distinct languages;

AND WHEREAS, pursuant to section 37.1 of the Constitution Act, 1982, a constitutional conference composed for the prime minister of Canada and the first ministers of the provinces was held on April 2 and 3, 1985, to which representatives of the aboriginal peoples of Canada and elected representatives of the governments of the Yukon Territory and the Northwest Territories were invited;

AND WHEREAS it was agreed by the government of Canada and the provincial governments, with the support of representatives of the aboriginal peoples of Canada and elected representatives of the governments of the Yukon Territory and the Northwest Territories, that

(a) the constitution of Canada should be amended to recognize and affirm the rights of the aboriginal peoples of Canada to self-government within the Canadian federation, where those rights are set out in negotiated agreements,

(b) the constitution of Canada should be further amended to clarify the provisions relating to equality rights for aboriginal men and women,

(c) direction should be provided for the continuing discussions leading up to the second constitutional conference required by section 37.1 of the Constitution Act, 1982,

(d) governments and aboriginal peoples would benefit from a greater degree of federal-provincial-territorial co-operation with respect to matters affecting the aboriginal peoples of Canada, including programs and services provided to them, and

(e) governments and the aboriginal peoples of Canada would benefit from better statistical information relating to the circumstances of aboriginal peoples, which could be achieved most efficiently by means of the proposed 1986 census of Canada;

NOW THEREFORE the government of Canada and the provincial governments hereby agree as follows:

PART I
SELF-GOVERNMENT [AND EQUALITY RIGHTS]

1 The prime minister of Canada will lay or cause to be laid before the Senate and House of Commons, and the first ministers of the provinces will lay or cause to be laid before their legislative assemblies, prior to December 31, 1985, a resolution in the form set out in Schedule I to authorize an amendment to the constitution of Canada to be made by proclamation issued by Her Excellency the Governor-General under the Great Seal of Canada.

2 The government of Canada and the provincial governments are committed, to the extent that each has authority, to

(a) participating in negotiations directed toward concluding, with representatives of aboriginal people living in particular communities or regions, agreements relating to self-government that are appropriate to the particular circumstances of those people; and

(b) discussing with representatives of aboriginal people from each province the timing, nature, and scope of the negotiations referred to in paragraph (a).

3 The government of Canada and the governments of the Yukon Territory and the Northwest Territories are committed to participating in negotiations directed toward concluding, with representatives of aboriginal people living in particular communities or regions, agreements relating to self-government that are appropriate to the particular circumstances of those people, and the minister of the government of Canada responsible for the negotiations shall invite elected representatives of the government of the Yukon Territory or the Northwest Territories to participate in those negotiations where, after consultation with representatives of the aboriginal peoples of Canada from the Yukon Territory or the Northwest Territories, as the case may be, the minister is of the opinion that those negotiations directly affect the Yukon Territory or the Northwest Territories, as the case may be.

4 The objectives of agreements negotiated pursuant to article 2 of this accord
shall be, where appropriate,
    (a) to allow aboriginal people increased authority over and responsibility
for lands that have been or may be reserved or set aside for their use;
    (b) to ensure increased participation of the aboriginal peoples of Canada
in government decision-making that directly affects them;
    (c) to maintain and enhance the distinct culture and heritage of the ab-
original peoples of Canada; and
    (d) to recognize the unique position of the aboriginal peoples of Canada.
5 The negotiations referred to in article 2 of this accord may have regard to
the following factors:
    (a) that agreements relating to self-government for aboriginal people may
encompass a variety of arrangements based on the particular needs and
circumstances of those people, including ethnic-based government, public
government, modifications to existing governmental structures to accommodate the unique circumstances of the aboriginal peoples of Canada
and management of, and involvement in, the delivery of programs and
services;
    (b) the existence of an identifiable land base for the aboriginal people
concerned;
    (c) aboriginal and treaty rights, or other rights and freedoms, of the ab-
original people concerned;
    (d) the rights and freedoms of the non-aboriginal people in the communi-
ties or regions where the aboriginal people live; and
    (e) any relationship between the matters being negotiated and land
claims agreements that have been, are being, or may be negotiated with the
aboriginal people concerned.
6 The negotiations referred to in article 2 of this accord may address any
appropriate matter relating to self-government including, among other
matters,
    (a) membership in the group of aboriginal people concerned;
    (b) the nature and powers of the institution of self-government;
    (c) responsibilities of, and programs and services to be provided by, the
institutions of self-government;
    (d) the definition of the geographic areas over which the institutions of
self-government will have jurisdiction;
    (e) resources to which the institutions of self-government will have access;
    (f) fiscal arrangements and other bases of economic support for the insti-
tutions of self-government; and
    (g) distinct rights for the aboriginal people concerned.
7 During the period between the date this accord is signed and the date the
constitutional amendment set out in Schedule I comes into force, the
government of Canada and the provincial governments, in consultation
with representatives of aboriginal people, shall take such measures as
may be appropriate to commence the negotiations contemplated in article
2 of this accord.

8 Periodic reports on the negotiations referred to in article 2 of this accord shall be made to the ministerial meetings referred to in article 10 of this accord.

PART II
PREPARATIONS FOR CONSTITUTIONAL CONFERENCE

9 In preparation for the second constitutional conference required by section 37.1 of the Constitution Act, 1982, the government of Canada and the provincial governments shall, with the participation of representatives of the aboriginal peoples of Canada and representatives of the governments of the Yukon Territory and the Northwest Territories, conduct such meetings as are necessary to deal with the items included in the agenda of the constitutional conference held on March 15 and 16, 1983 and listed in the 1983 constitutional accord on aboriginal rights and to deal with the constitutional proposals of the representatives of the aboriginal peoples of Canada.

10 Ministerial meetings, composed of designated ministers of the government of Canada and the provincial governments, representatives of the aboriginal peoples of Canada, and elected representatives of the governments of the Yukon Territory and the Northwest Territories, under the chairmanship of a designated minister of the government of Canada, shall be convened at least twice in the twelve-month period immediately following the date this accord is signed, and at least twice in the period between the end of that twelve-month period and the date on which the second constitutional conference required by section 37.1 of the Constitution Act, 1982 is held.

11 The ministerial meetings referred to in article 10 of this accord shall
    (a) issue directions as to work to be undertaken by technical or other working groups and review and assess that work on a periodic basis;
    (b) receive periodic reports, in accordance with article 8 of this accord, on the negotiations referred to in that article and consider further constitutional amendments relating to self-government; and
    (c) seek to reach agreement or consensus on issues to be laid before first ministers at the second constitutional conference required by section 37.1 of the Constitution Act, 1982.

PART III
SECOND CONSTITUTIONAL CONFERENCE REQUIRED BY
SECTION 37.1 OF THE CONSTITUTION ACT, 1982

12 The second constitutional conference required by section 37.1 of the Constitution Act, 1982 shall have included in its agenda an item relating to self-government for the aboriginal peoples of Canada.

PART IV
FURTHER UNDERTAKINGS RELATING TO THE ABORIGINAL PEOPLES
OF CANADA

13 The government of Canada and the provincial governments, with the participation of the aboriginal peoples of Canada and elected representatives of the governments of the Yukon Territory and the Northwest Territories, further agree on the matters affecting the aboriginal peoples of Canada set out in Schedules II and III.

PART V
GENERAL

14 Nothing in this accord is intended to preclude, or substitute for, any bilateral or other discussions or agreements between governments and the various aboriginal peoples of Canada.

SCHEDULE I
RESOLUTION

Motion for a resolution to authorize an amendment to the constitution of Canada
WHEREAS the Constitution Act, 1982 provides that an amendment to the constitution of Canada may be made by proclamation issued by the Governor-General under the Great Seal of Canada where so authorized by resolutions of the Senate and House of Commons and resolutions of the legislative assemblies as provided for in section 38 thereof;
NOW THEREFORE the (Senate) (House of Commons) (legislative assembly) resolves that an amendment to the constitution of Canada be authorized to be made by proclamation issued by Her Excellency the Governor-General under the Great Seal of Canada in accordance with the schedule hereto.

SCHEDULE
AMENDMENT TO THE CONSTITUTION OF CANADA
[Possible Equality Rights Amendment]

1 The Constitution Act, 1982 is amended by adding thereto, immediately after section 35 thereof, the following section:

35.01 (1) The rights of the aboriginal peoples of Canada to self-government, within the context of the Canadian federation, that are set out in agreements referred to in subsection (2) are hereby recognized and affirmed.
(2) Subsection (1) applies in respect of any agreement with representatives of aboriginal people that sets out rights of self-government and that

(a) includes a declaration that subsection (1) applies; and
(b) is approved by an act of Parliament and acts of the legislatures of any provinces in which those aboriginal people live.

(3) Nothing in this section abrogates or derogates from any rights to self-government, or any other rights, of the aboriginal peoples of Canada.

2 Section 61 of the said act is repealed and the following substituted therefor:

61   A reference to the Constitution Act, 1982, or a reference to the Constitution Acts 1867 to 1982, shall be deemed to include a reference to any amendments thereto.

3 This amendment may be cited as the Constitution Amendment, year of proclamation (Aboriginal peoples of Canada).

SCHEDULE II
FEDERAL-PROVINCIAL-TERRITORIAL CO-OPERATION ON MATTERS AFFECTING THE ABORIGINAL PEOPLES OF CANADA

1 The government of Canada and the provincial and territorial governments are committed to improving the socio-economic conditions of the aboriginal peoples of Canada and to co-ordinating federal, provincial, and territorial programs and services for them.
2 In order to achieve the objectives set out in article 1 of this schedule, the government of Canada and the provincial and territorial governments shall, with the participation of representatives of the aboriginal peoples of Canada, enter into regular discussions, on a bilateral or multilateral basis as appropriate, which shall have the following additional objectives:
   (a) the determination of the respective roles and responsibilities of the government of Canada and the provincial and territorial governments toward the aboriginal peoples of Canada;
   (b) the improvement of federal-provincial-territorial co-operation with respect to the provision of programs and services, as well as other government initiatives, to the aboriginal peoples of Canada so as to maximize their effectiveness; and
   (c) the transfer to institutions of self-government for the aboriginal peoples of Canada, where appropriate, of responsibility for the design and administration of government programs and services.

SCHEDULE III
STATISTICAL DATA RESPECTING THE ABORIGINAL PEOPLES OF CANADA

1 It is recognized that the government of Canada, the provincial and territorial governments, and representatives of the aboriginal peoples of Canada are in need of improved data relating to the socio-economic situation of the

aboriginal peoples of Canada, including the numbers and geographic concentrations of those peoples, so as to facilitate the structuring of initiatives to better meet their social, economic, and cultural needs.

2 In order to obtain data referred to in article 1 of this schedule, the government of Canada and the provincial governments, with the participation of representatives of the aboriginal peoples of Canada and representatives of the governments of the Yukon Territory and the Northwest Territories, shall forthwith establish a technical working group for the purpose of developing a proposal to use the 1986 census of Canada and, if considered necessary, to supplement information taken therefrom, which group shall present its recommendations to the participants no later than the end of May 1985.

3 The proposal referred to in article 2 of this schedule shall include recommendations for use of and access to the data obtained and for cost-sharing with respect to the implementation of measures to obtain data that are to be taken in addition to measures taken within the existing structure of the 1986 Census of Canada.

Table of Cases

1889 *St Catherine's Milling and Lumber Co.* v *The Queen* 14 AC 46

1897 *Attorney-General for Canada* v *Attorney-General for Ontario* AC 199

1910 *Dominion of Canada* v *Province of Ontario* AC 637

1921 *Attorney-General for Quebec* v *Attorney-General for Canada* (Star Chrome Case) 1 AC 401

1939 *In Re Eskimos* SCR 104

1964 *Sikyea* v *The Queen* 44 CR 266

1965 *Regina* v *White and Bob* 52 DLR (2d) 481

1970 *The Queen* v *Drybones* SCR 282

1972 *Regina* v *Pritchard* 32 DLR (3d)

1973 *Calder et al.* v *Attorney-General of British Columbia* SCR 313

1973 *Cardinal* v *Attorney-General of Alberta* 6 WWR 205

1973 *Kanatewat et al.* v *Attorney-General of the Province of Quebec and The Quebec Hydro-Electric Commission* QPR 38

1973 *In Re Paulette* 6 WWR 97

1978 *Attorney-General of Canada* v *Lavell* 38 DLR (3d) 481

1979 *Jack* v *The Queen* 100 DLR (3d) 193

1980 *Baker Lake et al.* v *Minister of Indian Affairs and Northern Development* 5 WWR 193

1984 *Guerin et al.* v *R. and the National Indian Brotherhood* 6 WWR 481 (Musqueam case)

Notes

WILSON Aboriginal Rights: The Non-status Indian Perspective

1 House of Commons Debates (29 June 1950) 3938
2 (1857) 20 Vict., c. 26
3 D.C. Scott *Evidence to Commons Committee to Consider Bill 14* (1920) Public Archives of Canada, record group 10

DALON An Alberta Perspective on Aboriginal Peoples and the Constitution

1 Robert Sheppard and Michael Valpy *The National Deal* (Toronto: Fleet Books 1982) 170
2 Letter dated 28 July 1982, quoted with the permission of the Honourable Peter Lougheed, the Honourable James D. Horsman, and the Honourable Milt Pahl.
3 The provincial elections were held on 2 November 1982, and the Progressive Conservative party was re-elected in another landslide victory. The Honourable Milt Pahl was given responsibility for the Native Secretariat, and the Honourable James D. Horsman was appointed minister of federal and intergovernmental affairs.
4 Kenneth M. Lysyk 'The Rights and Freedoms of the Aboriginal Peoples of Canada' in *The Canadian Charter of Rights and Freedoms* edited by W.S. Tarnopolsky and Gerald A. Beaudoin (Toronto: Carswell 1982) 477
5 John Locke *Two Treatises of Government* (New York: New English Library 1960) 336–7
6 Excerpt from the verbatim transcript of the 1983 first ministers' conference on aboriginal constitutional matters, 15–16 March 1983
7 Leslie C. Green 'Aboriginal Peoples, International Law and the Canadian Charter of Rights and Freedoms' 61 *Canadian Bar Review* (1983) 350–1
8 Professor Green makes an interesting, though I think erroneous, point in the article cited in note 7 when he says, 'Since section 25 of the Charter

already guarantees all aboriginal, treaty and other rights which pertain to the aboriginal peoples, whether they are "existing" or not, so that, presumably, new rights recognized by some future treaty as belonging to aboriginal peoples would be included, it is not easy to understand why, other than for ideological or political reasons, section 35 appears.' He mentions in several places almost nonchalantly that section 25 guarantees all aboriginal rights. I do not think this is the case. Section 25 says merely that if there are aboriginal rights the Charter cannot take anything away from them. It provides protection against internal forces but affords no protection at all from external forces that may create or deny aboriginal rights. For example, if the courts were to decide in the future that a particular aboriginal right – say hunting and fishing – no longer existed, I do not think anyone could appeal successfully to section 25 for help. One would, it seems to me, go to section 35(1) and hope that it offers the kind of guarantee that Professor Green thinks is contained in section 25. At most, section 25 might tend to give more credence to the kind of protection afforded in section 35(1). It is my view, in fact, that one must read section 25 in conjunction with sections 35 and 37. The three sections are intimately bound together, and any legitimate interpretation must place them in relationship to each other.

SLATTERY The Hidden Constitution: Aboriginal Rights in Canada

1 For standard survey accounts, see e.g. H.E. Driver *Indians of North America* 2d ed. (Chicago: University of Chicago Press 1969); Diamond Jenness *The Indians of Canada* 6th ed. (Ottawa: Queen's Printer 1963).
2 Following ordinary legal usage in Canada, I will use the term 'Indian' to refer to the full range of native American peoples, including the Inuit or Eskimo peoples. For legal background, see *Re Term Indians* [1939] SCR 104 (SCC).
3 Reported in Richard Zouche *Iuris et Iudicii Fecialis, sive, Iuris inter Gentes* vol. 2, edited by T.E. Holland and translated by J.L. Brierly (Washington, DC: Carnegie Institution 1911)
4 For varying accounts of European state practice regarding America, compare the following: Julius Goebel *The Struggle for the Falkland Islands* (New Haven: Yale University Press 1927) 47–119; John T. Juricek 'English Territorial Claims in North America under Elizabeth and the Early Stuarts' 7 *Terrae Incognitae* (1975); A.S. Keller, O.J. Lissitzyn, and F.J. Mann *Creation of Rights of Sovereignty through Symbolic Acts, 1400–1800* (New York: Columbia University Press 1938); M.F. Lindley *The Acquisition and Government of Backward Territory in International Law* (London: Longmans Green 1926) 24–44, 129–38; M.S. McDougal, H.D. Lasswell, and I.A. Vlasic *Law and Public Order in Space* (New Haven: Yale University Press 1963) 830–44; Max Savelle *The Origins of American Diplomacy: The International History of Angloamerica,*

1492–1763 (New York: Macmillan 1967); Brian Slattery 'French Claims in North America, 1500–59' 59 Canadian Historical Review (1978) 139; Friedrich A. von der Heydte 'Discovery, Symbolic Annexation and Virtual Effectiveness in International Law' 29 American Journal of International Law (1935) 448; The work by Keller et al. must be used with caution; the evidence presented is highly selective, and many of the authors' historical interpretations are doubtful.

5 See article 10 of the Treaty of Utrecht, 1713, in The Consolidated Treaty Series vol. 27, edited by Clive Parry (Dobbs Ferry, NY: Oceana Publications (1969–).

6 The Constitution Act, 1982, is set out in English and French in Schedule B of the Canada Act, 1982, c.11 (U.K.), which is the formal enacting vehicle. The Constitution Act, 1982, was brought into force by a proclamation issued by Elizabeth II as Queen of Canada on 17 April 1982 under section 58 of the act; see Canada Gazette (part I) vol. 116, no. 17 at 2927–8.

7 For background, see Peter Hogg, Canada Act 1982 Annotated (Toronto: Carswell 1982) 1–3, 83; Douglas Sanders 'The Rights of the Aboriginal Peoples of Canada' 61 Canadian Bar Review (1983) 314, 315–21.

8 House of Commons Debates (24 November 1981) 13203–4

9 1983 constitutional accord on aboriginal rights, first ministers' conference on aboriginal constitutional matters; document 800–17/041 (15–16 March 1983)

10 The new subsection states: '(3) For greater certainty, in subsection (1) "treaty rights" includes rights that now exist by way of land claims agreements or may be so acquired.'

11 '(4) Notwithstanding any other provision of this Act, the aboriginal and treaty rights referred to in subsection (1) are guaranteed equally to male and female persons.'

12 The new paragraph reads as follows: '(b) any rights or freedoms that now exist by way of land claims agreements or may be so acquired.'

13 For other discussions, see Kenneth Lysyk, 'The Rights and Freedoms of the Aboriginal Peoples of Canada' in The Canadian Charter of Rights and Freedoms edited by W.S. Tarnopolsky and Gerald A. Beaudoin (Toronto: Carswell 1982); Hogg Canada Act 1982 at 69, 81–3, 84–5; Kent McNeil 'The Constitutional Rights of the Aboriginal Peoples of Canada' 4 Supreme Court Law Review 255 (1982); Sanders 'Rights of the Aboriginal Peoples'; Brian Slattery 'The Constitutional Guarantee of Aboriginal and Treaty Rights' 8 Queen's Law Journal (1982–3) 232. For general background, see Native Rights in Canada 2d ed., edited by Peter A. Cumming and Neil H. Mickenberg (Toronto: Indian-Eskimo Association of Canada 1972); Kenneth Lysyk 'The Unique Constitutional Position of the Canadian Indian' 45 Canadian Bar Review (1967) 513; Lysyk 'Constitutional Developments Relating to Indians and Indian Lands: An Overview' in Special Lectures of the Law Society of Upper Canada The Constitution and the Future of Canada (1978) 201;

Lysyk 'The Indian Title Question in Canada: An Appraisal in the Light of Calder' 51 *Canadian Bar Review* (1973) 450.

14 For discussion, see Brian Slattery *Ancestral Lands, Alien Laws: Judicial Perspectives on Aboriginal Title* (Saskatoon: University of Saskatchewan Native Law Centre 1983).

15 8 Wheaton 543.

16 6 Peters 515.

17 34 DLR (3d) 145 (SCC) especially at 150–2, 156, 190–203, 208–11. See also *St Catherine's Milling and Lumber Co.* v *The Queen* (1885) 10 OR 196 (Ont. Ch.); (1886) 13 OAR 148 (Ont. CA); (1887) 13 SCR 577 (SCC); (1888) 14 AC 46 (PC); *Hamlet of Baker Lake* v *Minister of Indian Affairs and Northern Development* (1980) 1 FC 518 (FCTD); Lysyk 'The Indian Title Question in Canada'

18 11 LC Jur. 197 (Que. SC), also reported at 17 RJRQ 75. The decision was upheld on appeal sub nom. *Johnstone* v *Connolly* (1869) 17 RJRQ 266, 1 RLOS 253 (Que. QB). The judgments are reproduced in *Canadian Native Law Cases* vol. 1, edited by Brian Slattery (Saskatoon: University of Saskatchewan Native Law Centre 1980).

19 11 LC Jur. 197 at 204–5

20 For French state practice, see Brian Slattery 'The Land Rights of Indigenous Canadian Peoples, as Affected by the Crown's Acquisition of Their Territories (Saskatoon: University of Saskatchewan Native Law Centre 1979) 70–94; and Slattery 'French Claims in North America, 1500–59' 59 *Canadian Historical Review* (1978) 139. For other views, see Henri Brun 'Les droits des Indiens sur le territoire du Québec' 10 *Cahiers de droit* (1969) 415, 428–30; Cumming and Mickenberg *Native Rights in Canada* 75–85.

21 For state practice prior to the American Revolution, see Slattery *Land Rights* at 10–44 and 95–174. Compare with John T. Juricek 'English Claims in North America to 1660: A Study in Legal and Constitutional History' (PH D dissertation, University of Chicago, 1970); Juricek 'English Territorial Claims'; Geoffrey Lester 'The Territorial Rights of the Inuit of the Canadian Northwest Territories: A Legal Argument' (JD thesis, Osgoode Hall Law School, York University, 1981); Cyrus Thomas 'Introduction' in Charles C. Royce *Indian Land Cessions in the United States* 18th Annual Report of the Bureau of American Ethnology (1896–97) (Washington, DC: Government Printing Office 1899).

22 For a detailed discussion of the proclamation see Slattery *Land Rights* 165–349; Kenneth M. Narvey 'The Royal Proclamation of 7 October 1763: The Common Law, and Native Rights to Land within the Territory Granted to the Hudson's Bay Company' 38 *Saskatchewan Law Review* (1973–4) 123; Cumming and Mickenberg *Native Rights in Canada* 85–8; Jack Stagg *Anglo-Indian Relations in North America to 1763 and an Analysis of the Royal Proclamation of 7 October 1763* (Ottawa: Department of Indian and Northern Affairs 1981).

23 Treaty of Paris, 10 February 1763; see text in *Documents Relating to the*

Constitutional History of Canada, 1759–1791 2d ed., edited by Adam
Shortt and Arthur G. Doughty (Ottawa: King's Printer 1918).

24 In a secret treaty concluded at Fontainebleau, dated 3 November 1762;
text in Parry *Consolidated Treaty Series* vol. 42, 239

25 Alexander Henry *Travels and Adventures in Canada and the Indian
Territories between the Years 1760 and 1776* (1809), quoted in
Dorothy V. Jones *License for Empire: Colonialism by Treaty in Early
America* (Chicago: University of Chicago Press 1982) 71. The state-
ment was made at the post of Michilimackinac in the fall of 1761, after
Quebec and Montreal had been taken by English forces.

26 George Croghan 'Journals' 11 *Illinois Historical Collections* 47–8;
quoted in Jones *License for Empire* 73. The year was 1765.

27 The original text of the proclamation, as entered on the patent roll for
the regnal year 4 Geo. III, may be seen in the British Public Record
Office: c. 66/3693 (back of roll). The most authoritative printed version
is that given in *British Royal Proclamations Relating to America*
edited by Clarence S. Brigham 12 *Transactions and Collections of the
American Antiquarian Society* (Worcester, Mass.: American Antiquarian Society 1911), which is quoted here.

28 The proclamation was open to repeal by imperial statute; but there is
doubt as to whether it could be repealed by a local Canadian legislature, at least prior to the Statute of Westminster, 1931, which released
Canada from the bonds of ordinary imperial acts. In *R. v Secretary of
State for Foreign and Commonwealth Affairs* [1982] 2 All ER 118 (CA), at
124 and 125, Lord Denning MR said that the proclamation 'was equivalent to an entrenched provision in the constitution of the colonies in
North America' and continued to be constitutionally binding on the
dominion and provincial legislatures even after Confederation. See also
R. v White and Bob (1964) 50 DLR (2d) 613 (BCCA) per Norris JA at 662,
cited in *R. v Isaac* (1975) 13 NSR (2d) 460 at 485 (NSSC App. Div.). The
question is discussed in Slattery *Land Rights* 315–19.

29 For detailed treatment of this question, see Narvey 'The Royal Proclamation'; Slattery *Land Rights* 217–27 and 244–60.

30 The Indian Territory is described as the residue of British territories in
North America after certain named areas are excluded. The excluded
areas are the colonies of Rupert's Land, Quebec, East Florida, and West
Florida, as well as the area east of the Appalachian watershed. For
discussion, see Slattery *Land Rights* 191–203 and 268–82.

31 Canadian courts are divided on this point, but the dominant judicial
trend favours the view expressed here. See, for example, the following
cases regarding the Maritime provinces: *Warman v Francis* (1958) 20
DLR (2d) 627 at 634 (NBSC, QB Div.); *R. v Isaac* (1975) 13 NSR (2d) 460 at
478 (NSSC, App. Div.); *R. v Smith* (1980) 113 DLR (3d) 522 at 528, 548–50
(FCA). See also *Mitchel v United States* 9 Peters 711 at 748–9 (1835)
(USSC); *St Catherine's Milling and Lumber Co. v The Queen* (1888) 14 AC
46 at 54 (PC). For different views, see *Doe* d *Burk v Cormier* (1890) 30

NBR 142 at 148 (NBSC); *R.* v *Syliboy* [1929] 1 DLR 307 at 310 (NS Co. Crt.); *R.* v *Jacques* (1978) 34 APR 576 at 579–80 (NBPC). The Supreme Court of Canada stated in *Sigeareak* v *The Queen* [1966] SCR 645 at 649–50 that the proclamation did not apply to Rupert's Land; but that statement should probably be read as referring only to the extent of the Indian Territory, from which Rupert's Land was clearly excluded. The proclamation's land purchase provisions were not as issue.

32 See, for example, *R.* v *White and Bob*, supra note 28; *Calder* v *A.-G. of British Columbia* supra note 17.

33 See Slattery *Land Rights* 175–90.

34 See authorities and discussion ibid. 329–49.

35 See supra note 28.

36 Many of these treaties are collected in *Indian Treaties and Surrenders* 3 vols. (1905–12) and Alexander Morris, *The Treaties of Canada with the Indians of Manitoba and the North-West Territories* (Toronto: Bedfords Clarke & Co. 1880). For early treaties in the Maritime provinces, see *Source Materials Relating to the New Brunswick Indian* edited by W.D. Hamilton and W.A. Spray (Centennial Print Ltd. 1976). For background to the treaties, see, for example, Réné Fumoleau *As Long as This Land Shall Last: A History of Treaty 8 and Treaty 11, 1870–1939* (Toronto: McClelland and Stewart 1973); *The Spirit of the Alberta Indian Treaties* edited by Richard Price (Montreal: Institute for Research on Public Policy 1979); *As Long as the Sun Shines and Water Flows* edited by Ian A.L. Getty and Antoine S. Lussier (Vancouver: University of British Columbia Press 1983).

37 See *The James Bay and Northern Quebec Agreement* (Quebec: Editeur officiel du Québec 1976), implemented by SC 1976–77, c.32, and SQ 1976, c.46.

38 See, for example, the articles concluded at Fort Albany between the colony of New York and the Mohawk and Seneca nations on 24–25 September 1664, the first article of which provides that 'the Indian Princes above named and their subjects, shall have all such wares and commodities from the English for the future, as heretofore they had from the Dutch'; O'Callaghan (ed.), *Documents Relative to the Colonial History of the State of New York* vol. 3, edited by E.B. O'Callaghan (Albany: Weed Parsons & Co. 1856–61) 67.

39 See, for example, the treaty of Middle Plantation of 29 May 1677 in W.L. Grant and James Munro (eds.), *Acts of the Privy Council of England: Colonial Series* vol. 1, edited by W.L. Grant and James Munro (London: HMSO 1908–12).

40 See, for example, the treaty with the Indians of Nova Scotia drawn up at Boston on 15 December 1725, and later ratified at Annapolis Royal in *Indian Treaties and Surrenders* vol. 2 198–9; discussed in Slattery *Land Rights* at 139–41.

41 Many examples can be seen in *Indian Treaties and Surrenders*.

42 Text in Morris *Treaties of Canada* 320

43 Ibid. at 59

44 See, for example, section 10 of the Interpretation Act, RSC 1970, c. I-23, which provides: 'The law shall be considered as always speaking, and whenever a matter or thing is expressed in the present tense, it shall be applied to the circumstances as they arise, so that effect may be given to the enactment and every part thereof according to its true spirit, intent and meaning.' Technically, this section does not apply to the Constitution Act, 1982, which is a UK statute enacted for Canada, but it can be argued that the section merely expresses a common-law rule of construction that would apply here.

45 *Bouvier's Law Dictionary* (8th ed. 1914) says with regard to 'existing': 'The force of this word is not necessarily confined to the present. Thus a law for regulating "all existing railroad corporations" extends to such as are incorporated after as well as before its passage, unless exception is provided in their charters ...' (references omitted). Similarly, 35 *Corpus Juris Secundum* 224 (1960) states: 'The word "existing" has an ordinary meaning of the fact, or state, of being or living, and carries the implication of having existence now. However, the force of this word is not necessarily confined to the present' (footnotes omitted).

46 The French text simply states that the rights in question 'sont reconnus et confirmés.'

47 Under the principle that the crown cannot legally commit the public purse to expenditures without the sanction of Parliament.

48 See the definitions of 'recognize' in Fowler and Fowler *The Concise Oxford Dictionary of Current English* (5th ed. 1964), and *The Oxford English Dictionary* (vol. 7 1933; reissued 1961).

49 *British Pacific Trust Co.* v *Baillie* (1914) 7 WWR 17 (BCSC) at 21

50 See the *Concise Oxford Dictionary* and the *Oxford English Dictionary*.

51 *Dictionnaire alphabétique et analogique de la langue française* (rev. ed. 1981): 'Rendre certain; affirmer ... l'existence de (qqch)'

52 *Harrap's Standard French and English Dictionary* (1961)

53 See, for example, *Black's Law Dictionary*.

54 *Stroud's Judicial Dictionary of Words and Phrases* (4th ed. 1971)

55 Ibid. For an illuminating example, see *Byers* v *Wa-Wa-Ne* 169 P. 121 (1917) (Oregon SC), discussed in Slattery 'The Constitutional Guarantee' at 251–2.

56 Except, of course, when those rights were protected by constitutional provisions binding on the legislature in question. For an excellent review of the constitutional terms relating to native rights in Rupert's Land and the old North-Western Territory and the boundaries of those territories, see Kent McNeil *Native Claims in Rupert's Land and the North-Western Territory: Canada's Constitutional Obligations* (Saskatoon: University of Saskatchewan Native Law Centre 1982) and McNeil *Native Rights and the Boundaries of Rupert's Land and the North-Western Territory* (Saskatoon: University of Saskatchewan Native Law Centre 1982). For the position of the Royal Proclamation of 1763, see supra note 28.

57 This conclusion is supported by a series of cases interpreting the effect of provisions in the South African and Australian constitutions that preserve the 'existing' rights of certain public servants; see especially *Noble and Barbour* v *South African Railways and Harbours* [1922] AD 527 (S. Afr. Sup. Ct. App. Div.); *Le Leu* v *The Commonwealth* (1921) 29 CLR 305 at 314–15 (Aust. HC); *Lucy* v *The Commonwealth* (1923) 33 CLR 229 at 238, 243–4, 250, 253–4 (Aust. HC); *Pemberton* v *The Commonwealth* (1933) 49 CLR 382 at 388–9, 391, 392, 397 (Aust. HC). These and other cases are analysed in Slattery 'The Constitutional Guarantee' at 258–62.

58 See *R.* v *Secretary of State for Foreign and Commonwealth Affairs* supra note 28 at 129, where Lord Denning MR states: 'It seems to me that the Canada Bill itself does all that can be done to protect the rights and freedoms of the aboriginal peoples of Canada. It entrenches them as part of the constitution, so that they cannot be diminished or reduced except by the prescribed procedure and by the prescribed majorities.'

59 See the Robinson Superior Treaty (1850) and the Robinson Huron Treaty (1850) in Morris *The Treaties of Canada* 302 at 303 and 305 at 306.

60 See supra notes 10 and 12.

61 For further discussion see Slattery 'The Constitutional Guarantee' 270–3.

62 Section 91(24) of the Constitution Act, 1867 (formerly the British North America Act, 1867), gives the dominion Parliament exclusive jurisdiction over 'Indians and Lands reserved for the Indians.'

WEAVER Federal Difficulties with Aboriginal Rights Demands

1 The historic involvement of the federal government with the Metis during the Riel 'rebellions' is well known. See, for example, W.L. Morton *Manitoba: A History* (Toronto: University of Toronto Press 1957); George F.G. Stanley *The Birth of Western Canada: A History of the Riel Rebellions* (Toronto: University of Toronto Press 1936); and Stanley *Louis Riel* (Toronto: Ryerson Press 1963). For reliable studies on 'half-breed' land scrip, see Douglas N. Sprague 'The Manitoba Land Question, 1870–1882' 15 *Journal of Canadian Studies* (1980) 74–84 and 'Government Lawlessness in the Administration of Manitoba Land Claims, 1870–1887' 10 *Manitoba Law Journal* (1980) 415–41, and Joe Sawchuk, Patricia Sawchuk, and Theresa Ferguson *Metis Land Rights in Alberta: A Political History* (Edmonton: Metis Association of Alberta 1981).

2 Privy Council Office 'Native Policy: A Review with Recommendations' (Ottawa, 26 May 1976). For a description of the policy priorities exercise, see Richard D. French *How Ottawa Decides: Planning and Industrial Policy-Making 1968–1980* (Toronto: James Lorimer 1980) 75–85.

3 The Native Council of Canada (NCC) is the national organization representing the interests of the Metis and non-status Indians. The Joint

Cabinet–NCC Committee, which was established in 1977, was created to give the NCC an opportunity to express its demands and concerns directly to cabinet ministers. The committee met annually until 1981. It was less bureaucratic than its Indian counterpart, the short-lived Joint Cabinet–National Indian Brotherhood Committee (1975–8); see Sally M. Weaver 'The Joint Cabinet–National Indian Brotherhood Committee: A Unique Experiment in Pressure-Group Relations' 25 *Canadian Public Administration* (1982) 211–39.

4 The administration of research funds allocated by the Department of Indian Affairs and Northern Development [DIAND] to Metis and non-status Indian organizations was problematic for both the government and the native sides. Government policy was to keep 'expectations' down regarding the availability of funds and the likelihood of establishing legally valid claims. Furthermore, DIAND sought to keep a low profile in the activity of administering the funds lest status Indian organizations criticize its involvement with Metis and non-status Indians. Metis and non-status Indian organizations found the content of DIAND's research and its tight controls on the process objectionable, as Sprague's account accurately portrays: see 'Commentary: A Possible Alternative to Research Funding from DIAND' 1 *Canadian Journal of Native Studies* (1981) 141–9.

5 The Constitution Act, 1982, sections 35(2) and 35(1)

6 The extension of these principles through international law and United Nations conventions is described by Professor D. Sanders elsewhere in this book.

7 For examples of recent demands by Metis and non-status Indians for special recognition and rights, see *A Declaration of Metis and Indian Rights* (Ottawa: Native Council of Canada 1979); NCC Brief, Minutes of Proceedings and Evidence of the Special Joint Committee of the Senate and House of Commons of the Constitution of Canada, no. 17, 2 December 1980 at 105–33; *Native People and the Constitution of Canada* (Ottawa: Native Council of Canada 1981); *We Are the New Nation: The Metis and National Native Policy* edited by Harry W. Daniels (Ottawa: Native Council of Canada 1979) and *The Forgotten People: Metis and Non-status Indian Land Claims* edited by Harry W. Daniels (Ottawa: Native Council of Canada 1979).

BOLDT AND LONG Tribal Philosophies and the Canadian Charter of Rights and Freedoms

1 Menno Boldt 'Intellectual Orientations and Nationalism among Indian Leaders in an Internal Colony: A Theoretical and Comparative Perspective' 33 *British Journal of Sociology* (1982) 484–510

2 Although we use the term 'Indian,' we do not intend to imply that Canada's indigenous tribes constitute a single people in any socio-cultural or political sense. There continues to exist diversity in cultural heritage, political institutions, and so on. At the same time, the cultural traits

and values traditionally shared by most Indian tribes have existed and continue to exist today. Lurie identifies these traits and values as reaching decisions by consensus, spiritual unity, institutionalized co-operation and sharing, respect for personal autonomy, and a preference for impersonal controls: Nancy Lurie 'The Contemporary American Indian Scene' in *American Indians in Historical Perspective* edited by E.B. Leacock and N.O. Lurie (New York: Random House 1971) 443–8. It is these core values that are jeopardized by the new Charter.

3 Robert Vachon 'Traditional Legal Ways of Native Peoples and the Struggle for Native Rights' 15 *Inter-Culture* (1982) 1–18

4 Peter Laslett 'The Face-to-Face Society' in *Philosophy, Politics and Society* edited by Peter Laslett (Oxford: Basil Blackwell 1963) 167

5 Michael Melody 'Lakota Myth and Government: The Cosmos as the State' 4 *American Indian Culture and Research Journal* (1980) 1–19

6 Adamantia Pollis and Peter Schwab 'Human Rights: A Western Construct with Limited Applicability' in *Human Rights: Cultural and Ideological Perspectives* edited by Adamantia Pollis and Peter Schwab (New York: Praeger 1979) 1–18

7 David Miller *Social Justice* (Oxford: Clarendon Press 1976) 253–72

8 Jack Donnelly 'Human Rights and Human Dignity: An Analytic Critique of Non-Western Conceptions of Human Rights' 4 *American Political Science Review* (1982) 303 draws a distinction between human rights and human dignity. Donnelly conceives of human dignity as the more encompassing idea; that is, individualized human rights represent only one possible pathway to the realization of human dignity. Some societies choose other means of attaining human dignity, because individualized conceptions of human rights conflict with their values. Charles Beitz 'Human Rights and Social Justice' in *Human Rights and U.S. Foreign Policy* edited by G. Brown and D. McLean (Lexington, Mass.: Lexington Books 1979) holds that the concept of individualized human rights is a very limited one, because it is restricted largely to personal security and lacks an adequate concern for the broader issues of human dignity and collective well-being (at 45–63).

9 A.J. Gregor *Contemporary Radical Ideologies: Totalitarian Thoughts in the Twentieth Century* (New York: Random House 1968) 16

10 Leroy Little Bear, Menno Boldt, and J.A. Long *Pathways to Self-Determination: Canadian Indians and the Canadian State* (Toronto: University of Toronto Press 1984) xi–xxi

11 Menno Boldt 'Enlightenment Values, Romanticism, and Attitudes toward Political Status: A Study of Native Leaders in Canada' 18 *Canadian Review of Sociology and Anthropology* (1981) 545–65

12 W.B. Miller 'Two Concepts of Authority' 57 *American Anthropologist* (1955) 271–89

13 Assembly of First Nations 'Memorandum Concerning the Rights of the First Nations of Canada and the Canadian Constitution' (Ottawa, 16 June 1982) 10

14 G.V. LaForest 'The Canadian Charter of Rights and Freedoms: An Overview' 6 *Canadian Bar Review* (1983) 19–29

15 K.M. Lysyk 'The Rights and Freedoms of the Aboriginal Peoples of Canada' in *The Canadian Charter of Rights and Freedoms* edited by W.S. Tarnopolsky and G.A. Beaudoin (Toronto: Carswell 1982) 471–2

16 R.L. Barsh and J. Youngblood Henderson 'Aboriginal Rights, Treaty Rights and Human Rights: Indian Tribes and "Constitutional Renewal"' 17 *Journal of Canadian Studies* (1982) 79

17 Gordon Fairweather, chief commissioner of the Canadian Human Rights Commission, has asserted that the provisions of the Charter must extend to Indian governments because Indians are Canadians protected by the Charter's constitutional guarantees of rights. Douglas Sanders, a recognized authority on Indians and the law, holds that Indian governments might not be subject to the provisions of the Charter because Indian governments, unlike municipal and provincial governments, were not created by the constitution; they pre-date the federal and provincial governments in this country. The Canadian government could also, for example, withdraw its jurisdiction over certain aspects of Indian governance, thus freeing them from the applicable provisions of the Charter. For a fuller discussion of the legal relationship of the Charter to Indian rights, see *Sixth Report of the Standing Committee on Indian Affairs and Northern Development* (1982) 18; Douglas Sanders 'The Rights of the Aboriginal Peoples of Canada' 6 *Canadian Bar Review* (1983) 314–53; L.C. Green 'Aboriginal Peoples, International Law and the Canadian Charter of Rights and Freedoms' 6 *Canadian Bar Review* (1983) 339–53; and P.W. Hogg 'Supremacy of the Canadian Charter of Rights and Freedoms' 6 *Canadian Bar Review* (1983) 69–80.

18 P.E. Trudeau *Federalism and the French Canadians* (Toronto: Macmillan 1968)

19 Assembly of First Nations 'Proposal for Amendments and Additions to the Constitution Act, 1982'; 'Presentation of the Indian Nations of Hobbema to the Section 37(1) Conference on Aboriginal and Treaty Rights'; and 'Opening Remarks for Presentation by Dr David Ahenakew.' These papers were all presented at the first ministers' conference on aboriginal constitutional matters held at Ottawa, 15 March 1983.

20 *Sixth Report of the Standing Committee on Indian Affairs and Northern Development* (1982) 1–42

21 R.L. Barsh and J. Youngblood Henderson *The Road: Indian Tribes and Political Liberty* (Berkeley: University of California Press 1980) 241–6

22 Vernon Van Dyke 'Self-Determination and Minority Rights' 13 *International Studies Quarterly* (1969) 223–53; 'Human Rights and the Rights of Groups' 18 *American Journal of Political Science* (1974) 225–41; 'Justice as Fairness: For Groups' 69 *American Political Science Review* (1975) 607–14; 'The Individual, the State, and Ethnic Communities in Political Theory' 24 *World Politics* (1977) 343–69; 'The Cultural Rights of Peoples' 2 *Universal Human Rights* (1980) 1–21; 'Collective Entities

and Moral Rights: Problems in Liberal Democratic Thought' 44 *Journal of Politics* (1982) 21–40
23 *Report no. 22 to the Sub-committee on Indian Women and the Indian Act* (Ottawa 1982)
24 For a fuller discussion of the legal foundation of Indian group rights, including the historical and operational dimensions, see D. Sanders 'Group Rights: The Constitutional Position of the Canadian Indian' unpublished paper (1972).
25 Indians also constitute nations of peoples according to social science criteria. Walker Connor 'A Nation Is a Nation, Is a State, Is an Ethnic Group Is a ...' 1 *Ethnic and Racial Studies* (1978) 379 defines the essence of a nation as 'a psychological bond that joins a people and differentiates it, in the subconscious conviction of its members, from all other people in a most vital way.' He adds in another context that 'national consciousness is accompanied by a growing aversion to being ruled by those deemed aliens': 'Ethnic Nationalism as a political Force' *World Affairs* 23 September 1970, 93. Other social scientists have defined a nation as 'a social group which shares a common ideology, common institutions and customs and a sense of homogeneity': J.C. Plano and Ray Olton *The International Relations Dictionary* (New York: Holt, Rinehart and Winston 1969). The very high level of cultural uniqueness and homogeneity of Indian societies not only strengthens their political integration as nations, but also acts as a barrier to political integration into Canadian society. The fact that Indian cultural uniqueness has become politicized adds to Indians' sense of historic nationhood.
26 Pollis and Schwab 'Human Rights' xiii–xvi

YOUNGBLOOD HENDERSON The Doctrine of Aboriginal Rights in Western Legal Tradition

1 Walter Ullman *The Growth of Papal Government in the Middle Ages* (London: Methuen 1955)
2 *Anguns Documentos* edited by J. Ramos-Coelho (Lisbon: Academia Real das Sciencias de Lisboa 1892) 7–8
3 Cited in Lewis V. Hanke *Spanish Struggles in the Conquest of America* (Philadelphia: University of Pennsylvania 1949) 29–30
4 Vitoria *De Indis et de Jure Belli Relectiones* (1557) translated by J.P. Bate (1917)
5 Ibid. section 1, 128
6 Ibid. Accord: *Johnson* v *M'Intosh* 9 Peters 713 (USSC); *Worcester* v *Georgia* 6 Peters 515 (USSC)
7 Ibid. 134, 138, 157
8 Translated in F.A. MacNutt *Bartholomew de las Casas: His Life, His Apostolate, and His Writing* (New York: G.P. Putnam's Sons 1909). Compare to Royal Proclamation of 1763 and Indian Intercourse Acts of the United States: Act of 22 July 1790, 2 U.S. Stat.

9 Lewis V. Hanke *Aristotle and the American Indians* (Chicago: H. Regnery Co. 1959); Las Casas Debates (1552)

10 [1841 Madrid] Law 1, Title 3, Book 6, derived from Act of 21 March 1551; Law 9, Title 3, Book 6, derived from Law of 19 February 1560; Law 13, Title 31, Book 2, Instructions to Viceroys (1596) ch. 2; Law 35–36, title 18, Book 2, derived from Law of 24 May 1571; Law of 19 December 1593; Law 1, Title 17, Book 10, and Law 4, Title 8, Book 11, of *Novisima Recopilacion* [1805]; Article 13 of Treaty of 1784 between Spain and Tallapuche Indians, 2 *White's New Recopilacion of the Laws of Spain and the Indes* 318, 321.

11 Law of 22 June 1594, translated from 2 *White's New Recopilacion* 51.

12 Cited in Hanke *Spanish Struggles* 148.

13 W. Camden *The Historie of the Most Renowned and Victorious Princesse Elizabeth, Late Queen of England* vol. 2 (London: 1630) 116

14 Edited by T.E.H. Holland (Oxford: Clarendon Press 1877) xix

15 Grotius *Mare Liberum* (Amsterdam 1712) chaps. 5 and 8; *On the Law of War and Peace* (Cambridge 1853)

16 M.F. Lindley *The Acquisition and Government of Backward Territories in International Law* (London: Longmans Green 1926) 10–28

17 Ibid.

18 (Oxford 1776) 1029–32

19 Ibid. 104–6. Compare to status of American nations as 'separate and distinct' (see note 43 infra).

20 S.F.C. Milsom *Historical Foundation of the Common Law* (London: Butterworths 1969)

21 Letter of instruction to Captain Endecott (1629) cited in F. Jennings *The Invasion of America: Indians, Colonialism, and the Cant of Conquest* (Chapel Hill: University of North Carolina Press 1975) 135; *Royal Instructions to British Colonial Governors 1670–1776* edited by L.W. Labaree (Washington DC: American Historical Association 1973)

22 Articles of Capitulation of Montreal, 1760

23 NZPCC 387 at 390

24 I Andros Tracts (1868–74) 51

25 Jennings *The Invasion of America* 143

26 I Andros Tracts 50–1

27 *Governor and Company of Connecticut and Mohegan Indians, by Their Guardians* certified copy book of proceedings before Commissioners of Review 1743 (London 1769) at 24 (cited hereafter as 'Connecticut'). Copy in Houghton Library, Harvard University.

28 J.H. Smith *Appeals to the Privy Council from the American Plantations* (New York: Columbia University Press 1950) 425

29 Smith *Appeals to the Privy Council* 426

30 Ibid. 431

31 Connecticut 126–7 (emphasis in original)

32 Smith *Appeals to the Privy Council* 442

33 *Two Treatises of Government* (Cambridge: Cambridge University Press 1960) Second Treatise section 4
34 Ibid. First Treatise sections 144–5; Second Treatise sections 9, 105, 108
35 Ibid. Second Treatise section 14
36 Ibid. sections 73, 117, 121
37 *The Federal and State Constitutions, Charters, and Other Organic Law* edited by F.N. Thorpe (Washington, DC: HD 1909, vols. 87–91, 1909)
38 *Appalachian Indian Frontier: The Edmond Takin Report and Plan of 1755* edited by W.R. Jacobs (Lincoln: University of Nebraska Press 1967)
39 Labaree *Royal Instructions* 477–8
40 *Native Rights in Canada* edited by Peter A. Cumming and Neil H. Mickenberg (Toronto: Indian-Eskimo Association of Canada 1972) 291
41 Smith *Appeals to the Privy Council* 105–27
42 Ibid. 426. A copy of the opinion is in *Chalmer's Collections* Conn. vol. 1, fol. 16, New York Public Library.
43 Connecticut supra note 27 at 118. Aff'd 15 January 1771 (PC)
44 E. de Vattel *Droit des Gens* sections 5 and 6 (London: Chitty's 1834)
45 Protected states retain their international personality; *Rights of U.S. Nations in Mexico* (International Court of Justice Reports 1952) 176.
46 *Worcester* v *Georgia* 31 U.S. 515 (1832)
47 Ibid. 561
48 *United States* v *Mitchell* 9 Peters 711 (USSC) (1835)
49 *Freeman* v *Fairlie* 1 Moo. PC 305 (1828)
50 Ibid. at 325, aff'd (Lord Lynderst) on appeal: 1 Moo. Indian App. 305 (1828). See also *Advocate-General of Bengal* v *Ranee Surnomoye Dossee* 4 Bomb. HCR (Bomb. HC) (1867) at 17 et seq.; lex loci report of Indian Law Commissioners (1840) quoted in Sir George Claus Rankin *Background to Indian Law* (Cambridge: Cambridge University Press 1946) 22.
51 Supra note 50
52 Ibid. 61
53 13 Moo. PC 22
54 *Mayor of Lyon* v *East Indian Company* Moo. PC 175, 275–6 (1836)
55 Sir Francis Piggott *Exterritoriality* (London: W. Cloves and Sons 1907) 4
56 Ibid. 4–5
57 *R.* v *Crews, ex parte Sekgome* [1910] 2 KB 576; *01 Le Njogo* v *A.-G.* [1913] A11 ER 70
58 *R.* v *Crews, ex parte Sekgome* supra note 57, at 619. Also see *Nyali Ltd.* v *A.-G.* [1956] 1 QB (CA)
59 A.D. McNair, *Opinions of Law Officers*
60 53 & 45 Vict., c. 37, originally enacted 6 & 7 Vict., c. 94 (1843)
61 O.W. Phillips *Constitutional and Administrative Law* (London: Sweet and Maxwell 1967) 759; Felix Cohen in his *Handbook of Federal Indian Law* (Washington, DC: Government Printing Office 1934) bor-

rowed these principles to construct his theory of tribal sovereignty in the United States (at 22).

62 Articles 1 and 6 of U.S. Constitution, Act of 22 July 1790, 2 U.S. Stat. 137
63 10 U.S. 87, 142–3
64 Ibid. 146
65 21 U.S. 543, 574
66 Ibid. 594–5
67 Supra note 46
68 Ibid. 544
69 34 U.S. 711
70 Ibid. 745–6
71 Ibid. 758
72 Ibid. 749, 753–4
73 60 U.S. 366
74 Blackstone *Commentaries on the Law of England* 2d ed. book 2
75 *Selection from the Public Documents of the Province of Nova Scotia* edited by T.B. Akins (1869)
76 Nova Scotia Council Minutes 1819–25, minutes for 27 December 1819 and 8 May 1820 (Public Archives of Nova Scotia record group 1, Vol. 214 1/2A)
77 *Report of the Select Committee on Aborigines (British Settlements)* (1837) 1
78 Ibid. The Foreign Jurisdiction Act, 6 and 7 Vict., c. 94 (1843) confirmed the exclusive preprogative power of the crown over treaties of protection. Also see Foreign Jurisdiction Act 53 and 54 Vict., c. 37 (1890).
79 An Act to provide for the Instruction and Permanent Settlement of Indians, SNS 1842, c. 16
80 Legislative Assembly of Nova Scotia, Journal (1849) 356
81 Manuscript document (Public Archives of Nova Scotia, record group 5, 1855–8, vol. 3, n. 162 (12 July 1860)
82 A.E. Woodward *Aboriginal Land Rights Commission Second Report* (1974) 151–2
83 Lester and Parker 'Land Rights: The Australian Aborigines Have Lost a Legal Battle, But ...' 11 *Alberta Law Review* (1983) 189
84 Ibid. 210
85 Ibid. 211–12
86 Ibid. 214
87 Ibid. 218
88 NZPCC 387 at 391
89 Ibid. 388, 390
90 *Wi Parata* v *Bishop of Wellington* [1877] NZ Jur. (n.s.) 72, 75–6, 78
91 Ibid. 77–8, 79
92 AC 561 at 576
93 Ibid. 574
94 [1902] NZLR 655, 667

95 Ibid 754–5
96 *In Re Ninety Mile Beach* [1963] NZLR 461, 468
97 Letter from Associate Deputy Minister Ian Binnie to Paul Williams, 24 January 1984
98 55 ID 14, 25 October 1934
99 (1774) Loff 655, ER 1045; Cohen *Handbook of Federal Indian Law* (Washington, DC: Government Printing Office 1934) 122; Barsh and Henderson *The Road: Political Liberty and Indian Tribes* (Berkeley: University of California Press 1979)

HENDERSON   Canadian Legal and Judicial Philosophies on the Doctrine of Aboriginal Rights

1 (1832) 6 Peters 515, 31 U.S. 530, 8 L.Ed. 483
2 See, for example, *R.* v *Sikyea* (1964) 43 DLR (2d) 150 at 162 (NWTCA)
3 An appeal of this decision to the Supreme Court of Canada was heard 13–14 June 1983; the judgment of the Federal Court of Canada was reversed.
4 (1889) 14 App. Cas. 45 (PC)
5 (1979) 107 DLR (3d) 513 (Fed. Ct. TD)
6 [1973] SCR 313, 34 DLR (3d) 145
7 *A.-G.(Que.)* v *A.-G.(Can.)* (1921) 1 AC 401, 56 DLR 373 (PC)
8 [1903] AC 73 (PC)
9 I can find only six: the *James Bay Injunction* case, the *Paulette Caveat* case, the *Calder* case, and the *Baker Lake* case, all of which have run their course, plus the Lubicon Lake claim and the Temi-Augama claim, both of which are now being litigated. In November 1983 the Alberta Supreme Court denied an interim injunction against oil exploration to the Lubicon Lake claimants.
10 The 1983 constitutional amendment will ensure that aboriginal groups are at least consulted before any further amendments are made that affect their rights. The extent to which Parliament's traditional jurisdiction to enact simple legislation affecting native rights has been diminished will be the same as the courts' definition of the 'existing aboriginal and treaty rights' now protected by section 35 of the Constitution Act, 1982.
11 This rule is set out in *Francis* v *The Queen* [1956] SCR 618. A member of the St Regis Band was denied border-crossing rights originally protected by the Jay Treaty (1792) between Great Britain and the United States. While this was a recognized international treaty, it had not been enacted into force by Parliament and was therefore of no effect in Canada. The court also found that it was not a 'treaty' within the meaning of section 88 of the Indian Act, which would otherwise have constituted a parliamentary enactment of Jay Treaty rights.
12 With respect to land rights, some of the avoidance techniques are discussed in William B. Henderson 'Canada's Indian Reserves: The Usufruct in Our Constitution' 12 *Ottawa Law Review* (1980) 167.

Another useful treatise is J.C. Smith 'The Concept of Native Title' 24 *University of Toronto Law Journal* (1974) 1.

13 The watershed case is the decision of the United Nations Human Rights Committee in *Lovelace* v *Canada* 2 *Human Rights Law Journal* (1981) 158, in which an Indian woman's loss of status on marriage to a non-Indian was held to contravene article 27 of the International Covenant on Civil and Political Rights.

FLANAGAN Metis Aboriginal Rights: Some Historical and Contemporary Problems

1 *Manitoba: The Birth of a Province* edited by W.L. Morton (Altona: Manitoba Record Society 1965) 246
2 Louis Riel to N.J. Ritchot, 19 April 1870, in the hand of Louis Schmidt: Archives de l'Archevêche de Saint-Boniface, T7316–18.
3 G.F.C. Stanley 'Le Journal de l'Abbé N.J. Ritchot, 1870' 17 *Revue d'Histoire de l'Amérique Française* (1964) 546
4 Ibid. 547
5 Two copies of the draft with Macdonald's annotations are in the Public Archives of Canada, MG 26A, 40559ff.
6 Ritchot's protest is documented in his letter to G.E. Cartier (18 May 1870): Public Archives of Canada MG 26A, 41528–30. Cartier's disingenuous reply, dated 23 May 1870, is found ibid. 41531–4. While I am critical of the whole idea of Metis aboriginal rights, I certainly do not endorse the duplicity with which Macdonald and Cartier treated the Metis. My point is that the creation of Metis aboriginal rights was itself part of that double-dealing.
7 33 Vict., c. 3, cited in *Manitoba: The Birth of a Province* at 258
8 House of Commons *Debates* (2 May 1870) 1302
9 Ibid. (4 May 1870) 1359
10 36 Vict., c. 37
11 House of Commons *Debates* (6 July 1885) 3113
12 42 Vict., c. 31, s. 125[e]
13 For an overall description, see Joe Sawchuk, Patricia Sawchuk, and Theresa Ferguson *Metis Land Rights in Alberta: A Political History* (Edmonton: Metis Association of Alberta 1981) chap. 4
14 Harry W. Daniels *We Are the New Nation* (Ottawa: Native Council of Canada 1979) 9
15 Ivor Jennings *The Law of the Constitution* 5th ed. (London: University of London Press 1959) 136
16 *Native Rights in Canada* 2d ed., edited by Peter A. Cumming and Neil H. Mickenberg (Toronto: Indian-Eskimo Association of Canada 1972) 3, note 3
17 Ibid. 50; *United States* v *Seminole Indians* 180 ct. Cl. 375 (1967)
18 *Baker Lake* v *Minister of Indian Affairs and Northern Development* (1980) 1 FC 518 at 557–8

19 See 'Les Métix du Nord-Quest' originally published in the Montreal *Star* 28 November 1885.

20 Jacqueline Peterson 'Ethnogenesis: Settlement and Growth of a "New People" in the Great Lakes Region, 1702–1815,' paper presented at Conference on the Metis in North America, Chicago, 3–5 September 1981

21 Alpheus Henry Snow *The Question of Aborigines in the Law and Practice of Nations* (Northbrook, Ill.: Metro Books 1972) 7

22 *Riverlots and Scrip: Elements of Metis Aboriginal Rights* (Winnipeg: Manitoba Metis Federation 1978) 1

23 Clem Chartier, a lawyer and Metis spokesman, writes that Metis rights 'are on a higher plane than the legal fiction of aboriginal title'; they are the rights of national self-determination: 'Aboriginal Rights: The Metis Perspective' in *Aboriginal Rights: Toward an Understanding* edited by J. Anthony Long, Menno Boldt, and Leroy Little Bear (Edmonton: The Alberta Law Foundation 1983) 46–52

24 Sawchuk et al. *Metis Land Rights in Alberta* 258

25 Ibid. 198

26 Kenneth M. Lysyk 'The Rights and Freedom of the Aboriginal Peoples of Canada' in *The Canadian Charter of Rights and Freedoms: Commentary* edited by W.S. Tarnopolsky and G.A. Beaudoin (Toronto: Carswell 1982) 470

27 Cumming and Mickenberg *Native Rights in Canada* 203

28 Chartier 'Aboriginal Rights' 51

29 Sawchuk et al. *Metis Land Rights in Alberta* 246

30 D.J. Hall 'The Half-Breed Claim Commission' 25 *Alberta History* (1977) 1–8

31 D.N. Sprague 'Government Lawlessness in the Administration of Manitoba Land Claims, 1830–1885' 10 *Manitoba Law Journal* (1980) 415–41; ibid. 'The Manitoba Land Question' 15 *Journal of Canadian Studies* (1980) 74–84

32 That the Manitoba Act was a constitutional text, and that it could not be unilaterally amended by the Manitoba legislature, had already been decided by the Supreme Court of Canada in *Attorney-General of Manitoba* v *Georges Forest* [1979] 2 scr 1032.

33 Section 11 of the claim. Section 12 advances the potentially explosive claim that all regulations of the Manitoba government respecting Metis lands were ultra vires because they concerned 'Indians and Lands Reserved for Indians' (section 91(24) of the bna Act, 1876). A judicial victory on this point might have the unintended consequence of outlawing various provincial programs for Metis people – for example, the Alberta Metis reserves.

34 Harry W. Daniels *Native People and the Constitution of Canada* (Ottawa: Mutual Press 1981)

35 Thomas Sowell *Race and Economics* (New York: David McKay 1957) 128

DACKS The Politics of Native Claims in Northern Canada

1 The federal government insists that the Dene claim is a 'specific,' not a comprehensive, claim in that treaties 8 and 11 cover the area in question. The Dene strongly reject this reading of treaties that they view as treaties of peace and friendship, not documents terminating their rights. Ottawa has agreed to negotiate the Dene claim as if it were a comprehensive claim, but not to acknowledge it as such. It should also be noted that there are some comprehensive claims in the provinces, but these comprise a small fraction of the total number south of 60 degrees.
2 Ottawa: Department of Indian Affairs and Northern Development 1981
3 'Perspective in Native Land Claims Policy' background paper prepared for the Canadian Arctic Resources Committee Third National Workshop (Yellowknife: Office of Native Claims 1983) 7
4 Government of the Yukon 'Yukoners Deserve a Fair Deal: A Land Claims Information package' (Whitehorse 1983) 56
5 Ninth Legislative Assembly of the Northwest Territories *Debates* (29 November 1982) 2097
6 'Yukoners Deserve a Fair Deal' 29–38
7 Ibid. 38
8 'Our Land, Our Future: Discussion Paper on Political and Constitutional Development in the Northwest Territories' (Yellowknife: Government of the Northwest Territories 1981) ii
9 'Perspective in Native Land Claims Policy' 9
10 It may be that the government promoted this view to pressure native negotiators. This view is widely held in the North. It is substantiated by a review of the short-lived Conservative government of 1979 and 1980 contained in Gurston Dacks *A Choice of Futures: Politics in the Canadian North* (Toronto: Methuen 1981) 66.
11 *Yukon News* 28 December 1984
12 'Inuvialuit Nunangat' 6 *Northern Perspectives* (1978) 1–10
13 Inuit Tapirisat of Canada *Nunavut: A Proposal for the Settlement of Inuit Land Claim in the Northwest Territories* (February 1976)
14 Inuit Tapirisat of Canada 'Proposed Agreement-in-Principle for the Establishment of Inuit Rights between the Inuit and the Government of Canada (July 1977); 'Political Development in Nunavut' (September 1979); 'Parnagujuk' (November 1980)
15 For example, in April 1983 two agreements establishing guidelines for the selection of Inuit lands were initialled by TFN and the chief government negotiator: *Nunavut Newsletter* (May-June 1983) 2–4.
16 *Yukon News* 28 December 1984

DIAMOND Aboriginal Rights: The James Bay Experience

1 *Calder et al.* v *Attorney-General of British Columbia 1973* SCR 313; [1973] 4 WWR 1; 34 DLR (3d) 145

2 [1964] SCR 642; [1964] 43 DLR (2) 150
3 *Kanatewat, Chief Robert, et al.* v *Attorney-General of the Province of Quebec and the Quebec Hydro Electric Commission* Superior Court, District of Montreal (8 December 1972)
4 *Kanatewat, Chief Robert, et al.* v *Attorney-General of the Province of Quebec and the Quebec Hydro Electric Commission* Superior Court, District of Montreal (1974) *Quebec Practice Reports* 38
5 *In Re Paulette* 1 WWR 321
6 *Baker Lake et al.* v *Minister of Indian Affairs and Northern Development* [1980] 5 WWR 193; 50 CCC (2d) 377 (FCTD)
7 *Re Southern Rhodesia* [1918] AC 210 (PC)
8 [1886] 13 SCR 577
9 [1889] 14 AC 46
10 [1932] 4 DLR 774
11 [1975] 1 SCR 48
12 [1975] Que. CA 166
13 [1976–77] SC 32
14 [1976] SQ 46, [1977] RSQ 67

SANDERS Aboriginal Rights: The Search for Recognition in International Law

1 See Douglas Sanders 'The Indian Lobby' in Keith Banting and Richard Simeon *And No One Cheered* (Toronto: Methuen 1983) 301
2 See Patrick Thornberry 'Is There a Phoenix in the Ashes? International Law and Minority Rights' 15 *Texas International Law Journal* (1980) 421
3 Alexander Morris *The Treaties of Canada with the Indians of Manitoba and the Northwest Territories* (Toronto 1880; reprinted Coles Canadian Collection 1971) 118
4 Donald B. Smith *Long Lance: The True Story of an Imposter* (Lincoln: University of Nebraska Press 1982) 71–2
5 On the strategy of the Allied Tribes, see E. Palmer Patterson 'Arthur E. O'Meara, Friend of the Indians' 58 *Pacific Northwest Quarterly* (1967) 90. There is no account that isolates the supranational strategies of British Columbia Indians, but much information can be found in Forrest Emmanuel LaViolette *The Struggle for Survival* (Toronto: University of Toronto Press 1961).
6 British Columbia Lands and Works Department *Papers Connected with the Indian Land Question, 1850–75* (Victoria 1875).
7 *The Native Voice* (Vancouver) December 1946
8 Ibid. July 1953
9 'Chiefs get warm welcome from Queen' *Native People* (Edmonton) 9 July 1976
10 Quoted in Emerson S. Coatsworth *Treaties and Promises: Saulteaux Indians* (Toronto: Ginn & Co. 1971) 22

11 Quoted from a release by Canadian Press wire service 5 July 1973

12 *Native Press* (Yellowknife) 7 May 1975

13 See Douglas Sanders 'The Indian Lobby' in Keith Banting and Richard Simeon *And No One Cheered* (Toronto: Methuen 1983) 301; Douglas Sanders 'Indians, the Queen and the Canadian Constitution' *Survival International Review* (Summer 1980) 6.

14 'Schreyer told by Indians "They are fed up"' *Kainai News* (Standoff, Alberta) July 1979; 'Governor General told not just another meeting' *Native People* (Edmonton) 27 July 1979

15 Warwick A. McKean *Equality and Discrimination under International Law* (Oxford: Oxford University Press 1983) 14–15

16 Letter to Charles R. Crane, Woods Hole, Mass., dated 21 October 1924, League of Nations Archives, Geneva

17 See Richard Veatch *Canada and the League of Nations* (Toronto: University of Toronto Press 1975) chap. 7.

RYSER Fourth World Wars: Indigenous Nationalism and the Emerging New International Political Order

1 John Bodley *Victims of Progress* (Menlo Park, Calif.: Benjamin/ Cummings 1982) 40. I have drawn upon the following works in this paper: Michael Kidron and Ronald Segal *The New State of the World Atlas* (New York: Simon and Schuster 1984); Leopold Kohr *The Breakdown of Nations* (New York: E.P. Dutton 1978); Rudolph C. Ryser *The New International Economic Order: Promise or Peril for the Indigenous Peoples of the World* (Seattle: YMCA Metrocenter 1979); Rudolph C. Ryser and Ellie Menzies *Tribal Political Status: Finding a Place for Indigenous Peoples in the Family of Nations* (Ottawa: World Council of Indigenous Peoples 1980); and Rudolph C. Ryser *First Nations, States of Canada and the United Kingdom: Patriation of the Canadian Constitution* (Ottawa: World Council of Indigenous Peoples 1981).

TENNANT Aboriginal Rights and the Penner Report on Indian Self-Government

1 Daniel Raunet *Without Surrender, Without Consent: A History of the Nishga Land Claims* (Vancouver: Douglas and McIntyre 1984)

2 Wayne Daugherty and Dennis Madill *Indian Government under Indian Act Legislation 1868–1951* (Ottawa: Research Branch, Department of Indian and Northern Affairs 1980)

3 Orders of Reference, Special Committee on Indian Self-Government (Task Force) House of Commons, 22 December 1982.

4 Sally M. Weaver 'A Commentary on the Penner Report' 10 *Canadian Public Policy* (Spring 1984) 217

5 House of Commons *Report of the Special Committee on Indian Self-*

Government in Canada Minutes and Proceedings of the Special Committee on Indian self-government (no. 40) October 1983
6 Weaver 'A Commentary on the Penner Report' 217
7 The following five paragraphs appeared in different form in my article 'Indian Self-Government: Progress or Stalemate?' 10 *Canadian Public Policy* (Spring 1984) 211–15. All quotations in these paragraphs are from the Penner Report.
8 This information, and that concerning Bill C-52, was obtained in interviews with two officials who had direct access to the processes in Ottawa.

BOLDT AND LONG   Tribal Traditions and European-Western Political Ideologies

1 Menno Boldt 'Intellectual Orientations and Nationalism among Indian Leaders in an Internal Colony: A Theoretical and Comparative Perspective' 33 *British Journal of Sociology* (1982) 484–510; 'Enlightenment Values, Romanticism and Attitudes toward Political Status: A Study of Native Indian Leaders in Canada' 18 *Canadian Review of Sociology and Anthropology* (1981) 545–65
2 James Youngblood Henderson 'Comment' in *Indian Sovereignty: Proceedings of the Second Annual Conference on Problems and Issues Concerning American Indians Today* edited by W.R. Swagerty (Chicago: The Newberry Library 1979) 71– 2
3 Charles E. Merrian Jr *History of the Theory of Sovereignty since Rousseau* (New York: A.M.S. Press 1968) 83, and Sir Ernest Barker *Essays on Government* 2d ed. (Oxford: Clarendon Press 1960) 65
4 Henderson 'Comment' 58
5 W.J. Rees 'The Theory of Sovereignty Restated' in *Philosophy, Politics and Society* edited by Peter Laslett (Oxford: Basil Blackwell 1963) 58
6 Hannah Arendt 'What Was Authority?' in *Authority* edited by C.J. Friedrich (Cambridge, Mass.: Harvard University Press 1958) 102–4
7 Yves R. Simon 'Sovereignty in Democracy' in *In Defense of Sovereignty* edited by W.J. Stankiewicz (New York: Oxford University Press 1969) 244
8 Merriam *The Theory of Sovereignty* 202–3
9 Frances F. Hinsley *Sovereignty* (London: C.A. Walls 1966) 16
10 Quoted in Keith W. Werhan 'The Sovereignty of Indian Tribes: A Reaffirmation and Strengthening in the 1970s' 54 *Notre Dame Lawyer* (1978) 5–25
11 David Ahenakew, 'Aboriginal Title and Aboriginal Rights: The Impossible and Unnecessary Task of Identification and Definition' unpublished paper 1984
12 Kenneth D. McRae 'The Plural Society and the Western Political Tradition' 12 *Canadian Journal of Political Science* (1979) 677–8
13 See Vernon Van Dyke 'Human Rights and the Fights of Groups' 18

American Journal of Political Science (1974) 725–41; 'Justice as Fairness: For Groups?' 69 *American Political Science Review* (1975) 607–14; 'The Individual, the State, and Ethnic Communities in Political Theory' 29 *World Politics* (1977) 343–69; 'Collective Entities and Moral Rights: Problems in Liberal-Democratic Thought' 40 *Journal of Politics* (1982) 21–40.

14 Robert A. Nisbet *Community and Power* (New York: Oxford University Press 1962) 224

15 Wendell Bell *Jamaican Leaders* (Berkeley: University of California Press 1964); *The Democratic Revolution in the West Indies* edited by Wendell Bell (Cambridge, Mass.: Schenkman Publishing Company Inc. 1967); Wendell Bell and I. Oxaal *Decisions of Nationhood* Monograph Series in World Affairs (Denver: University of Denver 1964)

16 Walker Connor 'A Nation Is a Nation, Is a State, Is an Ethnic Group, Is a ...' 1 *Ethnic and Racial Studies* (1978) 377–400

17 Walker Connor 'Ethnic Nationalism as a Political Force' 133 *World Affairs* (1970) 91–7

18 Jack C. Plano and Ray Olton *The International Relations Dictionary* (New York: Holt, Rinehart and Winston 1969)

19 Menno Boldt 'Philosophy, Politics and Extralegal Action: Native Indian Leaders in Canada' 4 *Ethnic and Racial Studies* (1981) 205–21

Contributors

David Ahenakew is national chief of the Assembly of First Nations. He has
served as chief of the Federation of Saskatchewan Indians. Dr Ahenakew
was awarded an honorary doctor of laws degree from the University of
Regina in 1975, and was made a member of the Order of Canada in 1978.

Menno Boldt is a professor of sociology at the University of Lethbridge. He was
educated at the University of Alberta and Yale University. A specialist in
minorities, he has published widely on the subjects of Indian leadership,
politics, and philosophy.

Clem Chartier is vice-president of the Association of Metis and Non-status
Indians of Saskatchewan. A Metis lawyer, he is also a national representative of the Metis National Council.

Gurston Dacks is a professor of political science at the University of Alberta.
He was educated at the University of Toronto and Princeton University.
His research interests focus on political and economic development in the
Canadian North.

Richard Dalon is executive director of Social and Cultural Affairs, Federal and
Intergovernmental Affairs Department, Government of Alberta. His office is actively involved in developing aboriginal policy for the government
of Alberta. He was educated at Wilkes College and the University of
Alberta.

Billy Diamond is grand chief of the Grand Council of the Crees, Quebec. He
has served as chairman of the Cree Regional Authority and president of
Air NoCreeBec Inc. He has been active in the Cree justice and police systems
as well as in social and economic development programs.

Thomas Flanagan is a professor of political science at the University of
Calgary. Educated at Notre Dame and Duke universities, his research has
focused on Louis Riel and the history of the Metis in Canada. He is assistant
editor and volume editor of the Louis Riel Project.

James Youngblood Henderson is a legal strategist for the Grand Council of the
Micmac Nations, Cape Breton. He holds a BA from California State University at Fullerton and a JD from Harvard University. He has written widely

about political liberty and aboriginal peoples. He is a member of the
Chickasaw Nation and the Cheyenne Tribe.

William B. Henderson is a member of the Toronto law firm of LaForme,
Henderson, Jones. Educated at the University of Ottawa, he has served as
head of land entitlements for the Department of Indian and Northern
Affairs. He has conducted significant research on aboriginal land tenure.

Peter Ittinuar is a former member of Parliament for Nunatsiag, Northwest
Territories. Educated at Carleton University, he has been a professor of
Inuktituk linguistics and Inuit culture at the University of Ottawa. He has
served as executive director and special assistant for the Inuit Tapirisat of
Canada.

Leroy Little Bear is a professor of native American studies at the University of
Lethbridge. He holds a BA from the University of Lethbridge and a law
degree from the University of Utah. He has served as a consultant to DIAND
and several provincial and national Indian political organizations. His research is focused on aboriginal and treaty rights.

J. Anthony Long is a professor of political Science at the University of Lethbridge. Educated at the Universities of Montana and Missouri, he special-
izes in Canadian public policy. He has written on Indian self-government
and traditional Indian philosophy.

Oren Lyons is a professor of American studies at the State University of New
York at Buffalo. Educated at the State University of New York at Oneon-
ta, he focuses his research on treaty rights, land rights, and Indian sovereignty. He is a peace-keeper of the Turtle Clan of the Iroquois Nation.

Leon Mitchell, QC, is a member of the law firm of Taylor, Brazzell and
McCaffrey of Winnipeg. He has been broadly involved in both specific and
general Indian land claims. He has served as commissioner of the Indian
Treaty Land Entitlement Commission for the Government of Manitoba.

The Right Honourable Brian Mulroney is the prime minister of Canada. He
was educated at St Francis Xavier University and Laval University. During
the early stage of his term as prime minister, he has strongly advocated
negotiated aboriginal self-government with constitutional status.

Fred Plain is a policy analyst on intergovernmental relations for the
Nishnawbe-Aski Nation. He has served as president of the Union of Ontario
Indians and as chief of the Chippewas of Sarnia.

Roy J. Romanow, QC, is the former attorney-general and deputy premier of
Saskatchewan. In 1978–9 and 1980 he served as the provincial co-
chairman of the federal and provincial ministerial discussions on the patriation of the constitution. As visiting scholar at the University of Saskatchewan, he co-wrote a book on the constitution. Educated at the University of
Saskatchewan, Mr Romanow is currently a senior partner in the Saskatoon law firm of Mitchell, Taylor, Romanow, Ching.

Rudolph C. Ryser is a senior fellow with the Center for World Indigenous
Studies and public affairs adviser to the president of the Quinault Indian
Nation in the United States. He is editor of the Center for World Indigenous
Studies publication, *CWIS Journal,* and the author of numerous articles

and papers on international indigenous affairs. He is a member of the Cowlitz Tribe.

Douglas Sanders is a professor in the faculty of law, University of British Columbia. Educated at the University of Alberta and the University of California (Berkeley), he has served as a legal consultant for various aboriginal organizations, including the Assembly of First Nations, the Union of British Columbia Indian Chiefs, and the World Council of Indigenous Peoples.

Brian Slattery is a professor at Osgoode Hall Law School, York University. Educated at Loyola of Montreal, McGill, and Oxford universities, he has written numerous articles and native law and rights and on constitutional law and history in general.

John Snow is chief of the Wesley Band of Stoney Indians, Alberta. He was educated at St Stephen's Theological College, Edmonton, and was ordained in the United Church in 1963. He has delivered numerous addresses and has written on matters of Indian concern.

Paul Tennant is a professor of political science at the University of British Columbia. He was educated at the universities of British Columbia and Chicago. His research has focused on Indian organizations in British Columbia. He has served as an adviser to the Office of Native Claims on Indian Self-Government and is currently a consultant for the Council of Yukon Indians.

The Right Honourable Pierre Elliott Trudeau is a former prime minister of Canada. He was educated at the University of Montreal, Harvard University, the Sorbonne, and the London School of Economics. During his term as prime minister, aboriginal policy initiatives ranged from the 1969 White Paper to the 1983 constitutional recognition of existing aboriginal rights.

Sally Weaver is a professor of anthropology at the University of Waterloo. Educated at the University of Toronto, she has written on contemporary Indian policy-making, including attempts at joint policy-making by government and aboriginal peoples. She has researched and written on comparative aboriginal policy, focusing on Canada and Australia.

Bill Wilson is co-ordinator of the Musgamagw Tribal Council in British Columbia. He has been involved in the native Indian movement since the early 1960s, serving at senior levels with the Union of British Columbia Indian Chiefs, the Assembly of First Nations, and the Native Council of Canada. He was a member of the Special Committee on Indian Self-Government. He holds a BA from the University of Victoria and an LLB from the University of British Columbia.